P9-CLF-742

Emergence of the
Presidential Nominating Convention
1789-1832

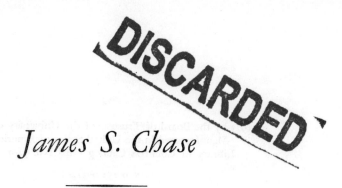

James S. Chase

———

Emergence
of the
Presidential Nominating
Convention
1789–1832

———

University of Illinois Press

URBANA   CHICAGO   LONDON

In memory of my Mother
Sue W. Chase

———

Contents

Preface

Preceding the election of 1832 the Antimasonic, National Republican, and Democratic parties selected their presidential tickets in national conventions. Except for the Whigs in 1836 all major and most minor parties have used the device ever since. The impact of the national convention on the development of American politics requires no underlining. The purpose of this volume is to reveal, insofar as it is possible, the circumstances responsible for the convention's nearly simultaneous introduction by three parties.

None of the men immediately involved realized they were founding a great American institution; their gaze extended no further than the next election. And in later years, when its significance had become apparent, no memoirists claimed credit for any of these initial conventions. Martin Van Buren did not even remember, when writing his autobiography, that the convention which nominated him for vice-president was the first in the history of the Democratic party. So obscure were its beginnings that in 1905 a political scientist could plausibly characterize the national convention as "neither a political inheritance nor a conscious contrivance" but "an unfathered institutional waif" (thereby turning the early national period into a modern equivalent of the Dark Ages).[1]

Notwithstanding the recentness of the convention's birth, this remark struck an appropriate evolutionary note, for well before the Antimasons met in 1831 knowledge of convention theory and practice was commonplace in all but a handful of the twenty-four states. In a sense the national convention has no origin. It emerged as the climax

1. Alfred Pearce Dennis, "The Anomaly of Our National Convention," *Political Science Quarterly*, XX (June, 1905), 186.

of a long process, dating from the eighteenth century, in which the local and state convention became the prevailing method of nominating candidates for public office. The transition was sufficiently advanced that proposals for holding a national convention received serious consideration in 1824 and 1828. No one claimed its creation in 1832 or subsequently because nothing about the national conventions seemed new at the time.

What is puzzling is why it was not used earlier. The answer lies in the nature of the institution. A national convention is a collection of delegates who purport to represent the full membership of a political party. They cannot be brought together unless there is a widespread conviction before the meeting that they will unite in pursuit of a common goal. A convention follows rather than precedes the formation of a party even though it may be the first formal and public demonstration of unity. The timing of the first nominating conventions was dependent, in other words, on the existence of national parties, not merely on the perfection of ways to appoint delegates, order agendas, and select nominees. In the election of 1832 the popularity of the convention form was matched for the first time with national parties capable of agreeing on candidates for president and vice-president.

Although politicians' familiarity with the convention technique prevents any one of them from advancing a clear title to discovery, someone or some group within the three parties, at a particular moment and place, had to decide that a national convention should be called. And in spite of the casual manner in which the decision was made in each case, enough facts are available to recreate the conditions and designate the men responsible.

These, then, are the questions I will be concerned with: Why did the convention gain steadily in popularity over other nominating methods until its involvement in presidential politics was almost a foregone conclusion? What impelled the revival of organized national parties that made the holding of conventions possible? Who made the decision for each party and for what reasons?

This is not a narrative of national politics from 1789 to 1832. Although it is not possible to disentangle the expansion of partisan organization from its broader context, I have touched only lightly on those larger events bearing on party maturation.

My debts for aid in writing this book are numerous. Walter Johnson, now at the University of Hawaii, gave generously of his time and good advice. I also benefited from the suggestions of Daniel J. Boorstin and Bernard A. Weisberger. My colleagues, Willard B. Gatewood, Jr. and James J. Hudson, were also most helpful. Albert Romasco, Mary Lynn McNulty, and Robert McAhren provided both encouragement and editorial assistance. My former assistant, Robert M. Peoples, kindly shared his own research with me and aided in other ways as well. Janie Johnson and Colleen Kain patiently endured my impatience when typing the manuscript. To these persons, and to others unnamed, I am most grateful. I am, of course, responsible for all errors.

I should also like to thank the library staffs of the Buffalo Historical Society, the University of Chicago, the Library of Congress, the New York Historical Society, the New York Public Library, the New York State Library, the Rochester Public Library, the University of Rochester Library, the Wisconsin State Historical Society, and the University of Wisconsin for their invaluable assistance.

The editors of *Mid-America* and *Social Science Quarterly* have kindly given me permission to use, in somewhat altered form, articles which were published in their journals.

Introduction

"Nominations are made from necessity. In an extended territory, comprising a numerous population, men having the same object in view, and governed by the same political principles, to give effect and success to their objects and principles, must act in concert. Meetings of some kind must be held—an interchange of sentiment take place, and the candidate agreed upon."

Albany Argus, June 2, 1826
(quoted from the Norwich *Journal*)

The Baltimore Athenaeum, erected in 1824 on the southwest corner of the intersection of St. Paul and Lexington streets, differed little from similar buildings in other cities whose libraries and lecture rooms sheltered those engaged in the serious business of self-improvement. But even though it was destroyed by fire only ten years after its completion, Baltimore's Athenaeum enjoys a unique historical distinction.[1] In its "splendid saloon" met the first national conventions to nominate candidates for president and vice-president of the United States. The Antimasons assembled on September 26, 1831, the National Republicans followed closely in December, and the Democrats were the last, meeting in May of the following year.

In the national convention the politicians of three parties hit upon a mechanism enabling a large and scattered membership to agree on men for the nation's top offices. They did more. The convention was the first national party organ fully integrated with state and local

1. Charles Varle, *A Complete View of Baltimore* (Baltimore, 1833), p. 35; J. Thomas Scharf, *The Chronicles of Baltimore* (Baltimore, 1874), pp. 405, 408, 440, 458–60, 473–74.

machinery and reflecting, with fair accuracy, the balance of power within each party. The national convention reproduced a federal form of party government modeled on that of the nation and states. It brought under one roof a series of local interests in quest of common denominators and represented the culminating step in the creation of a durable party organization which has withstood the test of 140 years.

At this point let me confess that I cannot define precisely what is meant by party. Many definitions are possible, but most of them turn out to be descriptions which can be applied to groups not generally conceded to be parties. If, for example, party is defined as a body of persons united in the pursuit of governmental power (and this is the best brief, albeit somewhat crude, definition), how is it differentiated from a faction or special interest?[2] If identified as those who share a set of principles or who are determined to enact certain laws, what can be said of our American parties so obviously lacking through much of their history in those inestimable qualities? An economic or class approach ignores other vital determinants such as race, religion, and parental preference.

One essential ingredient of a party is the group's self-consciousness that it is a party, even if (like the Federalists) it is not willing to own up to the label. It cannot perform any of the functions universally imputed to a party unless its members, or at least its leaders, are aware of their unity. Does this mean that the test of what constitutes a party is purely subjective, that because some miscellaneous collection of people styles itself a party that, therefore, it is? To escape an affirmative answer let me impose a qualification, one capable of some degree of objective testing, yet following reasonably from the fact of self-consciousness.

All admit that parties do certain things although they are not necessarily the exclusive functions of parties: they influence public opinion, run the government, conduct campaigns, nominate candidates, take voters to the polls when it rains, distribute patronage, and perform any number of other tasks a schoolboy can recite. In order to perform these functions decisions must be made; some individual or agency must assign jobs, establish priorities, raise money, and so forth. To make the decisions necessary to accomplish its work the party must have, in a word, organization. The geographic scope of the organization

2. For a concise discussion of this problem, see William Nisbet Chambers, *Political Parties in a New Nation: The American Experience, 1776–1809* (New York, 1963), pp. 44–48.

determines whether a party can properly be called national or local. Party status can be recognized only to the degree that the group's organization is commensurate with its desire for power. A national party must be capable not just of nominating candidates for president and for Congress but of waging effective campaigns in their behalf. In sum, a party is a group of men united for the purpose of controlling the legal government and organized in a manner which provides an opportunity for gaining the power it seeks.

In many ways the organization *is* the party since it furnishes the means for the party to fulfill the purpose responsible for bringing it into being. And although I would not exclude other concepts of party or underestimate the importance of ideas, personality, and economics I will tend in the following pages to equate party development with organizational development, placing special emphasis on the act of nomination as the key function of organization.[3] "Nomination can be regarded," writes Neil McDonald, "as a kind of professional *initiative-taking* in connection with the filling of public offices. The initiative-taking function is nowhere provided for in the Constitution or in law, and parties, it may be argued, have made it their most distinctive function in the political system."[4] Whatever else it may or may not do, the party must make nominations if it is to win office; designating candidates is virtually a condition of life.

The party system, as we know it today, is a product of the early national period. It grew out of a trial and error process aimed at building an adequate organization, the most critical feature of which was the devising of an acceptable way to nominate candidates for president and vice-president. "When the national convention was contrived to designate presidential candidates," V. O. Key wrote, "a viable national party came into existence."[5]

National parties were not inevitable. None existed prior to 1789. In the late eighteenth century the term conjured up an image of selfish

3. E. E. Schattschneider, *Party Government* (New York, 1942), p. 100; Avery Leiserson, *Parties and Politics: An Institutional and Behavioral Approach* (New York, 1958), pp. 44–50; Edgar E. Robinson, "The Place of Party in the Political History of the United States," *Annual Reports of the American Historical Association for the Years 1927 and 1928* (Washington, 1929), pp. 200–205; Vladimir Orlando Key, *Politics, Parties, and Pressure Groups* (New York, 1958), pp. 218–25, 345–46; Neil A. McDonald, *The Study of Political Parties* (New York, 1955), pp. 16–26.
4. McDonald, *The Study of Political Parties*, p. 26.
5. Key, *Politics, Parties, and Pressure Groups*, pp. 471–72.

and petty groups like the corrupt Whigs and Tories in England or
the bickering factions of state politics. The size of the new nation,
its regional differences, economic diversity, and strong tradition of
states' rights conspired to render their formation unlikely. James Madison's prophecy in the Tenth Federalist paper of a national politics
based on perpetually shifting alliances between numerous economic
and sectional interests was entirely reasonable and few persons could
have possessed the prescience to foresee a structure resting on two
permanent nationwide parties.

The two-party system began with the reaction to Alexander Hamilton's proposals during the first Washington administration for strength-
ening the central government and received additional impetus from
the almost continuous warfare raging in Europe from 1792 to 1815.
When the issues raised by these events had been settled partisan conflict subsided until new questions in the 1820s—the tariff, internal
improvements, public land policy, and the government role in banking—compelled the voter to take sides once again. After Jefferson's
election in 1801 Federalism declined, eventually expiring as a national
force with the Treaty of Ghent, and the party system started its
revival in the wake of John Quincy Adams's election in 1825.

But politics in the United States has seldom been determined solely
by appeals, either rational or emotional, to the issues. Personalities,
then as now, were never far beneath the surface. Men and policies
have been so inextricably entwined that parties, particularly in the
first years of the Republic, were often named for individuals. Contemporaries spoke of Jeffersonians and Hamiltonians, of Jacksonians and
the Friends of Adams or Clay. This resulted only partially from the
amorphous organization of the early parties. It flowed also from the
democratic features of American politics, the necessity of winning
over a mass electorate. On election day the voters had to choose between men, not issues, and even though candidates were often identified with certain policies, decision-making was humanized and simplified by reducing debate to a personal preference for one man or his
opponent.

The focus on men also has a technical cause rooted in the provisions
of the Constitution, provisions which contributed greatly to reducing
the number of national parties. The founders devised so powerful
a chief executive that competition for control of the government was
inevitably translated into a struggle to elect him. The White House
quickly became an indispensable adjunct to achieving national political

goals and public attention was attracted by the fight for its possession. Thus the Constitution turned American politics into a popularity contest between the contenders for the presidency around whom clustered lesser figures, the spokesmen for various interest groups, seeking control over the potential wielders of this vast power.

The potency of the office in combination with the Electoral College provided an invaluable assist to the growth of a two-party system.[6] The Constitution assigns each state the number of votes equal to its representation in Congress and requires that a successful presidential candidate receive a majority. As no one interest, be it regional or economic, can muster the requisite figure, the welter of minority groups generally coalesce behind two candidates. Multiple candidacies succeed only in fragmenting the electoral votes, resulting either in the triumph of the strongest contender or election by the House of Representatives where a different, and narrower, set of interests prevails. Third and fourth parties will almost inevitably be squeezed out of the College entirely since the electors go to the candidate who has a plurality of a state's popular vote. Rather than submit to a certain defeat, special interests subordinate their peculiar demands in the expectation of finding a combination of candidates and issues capable of producing the one-half plus one of the electoral votes.

The polarization resulting from the fight for the presidency slowly sifted down to the states, fashioning two parties from the chaos engendered by local factions based on personal, economic, or geographic rivalries. Candidates for sheriff or the state legislature increasingly aligned themselves after 1792 with presidential nominees in response to the voters' demands for such identification or in hopes of gaining additional support by clinging to the coattails of a popular figure. Following Washington's decision to retire, aspiring president-makers began their long search for the best way of insuring an electoral majority in advance of the election. The search ended in Baltimore.

6. *Ibid.*, pp. 228–31.

I

The Jeffersonian Legacy
1789–1824

"The constitution of the United States itself illustrates the mischief of a too powerful executive. All our great parties have taken their principal distinction from the measures of the existing administration. Nay, it may be said that the late disagreeable schism of the republicans takes its origin here; for let whatever may be said to the contrary, the principal question at bottom is, who shall be the next President? Were that officer possessed of less exorbitant power; were he, as he ought to be, a mere executive agent, except as to our foreign relations; with no share of legislation and little of patronage; were he elected for a shorter period than they now are, then, the candidates themselves, their friends or the people at large would be less agitated than they are at the prospect of an election."

Richmond Enquirer, May 2, 1806

ONE

The Rise and Decline of the First Republican Party, 1789-1820

Through most of the nineteenth century, and a part of the twentieth, the organizational structures of the major American political parties could be easily delineated. A layered pyramid of conventions in both parties—county, district, state, and national, each level composed of delegates chosen by the one immediately beneath it, and all ultimately based on the grass roots membership—nominated candidates for almost every elective office in the United States. These conventions also performed the important tasks of adopting the local and national platforms and appointing the hierarchy of committees which controlled the campaign machinery. Whatever corruptions this democratic facade might conceal, the convention system provided the parties with a uniform, legally responsible, and comprehensive means for making their most important decisions and carrying on their electioneering activities. Its adoption marked a considerable advance over the haphazard and ephemeral organization of the first national parties. It would not be much of an exaggeration to say that the use of the national convention by the Antimasons, National Republicans, and Democrats marked the beginning of political parties as we know them today.

The politicians of the Jackson era cannot, however, take exclusive credit for the convention's application to partisan purposes, for they built on foundations laid in an earlier age, only "topping" a structure that had been rising slowly for over forty years. They owe, in particular, a large debt to the Republicans who were the pioneers, if unwitting ones, of our modern parties. All three groups responsible for the introduction of the national convention were offspring of the party of Thomas Jefferson, drawing naturally on its precedents, since their leaders, with a few exceptions, began their careers as Republicans. Any account of the rise of the convention system must start with an examination of the organization of the old Republican party.

The methods by which the Jeffersonians arrived at the thousands of decisions implicit in the task of electing a president, vice-president, congressmen, governors, state legislators, and a host of local officials were various. Variety, indeed, was the distinctive feature of Republican organization. It could not be called systematic insofar as system implies a single, unified method of handling party business. Ostensibly at the apex, but really detached from everything below it, was the congressional caucus, a quadrennial meeting of Republican congressmen summoned to choose the nominees for president and vice-president. The caucus's ties with the state and local divisions of the party were informal and uncertain. Control over local politics was exercised by a confusing number of devices, varying not only from state to state, but often changing within each state from election to election. Furthermore, the lack of coordination between the mechanisms contrived for selecting nominees for statewide offices (e.g. the governor) and those used for county and district nominations (e.g. state legislators) was almost as great as the void existing between the national caucus and the state organizations.

The fluidity of nominating devices before the advent of the convention is so pronounced that it is extremely difficult to make an intelligible summary of the Republican party's organization. Even the congressional caucus, on its face the unquestioned way of nominating presidents, partakes of this general instability. Often pictured as the precursor of the national convention in terms of its procedures and general acceptance by party members, the caucus barely qualifies for institutional status.

Organizational development was, moreover, uneven. In the early years the struggle to attain power imposed on party leaders the necessity of finding ways of uniting all opponents of the Washington and Adams administrations. But the Republican unity forged in the decade of crises beginning in 1790 could not withstand the years of success following the victory of 1800.[1] Although cohesion was maintained nationally until the eve of Jefferson's departure from the White House,

1. Noble Cunningham's *The Jeffersonian Republicans in Power: Party Operations, 1801–1809* (Chapel Hill, 1963) is an invaluable study. Nothing comparable exists for the period between 1809 and 1820.

schisms within the branches of the party developed soon after his first inauguration and became a fixed condition of state politics. Jefferson was easily reelected in 1804, but four years later the caucus-sanctioned nominee, James Madison, faced challenges from two Republicans, James Monroe and George Clinton, as well as from the Federalists.[2] Even though he won handily, the double fissure was symptomatic of a fatal malady. Discipline in the congressional ranks of the party disappeared during the debate over the Embargo in the interregnum between Madison's election and inauguration. In 1812 Madison narrowly defeated fellow Republican De Witt Clinton, who ran with extensive and open support from disaffected Republicans in a tacit coalition with the Federalists. The virtually unanimous elections of Monroe signaled the extinction of the party, not its revitalization. Faced with only token opposition in 1816, Monroe had none at all in 1820. That the Republican party disintegrated at the moment of its greatest triumphs was ironic, yet it cannot be identified after 1816 by a legislative program, a consistent ideology, or an organizational structure that would embrace a majority of the professing members. It became so inclusive that it ceased to exist.

The deterioration of party fabric is usually blamed on the rapid decline of the Federalists following their narrow defeat in 1800. Never strong enough thereafter to compete seriously for the presidency, except as the junior partner in alliances with dissident members of the majority, the Federalists could not maintain, it is reasoned, a sufficiently steady pressure on the Republicans to prevent their fragmentation. So pervasive was the party's success that, in time, it encompassed men whose ideas once would have been judged heretical, "pleasantly drifting," in Henry Adams's phrase, "with the easy current of power."[3]

Without denying the basic validity of this view it could be argued that the Republican party might have withstood the effects of its own prosperity (and we today can appreciate that one-party government is not the anomaly once thought) if it had developed a sturdy organization during its early, creative years. But from an organizational standpoint the party after 1801 was living on the capital accumulated in the previous decade. That fund was publicly declared bankrupt

2. For brief accounts of these and subsequent elections, see Eugene H. Roseboom, *A History of Presidential Elections* (New York, 1964); Arthur M. Schlesinger, Jr., Fred L. Israel, and William P. Hansen (eds.), *History of American Presidential Elections, 1789–1968* (New York, 1971), vol. 1.

3. Henry Adams, *John Randolph* (Boston, 1883), p. 193.

by the failure of the congressional caucus meeting in 1820 to make nominations. The framework of the party proved inadequate to comprehend the political adjustments inevitable in a dynamic society. The failure of the leadership to settle upon a satisfactory organizational formula, as well as the corrosive effects of a monopoly of power, contributed to Republican degeneration. A well-defined exoskeleton of committees, caucuses, or conventions, invested with the power of decision, could conceivably have insured the future of the party by preventing its energies and ideas from dissipating.

The organizational weakness of the Republican party resulted, in some degree, from a conceptual failure. Neither Jefferson nor Madison, or anyone else, set out to create a party. The idea of a permanent, extralegal, and popular organization existing for the purpose of controlling the government would have repelled them in 1789 (provided they could have imagined such a novelty) and it continued to repel them after they had founded the Republican party. It has been frequently pointed out that the word *party*, as applied to politics in the eighteenth century, bore invidious connotations. What is perhaps more pertinent to understanding the organization of the Republican party is the fact that until the adoption of the Constitution national parties were not possible. The Articles of Confederation made no provision for the direct participation of the citizens in the central government. The election of congressmen by thirteen scattered legislatures diffused the source of national power and made it remote from the people.

Thus the states, under the Confederation, provided the only arenas for popular political activity, and even though power struggles developed everywhere the combatants have been more accurately described as factions or interest groups than as parties.[4] The distinction, admittedly, can be a fine one as in several states the cleavage was sharply defined, most notably in New York and Pennsylvania where it bore all the marks of party conflict: an established leadership, a legislative program, a philosophy of government, and a rudimentary organization.[5] Missing as a rule were party self-awareness and a high degree of institutional stability within these factions. There were no recog-

4. Merrill Jensen, *The New Nation: A History of the United States During the Confederation, 1781–1789* (New York, 1950) and *The Articles of Confederation* (Madison, 1948).

5. Alfred E. Young, *The Democratic Republicans of New York: The Origins, 1763–1797* (Chapel Hill, 1967); E. Wilder Spaulding, *New York in the Critical Period, 1783–1789* (New York, 1932); Forrest McDonald, *We the People: The Economic Origins of the Constitution* (Chicago, 1958), p. 164.

nized and consistent methods of decision-making, including how factional candidates should be nominated. State "parties" in the "Critical Period" were exceedingly loose affairs based on secret understandings between leaders of family cliques and narrow regional or economic blocs that changed with bewildering frequency.[6] Even so, the legislative caucus, the corresponding committee, and the public meeting—all fundamental to securing party unity—were not entirely absent, but organizational structure, when present, was highly unstable and excessively decentralized. No state factions, save in Pennsylvania, developed organizations which survived intact between elections or possessed sufficient self-awareness to give themselves distinctive names.[7]

The document offered by the Philadelphia convention to the nation in 1787 presented the first opportunity for waging a national campaign. A few historians have tended to treat the supporters and opponents of the Constitution, Federalists and Antifederalists, as though they were the first national parties, or at least the immediate ancestors of the Federalists and Republicans.[8] Yet contacts over state boundaries were minimal, and nothing approaching a national organization was formed by either group.[9] Only in New York did both sides resort to anything beyond the printed page in mustering popular backing.[10]

The first elections in 1788 under the provisions of the new Constitution were also conducted, by and large, without the use of formal party machinery.[11] George Washington was the choice of every elector and the second votes were widely scattered. The congressional elections were no less lacking in form. Only in Pennsylvania did the Federalist and Antifederalist leaders make serious efforts to unify their followings behind slates of candidates for the House of Representatives

6. The best accounts of politics during this period are Jensen's *New Nation* and *Articles of Confederation*. See, also, Allan Nevins, *The American States During and After the Revolution, 1775–1789* (New York, 1924), pp. 210–410. Forrest McDonald's *We the People* (pp. 22–36) contains a useful summary of state factions as they existed in 1787.

7. Jensen, *Articles of Confederation*, p. xi; Chambers, *Political Parties in a New Nation*, pp. 21–22.

8. This approach is closely associated with Charles A. Beard and receives full expression in his *Economic Origins of Jeffersonian Democracy* (New York, 1927). It is stated more succinctly in *The American Party Battle* (New York, 1928), pp. 29–30.

9. Jackson Turner Main, *The Antifederalists: Critics of the Constitution, 1781–1788* (Chapel Hill, 1961); McDonald, *We the People*, pp. 113–346.

10. Main, *The Antifederalists*, pp. 233–36; Spaulding, *Critical Period*, pp. 221–28.

11. Charles Oscar Paullin, "The First Elections Under the Constitution," *Iowa Journal of History and Politics*, II (Jan., 1904), 3–33.

by holding, in the fall of 1788, state conventions of county delegates to make nominations.[12] The Antifederalists, unsure of their strength, held their convention in secrecy and placed two of their opponents on the ticket so that no clear-cut party alignment was visible to the voters. These were the first nominating conventions ever held, the first application of the representative principle to party government. It would be years before the practice was fully accepted. Elsewhere, nominating devices other than occasional mass meetings were absent, and elections typically were either a free-for-all with many candidates or went by default to some preeminent leader. The preponderant majority of the members of both houses of Congress, including those destined to initiate the Republican party, were decided friends of the new government. The Federalist and Republican parties were an unforeseen development when Chancellor Livingston administered the oath of office to Washington.[13]

The process of party formation was, in a word, organic, and the parties changed continuously in response to new stimuli.[14] Nothing indicates this more forcefully than the diversity of answers given by historians to the question of when parties began. Plausible arguments can be made for the decisiveness of half-a-dozen events ranging in time over a decade.[15] Whatever occasion marks the birth of the first

12. *Ibid.,* 5–7; Harry Marlin Tinkcom, *The Republicans and Federalists in Pennsylvania, 1790–1801* (Harrisburg, 1950), pp. 22–24.

13. This is the opinion of almost every important historian except for the disciples of Beard. See, for example, Roy F. Nichols, *The Invention of the American Political Parties* (New York, 1967); John Spencer Bassett, *The Federalist System, 1789–1801* (New York, 1906), pp. 42–43; Noble E. Cunningham, *The Jeffersonian Republicans: The Formation of Party Organization, 1789–1801* (Chapel Hill, 1957), pp. 23–24; Harry Ammon, "The Formation of the Republican Party in Virginia, 1789–1796," *Journal of Southern History* (referred to hereafter as *JSH*), XIX (Aug., 1953), pp. 284–88; Edward Channing, *A History of the United States* (New York, 1917), IV, 150; Paul Goodman, *The Democratic Republicans of Massachusetts: Politics in a Young Republic* (Cambridge, 1964).

14. The most valuable work on the early history of the Republican party is Cunningham's *The Jeffersonian Republicans.* The following are also very helpful: Irving Brant, *James Madison: Father of the Constitution, 1787–1800* (Indianapolis, 1950); Chambers, *Political Parties in a New Nation;* Dumas Malone, *Jefferson and His Time,* vol. 3, *Jefferson and the Ordeal of Liberty* (Boston, 1962); Joseph Charles, *The Origins of the American Party System* (Williamsburg, 1956); Stuart Gerry Brown, *The First Republicans* (Syracuse, 1954).

15. See Herbert Agar, *The Price of Union* (Boston, 1950), p. 64; Bassett, *The Federalist System,* pp. 42–55; Wilfred E. Binkley, *American Political Parties* (New York, 1947), pp. 45–46; Brant, *James Madison: Father of the Constitution,* pp. 276–305; Chambers, *Political Parties in a New Nation,* pp. 36–42; Edward Channing, "Washington and Parties, 1789–1797," *Proceedings of the Massachusetts*

Republican party, not until the first congressional nominating caucus met in 1800 did it exist, in any formal or precise sense, as a national organization.

The presidential election of 1792 was the first to show the effects of the new partisanship. But the efforts of the "republican interest," as Jefferson termed it, were under the restrictions imposed by Washington's decision to run for a second term, a choice made with the approval of Madison and Jefferson.[16] National unity still carried a higher priority than the demands of party. Additional limitations resulted from the failure of Republican leaders to devise an inclusive national organization for conducting operations against the enemy, although given the gradual manner in which their opposition to Hamilton's reports on the public credit had unfolded this is not surprising. One historian has stigmatized the attempt to defeat John Adams for vice-president as an "intrigue."[17] George Clinton was the candidate selected to oppose Adams, a choice attributable to his strength in an important state and the belief that his fight against ratification of the Constitution would attract support from those dreading an overweening central government.[18] The nomination was highly informal, growing out of conversations among Republican congressmen and other party bigwigs in Philadelphia in conjunction with soundings taken

---

Historical Society, XLVIII (Oct., 1913), 40–41; Henry Jones Ford, *Washington and His Colleagues* (New Haven, 1921), p. 174; Orin G. Libby, "A Sketch of the Early Political Parties in the United States," *Quarterly Journal of the University of North Dakota*, II (Apr., 1912), 213–26, and "Political Factions in Washington's Administration," *ibid.*, III (July, 1913), 293–318; Edgar E. Robinson, *The Evolution of American Political Parties* (New York, 1924), p. 69; Claude G. Bowers, *Jefferson and Hamilton* (Boston, 1925), pp. 56–57, 140–206; John Bach McMaster, *A History of the People of the United States, from the Revolution to the Civil War* (New York, 1936), II, 49; William Miller, "First Fruits of Republican Organization: Political Aspects of the Congressional Election of 1794," *Pennsylvania Magazine of History and Biography*, LXIII (Apr., 1939), 118–43; Mary P. Ryan, "Party Formation in the United States Congress, 1789 to 1796: A Quantitative Analysis," *William and Mary Quarterly*, XXVIII (Oct., 1971), 523–42.

16. Jefferson to Washington, May 23, 1792, Paul Leicester Ford (ed.), *The Works of Thomas Jefferson* (New York, 1904), VI, 493–94; Memorandum, "Substance of a Conversation with the President," May 5, 1792, Gaillard Hunt (ed.), *The Writings of Madison* (New York, 1906), VI, 106–9.

17. Dumas Malone, *Jefferson and His Time*, vol. 2, *Jefferson and the Rights of Man* (Boston, 1951), pp. 478–83.

18. Monroe to Jefferson, July 17, 1792, Stanislaus M. Hamilton (ed.), *The Writings of James Monroe* (New York, 1898), I, 237; Jefferson to Madison, June 21, 1792, Ford, *Works of Jefferson*, VII, 123–24.

from state leaders.[19] Clinton received the second vote of all but five of those electors opposed to the Federalists, finishing a creditable third behind Washington and Adams.

Although there is no indication that Republican leaders were aware of it, by 1792 the main outline of party organization was already evident. Because the party unfolded in response to legislation backed by the executive branch, command fell initially on those congressmen opposing passage of the controversial bills. Often living in the same house, eating from a common table, and otherwise thrown together for hours out of each day, the legislative enemies of the Hamiltonian schemes inevitably assumed responsibility for directing party affairs. No one assigned them this power; it was theirs by necessity.

The method used to focus Republican votes on Clinton clearly fore-shadowed the congressional caucus even though there was never a called nominating meeting of Republican representatives and senators. Not only were members of Congress making the important decisions for the party by 1792, they were also serving individually as agencies for securing the necessary cooperation of politicians back in the states and for collecting grass roots opinion. But whereas the procedures for registering national decisions was eventually formalized, the congressional link with the localities was left to the interest or energy of each legislator. For those districts or states represented by Federalists there was no link at all. The loose connection joining the decision-makers at the center with those responsible for implementing their decisions in the provinces remained the weakest point in the party's line of command. It worked only as long as a consensus prevailed sufficient to insure that most party members would fall in line once the central agency, the congressional caucus, rendered its verdict.

In 1792, however, the party did not extend very far beyond the capitol.[20] Newspaper articles and congressional debates had helped acquaint the common man with the growing split within the government, but arguments over the funding of the debt were not the stuff to excite the average citizen to a very keen interest in government.[21] The events of the next eight years, especially those inspired by the cataclysm underway in France after 1789, would supply the missing

19. Monroe to Madison, Oct. 9, 1792; John Nicholson to Madison, Oct. 3, 1792, Hamilton, *Writings of Monroe*, I, 242–45; Brant, *Madison: Father of the Constitution*, p. 364; Cunningham, *The Jeffersonian Republicans*, pp. 45–49.
20. Cunningham, *Jeffersonian Republicans*, p. 49.
21. Monroe to Jefferson, June 17, 1792, Hamilton, *Writings of Monroe*, I, 231–32.

drama in sufficient quantity to convert the Republican party from a congressional faction into a broadly based national party.

Growing resentment against England's affronts to our national sovereignty turned many Americans against the neutrality policy of the administration. When neutrality ripened into a rapprochement, embodied in Jay's Treaty, opposition was so intense that the congressional leaders of the Republican party were not content merely to oppose its ratification in the Senate—they sought to scuttle the Treaty in the spring of 1796 by persuading the House of Representatives to refuse the funds necessary for carrying out its provisions. Strategy for the maneuver was devised at a meeting of the Republican members of Congress, the first time party policy was officially decided in caucus.[22] But as another caucus would not meet again for several years this was not a precedent of immediate importance.

In the poisonous atmosphere enveloping Jay's Treaty, Washington's prospective retirement assured a contest for the succession. Jefferson's unquestioned preeminence among the Republicans obviated the necessity of convening the newly founded caucus. When Madison wrote him in the spring of 1796 that he and other congressmen intended to "push" him for the presidency it was no more than an informal recognition of what everyone already assumed.[23]

For the vice-presidency no such unanimity existed even though most party leaders believed New York should again be the source. The question was discussed by the members of Congress, but no definite agreement was reached, a few preferring another try with Clinton, others attracted by the rising star of Senator Aaron Burr.[24] Evidently, it was not considered sufficiently important to bother about convening a caucus. Because there had been no need for deciding who the presidential nominee would be, there was no way of deciding upon a vice-presidential candidate. The second votes of the Republican electors were scattered among several men, and Burr, the choice of most of the Republican electors, finished well behind Thomas Pinckney, John

22. Cunningham, *Jeffersonian Republicans*, pp. 77–85.
23. Malone, *Jefferson and the Ordeal of Liberty*, p. 274; Brant, *Madison: Father of the Constitution*, p. 433; Cunningham, *Jeffersonian Republicans*, pp. 89–90.
24. Malone, *Jefferson and the Ordeal of Liberty*, pp. 274, 277; Cunningham, *Jeffersonian Republicans*, pp. 91–92; William Smith to Ralph Izard, May 18, Nov. 8, 1796, Ulrich B. Phillips (ed.), "South Carolina Federalist Correspondence, 1789-1797," *American Historical Review* (referred to hereafter as *AHR*), XIV (July, 1909), 780, 785; Brant, *Madison: Father of the Constitution*, p. 440.

Adams's running mate. This split had important repercussions. Burr later claimed that he was *the* vice-presidential nominee and was, consequently, offended when all the Republican electors, particularly those in Virginia, did not vote for him. Jefferson on the other hand received the united support of the Republican electors.

Agitation stemming from the French Revolution and the pro-English policies of Washington provided the Republicans with a widening base, but it took the events of 1797–1800 to hammer the party into its definitive shape.[25] Under Adams, worsening relations with France brought the United States to the edge of war without healing the deep division between the admirers of England and the supporters of France. The Federalist majority in Congress, egged on by Hamilton and upheld by President Adams, endeavored to suppress opposition through the Alien and Sedition Acts. Seeing in these laws, and in the government's military preparations, a concrete threat to individual liberties and states' rights, the Republicans redoubled their efforts to oust their opponents. Jefferson, elected vice-president in 1797, became the leader in fact as well as in name, and at every level—in Congress, among newspaper editors, in the states, counties, and towns—party consciousness increased many times over.

Yet organizational efforts retained an ad hoc quality. It is highly improbable that the forty-three senators and representatives attending the casual meeting at Marache's boarding house in the spring of 1800 appreciated the future significance of their actions. The gathering was called to prevent a repetition of the confusion occurring in 1796.[26] Jefferson was again the unquestioned choice for president. The sole purpose of the caucus was to designate a vice-presidential candidate. Since the leadership had already agreed upon Burr, his unanimous nomination by the caucus was largely a formality staged to place the official stamp of approval on him for the benefit of distant electors. Both men subsequently received the votes of all the electors opposed to Adams.

Neither before nor after 1800 was any sustained effort made to impose a uniform organization on the states. Despite an early recogni-

25. Stephen G. Kurtz, *Presidency of John Adams: The Collapse of Federalism, 1795–1800* (Philadelphia, 1957); Malone, *Jefferson and the Ordeal of Liberty*, pp. 322–490.
26. Cunningham, *Jeffersonian Republicans*, pp. 161–64; Carl Becker (ed.), "A Letter of James Nicholson, 1803," *AHR*, VIII (Apr., 1903), 511–13; Malone, *Jefferson and the Ordeal of Liberty*, pp. 473–74; E. Wilder Spaulding, *His Excellency George Clinton: Critic of the Constitution* (New York, 1938), pp. 241–42.

tion of what would happen if the Republicans did not pull together, nothing beyond the most informal prodding took place. "In New York there will be at least half republicans; perhaps more [in the state's congressional delegation]," Madison wrote Jefferson in 1794. "It has unluckily happened that in 2 Districts two *republicans* set up agst one Anti [-republican]. The consequence is that a man is re-elected who would not otherwise have taken the field; and there is some danger of a similar consequence in the other district."[27] As more and more people interested themselves in government, reliance on self-nomination or on a small, secret group of leaders to pick candidates and make other intraparty decisions became less and less satisfactory. Needed was an organ which could speak with authority for the whole party so that its decisions would be implicitly obeyed. Only then could the full force of the party's strength be marshaled behind a single candidate or slate. It was precisely this problem which the Jeffersonian Republicans never fully solved. Politicians below the national level continued to be on their own in devising methods of welding their followers into an effective bloc. Inevitably, they built with whatever materials were at hand, leftovers from the colonial and Confederation eras.

In 1792 open campaigning and organization existed, if at all, only in contests for Congress and the state legislatures.[28] In the South, where gentry politics was most evident, candidates announced themselves and presented their case to the citizenry without apparent party backing. New England campaigns were occasionally more complicated. Boston newspapers, for example, circulated tickets of preferred candidates, although there was considerable overlapping between them, and no group in Massachusetts offered a full slate of candidates. Legislative caucuses in New Hampshire made some congressional nominations, but there, as elsewhere in the region, "few signs" of real party organization appeared.[29] New Yorkers used public meetings and correspondence committees in the hot battle between the Federalist John Jay and old Antifederalist George Clinton for the governorship. On its face this election, above all others, seemed a party contest, but the organization behind it was "rudimentary" and it was, in reality,

27. Madison to Jefferson, December 21, 1794, Hunt, *Writings of Madison*, VI, 229.
28. Cunningham, *Jeffersonian Republicans*, pp. 29–45; Ulrich B. Phillips, "The South Carolina Federalists," *AHR*, XIV (April, 1909), 732–36.
29. Cunningham, *Jeffersonian Republicans*, p. 35.

more of a popularity contest than a match between Federalists and Republicans.[30]

The perennial pioneer in these early attempts at party organization was Pennsylvania, where presidential electors and congressmen were all chosen on a statewide basis. Pennsylvania Republican leaders compiled a list of congressional candidates from names submitted by county correspondence committees (chosen at public meetings), but seven of their candidates were the same as those nominated by the Federalists at a small state convention, and neither party had a substantial network of local organizations.[31]

Not until the approach of the election of 1800 was the organization so tentatively begun in 1792 further perfected, assuming in several states a relatively fixed pattern. Republicans in New York adopted the legislative caucus to select their nominee for governor, while candidates for lesser offices received the nod at public meetings.[32] Conferences among top leaders, including congressmen and state legislators, supplemented by popular ratification meetings, designated the gubernatorial candidate in Pennsylvania. A few counties in Pennsylvania initiated conventions of delegates from the townships to nominate local tickets.[33] There was relatively little organized Republican activity in New Jersey until 1800, when the party staged a series of county conventions climaxed by two state conventions, the second for the purpose of making nominations for Congress. As the practice was continued thereafter, New Jersey can claim the honor of holding the first "permanent state nominating convention."[34] Delaware Jeffersonians developed a conferee system closely resembling the delegated convention. Mass meetings in the counties appointed committees to

30. *Ibid.*, p. 38; Spaulding, *George Clinton*, pp. 199–200.
31. Cunningham, *Jeffersonian Republicans*, pp. 38–45; Tinkcom, *Republicans and Federalists in Pennsylvania*, pp. 55–67; Raymond Walters, Jr., "The Origins of the Jeffersonian Party in Pennsylvania," *Pennsylvania Magazine of History and Biography*, LXVI (Oct., 1942), 444–52. Republican electors were nominated through the newspapers. *Ibid.*, 457–58.
32. Cunningham, *Jeffersonian Republicans*, pp. 110, 176–81; Spaulding, *George Clinton*, p. 243.
33. Cunningham, *Jeffersonian Republicans*, pp. 110–14, 159–60; Tinkcom, *Republicans and Federalists in Pennsylvania*, pp. 164, 168, 185–87, 221–22, 257–80. In 1794 one Pennsylvania congressional district held what amounted to a district convention, the first example of a local nominating convention. Tinkcom, *Republicans and Federalists in Pennsylvania*, *pp.* 139–40.
34. Carl E. Prince, *New Jersey's Jeffersonian Republicans: The Genesis of an Early Party Machine, 1789–1817* (Chapel Hill, 1967), pp. 42–64; Cunningham, *Jeffersonian Republicans*, pp. 154–58.

consult with one another before approving candidates for state offices.[35] In Maryland, conventions nominated one Republican candidate for Congress and one presidential elector, but otherwise self-announcement was the prevailing mode.[36]

The increase in party feeling was not always accompanied by the adoption of formal arrangements. New England Republicans, unable to mount an effective counterattack against the large Federalist majority, continued (with an occasional exception) to shroud their operations.[37] In Virginia and South Carolina they employed a mixture of public meetings, committees, and clandestine conferences between legislators to reach their decisions, the line of command more strongly marked in the Old Dominion than elsewhere.[38] North Carolinians possessed no rudimentary structure; candidates simply announced themselves by placing a notice in the local paper.[39]

Deficiencies in organization were for a time masked by strong presidential leadership. Under Jefferson, possession of the White House served as a substitute for organization. Even though Jefferson never subscribed to modern notions of party, he was a thorough partisan who lavished much attention on eliminating the Federalists.[40] But Jefferson's concern could not be transmitted to his successors. In fact it failed before Jefferson retired. Although Madison was, in addition to being the nominee of the congressional caucus, the undoubted choice of the party leaders and membership, including the incumbent president, two separate groups of dissidents opposed his election. One, composed of extreme states' righters, put forward Monroe.[41] The other group, northerners jealous of southern domination or unhappy over the Embargo, backed Madison's running mate, Vice-President Clinton.[42] When Jefferson relaxed his hold on Congress following the elec-

35. Cunningham, *Jeffersonian Republicans*, p. 110; John A. Munroe, *Federalist Delaware, 1775–1815* (New Brunswick, 1954), p. 228.
36. Cunningham, *Jeffersonian Republicans*, pp. 158–59, 192–93.
37. *Ibid.*, pp. 114, 204–8; William A. Robinson, *Jeffersonian Democracy in New England* (New Haven, 1916), pp. 1–35.
38. Ammon, *JSH*, XIX, 309; John Harold Wolfe, *Jeffersonian Democracy in South Carolina* (Chapel Hill, 1940); Cunningham, *Jeffersonian Republicans*, pp. 149–54; 160–61; Malone, *Jefferson and the Ordeal of Liberty*, pp. 460–61.
39. Delbert Harold Gilpatrick, *Jeffersonian Democracy in North Carolina, 1789–1816* (New York, 1931), pp. 69–118.
40. Cunningham, *Jeffersonian Republicans in Power*, pp. 203–74.
41. Harry Ammon, "James Monroe and the Election of 1808 in Virginia," *William and Mary Quarterly*, XX (Jan., 1963), 33–56.
42. Spaulding, *George Clinton*, pp. 288–94.

tion, party lines vanished in angry debates over foreign policy and a squalid struggle for place and power within the new regime.[43] Irving Brant remarks that "the marvel was that the breakdown of administration control did not come several years earlier."[44]

Madison could not put the pieces together. He showed no more interest than Jefferson in organization and far less in other aspects of party business. He did not share Jefferson's partisan and frequently vindictive temperament. Neither could he command by virtue of his hold over the rank and file, for he did not inspire popular adulation. Had Madison possessed the Jeffersonian charisma it is still doubtful he could have kept the party together. To what authority or agency could he appeal? What standard existed against which rebelliousness could be measured? The constitutional landmarks of the 1790s had been defaced by the Republicans' partial assimilation of a neo-Hamiltonian program of internal improvements, protective tariffs, and a national bank.[45] The rise of Napoleon, and French as well as British maritime insults, had partially removed the ideological sting from the conduct of foreign relations. It is significant that the chief source of Madison's difficulties in formulating and carrying out his policies emanated from members of his own party.[46] Nor is it surprising that in 1812 he was reelected in a close and bitter race with another Republican.

The end of the War of 1812 removed from discussion most of the issues which had divided Republicans from Federalists and even Republicans from Republicans. It gave promise of a new age in politics. The results of the election of 1816 strengthened this hope. Monroe's overwhelming victory was achieved against an opposition so half-hearted as to suggest that the party of Washington was, at last, ready to die. Moreover, the new president made the ending of party strife the chief goal of his administration.[47] Because he kept himself above the party battles, a president of the whole nation, he tolerated a Speaker of the House (Henry Clay) who systematically attacked the adminis-

43. Irving Brant, *James Madison: Secretary of State, 1800–1809* (Indianapolis, 1953), pp. 469–81.

44. *Ibid.*, p. 481.

45. Hunt, *Writings of Madison*, VIII (1908), 126–27, 163–64, 341–43.

46. The story of these difficulties is most fully told in the last two volumes of Irving Brant's biography, *James Madison: The President, 1809–1812* (Indianapolis, 1956) and *James Madison: Commander in Chief, 1812–1836* (Indianapolis, 1961).

47. Monroe to John Taylor, Nov. 19, 1810, Hamilton, *Writings of Monroe*, V (1901), 152–53, 156–57; Monroe to Jackson, Dec. 14, 1816, *ibid.*, 342, 345–46.

tration's foreign policy, refused to intervene in the bitter congressional debate over the admission of Missouri, and kept his hands off the struggle over the presidential succession despite its disruptive effect within his cabinet.

Monroe certainly must have thought his nonpartisanship successful when only the caprice of a single elector prevented his unanimous reelection. Yet this unanimity was achieved at the expense of the party. The one means for reaching national decisions fell into disuse. Under Monroe the shaky congressional caucus broke down completely because the unanimity of the election of 1820 destroyed its function.

The fundamental cause for the failure to create a national organization was intellectual. Jefferson, Madison, and Monroe were very much men of their time so far as their concept of party was concerned. Although they occasionally talked about the advantages of parties in a democracy, on balance they were opposed to the idea of permanently organized groups competing for office. To Jefferson they were a "great evil," justifiable only when a vital principle was involved.[48] Madison viewed politics as the testing ground of ideas, not political machines.[49] Like his two predecessors, Monroe thought of the Republican party as comprising all who subscribed to republican government, and he was quite willing to include the mass of the Federalists within this literal definition.[50] The Federalists fell victim not so much to the superior organization of their opponents as to the mildness of the Jeffersonian policies which left them no constructive alternatives.[51]

48. Jefferson to William Branch Giles, Dec. 31, 1795, Ford, *Works of Jefferson*, VIII, 203; Jefferson to James Sullivan, Feb. 9, 1797, *ibid.*, 281; Jefferson to Arthur Campbell, Sept. 1, 1797, *ibid.*, 337–38; *ibid.*, IX (1905), 193n; Jefferson to Thomas Mann Randolph, Feb. 19, 1801, *ibid.*, 185–86; Jefferson to Monroe, Mar. 7, 1801, *ibid.*, 203–4; Jefferson to Benjamin Rush, Mar. 24, 1801, *ibid.*, 230–32; Jefferson to Henry Knox, Mar. 27, 1801, *ibid.*, 236–38; Jefferson to Samuel Adams, Mar. 29, 1801, *ibid.*, 239–40; Jefferson to Gideon Granger, Mar. 29, May 3, 1801; June 1, 1803, *ibid.*, 244–47, 249–50, 469–70; Jefferson to Theodore Foster, May 9, 1801, *ibid.*, 251–52; "Fair Play," *ibid.*, 470–74; Jefferson to E. Gerry, Mar. 29, 1801, *ibid.*, 242. For a full discussion of the attitudes of Jefferson and other Republican leaders, see Richard Hofstadter, *The Idea of a Party System* (Berkeley, 1969).

49. Brant, *Madison: Father of the Constitution*, pp. 347–48; Hunt, *Writings of Madison*, VI, 106–19.

50. Monroe to Jefferson. July 27, 1817, Hamilton, *Writings of Monroe*, VI (1902), 27–28; Monroe to Madison, May 10, 1822, *ibid.*, 289–90; Monroe to George Hay, Aug. 5, 1817, Monroe to Henry Dearborn, Apr. 22, 1820, James Monroe Papers (New York Public Library), cited hereafter as Monroe MSS.

51. Anson D. Morse, "Causes and Consequences of the Party Revolution of 1800," *Annual Report of the American Historical Association for the Year 1894* (Washington, 1895), pp. 538–39.

Only in the states was there an improvement in Republican organization after 1800.

What of the congressional caucus? Did it not provide the same kind of national authority within the party before 1824 that the national convention has supplied since 1832? To all outward appearances it did. From 1800 to 1820 the caucus candidates for president and vice-president were acceptable to the preponderant majority of Republicans and were successful in the Electoral College. Yet the similarities between the two are more apparent than real.

The differences are not just differences of form, although these are significant. On its face the caucus amounted to a selection of the executive by the legislature, a mixing of the two branches of government that could lead, as contemporary critics pointed out, either to the domination of the president by Congress or the corruption of Congress by presidents or would-be presidents. A national convention consists of delegates who have usually played no important role in national affairs and whose primary concerns are often parochial. The convention enlarged and dispersed the process of naming presidential candidates, in effect transferring power from a small number of nationally oriented legislators to a relatively large body of full- and part-time politicians concerned chiefly with local or state patronage. To put it another way, nominating the presidential candidate became the prerogative of the state house and county courthouse crowd instead of remaining the preserve of a small group of congressmen.

Whether the change was salutary remains a moot question, but the convention does reflect the structure of political power more accurately than the caucus. Congressmen did not directly represent or necessarily speak for the state leaders and organizations which operated below them. Few of those manning the state and local nominating machinery, which controlled thousands of elective offices and through them a vast amount of patronage, sat in Congress. Republican voters in districts that elected Federalists had no voice at all in the caucus, a circumstance favoring the South and West where the Federalists were weak or nonexistent. The congressional nominating caucus moved in a sphere entirely separated in any formal or official sense from the great bulk of the party apparatus encompassing the mass of the professional politicians.

But this theoretical weakness of the caucus—its exclusion of the state politicians—was not the immediate cause of its downfall even though it would undoubtedly have proved fatal in the long run. Rather the caucus fell, perhaps faded away would be more apt, because, unlike the national convention, it never succeeded in becoming fully established as the arbiter of the party. The myth of "King Caucus" was the product of a unique contest in 1824 by which time it was, in actuality, already dead. The caucus failed to achieve complete acceptance because its activities were largely superfluous. No one seriously contends that Jefferson, Madison, or Monroe reached the White House as the result of a caucus nomination, something which cannot be said of many of the national convention nominees. It took a very special mechanism to give the presidency to such relatively obscure men as Pierce, Lincoln, and Harding.

Jefferson had received the undivided support of his party in 1796 before the caucus existed. His nominations in 1800 and 1804 were perfunctory, these first caucuses having been summoned to choose his vice-president. The compelling force behind both meetings was the failure of the Constitution to distinguish between the two offices. Unless an agreement was reached before the election there was danger either that the Federalists would win the second office or that the Republican candidates would tie (as happened in 1800).[52] Had Burr not ruined himself by his supposed intrigue with the Federalists in 1801 it is conceivable that a caucus would not have been called in 1804. Everyone would have assumed that the incumbents would be supported for reelection. In any event, the caucus of 1804 met in response to pressures to remove Burr from the ticket, not because anyone believed it necessary to renew Jefferson's title to party leadership. As in 1800 his nomination was unanimous. George Clinton was chosen for vice-president after a single ballot, a number of names being under consideration.[53]

The caucus of 1808 was the first with any claim to have designated the party's standard-bearer. Yet Madison's elevation was as widely taken for granted before the caucus met as Jefferson's had been. His indispensable services in Congress during the party's formative years and his long tenure as Secretary of State had unmistakably marked him as the heir apparent. That he was Jefferson's personal choice was so obvious that it "needed no words."[54] But since opposition to

52. As it turned out, the Twelfth Amendment was implemented before the election of 1804, but its ratification was not a certainty at the time the caucus met.

53. Cunningham, *Jeffersonian Republicans in Power*, pp. 103–5.

54. Brant, *Madison: Secretary of State*, p. 419.

Madison from within the party did exist it could be argued that it was the caucus which put the official party seal of approval on his candidacy, and thereby suppressed any serious threat to his success.[55]

Two intraparty obstacles were raised against Madison. One grew out of northern jealousy over Virginia's presidential monopoly. These malcontents fastened on to the aging vice-president. Clinton's hopes, however, lay more in a union with the Federalists than in diverting Republicans from Madison. The greater menace so far as the caucus nomination was concerned stemmed from a group of Virginians. John Randolph and a considerable number of others, distressed over the administration's detour off the narrow path of strict construction, for which they held Madison responsible, rallied behind Monroe. Monroe did not actively seek the presidency, but, stung by Jefferson's repudiation of his diplomatic labors in London, permitted his name to go before the public in opposition to his former friend.[56]

While it is true that Monroe's candidacy faded rapidly, even in Virginia, after the congressional caucus met, it is not clear that this resulted from the caucus's nomination of Madison. Monroe's prospects were doomed by his lack of support in his own state rather than by what happened in Washington. Clear evidence of this is provided by the results of two legislative caucuses held at Richmond two days before the Washington caucus. At these meetings Monroe was able to garner only 57 legislators to 134 for Madison.[57] Without more substantial support from Virginia, Monroe's candidacy could not be a reasonable undertaking, although a slate of electors pledged to him was subsequently nominated. The congressional caucus which convened on January 23 merely reflected the prevailing Madisonian sentiment in Virginia and elsewhere. Of the 94 persons attending it, 5 abstained, 3 voted for Clinton, 3 for Monroe, and 83 for Madison. Twelve other congressmen were known to be favorable to the Secretary of State.[58] It could hardly be called a contest.

For many years it was commonly believed that in 1812 the caucus nomination had been held over Madison's head by the War Hawks

55. *Ibid.*

56. Ammon, *William and Mary Quarterly,* XX (Jan., 1963), 33–56, relates the whole story behind Monroe's candidacy.

57. *Ibid.,* pp. 45–46; *Richmond Enquirer,* Jan. 23, 26, Feb. 2, 1808.

58. *Richmond Enquirer,* Jan. 28, 30, 1808; Brant, *Madison: Secretary of State,* p. 426.

in order to force his consent to a declaration of war against England.[59] Implicit in this interpretation is a belief in the absolute invincibility of the caucus, that without its sanction Madison could not have been reelected. Irving Brant, in his careful and detailed biography, has shown that the War Hawks had neither the motive nor the desire to withhold the caucus nomination from Madison. No political black-mail lay behind the caucus which renominated the president unani-mously.[60] Senator John Langdon of New Hampshire was chosen to replace the deceased Clinton as Madison's running mate, but a second caucus was required when Langdon declined the honor. Elbridge Gerry was substituted.[61] So again it was the vice-presidency rather than the presidency which revived the caucus. Madison's foes, both Federalists and Republicans, rallied around De Witt Clinton, but they chose to fight their battle outside the caucus walls.

By 1816 Monroe possessed the same imposing credentials that Madi-son carried eight years earlier. His lapse from party regularity had been atoned for by service under Madison as Secretary of War and Secretary of State. "He is certainly the most prominent public charac-ter," one observer wrote in 1815, adding that "public opinion centers upon him, as unhesitatingly, generally, and steadily, as it did upon Mr. Jefferson, or Mr. Madison."[62] Yet the caucus of 1816 came closest to acting like a national convention in that it almost made a nomination not dictated to it in advance. But instead of demonstrating its power, this near exercise of independence confirms the view that caucus con-trol was tenuous.

The principal objection to Monroe had a familiar ring: he was a Virginian. New York Republicans endorsed Governor Daniel D. Tompkins in a state legislative caucus, yet loyally promised to support the choice of the whole party.[63] Tompkins's failure to attract support outside his own state led a number of New York congressmen to cooperate with the advocates of Monroe's more formidable rival, Wil-liam H. Crawford of Georgia. Formerly senator, minister to France, Secretary of War, and, at this time, Secretary of the Treasury, Craw-

59. Roseboom, *A History of Presidential Elections*, p. 68; McMaster, *A History of the People of the United States*, IV, 191.

60. Brant, *Madison: The President*, pp. 452–59.

61. *Richmond Enquirer*, May 26, June 9, 12, 1812.

62. Jonathan Fish to J. W. Taylor, Dec. 15, 1815, John W. Taylor Papers (New York Historical Society), cited hereafter as Taylor MSS.

63. *Niles' Weekly Register*, X (Mar. 16, 1816), 48; "Resolutions of the Republi-can Members of the New York Legislature" [Feb. 14, 1816], in Taylor MSS.

ford obscured his own part in tying to upset Monroe, but there can be no question that his friends made a determined effort in his behalf.[64]

On March 10, 1816, congressmen received an anonymous notice informing them that a caucus would meet in two days to nominate candidates. So few responded to this mysterious invitation, which was interpreted as a Crawford maneuver designed to catch the Monroeites off-guard, that the meeting adjourned after summoning another caucus to meet in four days.[65] At the second caucus a much larger attendance was secured and, after beating back two attempts to prevent nominations, proceeded to ballot. Monroe bested Crawford by the relatively close margin of 65 votes to 54. To mollify the New Yorkers, Tompkins was nominated for vice-president.[66]

Here was a genuine contest for the presidential nomination, the first and only one in the history of the caucus. Does it not prove that the caucus was, after all, the decisive voice of the party? Would not the switch of six votes have resulted in Crawford's election? Perhaps, but it seems more likely that had Crawford won those votes he would still not have become president. The caucus nominee depended ultimately on the acquiescence of the state party leaders and the voters. John W. Taylor, member and later Speaker of the House of Representatives, predicted early in 1816 that "should they [congressional caucuses] ever attempt to *control* the public sentiment instead of *expressing* it, their doings would have little influence in the nation other than to embitter party animosity and to sharpen the edge of political strife."[67] A correspondent of Taylor's warned: "Let a caucus once nominate him who is not the favorite of the people, and then it will be seen that a caucus nomination does not make the president of these United States."[68]

These remarks indicate that not everyone was necessarily prepared to accept the caucus decision as final; more, that the caucus itself

64. S. R. Betts to Van Buren, Mar. 17, 1816; W. W. Bibb to Van Buren, Feb. 5, 1816, Martin Van Buren Papers (Library of Congress), cited hereafter as Van Buren MSS (LC); Barttell Yancey to Thomas Ruffin, Feb. 17, 1816, J. G. De Roulhac Hamilton (ed.), *The Papers of Thomas Ruffin* (Raleigh, 1918), I, 167–68.

65. Nathan Sandford to Van Buren, Mar. 14, 1816, Van Buren MSS (LC); *Richmond Enquirer*, Mar. 16, 20, 1816.

66. J. W. Taylor to Jane Taylor, Mar. 17, 1816; Victory Birdseye to J. W. Taylor, March 13, 1816, Taylor MSS; *Niles' Weekly Register*, X (Mar. 23, 1816), 59–60.

67. J. W. Taylor to John Taylor, draft, Feb. 28, 1816, Taylor MSS.

68. Jonathan Fish to J. W. Taylor, Feb. 20, 1816, Taylor MSS.

was viewed with some distaste. Intraparty attacks on the caucus dated, in fact, from 1800 when some Republican newspapers had denounced the idea of congressional nominations as a usurpation of the Constitution, unaware that their party, and not just the Federalists, had secretly resorted to them.[69] Even the 1804 caucus did not pass completely unchallenged despite the general satisfaction with the ticket.[70] In 1808 it was subjected to a stinging attack by those unhappy over Madison's lockhold on the nomination. All of the anti-caucus arguments destined to gain wide currency in 1824 were enunciated at that time.[71] In 1812 the assault on the caucus was intensified by the Clintonians.[72]

Could the caucus have survived a Crawford nomination? Many were of the opinion that it could not. A letter in the Baltimore *Patriot* cautioned Congress that "should it *in contempt of public opinion* decide on putting Crawford in nomination . . . it will strike upon the public mind like an earthquake and give a shock to the Republican cause the consequences of which cannot be foreseen or easily calculated."[73] The *Kentucky Argus* was more direct: if Monroe were not selected then "the western states will disregard the caucus recommendation."[74] Every tangible sign of public opinion indicated a preference for Monroe.[75] Even more important than newspaper support was the strength Monroe exhibited in the state organizations. Prior to the congressional caucus he had been endorsed by the Republican legislators (in caucus meetings) in Rhode Island, Massachusetts, Pennsylvania, and North Carolina.[76]

The reaction of Virginia, however, would have been critical in determining the fate of a Crawford nomination. The state still held a powerful political position not only because it possessed the second largest number of electoral votes, but also because it occupied a special place in the history of the party. It had reaped the greatest advantage from the caucus system and might, therefore, be expected to support

69. Cunningham, *Jeffersonian Republicans*, pp. 165–66.
70. Cunningham, *Jeffersonian Republicans in Power*, pp. 106–8.
71. *Richmond Enquirer*, Feb. 16, 23, Mar. 22, Apr. 5, May 6, Sept. 30, 1808; James Cheetham, *The Life of Thomas Paine* (New York, 1809), p. iv.
72. *Richmond Enquirer*, June 16, Sept. 4, 8, 1812; *Niles' Weekly Register*, III (Oct. 31, 1812), 131–33; *Touchstone to the People of the United States, on the Choice of a President* (New York, 1812).
73. Holograph copy of a letter printed in the *Baltimore Patriot*, dated Feb. 16, 1816, Monroe MSS.
74. *Richmond Enquirer*, Mar. 23, 1816.
75. *Ibid.*, Jan. 23, Feb. 8, 20, 1816.
76. *Ibid.*, Feb. 8, 24, Mar. 20, 1816.

the caucus even though it rejected, for the first time, the state's favorite son. Such was not the case. Virginia's political leaders made plans in advance to repudiate the caucus should Crawford be nominated and to run Monroe in defiance of it on the grounds that he was the choice of the people. The purpose of the caucus, they asserted, was "merely to give concert to public opinion and not to influence it. . . ."[77] As part of the anticipated revolt, Virginia's congressmen were to boycott the caucus if it seemed likely the Georgian would win.

Of course, we can never know for certain what would have happened had Crawford been nominated. But all sides agreed that the function of the caucus was to concentrate the party behind the man already marked out by public favor. This is what it had done in the past. That man in 1816 was unquestionably Monroe. The success of the caucus nominee depended on the voluntary submission to the caucus edict by the state politicians who controlled the selection of the electors, usually by means of legislative caucuses. Unless the prestige of the congressional caucus nomination was sufficient to command the cooperation of state leaders the mere act of nomination would avail nothing. The prestige of the caucus per se was certainly not great in 1816 and the alternative to Crawford would not have been a fatal division in the party, but a rival candidate far more popular than he.

The full impact of the 1816 caucus became apparent four years later. For the first time in the party's history both the incumbent president and vice-president were candidates for reelection. So pervasive was the disapproval of the caucus by 1820 that only some forty out of over two-hundred members showed up on the appointed day.[78] That it was summoned at all occasioned surprise and the circumstances surrounding the meeting were heavy with intrigue. The object of the caucus's sponsors was, apparently, the vice-presidency. No one, not even the Federalists, thought of opposing Monroe. But Tompkins was then running for governor of New York against De Witt Clinton. The Clintonians saw a chance to embarrass Tompkins by forcing him to declare explicitly his intentions toward the vice-presidency.[79] They

77. James Barbour, Armistead T. Mason, James Pleasants, Jr., Thomas Newton, William H. Roane, Hugh Nelson to the Virginia Legislature, Feb. 9, 1816; Spencer Roane to James Barbour, Feb. 12, 1816, James Barbour Papers (New York Public Library), cited hereafter as Barbour MSS.

78. *Niles' Weekly Register*, XVIII (Apr. 8, 15, 1820), 97, 113; *Richmond Enquirer*, Apr. 11, 14, May 2, 1820.

79. Smith Thompson to Martin Van Buren, Apr. 9, 1820, Van Buren MSS (LC).

were aided in this scheme by admirers of Henry Clay who wanted
to substitute him for Tompkins to give him a head start for the presidency in 1824.[80] Both of these aims were frustrated. The Pennsylvania
and North Carolina delegations formally condemned the caucus and
refused attendance. Only two representatives from Virginia appeared.
With less than a fifth of those invited present any nominations would
have been farcical. A majority of those who did go voted in favor
of Kentucky Congressman Richard M. Johnson's resolution that nominations were unnecessary.

Without a voice being raised in its defense the congressional nominating caucus, as a party institution, passed into oblivion. Monroe and
Tompkins (defeated for the governorship) were reelected all but unanimously without the benefit of its nomination. When a caucus met
again in 1824 it would be the instrument of a faction not a party.

The unlamented end of the caucus in 1820 verified the weak position
it occupied, and the failure to replace it with another organ under-
scored the inherent flaw in the Jeffersonian concept of the party.
Compare it for a moment with the present position of the national
convention. The national convention has been subjected to the severest
criticism, yet its existence has never been seriously menaced because
almost everyone recognizes the need for some means of choosing the
presidential nominees. The convention, thus far at least, seems better
than the alternatives. There have been numerous elections like that
of 1820 when the party nominees were so clearly indicated that the
convention has been a dull superfluity, but no one suggested that it
should be abandoned. It could not be abandoned without jeopardizing
the party as a national organization. But the caucus was abandoned,
and without much thought. So feeble was its institutional grip that
it slipped from life at the first opportunity, taking the Jeffersonian
Republican party with it to the grave.

In retrospect the caucus's lack of acceptance, particularly after 1804,
is unmistakable. First, there is the poor attendance. Every time the
caucus met, a considerable number of congressmen stayed away. Some
of these frankly expressed their dislike of caucuses as improper assemblies, but most, one suspects, did not bother to go because their pres-

80. *Ibid.*; Henry Clay to Amos Kendall, Apr. 16, 1820, in the *United States
Telegraph*, July 25, 1828; William Plumer, Jr. to his Father, Apr. 7, 10, 11,
1820; Plumer to Salma Hale, Apr. 5, 1820, in Everett Sommerville Brown (ed.),
The Missouri Compromises and Presidential Politics, 1820–1825 (St. Louis, 1926),
pp. 17, 47–50; Charles Francis Adams (ed.), *Memoirs of John Quincy Adams*
(Philadelphia, 1875), V (Apr. 6, 9, 1820), 57–58, 60–61.

ence would not have affected the outcome.[81] Measured by attendance, approval of and interest in the caucus reached its peak in 1800 and 1804 and declined steadily thereafter, except in 1816, until 1820. The caucuses of 1800 and 1804 were held before the ratification of the Twelfth Amendment separated the vice-presidency from the presidency in the Electoral College, undoubtedly a factor in the high level of interest. In 1808 attendance fell to 65 percent of those invited (52 absent out of 149) and for the two caucuses of 1812 the percentages were 58 and 56. The first caucus of 1816 drew less than half the Republicans while 24 members (out of a potential of 143) absented themselves from the spirited contest between Monroe and Crawford. The turnout in 1820 was so pathetic that, as we have seen, the caucus adjourned immediately.

A second test of the caucus's acceptance was its procedural stability. When a decision-making body acquires permanence, rules are necessary to regulate its proceedings in order to assure that the individuals or groups contesting for its control will receive fair treatment, or at least know the conditions under which they must compete. The national convention has evolved such rules and it is over them that the fight for party supremacy is often waged. Nothing about the congressional caucus, however, was firmly established. Not the time of its meeting, for it was held as early as January and as late as June. Nor the method of its calling, a very important consideration since the right to convene the caucus amounted to the power to suspend it entirely. The other arrangements of the caucus were in a similar state of flux.

Very little is known about the first caucus because of its informal and secretive nature. We do not know who called it, how it was organized, or how the proceedings were conducted, and no one asked until it was too late to find out.[82] The caucus of 1804 was the first held publicly, but on whose authority it was summoned is equally unclear. It elected a chairman, formally balloted to choose a vice-president, and appointed a national committee of correspondence to oversee and coordinate the campaign.

The highpoint of caucus organization occurred in 1808. Senator

81. *Richmond Enquirer*, Jan. 30, 1808; May 26, 1812; Mar. 20, 1816; Wolfe, *Jeffersonian Democracy in South Carolina*, p. 259; Philip Shriver Klein, *Pennsylvania Politics, 1817–1832* (Philadelphia, 1940), p. 110.

82. T. W. Cobb to Albert Gallatin, Apr. 28, 1824; Gallatin to Walter Lowrie, May 22, 1824, Albert Gallatin Papers (New York Historical Society), cited hereafter as Gallatin MSS.

Stephen R. Bradley of Vermont, chairman of the previous caucus, took it upon himself ("by virtue of the powers vested in me") to call the caucus, although the caucus of 1804 had not authorized such a procedure. A chairman and a secretary were chosen and a committee to notify and secure acceptances from the nominees, as well as a correspondence committee, was appointed. The notification committee was authorized to call another caucus should either of the nominees decline. Bradley's assumption of power did not go unchallenged. A group of seventeen congressmen, headed by Randolph and including many of the opponents of Madison, attacked not only the caucus but singled out the method of calling it for special abuse.[83] Those in favor of the caucus exerted no effort to defend Bradley, preferring to pass off his announcement as a personal eccentricity. One expressed the opinion that the senator was "fitter for Bedlam than the Senate Chamber."[84]

The first caucus of 1812 met in response to an unsigned notice posted to all Republican members which indicated that the barbs aimed at Bradley had found their target. Nothing perhaps betrays the institutional weakness of the caucus more quickly than this inability to solve the simple but basic problem of who would call it. No one thought in terms of continuing party organization. The committee of correspondence was for the campaign only, and even it was abandoned after 1812. Investing the chairman of the previous caucus with the status of a national committee was obviously unsatisfactory since there would always be a fair chance that he would not be around four years later, but at least it had been a start toward a solution. Seemingly, the caucus was simply not worth working out procedures for.

The deterioration of the caucus continued in 1816. So few representatives responded to an unsigned circular that had been mailed that the meeting adjourned after it had authorized printing a notice in the *National Intelligencer* calling another caucus. At the end of the second meeting Henry Clay and John W. Taylor introduced resolutions which would have forced the caucus to adjourn without proceeding to nominations, but these were defeated.[85] Absent congressmen were permitted to cast ballots by proxy, a precedent established in 1808 but disallowed in 1812. Samuel Smith of Maryland, who had

83. *Richmond Enquirer*, Mar. 11, 1808; Mathew Carey, *The Olive Branch* (Philadelphia, 1818), pp. 441–44.
84. *Richmond Enquirer*, Mar. 25, 1808; also, Jan. 26, Mar. 18, 1808.
85. *Niles' Weekly Register*, X (Mar. 23, 1816), 59–60; J. W. Taylor to Jane Taylor, Mar. 17, 1816, Taylor MSS.

signed the Randolph anti-caucus manifesto in 1808, presided. No committee of correspondence was appointed.

The abortive caucus of 1820 reverted to the practice of having the previous chairman issue the call.

A third test of the caucus's acceptance was its ability to unite the party. It had no other raison d'etre. But instead of providing a rallying point, the caucus furnished those who opposed its nominee with an excuse to support another candidate.[86] The caucus did not prevent Monroe or George Clinton from running in 1808.[87] Nor did it stop a number of Republican electors in 1808 from withholding their votes from Clinton, the caucus nominee for vice-president.[88] It did not prevent eighty-seven out of ninety-five Republicans in the New York legislature from nominating De Witt Clinton in 1812, or keep a large body of the party rank and file in other states from voting for him.[89] Such opposition as Monroe faced in the general election of 1816 was based on dislike of the caucus.[90] As the acid test of party regularity, the caucus failed. Far more effective in unifying the party was the transcendent popularity of its presidential nominees.

Republican domination nationally after 1801 was not matched locally. Federalists in the North vigorously, and sometimes successfully, contested for local offices, congressional seats, and governorships. Abandoning their elitist mentality, Federalists in the middle Atlantic and New England states increasingly imitated their opponents by resorting to public meetings, correspondence committees, and nominating conventions. Indeed, "the practical ease" with which the national convention was taken up was "made possible by long experience with low level conventions" held by both parties.[91] But the foundation-laying was primarily Republican work. The Federalists were late-comers and

86. Ammon, *William and Mary Quarterly*, XX (Jan., 1963), 48–49.

87. "Letters of James Monroe, 1798–1808," *Bulletin of the New York Public Library*, IV (Feb., 1900), 56–60; *Richmond Enquirer*, Mar. 18, 1808; Brant, *Madison: Secretary of State*, pp. 430–50.

88. Cunningham, *Jeffersonian Republicans in Power*, pp. 121–23.

89. *Niles' Weekly Register*, II (June 6, 1812), 235; *Address of the General Committee of Correspondence to the Democratic Citizens of the State of Pennsylvania on the Subject of the Presidential Election, 1812* (Philadelphia, n.d.); Brant, *Madison: Commander in Chief*, pp. 96–112.

90. Nicholas Biddle to James Monroe, Nov. 25, 1816, Monroe MSS; *Richmond Enquirer*, Nov. 6, 1816; McMaster, *A History of the People of the United States*, IV, 364–65.

91. David Hackett Fischer, *The Revolution of American Conservatism: The Federalist Party in the Era of Jeffersonian Democracy* (New York, 1965), pp. 81–82 ff.

their apparatus did not survive long after the Treaty of Ghent. By contrast most of the Republican state and local conventions continued functioning and merged into the structures of the new parties which developed after 1825.

In the counties, towns, and states above the Potomac after 1801 the search for votes continued and with it the quest for better ways of gathering them. Where competition between parties did not furnish adequate incentive, factional disputes between Republicans frequently achieved the same result—growing adoption of the convention.

The middle Atlantic states were most advanced along the convention road. Of these, Pennsylvania was well in the lead. The years from 1801 to 1820 in Pennsylvania marked a steady but uneven drift toward the convention system.[92] Many of the factors conducive to the adoption of the convention were present. Popular participation in politics and group competition were traditional by 1800. Antipathy to self-nominated candidates was widespread, based on the belief that in a democracy the office should seek the man.[93] Frequent elections meant incessant, virtually year-round campaigning.[94] Set against Republican factional conflict these conditions resulted in the rapid diffusion of the delegated convention.

The most interesting and significant contests in Pennsylvania after Jefferson's election were between Republicans, with the Federalists reduced to the position of makeweights. Only during presidential campaigns, when the Federalists temporarily came to life, did the Republicans show a semblance of unity. After the War of 1812 multiple factionalism prevailed within the Republican ranks. Before 1801 nomination by delegates, called conferees, elected in county, township, or ward public meetings had received limited use, chiefly in the Philadelphia area. The technique was gradually extended thereafter, first to

92. The indispensable references for Pennsylvania politics for this period are Sanford W. Higginbotham, *The Keystone in the Democratic Arch: Pennsylvania Politics, 1800–1816* (Harrisburg, 1952), and Klein, *Pennsylvania Politics, 1817–1832*. Noble Cunningham's *The Jeffersonian Republicans in Power* (pp. 156–66) contains an able analysis of Republican organization in the state for the years from 1801 to 1809. George D. Luetscher, *Early Political Machinery in the United States* (Philadelphia, 1903); Frank Hayden Miller, "The Nominating System in Pennsylvania" (M.A. thesis, University of Wisconsin, 1894); William M. Meigs, "Pennsylvania Politics Early in This Century," *Pennsylvania Magazine of History and Biography*, XVII (No. 4, 1893), 466–75; and Russell J. Ferguson, *Early Western Pennsylvania Politics* (Pittsburgh, 1938) also contain useful information. In addition see Raymond Walters, Jr., *Alexander James Dallas: Lawyer–Politician–Financier, 1759–1817* (Philadelphia, 1947), pp. 119–46.

93. Higginbotham, *Pennsylvania Politics, 1800–1816*, p. 21.

94. *Ibid.*, p. 28.

combat the Federalists and then by dissident Republicans in order
to discredit the nominations made by the ruling faction's committees,
caucuses, or public meetings. After 1810, county and district conventions were choosing the candidates for the state and national legislatures, although mass meetings were still used for certain county
officials.[95]

The legislative caucus, occasionally employed in the 1790s but not
fully developed and accepted until 1804, nominated the Republican
candidates for governor and presidential electors until 1808.[96] In 1805
and again in 1808 the faction in the minority in the caucuses, the
"Old School" Republicans, sought to switch to a state convention for
the governor's nomination on the grounds that it would be more reflective of the wishes of the party members. In response to this pressure
the leaders of the majority, the "New School" Republicans, in 1808
substituted a "mixed" caucus composed of Republican legislators plus
delegates from those districts represented by Federalists.[97] The mixed
caucus was used again in 1811 following another abortive Old School
attempt to hold a convention. Simon Snyder's uncontested reelection
in 1814 brought a temporary halt to intraparty warfare over how
to nominate a gubernatorial candidate.[98]

Three years later the state convention permanently replaced the
caucus, completing the adoption of the convention system in Pennsylvania.[99] The issue was forced, as usual, by the Old School men. In
1816 they had met in a small and secret convention at Carlisle to
nominate electors hostile to Monroe. At the same time they made
plans to hold another convention in 1817 to select an opponent to
Snyder. The excuse given for creating this schism lay in the supposedly
undemocratic character of the caucus. But the New School faction
parried this thrust by calling their own convention of county delegates
to renominate Snyder. Both groups repeated the technique in 1820.
Subsequently, all major parties and factions used the convention to
nominate candidates for statewide offices as well as for local ones.[100]

95. *Ibid.*, pp. 36–39, 58–63, 70–71, 115–17, 139, 202, 263–64, 282–83, 297–98, 304,
312–20.
96. *Ibid.*, pp. 41, 74, 87–89, 115–17, 139, 332.
97. *Ibid.*, pp. 153–54; Cunningham, *Jeffersonian Republicans in Power*, pp.
163–65; *Richmond Enquirer*, Mar. 8, 15, 1808.
98. Higginbotham, *Pennsylvania Politics, 1800–1816*, pp. 226–27, 297.
99. *Ibid.*, pp. 317–23.
100. Klein, *Pennsylvania Politics, 1817–1832*, pp. 58, 195–97. Large numbers
of state legislators served as delegates to state conventions, so they did not
entirely lose their caucus flavor.

New York repeated the Pennsylvania experience of growing Republican factionalism, although the Federalists were able to maintain their separate identity for a longer period. Competition, both inter- and intraparty, resulted in an improvement and extension of party organization, but the state lagged behind its southern neighbor in the use of the convention. Before 1801 nominations for local offices were made at public meetings or by committees chosen at such gatherings. Legislative caucuses selected the candidates for governor and lieutenant governor. This pattern remained fundamentally unchanged until around 1809.[101] In New York City and in a few congressional districts there developed the practice of referring nominations to a joint meeting of the committees elected at the mass meetings in the wards or counties. Within the next few years this introduction of the representative principle led to the widespread employment of the convention for the nomination of state and national legislators.[102]

The dominant force in New York politics for more than two decades after 1801 remained the caucus. Within the Republican party caucus supremacy did not meet serious challenge until 1817, and the state convention was not introduced by one faction until 1824. The caucus not only designated candidates for governor and lieutenant governor, it also chose the nominees for the state senate, approved the holders of major appointive offices, and umpired the disputes between the various sections of the party. It was, in short, the ruling agency of the party to whose decisions all who hoped for preferment bowed.[103] Prior to 1817 periodic revolts against the caucus nominee occurred, but the minority faction merely held its own caucus, leaving the institution undisturbed.

The breakup of the caucus occurred gradually and was intimately connected with the struggle for party leadership between the Clintons (first George and then his nephew De Witt) and their opponents, dubbed Bucktails from an insignia worn on their hats.[104] In 1811 and 1813 the Bucktails, closely associated with Tammany in New York

101. Cunningham, *Jeffersonian Republicans in Power*, pp. 148–56.

102. *Ibid.*, pp. 150, 154–56; *Richmond Enquirer*, Mar. 31, 1807; Apr. 15, 1808.

103. Jabez D. Hammond, *The History of Political Parties in New York* (Albany, 1842), I, 294–95, 393, 458, 480–81, 561–64; *ibid.*, II, 114, 191–95, 208–11, 214–15; Van Buren to ——, draft, Mar., 1818, Van Buren MSS (LC); Robert V. Remini, *Martin Van Buren and the Making of the Democratic Party* (New York, 1959), pp. 10–11.

104. The best general accounts of New York politics in this period are Hammond, *Political Parties in New York* and Alvin Kass, *Politics in New York State, 1800–1830* (Syracuse, 1965).

City, threatened to bolt the caucus rather than submit to De Witt's nomination for lieutenant governor.[105] When Tompkins moved from the governorship to the vice-presidency in 1817 the two groups locked horns over the succession. A majority of the Republican legislators were Bucktails, but as De Witt was strong in the Federalist counties, his friends suggested that those counties be allowed to elect delegates to the caucus. The Bucktails could not refuse without offending a large segment of the party, and even though they forced a second election of delegates in an effort to secure a favorable result, Clinton was nominated for governor by a mixed caucus of 95 legislators and 32 delegates.[106]

Animosity between the Republican factions after this election prevented the restoration of party harmony. After 1817 Clintonians and Bucktails ceased to attend the same caucus. Since the Bucktails controlled the legislature they assiduously tried to make their majority caucus the standard of Republican regularity.[107] In 1820 the Bucktails nominated Tompkins for governor in a pure caucus, laying exclusive claim to the Republican title.[108] An attack on the caucus, they asserted, constituted an assault on the integrity of the Republican party; the Clintonians were accused of denouncing the caucus only because it did not serve their ambitions.[109] Clinton, nominated at a public meeting, narrowly won reelection in 1820, but did not seek a third term. The caucus was successfully reestablished in 1822 when its candidate, Joseph C. Yates, was elected over feeble opposition.[110] Not until the upheaval in New York attendant upon the election of 1824 would the convention rise to challenge the caucus.

New Jersey Republicans had experimented with conventions before 1800, but it was not until after Jefferson's election that the state was

105. Hammond, *Political Parties in New York*, II, 291–94, 342–43.
106. *Ibid.*, I, 433–34; *Niles' Weekly Register*, XII (Apr. 5, 1817), 96; John C. Fitzpatrick (ed.), *The Autobiography of Martin Van Buren* (Washington, 1920), pp. 79–82; Peter B. Porter to Van Buren and Moses I. Cantine, Feb. 13, 1817; S. R. Betts to Van Buren, Feb. 24, 1817; Enos T. Throop to Van Buren, Mar. 15, 1817, Van Buren MSS (LC).
107. *Richmond Enquirer*, Apr. 8, 1817; Hammond, *Political Parties in New York*, I, 484–87, 504–5, 576–77; Ivor Debenham Spencer, *The Victor and the Spoils: A Life of William L. Marcy* (Providence, 1959), pp. 27–30.
108. *Albany Argus*, Feb. 25, 1820; *Niles' Weekly Register*, XVII (Jan. 29, 1820), 376; *Republican Nomination for Governor and Lt. Governor. With an Address to the Electors of the State of New York*. n.p., n.d.
109. *Republican Nomination for Governor* . . . . , pp. 7–12.
110. Hammond, *Political Parties in New York*, I, 527; *ibid.*, II, 100–101; *Albany Argus*, Mar. 29, 1822.

systematically and thoroughly organized.[111] County conventions in the northern part of the state (composed of delegates chosen in the township), some of which operated under detailed rules of procedure drawn up by associations of party members, made local nominations and appointed delegates to a biennial state convention which designated candidates for Congress and for presidential electors. The southern counties were not so well organized and depended on public meetings to perform these tasks. The legislative caucus controlled patronage and nominated the gubernatorial candidate (elected by the legislature, not by popular vote). Decline of the Federalists beginning in 1812 caused the county associations and their convention-committee structure to fall apart, a process largely completed by 1817. The state convention, nevertheless, continued to meet until 1826 when its continuity was broken by a split which heralded a new party system.

Delaware enjoyed all the requisites for an early development of the convention. Its three counties were broken down into smaller governmental units called "hundreds" which functioned politically much as the northern township; the governor and the one member of Congress were popularly elected; and Delaware Republicans and Federalists kept up party competition well after Federalism elsewhere had yielded up the ghost.[112] Use of a convention-type format went back to the 1790s when conferees appointed at public meetings consulted over the selection of the Republican gubernatorial standard-bearer. In 1801 the party again held a state convention for the governorship and followed the same procedure the next year in nominating the congressional ticket. At the same time, the counties adopted the convention, the delegates chosen at mass meetings in the "hundreds." Delaware thereby became the first state to employ fully the convention system.[113]

New England tarried behind the middle states in the utilization of the convention, but it made considerable progress after 1801 in developing an efficacious system of centralized control over party affairs.

111. Luetscher, *Early Political Machinery*, pp. 83–94, 137–43; Cunningham, *Jeffersonian Republicans in Power*, pp. 166–71; Prince, *New Jersey's Jeffersonian Republicans*, pp. 68–209.

112. Shaw Livermore, Jr., *The Twilight of Federalism: The Disintegration of the Federalist Party, 1815–1830* (Princeton, 1962), pp. 123–24; John A. Munroe, *Federalist Delaware*.

113. Munroe, *Federalist Delaware*, pp. 228–30; Cunningham, *Jeffersonian Republicans in Power*, pp. 171–74; Luetscher, *Early Political Machinery*, pp. 94–103, 146–50.

Connecticut was the only state which attempted a close supervision, by law, over the nomination process. At the poll preceding the election of congressmen and state senators every freeman was entitled, when casting his ballot, to nominate in writing his choice for the office to be voted on in the next election. By a varying formula, usually twice the number to be elected, the persons most frequently named were officially nominated.[114] Unless party leaders were willing to relinquish control over nominations some device was needed to guide the rank and file in the exercise of their statutory prerogative.

A highly centralized caucus-committee system served the purpose. An annual meeting at the state capitol of Republican legislators and other leaders either made the nominations for the statewide offices or turned the responsibility over to a general committee designated by the caucus. The general committee, in turn, appointed the county committees (divided into town and election district subcommittees) which made the selections for local offices. Republican voters participated in this process only if they attended a great rally held for their benefit each year in order to sanction what the leaders had already decided.[115]

Party choices for state offices in Rhode Island had been dictated by caucuses since the late eighteenth century. In 1808 the Republicans began electing delegates to join with the legislators for making nominations. This mixed caucus (styled a "convention") continued in operation for over twenty years before being replaced by the pure convention. The governor and other state officials, congressmen, and presidential electors fell under the sway of these caucuses.[116] Rhode Island was one of the earliest and most persistent users of the mixed caucus, a transitional stage between the caucus and the convention.

Republican organization made considerable headway in Federalist-dominated Massachusetts after 1801. As in other New England states, the directing agency consisted of the caucus which nominated the governor and lieutenant governor and appointed the members of the county committees on whom the burden of campaigning rested.[117]

114. Luetscher, *Early Political Machinery*, pp. 117–19.
115. *Ibid.*, pp. 119–20; Cunningham, *Jeffersonian Republicans in Power*, pp. 125–30; Robinson, *Jeffersonian Democracy in New England*, pp. 38, 59, 63–64.
116. *Republican Prox* [Feb. 28, 1815], handbill, Library of Congress; *Richmond Enquirer*, Nov. 14, 1816; Neil Andrews, Jr., "The Development of the Nominating Convention in Rhode Island," *Publications of the Rhode Island Historical Society*, I (1893), 260–67; Luetscher, *Early Political Machinery*, pp. 120–21.
117. Cunningham, *Jeffersonian Republicans in Power*, pp. 133–37; *Richmond Enquirer*, Feb. 1, 1814; Feb. 24, 1820.

For state legislators, congressmen, and electors, county and district public meetings sufficed in most instances, but delegate conventions appeared shortly after the turn of the century. By 1810 the local convention had become common, although not universal, throughout the state.[118]

The Republican caucus in New Hampshire attained a relatively early supremacy. By 1804 legislators, in conjunction with other party chiefs, selected the candidates for the governorship, state senate, and Congress. These leaders also supervised the formation of a county convention and committee network similar to that in the neighboring states of the region.[119]

Vermont, still largely a frontier state in the period before 1820, was the least well organized. As in the western states, the Federalists were not able to offer much in the way of a sustained opposition, thus depriving the Republicans of their greatest incentive to establish partisan machinery. Party feeling was sufficiently present, however, that the Republicans were compelled to use the legislative caucus for marking out their nominees for statewide offices.[120]

The Southeast manifested the least concern with formal political organization of any of the sections bordering on the Atlantic, evidence of the lack of a competitive two-party system. But the degree of deficiency varied from state to state.

Maryland, true to its tradition, bore the characteristics of both North and South in the development of an electioneering apparatus. In some areas of the state the convention appeared relatively early. Baltimore, for example, held a city convention in 1804, seven years after it had been divided up into wards. A number of counties and congressional and presidential electoral districts also adopted the convention. In most places, though, self-nomination, public meetings, and committees prevailed, and the convention, even where introduced, was irregularly used.[121] The absence of popularly elected state officials hindered the growth of centralized nominating devices.

118. Cunningham, *Jeffersonian Republicans in Power*, pp. 138–42; *Richmond Enquirer*, Nov. 12, 1812; Robinson, *Jeffersonian Democracy in New England*, pp. 60–62; Samuel Eliot Morison, *The Life and Letters of Harrison Gray Otis* (Boston, 1913), I, 90–91; *Statement of Votes in Congress Given by the Hon. Ebenezer Sage* (Boston, 1812).

119. Cunningham, *Jeffersonian Republicans in Power*, pp. 142–45; Luetscher, *Early Political Machinery*, p. 122.

120. Cunningham, *Jeffersonian Republicans in Power*, pp. 145–46.

121. *Ibid.*, pp. 176–80; Luetscher, *Early Political Machinery*, pp. 103–5, 107–11; *Richmond Enquirer*, May 22, 1816.

Among southern Republicans, the Virginians maintained the most efficient organization. A general state committee, composed of Richmond residents, managed party affairs and oversaw election campaigns, relying on a network of county committees to carry out its orders. But the ultimate voice belonged to the legislative caucus which appointed both the general and local committees.[122] This pyramidal structure, constructed initially for the election of 1800, provided the "Richmond Junto," a small coterie of leaders who dominated the caucus and usually served on the central committee, with the means for extending its sway throughout the state.[123] Yet little existed in the way of formal nominating machinery. Only the presidential electors were chosen popularly on a general ticket and these were picked by the caucus. Candidates for legislative and other positions were normally announced in the newspapers, the notice either authorized by the aspirant or placed by his friends. Even public meetings for nominating purposes were rare before 1820.[124] In a few isolated instances committees from the counties in a particular congressional district met to designate a nominee, but this procedure was so seldom used that it did not indicate a trend to the convention system.[125] Not until 1828 would the domination of the caucus be seriously challenged in Virginia.

Until North Carolina switched from district electors to a general ticket in 1815 there were no statewide elections. This, in addition to the fact that (as in Virginia) the governor and other state officers were chosen by the legislature, retarded the growth of overt organization. Then, too, after 1803 the Federalists were a negligible factor.[126] With an occasional exception self-announcement was the only way candidates had of getting their names before the public.[127] The predictable result of these conditions was the multitude of candidates indicative of an unstructured politics.

Popular elections in South Carolina existed only for the state and

122. Cunningham, *Jeffersonian Republicans in Power*, pp. 180–83; *Richmond Enquirer*, Aug. 9, Oct. 11, 1808.

123. Harry Ammon, "The Richmond Junto, 1800–1824," *Virginia Magazine of History and Biography*, LXI (Oct., 1953), 395–418.

124. Cunningham, *Jeffersonian Republicans in Power*, pp. 86, 185–87; *Richmond Enquirer*, Apr. 29, 1806; Apr. 10, 1807; Mar. 22, 1811; June 25, 1814; Mar. 2, 1816; Apr. 18, 1817; Mar. 6, 1818; Sept. 19, 1820.

125. *Richmond Enquirer*, Feb. 15, 1815; Aug. 10, Oct. 26, 1816.

126. Henry M. Wagstaff, *States' Rights and Political Parties in North Carolina, 1776–1861* (Baltimore, 1906), pp. 38–40.

127. Gilpatrick, *Jeffersonian Democracy in North Carolina*, pp. 127–78; Cunningham, *Jeffersonian Republicans in Power*, pp. 187–88.

national legislatures and for local offices. And for these the masses had little opportunity for expressing their preferences in the selection of the party's candidates. The nominees were agreed upon informally by small clusters of leaders who indicated their decisions through newspaper columns. Now and then a public meeting did venture to make nominations, but these were exceptions. South Carolina was to remain one of the most backward states in the adoption of an institutionalized party organization.[128]

In distant and sparsely populated Georgia the Federalists were never able to compete effectively as a party. Politics, personal and factional in nature, was conducted under the broad banner of Republicanism. The ambitious nominated themselves or were put forward by their friends. Public meetings for nominating purposes convened with great rarity. Congressmen were elected on a general ticket (the only office holders who were), but party leaders at the capitol managed their selection without bothering to involve the public. Formal party organization was, in brief, nonexistent in this period.[129]

With one exception the same general inattention to organization that prevailed in the South also characterized the West. The exception was Ohio. The convention technique was employed as early as 1802 to nominate delegates to the state constitutional convention.[130] For five or six years following the territory's admission to the Union in 1803 a legislative caucus picked the party's nominees for governor, electors, and congressman. Those running for the state legislature were approved by county conventions made up of delegates chosen by township meetings. These early conventions were held only in the more settled areas, most frequently in Hamilton County, which supported a full-blown convention-committee system, where the population was sufficiently dense to make the system feasible. Rival tickets frequently challenged the convention's nominees so that the system was far from secure.[131] This early organizational sophistication did not last as diminishing competition from the Federalists removed its main cause. For a time after 1803 the Federalists had been able to maintain enclaves of strength in those towns settled by New Englanders, retaining a

128. Cunningham, *Jeffersonian Republicans in Power*, pp. 189–90.
129. *Ibid.*, pp. 190–92; Paul Murray, "Party Organization in Georgia Politics, 1825–1853," *Georgia Historical Quarterly*, XXXIX (Dec., 1945), 195–97.
130. William T. Utter, *The Frontier State, 1803–1825*, vol. II, *The History of the State of Ohio* (Columbus, 1942), p. 7.
131. *Ibid.*, pp. 30–36; Cunningham, *Jeffersonian Republicans in Power*, pp. 196–200; *Richmond Enquirer*, Nov. 14, 1804; Mar. 15, 1808.

measure of influence by supporting one Republican faction against another.[132] As this external pressure abated, the importance of party among Republicans receded in favor of personality cults and regional interest groups. Weakening party discipline was highlighted by the decline of the caucus; after 1808 gubernatorial and congressional candidates relied on self-announcement.[133]

An unusual characteristic of Ohio Republicanism was the attempt of closed associations to preempt party decision-making. Prior to 1803 party organization had been synonymous with certain Republican Societies, modeled apparently on the Democratic Societies of the 1790s. It was delegates from these clubs who had met in conventions to nominate the delegates to the constitutional convention in 1802. Afterward, their nominating activities atrophied. Then for a few years, roughly from 1810 to 1812, a transplanted version of New York City's secret Tammany Society attempted to impose its will on the party by nominating state officers and an electoral ticket. Although it enjoyed some initial success, the influence of Tammany waned rapidly.[134]

Indiana became a state too late (1816) to feel the impact of the first national parties. Every politician acknowledged allegiance to the great Republican family. The state was run by a triumvirate whose control was exercised informally; no agency preselected the candidates for any office.[135] Election contests were pell-mell affairs with a large number of candidates who entered the lists by having their friends announce their intentions in a newspaper. An attempt in 1817 to introduce a caucus nomination for Congress had to be abandoned because of the hostility to such control. A hint of a new era occurred in 1820, however, when a convention of representatives from county militia companies nominated a candidate for the legislature.[136] And a year later a more regular form of the convention, with delegates from the townships, made its appearance. A local editor hailed its coming as a moral event, and hoped it would "have a tendency of

132. Utter, *Frontier State*, pp. 32–62; Roscoe Carlyle Buley, *The Old Northwest: Pioneer Period, 1814–1840* (Bloomington, 1955), I, 4; Eugene H. Roseboom and Francis P. Weisenburger, *A History of Ohio* (Columbus, 1953), pp. 78–79.

133. Utter, *Frontier State*, pp. 43, 57–58, 117, 296–97, 326; Buley, *Old Northwest*, II, 8–9.

134. Utter, *Frontier State*, pp. 55–62.

135. Buley, *Old Northwest*, II, 5–6, 36; Adam A. Leonard, "Personal Politics in Indiana, 1813–1823," *Indiana Magazine of History*, XIX (Mar., 1923), 1–12; Logan Esarey, "Pioneer Politics in Indiana," *Indiana Magazine of History*, XIII (June, 1917), 103.

136. Esarey, *Indiana Magazine of History*, XIII (June, 1917), 111–13.

putting down that uncouth and baneful method of a candidate starting up, and to gain popularity all around the country to electioneer for himself, treating at every town or grog shop he comes to as long as he has money or credit."[137]

Illinois politics in the first few years of its statehood bore a close resemblance to that of Indiana. Parties did not exist. Elections after 1818 continued the petty quarrels of territorial days. Weak focal points were provided by a running, undercover battle on the part of those seeking to introduce slavery and by the predominance of Ninian Edwards, territorial governor and then United States Senator. Both sides in the dispute over slavery were sufficiently well organized to nominate delegates to the constitutional convention and for other offices by holding public meetings and local conventions. But these vanished after a few years. Not until the 1830s would the nominating convention win a permanent place in the political scheme. In the meantime, self-announcement by the candidates sufficed.[138]

Of the remaining states of the nation of 1820—Kentucky, Tennessee, Louisiana, Alabama, and Mississippi—little can be said because they possessed no political organization worthy of the name. Politics in these southwestern states was an intensification of the individualistic tendencies already noted in the Southeast and Northwest: the absence of a two-party system and the ensuing prevalence of candidacies supported, at most, by narrowly based cliques. No conventions, no caucuses (of a formal nature) gave central direction to this factionalism. The mass meeting, called on an ad hoc basis, was the only form of open activity which these states could muster.[139] Regular party organization would not be incorporated into the politics of these sparsely populated states until the national revival of parties in the 1820s.

The trend in most states, despite occasional reverses, was toward greater control over nominations by party leaders. Yet no improvement in the national organization accompanied the increase in power of

137. *Ibid.*, p. 113.
138. Buley, *Old Northwest*, II, 7–8, 15–17, 20; Theodore Calvin Pease, *The Frontier State, 1818–1848*, vol. II, *The Centennial History of Illinois* (Springfield, 1918), pp. 70–92, 136, 251–54; Charles Manfred Thompson, "Elections and Election Machinery in Illinois, 1818–1848," *Journal of the Illinois State Historical Society*, VIII (Jan., 1915), 379–82.
139. Cunningham, *Jeffersonian Republicans in Power*, pp. 192–96; Thomas Perkins Abernathy, *Formative Period in Alabama, 1815–1828* (Montgomery, 1922); Edwin Arthur Miles, *Jacksonian Democracy in Mississippi* (Chapel Hill, 1960).

the state and local leaders. The congressional caucus originated when the party was largely coterminus with a minority in the Congress. Within a few years the state and local branches had grown tremendously, but the most important decision—the selection of the presidential nominee—remained, ostensibly, the prerogative of a few men at the top who were under no compulsion to consult with those beneath them. This lack of balance inevitably bred discontent that revealed itself in periodic revolts. The rebels were contained only because the line of inheritance was so distinct, the caucus's function being that of naming the vice-president. No one thought about the caucus except during the few months immediately preceding its meeting. No sustained effort was made to replace the caucus with a more satisfactory institution or even to initiate fixed rules of proceeding. An air of subterfuge always surrounded its meetings. Out of sight for four years, it remained out of mind. The only persons who could have effectively remedied the organizational weakness of the party, the three Republican presidents, failed to do so because they were prisoners of an archaic concept of parties and looked forward to, indeed encouraged, their extinction. The election of 1824, by reviving competition for the presidency, would result in sweeping the congressional nominating caucus into the discard once and for all.

TWO

The Nadir of Party, 1821–24

If the election of 1820 reduced the number of candidates for president to the absolute minimum, that of 1824 achieved the opposite distinction. The list of possibilities seemed inexhaustible. Hezekiah Niles observed in 1822 that no less than sixteen persons were under consideration, and ventured the sarcastic prediction that since "each has a reasonable quantity of friends, with long purses or extensive patronage to keep the press a going we may expect a great deal of *ink-shed* before the 4th of March, 1825."[1] The campaign and election of 1824 provided a rare demonstration of what happens when a triumphant party, having vanquished its opposition, also exhausts its ideology, heroes, and organization.

The party did not have and did not need until 1824 an efficient tribunal to referee conflicting claims on the presidency. During the long campaign prior to the election of 1824 an attempt was made to resurrect the congressional caucus. It failed miserably. Yet the abortive effort became the central issue of the contest, elevating the caucus to an importance it never had previously enjoyed. The most consequential result of the campaign, though, was not the death throes of the discredited caucus, but the impetus it provided for the spread of the convention idea. Out of the competition for the presidency came a revived interest in ways of concentrating mass support, a pursuit that had been neglected for over twenty years. Significantly, 1824 was the first election in which a proposal for holding a national nominating convention received serious and sustained attention. The suggestion was premature, but as a result of the discussion and of organizational

1. *Niles' Weekly Register*, XXII (Apr. 27, 1822), 129-30.

developments in the states the election of 1824 moved the national convention measurably closer to realization.

The acknowledged front-runner was William H. Crawford, the Secretary of the Treasury, whose supporters styled themselves "Radicals" in order to advertise their devotion to states' rights and economy. John Quincy Adams, by virtue of his position as Secretary of State and as the only northern candidate, was assured of substantial support. Another cabinet member, Secretary of War John C. Calhoun, also received serious consideration. Still in the nationalist phase of his long career, the South Carolinian enjoyed broad but (as it turned out) shallow backing. Speaker of the House Henry Clay was looked upon as the natural leader of the new West. The most lightly regarded of the major contenders, Andrew Jackson, the folk hero of New Orleans, began the campaign as an unknown political quantity.

Crawford's place at the head of the pack rested in large measure on the myth of caucus invincibility. Failing to grasp fully the difference between his position and that of Jefferson, Madison, and Monroe before their elections, Crawford's opponents feared that if the caucus nominated him, Republicans throughout the nation would dutifully fall into line. This fear not only overestimated Crawford's appeal and the caucus's power, it was based on a gross misunderstanding of the nature of the Republican party. It implied a degree of cohesiveness which simply did not exist. The Republicans were no longer bound together by doctrine or platform nor pressed together by Federalist opposition. The congressional caucus could not have delivered the presidency to any of the candidates in 1824.

All agreed that if a caucus did meet the Georgian would receive its endorsement. "Crawford," wrote Senator Rufus King early in 1823, "is the favorite of Congress."[2] His impressive showing eight years earlier seemed proof of his strength. His enemies conceded that he had more congressmen pledged to him than any one of his antagonists. It was, therefore, to the mutual interest of the other aspirants to discredit the caucus. By damaging the chief prop of the leading contestant they would advance their own prospects. Maintaining a united front against Crawford was no easy task as the relationships between Adams, Clay, Calhoun, and Jackson were plagued by suspicions born of con-

2. King to Christopher Gore, Feb. 9, 1823, Charles R. King, *Life and Correspondence of Rufus King* (New York, 1900), VI, 499.

flicting ambitions and, in several instances, personal animosities. A limited cooperation was made possible, however, by their common and intensive dislike of Crawford, reinforced by their individual self-interest. "It strikes me that many of the voices now raised against caucusing," a correspondent of the *Richmond Enquirer* wrote, "do not proceed so much from an objection to the principle, as from the consequences—they foresee that William H. Crawford *will be* the favorite of the Republicans."[3] Virtually all of the anti-caucus rhetoric that filled the newspapers between 1821 and 1824 was aimed as much at Crawford as at the caucus, and emanated from editors enlisted under the banner of one or another of his presidential rivals. Crawford's strong suit, in the estimate of the opposition, was highly assailable.

The Crawfordites, for their part, accepted the role assigned them. No effort was made to disguise Crawford's dependence on the caucus nomination for success in the election. Yet his friends tried very hard to pretend that the caucus was not merely a Crawford tool. Legislative caucuses in Virginia and New York, known to favor Crawford, endorsed the congressional caucus as the best method of selecting the Republican nominee, but scrupulously refrained from mentioning their preferred candidate.[4] The Georgia legislators permitted themselves to endorse the state's favorite son, nobly agreeing to sacrifice "their personal predilections" if "necessary to preserve undivided the Republican interest of the Union. . . ."[5] Reports circulated that he would withdraw if he failed to receive the caucus nomination.[6] Nothing though could mask the fact that almost all of those upholding the caucus were friends of the Treasury secretary. Thus the pattern for the campaign was fixed early: the defenders of the caucus against its attackers, Crawford versus the field.

The chief argument used in 1824 against the caucus was familiar enough—it violated the spirit, if not the letter, of the Constitution. Members of the national legislature were barred from serving in the Electoral College and the power to choose electors had been given to the state legislatures to dispose of as they saw fit. By 1824 all but six of them had placed the selection in the hands of the voters.

3. *Richmond Enquirer*, Nov. 11, 1823.
4. *Niles' Weekly Register*, XXI (Jan. 10, 1823), 292; *ibid.*, XXIV (May 3, 1823), 131; *Daily National Intelligencer*, Jan. 24, 1824; *Albany Argus*, Jan. 29, 1824; John Tyler to James Barbour, Jan. 5, 1824, Barbour MSS.
5. *Albany Argus*, Jan. 6, 1824.
6. *Richmond Enquirer*, May 9, 1823.

If the mandate of the Republican caucus were obeyed, resulting in the almost certain election of its nominee, then not only would the Electoral College be bypassed, but the rights of the people of the states would be preempted as well. The caucus was "a nocturnal assembly convoked at short notice, after long preparation, bound by no rule, acting without authority . . . within the immediate reach of every sort of influence, calculated, if exerted, to mislead, to deceive, or to corrupt, guarding the people of these United States from the mischief threatened by their own Constitution!!"[7] Unknown to the Constitution or the statute books, the caucus opened the door to a veritable host of evils and dangers.[8]

Defenders of the caucus denied the charges that it was unconstitutional, undemocratic, or corrupt. "Surely no man supposes," intoned a pro-Crawford paper, "that the proceedings in caucus are to be in their character as legislators of the nation, or to partake in any degree of the official functions of the congress."[9] The caucus nomination was but an expression of opinion by individuals, citizens exercising their constitutional right to state a preference for the presidency. "Their recommendation has neither the force of a law nor the authority of a command, . . . and which the people are at perfect liberty to treat with contempt."[10] What could be the harm in such a proceeding? No provision of the Constitution, no law forbade congressmen this privilege just as none obligated other voters to support their nomination.[11]

Lest they destroy the foundation for the caucus, its advocates were quick to point out, even while denying its official character, that the participants in a congressional caucus accurately reflected the thinking of the party rank and file. Admitting that a nomination by congressmen was "not entirely free from some objections," the New York legislative caucus asserted, "that assembled as they are from the different quarters of the Union—coming from the various classes of the commu-

7. *Daily National Intelligencer*, Dec. 5, 1823.
8. *Ibid.*, Dec. 24, 1823; Jan. 13, 14, 19, February 10, 1824; *Niles' Weekly Register*, XXV (Sept. 30, Oct. 4, Nov. 1–Dec. 27, 1823), 2–4, 49, 65, 97–103, 130–31, 137–39, 260; *Richmond Enquirer*, May 6, Aug. 8, 1823. These newspapers quoted extensively from other journals.
9. *Albany Argus*, July 8, 1823.
10. *New Hampshire Patriot*, May 19, 1823.
11. *Albany Argus*, June 17, Aug. 15, Sept. 2, 16, 19, Nov. 28, Dec. 23, 1823; *Daily National Intelligencer*, Aug. 5, 14, 16, Sept. 6, Dec. 17, 20, 22, 1823; Jan. 23, Feb. 5, 10, 12, 13, 1824; *Niles' Weekly Register*, XXIV (Jan. 10, 1824), 292–93; *Richmond Enquirer*, Aug. 12, Oct. 3, Dec. 9, 20, 1823; Jan. 1, 1824.

nity—elected during the pendency and discussion of the question, and in a great degree with reference to it, they bring into one body as perfect a representation as can be expected of the interests and wishes of all . . . ."[12] Far from being a repudiation of democracy, the caucus was the very embodiment of the principle of representative government.

To answer the imputations of corruption, the caucusites switched to less abstract arguments. They challenged their critics to cite a single example from the past of the pernicious effects alleged to accompany caucus nominations. "And whereas Experience is one of the best and surest guides in all political proceedings," one resolution offered at a public meeting began, "and the experience of an age has proved, that the Democratic members of Congress have, at all times, selected as candidates for the Presidency, Wise, Good, and Patriotic men . . . ."[13] The *Eastern Argus* reminded its readers that "It was in this way that Mr. Jefferson was elected, it was in this way that Mr. Madison was elected, and finally in this way it was that Mr. Monroe was elected."[14] The trinity of Jefferson, Madison, and Monroe was invoked with ritualistic frequency by the defenders of the caucus as irrefutable evidence that the caucus was "crowned with happiest results" rather than sunk in obloquy.[15]

The appeal to experience highlighted the main positive argument in behalf of the caucus: its necessity to preserve party unity. Cried the *Albany Argus* in alarm: "Perhaps at no former period of history has the democratic party been more seriously assailed, or its interests and distinctive character more dangerously menaced."[16] Unless a caucus concentrated Republicans behind a single candidate the party would be dissolved, and a victory for the Federalists or a referral of the election to the House of Representatives would result. Fear of the Federalists could not have excited many voters, but the probability of an election in the House was certainly real. The possibilities for intrigue in such an event, as in 1801, seemed endless. Moreover, in a House election each state delegation would have one vote, greatly favoring the small states against the larger ones like New York and

12. *Albany Argus*, Apr. 25, 1823. Also, *New Hampshire Patriot*, May 19, 26, Dec. 1, 15, 1823; *Richmond Enquirer*, Aug. 12, Sept. 2, 30, Oct. 3, Dec. 23, 27, 1823.
13. *Richmond Enquirer*, Jan. 3, 1824.
14. Quoted in the *New Hampshire Patriot*, June 2, 1823.
15. *Richmond Enquirer*, Dec. 18, 1823.
16. Jan. 6, 1824.

Virginia, just the reverse of the Electoral College. The caucus was "absolutely essential to preservation of the Republican party," which, in turn, was essential to preserve the unity of the nation.[17]

To buttress their plea for party unity, the Radicals fell back on appeals to tradition. No reference to the caucus was complete without mentioning that the party had always used it to nominate its candidates. No effort was spared before the meeting of the Crawford caucus to give it historical continuity from the party's earliest beginning down to 1824.[18] Because of the caucus the party had achieved its first success in 1800. It had been responsible for all of its succeeding victories. It was described as "the good old way," "the invariable usage, in the purest days of democracy," an "old landmark." If its advocates in 1824 were usurpers, so then were Jefferson, Madison, John Langdon, Nathaniel Macon, and the other great patriots who had founded the party.

The caucusites were the self-appointed keepers of the Jeffersonian flame. Eighteen cheers followed this toast to the caucus at a dinner in Philadelphia: "The best method of uniting our whole force; it has advanced to the presidential chair a Jefferson, a Madison, and a Monroe; may it supply a successor who will re-survey the grounds, re-establish the boundary lines, and repair the ancient land marks of the democratic party."[19] The determination to keep the spirit, as well as the organization, of the party alive was one of the most significant long-range results of the 1824 campaign, for it sustained the illusion that the party still survived. And it was this conviction which supplied the basis for the new and more lasting party that arose after the election. The vision of a nation without parties held no charm for these men. Monroe's policy of seeking a reconciliation of all parties they contemptously called "amalgamation." The supporters of the 1824 edition of the caucus were fated to play a decisive hand in the creation of the Democratic party.

Who were they? Only a few of them joined the caucus ranks out

17. *Richmond Enquirer*, Nov. 14, 1823; also *ibid.*, Aug. 16, Sept. 3, Oct. 24, 1822; July 8, Nov. 18, Dec. 18, 27, 1823; *Albany Argus*, Nov. 12, 1822; Mar. 25, June 24, July 4, Sept. 2, 12, 16, 19, 1823; *Daily National Intelligencer*, Apr. 1, 3, May 30, June 18, July 23, Aug. 16, Sept. 25, Dec. 13, 1823; *New Hampshire Patriot*, Feb. 3, Apr. 21, May 5, Sept. 22, Oct. 27, Nov. 3, Dec. 15, 1823.

18. *New Hampshire Patriot*, May 5, June 2, 1823; Jan. 5, 1824; *Richmond Enquirer*, Feb. 7, Sept. 24, Nov. 15, 1822; June 24, Aug. 8, Nov. 14, Dec. 27, 1823; Jan. 8, 13, 17, Feb. 10, 12, 1824.

19. *Richmond Enquirer*, Dec. 27, 1823.

of personal admiration of Crawford. Their motivation was narrowly political. It suited their own purposes to maintain that a Republican party capable of agreeing on a single candidate for the presidency still existed. The most important clusters of Crawford supporters were those in Virginia, representative of a whole group of southern leaders, and New York, typical of a certain breed of northern politician. These two states were the main pillars of Crawford's candidacy outside his native Georgia.

Virginia was in many ways the body and soul of the party of Jefferson. Here the party had found the leaders responsible for its birth, furnishing in the process the first three Republican presidents who had guided the nation as well as the party for twenty-four years. Here, too, could be found the milieu which had produced its distinctive tenets—the distrust of central power and the glorification of states' rights—positions that not incidentally served the interests of most of the state's inhabitants and those of a large portion of the South.

There were no more Jeffersons or Madisons, or even Monroes, but the particularist tendencies of Virginia remained strong, impervious to the growing demands from the Northeast and West for economic aid from Washington. The continuity of leadership and political ideas in Virginia was remarkable. Almost the only changes in the power structure were those caused by death. The same men, or ones with the same attitudes, who controlled the state in 1801 dominated it a generation later, using the same means—the caucus-appointed central committee, nicknamed the Richmond Junto, which spoke through the *Richmond Enquirer*, edited since 1804 by Thomas Ritchie.[20]

These guardians of southern gentry understood instinctively the political value of tradition. The knew that the great body of the voters in the North and West considered themselves, if only vaguely, Republicans. They sought to take advantage of this massive identification in order to control the national government in behalf of their own section. They could do this by insisting that a Republican party wedded to strict construction was still in being. If the Radicals could arrogate the remains of the Jeffersonian estate, both its historic ideology and organization, they might check the trend toward centralization by rekindling the fires of party loyalty. Those outside the South with no pressing concern for states' rights, stirred by memories of their

20. Charles Henry Ambler, *Thomas Ritchie: A Study in Virginia Politics* (Richmond, 1913).

heritage, might automatically join the Radical cause. And through the party the Radicals might control the nation.

A general acceptance of the congressional caucus was an essential part of the Junto's plan even though its members were basically indifferent to formal nominating machinery. Their domination within Virginia was sufficiently complete that they had no need for an extensive visible organization. In 1816 they had shown their contempt for the congressional caucus when it did not match their ambition. But in 1824 it was the most tangible link with the past. The caucus was also the only means at hand for uniting the party so that it could become an effective instrument for controlling the national government. That Crawford, the candidate with the most congressional support, paid homage to the "Old Republican" ideals was the final factor in winning Junto support for the caucus. His nomination would make him the official standard-bearer of the party and Republicans everywhere would then be committed to a candidate congenial to Virginia and her southern neighbors.

The motivation of the northern Radicals, strongest in New York, differed from that of their allies below the Potomac, although they also pursued the party phantom. While the New York Bucktails, a tightly knit band of seasoned professionals, were not oblivious to states' rights, their support of Crawford owed less to ideology.[21] And they were far more conscious of the importance of organization, as their success in New York depended on the maintenance of a powerful electioneering apparatus. The Bucktails did not possess the easy mastery over their state that the Junto did in Virginia. They did not even exercise undisputed sway over the Republican party of New York. State politics was a many-sided affair which featured the Bucktails against the followers of De Witt Clinton, with other groups, Federalists and independent Republican factions, throwing their weight from one side to the other.

The Bucktails' greatest advantage lay in their superior organization, which enabled them, in most instances, to control the nominating machinery of the party, the county and district conventions, and the legislative caucus.[22] With agents loyal to the Bucktail-controlled state central committee in almost every community, they were able to muster the numbers necessary to dominate the public meetings that made nominations or selected the delegates to the nominating conventions.

21. Robert V. Remini, "The Albany Regency," *New York History*, XXXIX (Oct., 1955), 341–55.
22. *Richmond Enquirer*, Nov. 21, 1823.

One important advantage of the formal nomination was that it entitled the nominee to proclaim himself the authentic Republican candidate. The imprimatur of regularity was worth a good many votes on election day, and the Bucktails were not slow in exploiting it.[23] Hence their great interest in preserving the image of the party as a going concern. And, therefore, their allegiance to the congressional caucus. The caucus was the appropriate capstone of a system which they were at pains to foster. Only if there were a national Republican party would party regularity at the state level make sense.

Equally important, Bucktail leaders believed that the congressional caucus gave them the best chance to place in the White House a man committed to recognizing their claim to be the Republican party of New York. Azariah C. Flagg, state comptroller and a key figure in the organization, wrote Senator Martin Van Buren in 1823 that "I consider it highly important to the rep. party and to the State that the person elected [president] should feel himself indebted to this State in a considerable degree for his appointment: and if so, whatever may be his location, our interests will be well attended to."[24] What better way to obligate him than by using New York's large congressional delegation to nominate him? After flirting with several of the candidates, Van Buren, the faction's master strategist and national spokesman, gave the almost inevitable signal for the Bucktails to support the caucus and Crawford. Support of the "regular" candidate for the presidency had the merit of consistency, but it also put them in line to receive national patronage which would be useful in their intraparty struggles in New York.[25]

Unfortunately, the Bucktails badly misjudged the course of events in New York and the nation.[26] Crawford proved to be an unpopular

---

23. *Albany Argus,* Oct. 29, 1822; J. W. Taylor to J. T. Adams, draft, Apr. 8, 1823; J. B. Stuart to J. W. Taylor, Jan. 28, 1824, Taylor MSS; R. W. Walworth to A. C. Flagg, Jan. 27, 1822, Azariah C. Flagg Papers (New York Public Library), cited hereafter as Flagg MSS. For a discussion of the Bucktails' concept of party, and their application of it in New York and national politics, see Michael Wallace, "Changing Concepts of Party in the United States: New York, 1815–1828," *American Historical Review,* LXXIV (Dec., 1968), 453–91.

24. A. C. Flagg to Van Buren, Nov. 12, 1823, Van Buren MSS (LC).

25. Van Buren to Johnston Verplanck, Dec. 22, 1822, *ibid.;* Fitzpatrick, *Autobiography of Van Buren,* pp. 28–108; Remini, *Martin Van Buren,* pp. 12–29, 36, 45–46, 92; Rufus King to Christopher Gore, Feb. 26, 1823; Charles R. King, *Memoranda,* Feb., Apr. 7, 1823, King, *Life and Correspondence of Rufus King,* VI, 504.

26. C. H. Rammelkamp, "The Campaign of 1824 in New York," *Annual Report of the American Historical Association for the Year 1904* (Washington, 1905), pp. 175–201; Hammond, *Political Parties in New York,* II, 157–74.

candidate and the congressional caucus a dubious means of solidifying support for him. The Georgian's adherence to states' rights shibboleths did not sit well with the many advocates of tariffs and internal improvements in New York who found Clay or Adams more congenial to their point of view. Others were tired of the string of southern presidents. The largest state in the Union had received only the vice-presidency in return for its cooperation with Virginia.

Deliverance of the state's votes to Crawford by the Bucktails was contingent on the legislature's retaining the right to appoint the electors, a procedure falling into growing disfavor as state after state abandoned it for a popular election. In the face of voter discontent the Bucktail leadership resolutely refused to alter the electoral law. This determination to hand New York's thirty-six electoral votes over to Crawford alienated many of those who had previously supported the Bucktails. When the local conventions met preparatory to the state elections in 1823 innumerable schisms occurred when the anti-Crawford delegates bolted the conventions they could not control. Allying themselves with the Bucktails' old foes, the Clintonians, they made separate nominations under the title of the People's party. In the election they won an impressive victory, gaining control of the lower house of the legislature. This did not, however, deflect the Bucktails, now styled the "Regency" for their defiance of the popular will, from their determination to vindicate the existence of a Republican party by supporting a caucus nomination in Washington.

No organizations quite like the Junto and the Regency existed outside Virginia and New York, but imitators elsewhere were ready to back the congressional caucus for the same basic reasons. In North Carolina, for example, most of the conservative, old-line Republican leadership was prepared to support Crawford. But the structure of Tarheel politics was too amorphous to permit them the same degree of control as in Virginia. The planter class could not contain the yeoman who showed a disposition to go for Jackson. In New England, Isaac Hill, editor of the *New Hampshire Patriot*, operated as a one-man Regency combating the idea of party amalgamation. Hill and other New England Republicans had fought the Federalists too long and too hard to call a halt to party warfare. They were always able to penetrate the subtle disguises the "aristocracy" used to cloak its designs. They were still capable of genuine zeal and not a little spite in political combat. In all of the states outside the West a group of well placed and experienced professionals stood by, with varying degrees of popular backing, to further the cause of Republican regularity and their own careers by proclaiming lineal descent from Jefferson.

To prove the point that they alone were truly interested in the survival of the party, the caucusites challenged their opposition to devise another means of keeping the party together.[27] If they found a nomination by members of Congress objectionable, what practical alternative did they offer that could prevent the breakup of the party implicit in the plethora of candidates? It was a relatively safe challenge. The knew that the other candidates had little interest in promoting a "national" nomination. Since 1821 the friends of Adams, Clay, Calhoun, and Jackson had been pushing them forward by the most convenient methods at hand. Well before the meeting of the congressional caucus in February, 1824, the names of all of them had been formally presented as candidates for the presidency. Late in 1823 Calhoun was nominated by a legislative caucus in South Carolina.[28] Jackson was nominated by official resolutions passed by the Tennessee and Alabama legislatures.[29] Adams won approval of legislative caucuses in Maine, New Hampshire, Connecticut, Rhode Island, and Massachusetts.[30] Caucuses in Kentucky, Ohio, Louisiana, Virginia, Illinois, and Missouri, some representing only a minority of the legislature, nominated Clay.[31]

These "partial" nominations were derided by the friends of Crawford. How could they do other than divide the party? Indeed, how could they do other than divide the nation? Each state and section was encouraged under a system of local nominations to bring forward a favorite, thereby exciting state and regional jealousies instead of harmonizing them behind a single man. The Union as well as the party might be jeopardized.[32] It had been objected that the caucus was undemocratic. Could anyone seriously contend that a state caucus was more representative of the people than a national one? What could state legislators chosen from small districts in reference to purely local questions know of the will of the people concerning the presi-

27. *Richmond Enquirer,* July 9, 1822.
28. *Daily National Intelligencer,* Dec. 12, 1823.
29. *Ibid.,* Aug. 23, 1823; Jan. 19, 1824; *Richmond Enquirer,* Aug. 16, 1822.
30. *Niles' Weekly Register,* XXIII (Jan. 25, Feb. 1, 1823), 322, 342–43; *Richmond Enquirer,* Jan. 27, 31, 1824.
31. *Niles' Weekly Register,* XXIII (Dec. 21, 1822; Jan. 18, 1823), 245, 305; *ibid.,* XXIV (May 3, 1823), 136; *ibid.,* XXVI (Mar. 20, 1824), 42–43; *Richmond Enquirer,* Dec. 17, 1822; Jan. 21, Apr. 18, 1823.
32. *New Hampshire Patriot,* Feb. 3, Nov. 3, 1823; *Richmond Enquirer,* July 11, Dec. 27, 1823; Jan. 20, 1824.

dency? State caucuses only multiplied the allegedly offensive features of a congressional caucus.[33]

Those responsible for these state nominations wasted little energy on defending them except as evidence of the popularity of their respective candidates.[34] Crawford's opponents preferred to stay on the attack, to keep attention focused on the iniquities of the congressional caucus while they gathered support in bits and pieces wherever they could. Local nominations by their very nature did not provide a clear counter target to shoot at since they were made at widely varying times.

Out of this debate over the best method of nominating presidential candidates arose the first protracted discussion of holding a national nominating convention.[35] State and local conventions were sufficiently commonplace by the early twenties that the application of the convention to the presidency required little imagination.

The suggestion came from three mutually antagonistic groups. The first source was a rather curious one. Early in January, 1822, the New York *American*, finding the caucus open to criticism because of the "influences" it subjected congressmen to, asked, "Why should not a general convention of Republican delegates from the different states assemble at Washington a few months prior to the period for electing a President and decide, by a majority, the choice of an individual for that elevated office."[36] The *American* was published and edited

33. *Richmond Enquirer*, Aug. 16, 1822.

34. One writer argued that state nominations were in actuality a winnowing process designed to eliminate the weaker candidates. To make certain that the shakedown took place he suggested that each state hold two caucuses, one two years prior to the election, the other one year before. This, apparently, was the best the opponents of the congressional caucus could come up with. From the *Lexington Reporter*, as quoted in the *Richmond Enquirer*, Nov. 5, 1822.

35. As early as 1806 the *Enquirer* (May 23) had hinted at a national convention when it suggested that "*nominators* appointed by the different states who might convene at a central place." In 1816 Mathew Carey, acting on the suggestion of John Binns, proposed a "mixed" congressional caucus with special delegates elected to represent districts and states with Federalist representatives. As a permanent solution, Carey recommended a procedure modeled on Connecticut's law governing nominations. At the general election in each state preceding the presidential election, the voters would indicate their preference for president. From these nominations "the sense of the nation would be fairly taken; and from the candidates thus designated, the electors might finally fill the offices." This proposal may be regarded as the ancestor of the presidential preference primaries. See Carey, *The Olive Branch*, pp. 451–52; John Binns, *Recollections of the Life of John Binns* (Philadelphia, 1854), p. 244.

36. As quoted in the *Richmond Enquirer*, Jan. 12, 1822.

by a group of young men bearing famous Federalist names, including Charles King (son of Senator Rufus King) and James A. Hamilton (son of Alexander Hamilton).[37] They were bitter foes of De Witt Clinton and on friendly terms with Van Buren. What inspired their advocacy of a national convention is unclear. Most of the Federalists, or former Federalists, still active in public life opposed the caucus because it served to maintain party distinctions which they were anxious to obliterate. A convention would serve them but little better in this regard. There is no indication though that the *American* was a stalking horse for the Regency, as none of its members or organs countenanced the proposal. In any event the *American*'s support was not critical in forcing a public discussion of the idea.

It was Thomas Ritchie of the influential *Richmond Enquirer* who, by endorsing a national convention, caused others to take notice. Ritchie was a prominent member of the Junto, which was widely assumed to stand squarely behind Crawford and, hence, the caucus. His reasons for advocating a convention can only be guessed at. Possibly, he was demonstrating the purity of the Radicals' devotion to the party by exposing the hypocrisy of their opponents. Willingness to embrace a substitute for the caucus would prove that it was the end—a united party and nation—not the means that was foremost in Radical thinking. Or perhaps, as one writer suggests, Ritchie was providing "an avenue of escape" in case the caucus should fail to meet or not nominate Crawford if it did.[38] But there is probably no need to look behind Ritchie's declared motive. His aversion to congressmen making presidential nominations was of long standing and he was simply casting about for a substitute.[39]

Ritchie copied the *American*'s proposal in the *Enquirer*, renewed his reservations about the caucus, and pronounced the national convention a sensible alternative.[40] For the remainder of the year the *Enquirer* reprinted editorial comments from other papers, both favorable and unfavorable, while urging that steps be taken to implement the holding of a convention.[41] But neither side in the controversy over the congressional caucus embraced his suggestion, at least until it was too late to act. By and large, those supporting candidates other than Craw-

37. Livermore, *Twilight of Federalism*, pp. 57–58, 74–75.
38. Ammon, *Virginia Magazine of History and Biography*, LXI (Oct., 1953), 415.
39. *Richmond Enquirer*, May 23, 1806.
40. *Ibid.*, Jan. 15, 19, July 23, Aug. 13, 1822.
41. *Ibid.*, Sept. 6, Nov. 5, 29, Dec. 12, 21, 1822.

ford ignored it. They were unwilling to risk their candidacies on an all-or-nothing decision whether made by a national caucus or a convention, preferring instead an every-man-for-himself approach. If it had been Ritchie's purpose to expose the selfishness behind the opposition to the caucus, he succeeded. It was also clear that no irresistible demand for a convention had developed.

Those favoring the caucus were generally hostile to a convention when they chose to comment on it at all. A few admitted that a convention might be superior in theory to a caucus, but pointed out its "utter impracticability."[42] In Georgia the Augusta *Constitutionalist* found "A thousand difficulties unnecessary to detail are opposed to the measure. . . ."[43] Other Crawford papers were explicit. Who, it was asked, would summon such a meeting? How would a time and place be agreed upon? Did time permit a gathering of delegates from all parts of the Union? Who would bear the financial burden? Would not delegates be just as susceptible to corrupt influences, the promise of jobs, as congressmen? And, finally, why would delegates be any more responsive to the popular will than the people's regular representatives?[44]

Ritchie was disappointed in the reaction of those he hoped would be his allies in replacing the caucus. Even before the debate on the national convention had run its course the *Enquirer* abandoned its stepchild. In March, 1823, Ritchie announced his support of the congressional caucus on the grounds that no one had taken up the convention.[45] In July he complained that the response had been so poor that he might as well have kept the idea to himself.[46] Two months later the New York (Regency) caucus formally pledged itself to support the nominee of the national caucus.[47] Isaac Hill added his approval of the Washington meeting shortly thereafter.[48] In January, 1824, the Junto caucus passed resolutions placing its seal of approval on its national counterpart.[49] The troops were falling into line; it became certain that the Crawfordites would persist in summoning a caucus.

42. From the *Harrisburg Intelligencer*, as quoted in the *Richmond Enquirer*, Sept. 6, 1822.
43. As quoted in the *Richmond Enquirer*, Oct. 3, 1823.
44. *Ibid.*, Sept. 6, 1822; Oct. 23, Dec. 27, 1823; *New Hampshire Patriot*, May 26, Nov. 17, 1823; Jan. 12, 1824; *Albany Argus*, Sept. 19, 1823; *Daily National Intelligencer*, Sept. 29, Dec. 20, 22, 1823.
45. *Richmond Enquirer*, Mar. 28, 1823.
46. *Ibid.*, July 8, 1823; also Oct. 7.
47. *Ibid.*, Apr. 29, 1823.
48. *Ibid.*, May 2, 1823; *New Hampshire Patriot*, May 29, 1823.
49. *Richmond Enquirer*, Jan. 6, 1824.

Just when the national convention idea appeared to have withered for lack of nourishment it was suddenly revived in the winter of 1824 by a group of Calhoun supporters in Pennsylvania seeking a strategem to bolster Calhoun's candidacy against a surge of Jackson fever. The maneuver was also part of a larger and more complex strategy to forestall a meeting of a congressional caucus which appeared imminent. Calhoun had campaigned more aggressively than any other candidate against the caucus and its likely nominee.[50] He relied for success on his moderate nationalism which, if it did not make him the favorite of any one section, gave him some support in all of them. "As to my own prospect," Calhoun observed in June of 1823, "my friends are quite confident that taking first and second choice together, I am decidedly the strongest of the candidates. In all New England, and for the greater part of the West w[h]ere I am not the *first*, I am clearly the second choice. Perhaps, at this early period, no position can be more safe."[51] Until eclipsed by the meteoric rise of Jackson, Calhoun stood to benefit the most from a national reading of the relative popularity of all the candidates.

The vital center of Calhoun's strength was Pennsylvania (with twenty-eight electoral votes), where he had the backing of important and well-established political leaders.[52] But in 1823 evidence began to accumulate of a groundswell for the Hero of New Orleans. Public meetings, largely uncontrolled by the reputable politicians, began declaring for Jackson. South Carolina representative George McDuffie's sneer that the Jackson movement was composed of "the grog shop politicians of villages & the rabble of Philadelphia & Pittsburgh" bore witness to its grass roots character.[53] Sentiment for the Tennessean

50. Charles M. Wiltse, *John C. Calhoun: Nationalist, 1789–1828* (Indianapolis, 1944), pp. 238–39; Fitzpatrick, *Autobiography of Van Buren*, p. 513; Calhoun to Joseph Gardner Swift, Apr. 29, May 10, Oct. 14, 26, 1823, Thomas R. Hay (ed.), "John C. Calhoun and the Presidential Campaign of 1824: Some Unpublished Calhoun Letters," *AHR*, XL (Oct., 1934), 85–87, 94–95; Calhoun to M. Stanly, July 23, 1823, J. Franklin Jameson (ed.), *Correspondence of John C. Calhoun*, vol. II, *Annual Report of the American Historical Association, 1899* (Washington, 1900), pp. 210–11; Klein, *Pennsylvania Politics, 1817–1832*, pp. 150–51.

51. Calhoun to Charles Fisher, June 11, 1823, A. R. Newsome (ed.), "Correspondence of John C. Calhoun, George McDuffie and Charles Fisher, Relative to the Presidential Campaign of 1824," *North Carolina Historical Review*, VII (Oct., 1930), 481.

52. Calhoun to John Ewing Calhoun, Mar. 19, 1822, Jameson, *Correspondence of Calhoun*, p. 202.

53. George McDuffie to ———, Jan. 13, 1823, Newsome, *North Carolina Historical Review*, VII (Oct., 1930), 486; Wiltse, *John C. Calhoun: Nationalist*, pp. 273–74; Klein, *Pennsylvania Politics, 1817–1832*, pp. 119–29, 130–41.

had been sufficiently well developed by the spring of 1823 to prevent an expected endorsement of Calhoun at the state gubernatorial convention. Calhoun, however, ignored this rebuff and continued to believe that Pennsylvania would eventually declare for him.[54]

Faced with a deteriorating situation in Pennsylvania, and amid rumors that a congressional caucus would soon be called to nominate the hated Crawford, Calhoun's friends in the Pennsylvania congressional delegation counseled among themselves to find a way of regaining the initiative. Guided by Representative Samuel D. Ingham, Calhoun's chief lieutenant in Pennsylvania, thirteen representatives and one senator issued an address to their constituents early in January, 1824, stating that it had become clear that if a congressional caucus did meet it would not muster an attendance sufficient to make it reflective of the people's wishes.[55] They therefore sought the advice of the voters as to what course they should pursue. Should they attend the caucus or avoid it? Was there a better method of nominating the party's standard-bearer? They asked that the voice of the people be recorded at the public meetings scheduled to convene shortly for the purpose of choosing delegates to a state convention in March.

This appeal was not entirely ingenuous. Accompanying the address (printed as a circular), were letters signed by individual congressmen and directed to persons in their home districts. These left little to the people's imagination. " 'I sincerely hope,' " read one, " 'that Pennsylvania will take the lead in recommending a national convention. It is the only plan calculated to conciliate and harmonize the republican party throughout the union.' "[56] In this manner the Calhoun leaders tried to salvage his candidacy. At the least it would sow confusion in the ranks of his rivals. Even if it were not held, plans for it might forestall a congressional caucus, thus delivering a blow to Crawford. If held, it would, presumably, advance Calhoun over the sectional appeals of Adams and Clay and the passing enthusiasm for Jackson.

The county meetings which followed the hint from Washington were not encouraging. According to one Philadelphia newspaper report, out of thirteen gatherings only one recommended a national convention to the exclusion of a congressional caucus, while meetings

---

54. Calhoun to ———, Mar. 18, 1823, Newsome, *North Carolina Historical Review*, VII (Oct., 1930), 478.

55. Klein, *Pennsylvania Politics, 1817–1832*, p. 151; *Niles' Weekly Register*, XXIV (Jan. 17, 1824), 306–7; *Richmond Enquirer*, Jan. 17, 1824.

56. *Richmond Enquirer*, Jan. 15, 1824. See also Klein, *Pennsylvania Politics, 1817–1832*, pp. 153–54.

in seven counties approved a caucus without expressing overt hostility to a convention.[57] Most of the meetings failed to take a stand one way or the other. The general tone of the resolutions that were passed relating to the convention, however, was distinctly friendly even when they did not endorse it. A Philadelphia assembly resolved that "a national convention composed of delegates from each congressional district presents at once the most practical and most republican mode of effecting a nomination for the presidency."[58] The Lancaster meeting resolved that "the best and most unexceptionable mode of concentrating the views of the Democratic Party . . . would be a convention of Delegates from all States of the Union . . . ," but added that it was "entirely impracticable, from the immense extent of our country, and from the great expense" involved.[59] The *Philadelphia Sentinel* agreed that a convention might be "preferable in theory," but doubted "whether there is time sufficient to carry it into effect, or a disposition in the republicans of many of the states to go to the necessary trouble and expense."[60]

How did Ritchie react, now that, at last, his suggestion was being acted on? He bubbled with newfound objections. "Is a Convention better?", he asked. Who would pay its expenses? How were the delegates to be selected, or a time and place to be fixed? Suppose competing delegations appeared from the same state? What would prevent Federalists from participating in the selection of delegates? What guarantees existed that all the congressional districts would be represented? Finally, by citing incidents from past Pennsylvania conventions, he insinuated that "violence, menace, disorder" would surround the whole affair.[61]

So far as Calhoun was concerned the proposal for a national convention soon lost its urgency. At a Philadelphia meeting in February, called to appoint the delegates to the state convention, he was unexpectedly eliminated from the race. His most prominent backer in the state, Senator George M. Dallas, moved that Calhoun's name be withdrawn as a candidate for the presidential nomination to be made at Harrisburg and that Jackson's be substituted. The Secretary of War was, on the same motion, relegated to the vice-presidency. Dallas's

57. As reported in the *Richmond Enquirer*, Feb. 14, 1824.
58. Quoted in Klein, *Pennsylvania Politics, 1817–1832*, p. 154. See also *Richmond Enquirer*, Jan. 27, 1824.
59. *Richmond Enquirer*, Jan. 20, 1824.
60. Quoted in *ibid.*, Feb. 14, 1824.
61. *Ibid.*, Feb. 12, 1824.

motion was less treachery to Calhoun than a tardy recognition by Pennsylvania's leaders that Jackson was the popular choice. Several weeks later the state convention, responding to this and similar meetings, nominated a Jackson-Calhoun ticket.[62] After the loss of Pennsylvania Calhoun was finished. Squeezed out in the South by Crawford and Jackson, in the West by Jackson and Clay, and in the Northeast by Adams, he submitted to his demotion.

Although the national convention was occasionally mentioned between Calhoun's enforced withdrawal and the election, it had died with his candidacy.[63] The idea had never been feasible. It assumed that all of the losing contenders for the nomination would retire once the convention made a choice. But none except Calhoun, who was desperate, was willing to defer to his opponents under any conditions. And none would have been willing to allow his rivals the exclusive use of the Republican title. One (or more) of the candidates could conceivably have held a national convention restricted to his supporters, but this would have been tagged as factionalism. Furthermore, it would have proved embarrassing politically as not one of them had sufficient strength to mount a truly national convention. There could be no convention in 1824, no national nomination of any kind by the Republican party, because there was no party capable of holding it.

During the winter of 1823–24 Washington was awash with plots and rumors of plots. Credulous politicians repeated countless tales of intrigues, deals, and combinations, many of them utterly contradictory. Members of Congress were canvassed time and again on their attitude toward a caucus. Van Buren directed the strategy for the Crawfordites while the friends of Adams, Calhoun, Clay, and Jackson met constantly in an effort to arrive at a united front against the common enemy.[64]

62. Klein, *Pennsylvania Politics, 1817–1832*, pp. 152–53, 158–65.
63. *New Hampshire Patriot*, Mar. 15, 1824.
64. Journal of Henry R. Storrs (Buffalo Historical Society), Dec. 10, 1823, cited hereafter as Storrs MS; Clay to Francis Brooke, Jan. 22, Feb. 23, 1824, Calvin Colton (ed.), *The Private Correspondence of Henry Clay* (Cincinnati, 1856), pp. 86–87; William Plumer, Jr., to Levi Woodbury, Dec. 29, 1823; Feb. 2, 1824; Samuel Bell to Woodbury, Feb. 5, 1824, Levi Woodbury Papers (Library of Congress), cited hereafter as Woodbury MSS; Calhoun to John Ewing Calhoun, Jan. 30, 1824, Jameson, *Correspondence of Calhoun*, p. 317; George McDuffie to ———, Jan. 7, Nov. 21, 1823, Newsome, *North Carolina Historical Review*, VII (Oct., 1930), 485, 488–89; Calhoun to Joseph Gardner Swift, Jan. 5, 25, 1824, Hay, *AHR*, XL (Jan., 1935), 289; [Henry] W. W[heaton]

For the anti-caucus forces the question was whether they should boycott the caucus or attend in order to vote down a nomination. The latter would eliminate Crawford and kill the caucus forever, but attendance would also compromise the high moral position they had taken against it. Moreover, there was always the possibility that the ranks might break. Clay and Adams, for example, were both reportedly tempted with promises that they would receive Crawford's votes in the caucus if the Georgian faltered, or, failing that, would be nominated for vice-president.[65] Virtually daily, bulletins gushed forth from each side giving estimates as to the number of congressmen who would or would not go.[66] Before it met, however, the anti-Crawford managers decided to administer "a death blow" by not attending.[67]

On February 6, 1824 an announcement signed by eleven members of Congress invited their colleagues to a caucus to be held in eight days for recommending candidates for president and vice-president. The invitation indicated the weakness of their position. The summons itself was novel. No previous caucus had been announced in that way. And this from those professing to act out of respect for tradition. They had originally planned to have the invitation signed by one congressman from each state, or at least a majority of them, to give the appearance of wide support.[68] Their failure to achieve even the barest semblance of national backing forecast the disaster which followed.

---

to Samuel L. Gouvernor, Feb. 3, 1824, Samuel L. Gouvernor Papers (New York Public Library), cited hereafter as Gouvernor MSS; Samuel D. Ingham to Ninian Edwards, Aug. 20, 1830, Ninian W. Edwards, *History of Illinois, from 1778 to 1833: And Life and Times of Ninian Edwards* (Springfield, 1870), p. 497; Joseph E. Sprague to John Bailey, Feb. 2, 1824, John Bailey Papers (New York Historical Society), cited hereafter as Bailey MSS; *Niles' Weekly Register,* XXV (Jan. 10, 17, 31, 1824), 291, 309, 357; Adams, *Memoirs,* VI, 235–36, 240–42, 244; William Plumer, Jr., to William Plumer, Sr., Dec. 12, 22, 1823; Charles Rich to William Plumer, Jr., Feb. 4, 1824, in Brown, *Missouri Compromises,* pp. 89, 90, 95; *Richmond Enquirer,* Feb. 3, 10, 12, 1824.

65. William Plumer, Jr., to William Plumer, Sr., Dec. 31, 1823; Feb. 5, 1824, in Brown, *Missouri Compromises,* pp. 92–93, 96; Adams, *Memoirs,* VI, 234–35, 239, 246–47; Rufus King to Charles King, Dec. 19, 1823, King, *Life and Correspondence of Rufus King,* VI, 539–40.

66. See, for example, the *Richmond Enquirer,* Feb. 3, 10, 1824.

67. "Caucus Statement," dated Feb. 2, 1824, in Taylor MSS; George McDuffie to Charles Fisher, Dec. 14, 1823, Newsome, *North Carolina Historical Review,* VII (Oct., 1930), 491; *Daily National Intelligencer,* Feb. 2, 7, 1824.

68. Romulus M. Saunders to Thomas Ruffin, Feb. 5, 1824, Hamilton, *Papers of Thomas Ruffin,* I, 288–89.

Shortly after seven o'clock in the evening of February 14 the caucus convened in the House of Representatives. Impatient and hostile spectators packed the gallery, thumped the floor with walking sticks and shouted "Adjourn, Adjourn" as the caucusers assembled below. The full gallery contrasted with the empty seats on the main floor—only 66 members out of 240 appeared, some of those seeking out the obscurity of "the sheltering shadow of a friendly column."[69] Four states accounted for more than two-thirds of those present: New York (16), Virginia (15), North Carolina (9), and Georgia (8). Ten states were unrepresented, and five others had only one member in attendance. It was not an impressive gathering.

The caucus quickly elected a chairman. A Pennsylvania member then submitted resolutions commending the caucus, but proposing that it adjourn until March 20 in order to secure a fuller attendance and to await the results of the presidential nomination which would be made at the state convention in Harrisburg. Senator Van Buren opposed the motion because the caucus "had already been delayed to a later period than had been usual on former occasions, and as *it was of some importance that our course conform, as nearly as might be, to that which had been heretofore pursued*, and which had led to such auspicious results."[70] The motion defeated, the caucus proceeded to the nominations. The roll was called by states in geographic order, north to south, the members of each delegation stepping forward to cast their ballots individually. Crawford received 64 votes, Adams 2, Jackson 1, and Nathaniel Macon 1.[71] Scattered applause and a general hissing from the gallery greeted the announcement of the result. Before balloting for vice-president, Van Buren disclosed that the incumbent, Daniel Tompkins, had no wish to retain his position. Albert Gallatin of Pennsylvania, colleague of Jefferson and Madison, received 57 votes while 8 were widely scattered. In making these nominations, the delegates resolved that they "acted in their individual characters, as citizens."[72]

Before dissolving, the caucus members voted to publish an address justifying their actions. Moderate and conciliatory in tone, it recalled that the unity provided by the caucus had enabled the party to triumph over its adversaries. It admitted that the Federalists were not

69. *Niles' Weekly Register*, XXV (Feb. 28, 1824), 404–5.
70. Italics mine.
71. There were two votes cast by proxy.
72. *Daily National Intelligencer*, Feb. 16, 1824.

"as efficient as formerly," but denied that party distinctions no longer existed. The lack of concert among Republicans opened a path that their enemies could tread to victory. At issue was nothing less than the preservation of the Republican party. Those departing from "the ancient usages of the party" were engaged in an attack upon the party itself.

For the duration of the campaign attention remained focused on the caucus.[73] Crawford's enemies never wearied of repeating the numerous arguments against it, fortified now with references to the February meeting. No Republican, so the critics maintained, need feel the slightest obligation to support the nominations of so pitifully small a group of self-annointed kingmakers. The Radicals covered their embarrassment over the numbers attending the caucus by claiming that many other congressmen actually favored Crawford, but were prevented from being present by one circumstance or another. If these names were added to the sixty-six, they concluded, then Crawford and Gallatin could be properly accorded full honors as the true Republican candidates.

No detail was overlooked in the effort to invest the caucus with historical authenticity. Even the date had been selected in order to conform to past practices. Earlier, Van Buren had sought to implicate two of the legendary figures from the past, Nathaniel Macon and John Taylor of Caroline, in the caucus. But Macon, Speaker of the House during Jefferson's first term, declined the invitation to attend because, in his opinion, the caucus bordered "on intrigue & bargain" and was "unknown to the constitution."[74] Taylor, the great philosopher of Republicanism, tartly replied that "If the habit of choosing presidents by Congressmen instead of the electors provided for by the constitution, should induce the country to compare it with the eight years rotation habit, it may not be unprofitable."[75] So the best caucusites could come up with in the way of a human link with the past was Senator Samuel Smith of Maryland who had been a member of either the House or the Senate since 1793. He had attended the sacred caucus of 1800 and had long been conspicuous in party councils. Yet his bitter and prolonged opposition to the Madison administration

---

73. *Albany Argus*, Feb. 24, May 13, July 25, Aug. 8, 15, 19, 1824; *Daily National Intelligencer*, Aug. 10, 11, 21, 25, Sept. 3, 28, 1824; Walter Lowrie to Albert Gallatin, Feb. 20, 1824, Gallatin MSS.
74. Macon to Van Buren, May 9, 1823, Van Buren MSS (LC).
75. Taylor to Van Buren, May 12, 1823, *ibid*.

hardly qualified him as a model of party regularity. He had, in fact, been one of the signers of Randolph's anti-caucus manifesto in 1808, although he subsequently served as chairman of the 1816 caucus. With such an elder statesman the caucus directors had to be content.

After the caucus adjourned the search for authentication continued. Macon was pressed for details about the caucus of 1800. How many persons had attended?; "what known or distinguished republicans were there?;" who were its officers? Macon could not recall.[76] Gallatin responded to similarly motivated inquiries about the past procedures of caucuses by denying that such procedures existed. The formality of the 1824 caucus, far from being based on historic precedent, only "furnished a pretence," Gallatin thought, "to attach to the whole the odium of being an attempt to dictate to the people."[77] Most of those at the caucus Gallatin was told agreed with him, but Senator Smith had insisted that he knew how things had been done in the old days and had prevailed because "many members thought it hard to vote the old man down. . . ."[78] Thus stood the ancient usage of the party in 1824, its ways so tenuously established that they had never been recorded and no one could accurately remember what they had been.

Failure dogged the attempt to pass Crawford off as the regular Republican nominee. No state or important politician switched to the Georgian following the caucus.[79] The caucus endorsement, if anything, was a liability. Of course, none of the other candidates withdrew. The Radicals were compelled to undertake new maneuvers to bolster their sagging cause. Gallatin, placed on the ticket as irrefutable evidence of the caucus's pedigree, added no strength to the ticket.[80] His

76. T. W. Cobb to Gallatin, Apr. 28, 1824, Gallatin MSS.
77. Gallatin to Walter Lowrie, May 22, 1824, *ibid.*
78. Lowrie to Gallatin, June 17, 1824, *ibid.*
79. *Daily National Intelligencer*, Feb. 23, 24, 1824; *Niles' Weekly Register*, XXV (Feb. 21, 28, 1824), 385, 407-8; Klein, *Pennsylvania Politics, 1817-1832*, pp. 155-56; Harry R. Stevens, *The Early Jackson Party in Ohio* (Durham, 1957), pp. 85-86; Binns, *Recollections*, p. 244; Everett S. Brown, "The Presidential Election of 1824-1825," *Political Science Quarterly*, XL (Sept., 1925), 395; A. C. Flagg to Silas Wright, Jr., Oct. 28, 1823, Flagg MSS.
80. Henry Adams, *Life of Albert Gallatin* (Philadelphia, 1879), pp. 590-91, 599; W. H. Haywood, Jr. to Willie Mangum, Feb. 23, 1824; James McBane to Mangum, Feb. 29, 1824, Henry Thomas Shanks (ed.), *The Papers of Willie Person Mangum* (Raleigh, 1950), I, 121-22; *Albany Argus*, Mar. 5, 1824; *Niles' Weekly Register*, XXVI (Apr. 10, 1824), 97-98; *Daily National Intelligencer*, Feb. 17, 19, 23, 1824; Brown, *Political Science Quarterly*, XL (Sept., 1925), 396; Walter Lowrie to Gallatin, Feb. 10, 17, 1824, Gallatin MSS.

home state of Pennsylvania was lost to Jackson. The South objected to his pro-tariff views, and, cruelest of all, he was attacked as a foreigner. In the fall of 1824 the veteran Republican was callously brushed aside by the Crawford managers despite their earlier assurances that he would be elected even if Crawford were not.[81] Initially, the strategy called for the substitution of Clay, but he stubbornly insisted on running for president so the slot was left vacant to be filled as local sentiment dictated.[82] The shabby treatment of Gallatin, who had not sought the office, reflected the desperation of the Radicals and it availed them nothing. The vaunted caucus sputtered to an ignominious conclusion by repudiating the very nomination that lent some credence to its historical pretensions.

The attention given by historians to the collapse of the congressional caucus has obscured the impetus which the election of 1824 provided for the development of political organization at the state and local levels. Public meetings in the towns and counties, legislative caucuses, and statewide rallies and conferences, promoted by the friends of the presidential candidates, abounded in unprecedented numbers. Inevitably, the convention also found increased employment as it was ostensibly the most democratic in form. There was a growing tendency for the sponsors of all types of gatherings to call them conventions even though they might actually be caucuses or public meetings. In New York and the Northwest, however, the election of 1824 spurred the initiation of bona fide state conventions where none had previously existed.

Conventions had long been used in New York for nominating candidates for local offices, but the legislative caucus survived for the governorship in spite of periodic revolts against its dominance. In 1823 opponents of the Regency, including erstwhile supporters who balked at the decision to champion Crawford, had coalesced into an amorphous

81. Andrew Steward to Gallatin, Feb. 6, 1824; Walter Lowrie to Gallatin, Feb. 10, 1824, Gallatin MSS.

82. C. W. Gooch to Van Buren, Sept. 14, 1824; Walter Lowrie to Van Buren, Sept. 14, 24, 1824; Joseph Gales to Van Buren, Oct. 17, 1824; P. N. Nicholas to Van Buren, Oct. 31, 1824; Gallatin to Van Buren, Oct. 2, 1824; Gallatin to Walter Lowrie, copy, Oct. 2, 1824, Van Buren MSS (LC); Fitzpatrick, *Autobiography of Van Buren*, p. 665; Clay to J. S. Johnston, Sept. 10, 1824, Colton, *Correspondence of Clay*, p. 103; Walter Lowrie to Gallatin, Sept. 24, 25, 1824; Adams, *Life of Albert Gallatin*, pp. 602-4; Gales and Seaton to James Barbour, Oct. 17, 1824, Barbour MSS.

group called the People's party. They challenged the Regency's candidates for the state legislature who had been nominated in district conventions. The next year they continued this tactic, denouncing the regular Republican county and district conventions as frauds. "It is a fact," proclaimed an anti-Regency broadside, "that what are called 'Regular Nominations' are a mere *hack*, a *machine*, which only serves to effect the purposes of the lordlings and office holders, to harness, hoodwink and break us in, to draw them coach like into office."[83] The propagandists of the new (and very ephemeral) party also attacked the Regency's use of the caucus to nominate its candidate for governor as "a dark and foul *aristocracy* in disguise. . . ."[84] To dramatize the point leaders of the People's party called a state convention to nominate their gubernatorial candidate. Under their auspices the convention format was transformed into a meeting "of delegates freely chosen from almost all the counties in the state" instead of being "a mere *hack*." The convention "ought to be regarded as the highest attainable evidence of public sentiment among that portion of our fellow citizens who are determined to emancipate themselves from degrading thraldom to an unprincipled faction."[85]

In the fall elections the nominee of the state convention, De Witt Clinton, beat the nominee of the caucus and in the process doomed the legislative caucus in New York. More immediately, Clinton's victory, coming on top of losses in the legislative races, temporarily broke the Regency's hold on the state. When the legislature convened in Albany to ballot for the presidential electors it was able to salvage only five of the state's thirty-six electoral votes for Crawford.[86] The Regency politicians were too astute not to see that the electoral law and the caucus would have to be sacrificed as the price of regaining popular favor.

In the Northwest the 1824 election triggered the formation of sys-

83. Handbill, "The People's Nomination," Apr. 15 [1824], in Taylor MSS. See also *Buffalo Emporium and General Advertiser*, Sept. 17, 1824.

84. *Albany Daily Advertiser*, Apr. 24, May 10, 14, 1824; *Proceedings of a Meeting of the Citizens of Albany, Held at the Capital, on the Evening of the 28th September, 1824*, n.p., n.d.; *Buffalo Emporium and General Advertiser*, Oct. 2, 1824; George E. Baker (ed.), *The Works of William H. Seward* (Boston, 1887), I, 335-37.

85. *Proceedings of a Meeting of the Citizens of Albany . . .* , p. 3.

86. Hammond, *Political Parties in New York*, II, 130-32, 139-66, 169-74, 177-78; Fitzpatrick, *Autobiography of Van Buren*, pp. 108-9, 131, 142-44; Dorothie Bobbé, *De Witt Clinton* (New York, 1933), pp. 263-66; Rammelkamp, *Annual Report of the AHA for 1904*.

tematic organization in Ohio and Indiana. Activity in Illinois, just beginning to emerge from personal factionalism, had not by 1824 progressed much beyond the point of nominating candidates at county public meetings. The only exception appears to have been a district convention which, rather curiously, nominated an elector pledged to vote for either Jackson or Clay.[87]

Ohio, older and more settled, was the most progressive. Both Adams and Clay were nominated by portions of the state legislature. The endorsement of Clay was followed by county public meetings, a number of which nominated electors pledged to him. Efforts in behalf of the Kentuckian culminated in July, 1824, in a hastily arranged mass meeting (dubbed a convention) held in Columbus, but including persons from elsewhere in the state.[88] The meeting was necessary in order to agree upon a single ticket of Clay electors. But it was the friends of Jackson who held the first genuine state convention. As elsewhere, most of Ohio's leading politicians (especially the officeholders) were committed to the early favorites before the Jackson boom got started. Consequently, Jackson's campaign suffered at first from lack of central direction. Locally called county meetings and district conventions met to nominate electors, producing a redundancy of candidates devoted to the general. The obvious need to pull this diffuse movement together eventuated in a state convention of delegates (chosen in the counties) in July, 1824.[89] Thus initiated, the convention system became a permanent feature of Ohio politics.

Developments in Indiana paralleled those in Ohio. Electors pledged to Adams and Clay were selected by legislative caucuses.[90] The Jacksonians, devoid of prominent backing, held public meetings at the county seats that put forward an overlapping slate of electors. Editors of pro-Jackson newspapers, foreseeing the need of coordinating these nominations, suggested that delegates be elected to a state convention. Even though delegations from only thirteen of the fifty-one counties

87. Pease, *The Frontier State, 1818–1848*, p. 106.

88. Stevens, *Early Jackson Party in Ohio*, pp. 78, 82, 107, 114–15, 128–32.

89. *Ibid.*, pp. 62–63, 94–136; Homer Webster, *History of the Democratic Party Organization in the Northwest* (Columbus, Ohio, 1915), pp. 7–11; *An Address to the People of Ohio on the Important Subject of the Next Presidency; by the Committee Appointed for that Purpose at a Convention of Delegates from the Different Sections of the State, Assembled at Columbus, on Wednesday, the 14th Day of July, 1824* (Cincinnati, n.d.).

90. Logan Esarey, "The Organization of the Jacksonian Party in Indiana," *Proceedings of the Mississippi Valley Historical Association for the Year 1913–1914*, VII, 221–27.

attended the convention at Salem, its meeting marked the first use of delegates for the conduct of party business in Indiana.[91]

The results of the November election fully justified those who had predicted that no candidate would receive a majority. Only the distribution of the vote occasioned surprise. Adams ran about as expected, carrying all of New England and most of New York, plus scattered votes in four other states, for a total of 84. Neither Crawford nor Clay did as well as anticipated. The Georgian finished a poor third with 41 votes, mostly from Georgia and Virginia. Clay's 37 placed him last in the field. He captured only Kentucky, Missouri, Ohio, and a handful from New York. Jackson's front-running total of 99 was the biggest upset. His votes were widely distributed geographically. He won the undivided vote of Alabama, Indiana, Mississippi, New Jersey, North Carolina, Pennsylvania, South Carolina, and Tennessee, while picking up partial support in four other states. He had, nevertheless, far less than the 131 votes necessary for election without resort to the House of Representatives.

The vote totals of the Electoral College confirmed the final dismemberment of the Republican party. This was the most obvious result of the election. Yet the election of 1824 did not quite mark the end of the party, since the campaign had revealed that one group of politicians was unwilling that it should die. The outlook for the Radicals did not appear promising in view of their poor showing in November; despite the prominence of their leaders they were deficient in popular support. The Radicals' refusal to accept the obvious, their determination to keep alive the party spirit, had potentially important repercussions for the future. If they could find a candidate whose personal popularity could supply what they lacked, then the Republican collapse might not be as final as it appeared.

No one during the uncertain months following the counting of the votes in the states could accurately predict the shape which political alliances would assume in the years ahead. That parties would revive was far from certain, for just as there were those seeking to reestablish them there were many who fervently opposed their renewal. What would develop depended in large measure on the outcome of the election in the House. By the spring of 1825 those committed against the return of the party system seemed to be in the ascendant.

91. *Ibid.*, 228–31; Webster, *Democratic Party Organization*, pp. 11–12; Leonard, *Indiana Magazine of History*, XIX (Mar., 1923), 22–28.

II

The Revival of Parties
1825–28

"A stranger would think that the people of the United States have no other occupation than electioneering."

John Quincy Adams, *Memoirs*, August 5, 1828

The idea of an amalgamation of parties in a free state, is chimerical, and the notion that three great parties can for any considerable time exist, is ridiculous.

Jabez D. Hammond, *The History of Political Parties in the State of New York*, 1842

THREE

The Friends of the Administration

The general election of 1824 ended forever the illusion of a coherent Republican party; the "run off" election in the House of Representatives the next year set the stage for new parties. By 1828 the process had advanced sufficiently that the outline of a "second American party system" was clearly visible.[1] But this fresh grouping was still poorly defined in 1828 compared to the first party system. The major parties lacked names, not to mention programs, to distinguish them. The Democratic and Whig labels would not predominate over other titles until after 1832. It was not even certain that the second system would include only two parties, as an ambitious and aggressive third party, the Antimasons, appeared to contest the field in the early 1830s. And none of them had developed a truly national organization which could bind the local units together. It might be more correct to call the parties formed during 1825–28 period "interests," the word Jefferson had used in 1792 to describe the incipient Republican party.

Yet the new alliances were more than just "interests." Consciousness of the party concept had become part of the American experience. It no longer carried the odious implications that it had in 1789. Many thoughtful persons never accepted parties as either necessary or desirable, but everyone had become accustomed to their existence. More than the concept was familiar. Partisan machinery for conducting elections and managing the government was still extant in many states (even where the parties themselves were no longer viable) and was available to those politicians involved in constructing the new national parties.

1. This idea is fully explored in an excellent monograph, Richard P. McCormick's *The Second American Party System* (Chapel Hill, 1966).

The most important step in the creation of the second party system was the way John Quincy Adams was elected president. Speaker of the House Henry Clay, no longer a contender, was auspiciously placed to decide which of the top candidates should prevail. His personal relations with Jackson, Adams, and Crawford were, to understate the matter, poor. No earlier clash of personalities or principles, however, seemed strong enough to rule out the possibility of Clay selecting any of the three. The details of his decision to support Adams need not be repeated here. Given Clay's position on the tariff and internal improvements, and his own undiminished ambition for the presidency, Adams's election made more sense than that of Jackson or Crawford whose views were ambiguous and who, like Clay, resided in slave states. No bargain in the sense charged by their enemies took place between Adams and Clay, although some sort of understanding was reached in a face-to-face encounter.[2] Even before the announcement that the Speaker would become Secretary of State, backers of General Jackson raised the cry that the presidency had been sold to the highest bidder.

These two occurrences—the Adams-Clay "bargain" and the instant, hostile reaction to it—are of cardinal importance in explaining the revival of parties. The first fused the fortunes of Adams and Clay, wedding their numerous followers into a political unit insofar as national politics was concerned. Wrote one contemporary after the election: "The interest of Clay & Adams are, at any rate identified. . . . What is good for one, is, therefore, good for both—"[3] The Adams-Clay merger, by an almost classic application of a physical law to human events, produced a counteralliance among those who had not been included in the arrangements leading to Adams's victory.

In large measure the 1828 election campaign initiated the modern party system, including most of our organizational and campaign techniques. It determined, also, the voting patterns for the next generation. The linking of Adams with Clay established a party committed to a program of economic nationalism that had its greatest appeal in the Northeast and the older West. The coalition of Jackson, Crawford, and Calhoun furnished the materials for a states' rights party strongest in the South and West, but not without powerful adherents in the middle Atlantic states. There was nothing foreordained about this division. Had Jackson become president in 1825, and Clay or Adams

2. Adams, *Memoirs*, VI (Jan., 1825), 464.
3. William Plumer, Jr., to William Plumer, Sr., Feb. 16, 1825, Brown, *Missouri Compromises*, p. 142.

members of his administration (and this was not at all unlikely given the volatile state of affairs existing in the early weeks of 1825), then the whole configuration of politics would have been drastically altered. Furthermore, the Jackson inaugurated in 1825 would have been far different than the man who took office in 1829. He would have brought to the presidency an entirely different set of prejudices, and he would have come in under totally different sponsorship. The Jackson of 1829 was the prisoner of rhetoric and managers that did not, so far as he was concerned, exist four years earlier.

It is one of the greater ironies of American politics that John Quincy Adams should be the central figure in the renewal of party strife. No man alive in 1825 had a deeper dislike of partisanship. In his diary he scorned the narrow political motives which he invariably detected in everyone except himself. No doubt it was the bitter fruit of his personal experience as a party member, first as a Federalist and then as a Republican. Devotion to the nation and to one's principles were the only worthy guides in determining a course of action; his own rise, as he saw it, had been achieved in spite of the existence of parties. The Federalists never forgave his transfer of loyalties while the Republicans could never fully accept a son of the hated John Adams.[4] To Adams, indifference, hostility even, to party was worn like a merit badge. It was an attitude fated to have an important and unhappy bearing on his presidency.

Adams's approach to the election of 1824 had been composed of one part high-mindedness, one part ambition (in equal measure), with a dash of paranoia. Time and again he pledged himself not to lift a finger to aid his own cause. No appointments, no favors of any kind, with a view toward self-advancement would emanate from him.[5] "Whatever talents I possess, that of intrigue is not among them," he wrote in 1819.[6] To his opponents he attributed no such innocence. They were constantly spinning webs, usually at his expense. He pictured himself surrounded by enemies, alone, clad only in righteousness.[7] One of his supporters characterized his unique approach to campaign-

4. Adams, *Memoirs.* IV (Sept. 20, 1818), 131; *ibid.,* VI (Summer, 1822), 136; Livermore, *Twilight of Federalism,* pp. 139–43.

5. Adams, *Memoirs,* IV (Mar. 18, 1818), 62–64; *ibid.,* V (May 2, 1820; Feb. 25, 1821), 89–90, 298.

6. *Ibid.,* IV (Jan. 25, 1819), 231.

7. *Ibid.,* IV (Mar. 18, 1818; Jan. 5, 6, Nov. 2, 1819), 62–64, 212, 214–15, 429; *ibid.,* VI (July 8, 1822), 42–43.

ing as "calculated to chill and depress the kind feeling and fair exertions of his friends."[8]

But this does not tell the whole story, for Adams's ambition burned too brightly to be quenched by his obsession with his own purity. Indeed, his self-righteousness betrayed the depth of his yearning to be president. Yet nothing but defensive measures were allowable. A friendly congressman asked permission to sound out his colleagues about Adams's candidacy. Adams consented only after rehearsing him in a cover story that would make the proposed canvass the result of a similar move by Calhoun.[9] On another occasion he was willing to angle for Federalist support by assuring a Massachusetts representative that "never under any circumstances, would I be made the instrument of a systematic exclusion" of Federalists from office under the national government.[10] Again, he blamed the activities of one of his rivals, Crawford this time, as responsible for his own maneuvering. Adams's handling of the Federalists in this instance foreshadowed his later dealings with them.

But if he carefully avoided giving offense to Federalists when they could help him, he was not, despite his proud indifference to labels, insensitive to Republican pretensions. Early in 1822 Adams was advised that some manifestation of support from his native New England would be helpful. The current sessions of the legislatures of Maine and Massachusetts were suggested as providing the proper setting. The candidate concurred, but cautioned that in Massachusetts, where party antagonism was still sharp, it would be best to let the initiative come from the Republicans. Adams believed "that the presence of the Federalists in such a caucus ought to be avoided, as likely to do much more hurt than good—"[11] And in framing his electoral tickets in New England, his managers carefully excluded all but Republicans in order to avoid the Federalist stigma.[12] Had he continued this policy he could have escaped many of the difficulties which beset his administration. Why he did not can be explained, in part, by the circumstances attending his election by the House. Clay, it turned out, was not the only person with whom Adams was willing to deal. Ambition triumphed over purity more than once.

8. Joseph Hopkinson to Mrs. Adams, *ibid.*, VI (Summer, 1822), 130.
9. *Ibid.*, V (Dec. 31, 1821), 468–69.
10. *Ibid.*, VI (May 3, 1824), 315–16.
11. William Plumer, Jr., to William Plumer, Sr., Jan. 3, 1822, Brown, *Missouri Compromises*, p. 74; Adams, *Memoirs*, V (Jan. 3, 1822), 478.
12. Livermore, *Twilight of Federalism*, pp. 168–69.

The Federalists had not vanished with the signing of the Treaty of Ghent, although their numbers did dwindle until it became hopeless for them to contend for public favor under their old name. Those remaining active in politics were eager to declare an end to party warfare which operated so disasterously against them. Ostensibly, they were motivated by a desire for national unity, but their actual object was the enjoyment of the honors and fruits of office-holding. The wish to end their proscription was, according to Shaw Livermore, Jr., "the rock upon which Federalist thought and action was shaped" after 1816.[13] The election of 1824 provided them with an excellent opportunity to break down the Republican monopoly on office since Federalist support might be vital in an election with so many candidates. All of the contenders, in fact, sought the votes of the Federalists, although none but Calhoun dared do so openly. Each of the candidates, including Crawford (whose supporters made a fetish of maintaining old party lines), received some Federalist votes. No consensus existed among the Federalists even though all believed that the paramount factor in making their choice was which of the candidates would be most likely to end their exile.[14]

Adams received a large share of Federalist support, especially, in New England, but suspicion of him remained strong among many Federalist leaders who feared he might retain a personal grudge against the party.[15] When the election was referred to the House of Representatives they were well situated to secure a plain reading of his feelings. In two of the delegations, Maryland and New York, the deciding vote was held by a Federalist congressman, and so close was the division of states between Adams and Jackson that these two men were thought to have it in their power to name the next president.

Early in February, Henry Warfield, the Maryland Federalist, wrote his colleague Daniel Webster that his friends "constantly express to me their apprehensions that, should Mr. Adams be the President, he will administer the government on party considerations; that the old landmarks of party distinction will be enforced with regard to those who have hitherto been denominated Federals."[16] Webster, a supporter of Adams, drafted a reply to Warfield and then went calling on the

13. *Ibid.*, p. 24.
14. *Ibid.*, pp. 132–70.
15. Adams, *Memoirs*, VI (Jan. 21, 1825). 474.
16. Henry R. Warfield to Webster, Feb. 3, 1825, Fletcher Webster (ed.), *The Private Correspondence of Daniel Webster* (Boston, 1857), I, 377.

candidate. The draft, written for Adams's approval, assured Warfield that his fears were groundless, that "a portioning, parcelling out, or distribution of trust among men called by different denominations" would not occur. Webster went on to say that Adams, as a token of sincerity, would appoint a Federalist to a high position in the new administration. Adams did not fall into that trap, which was part of Webster's campaign to get himself appointed minister to England, but he did endorse the general statements of goodwill that Webster had penned.[17] The next day Representative Stephen Van Rennselaer of New York paid his respects in person, and for an identical purpose. He received the same guarantee that Adams had given Warfield through Webster and went away completely satisfied.[18] On the crucial day Maryland and New York cast their votes for Adams, electing him on the first ballot and ending the fears of a protracted struggle like that of the Jefferson-Burr contest in 1801.

The new president had thus committed himself to the "no party" concept as a condition of his election, although his course squared with his long-standing ideas on the subject. The implications for the future of his administration were enormous, determining, for example, his patronage policy. It would also critically affect his reelection. Adams's alliance with the Federalists undoubtedly seemed to him the child of his generosity, a piece of his larger policy to reunite the nation. Yet it also bore the curse of expediency and, in the end, imprisoned him within a politically damaging coalition. The price of power came high. It would cost him the support of Republicans who were essential to his success. Ironically, it was Webster who gave this as the very reason why Adams should seek a union with the Federalists. Shortly after his election, Webster cautioned that opposition was "likely to rise in an unexpected quarter, and unless the administration has friends, the opposition will overwhelm it."[19] The warning became a self-fulfilling prophecy.

Adams's opinions concerning parties were drawn from an earlier generation. Like Jefferson, Madison, and Monroe, he viewed parties as temporary and dangerous combinations. Unlike his predecessors, however, he intended offering the nation a positive leadership to over-

17. Webster to Warfield, Feb. 5, 1825, *ibid.*, 279–80; Adams, *Memoirs*, VI (Jan. 17, 1825), 469.
18. Adams, *Memoirs*, VI (Feb. 4, 1825), 493.
19. Webster to Jeremiah Mason, Feb. 14, 1825, Daniel Webster, *The Writings and Speeches of Daniel Webster* (Boston, 1903), XVI, 100.

come these ghosts. Through appointments and legislative recommenda-
tions he would provide the example and the means requisite to the
achievement of national unity. To implement his program, he counted
on the support of a majority of those still calling themselves Republicans, believing they would be willing to lay aside old and meaningless
quarrels. If they did not back him in his high endeavor, at least he
would have done his duty. The inaugural address announced in unmistakable language that he would not permit narrow partisan considerations to rule his actions.[20] Even though he was painfully aware that
he was a minority president, he would not attempt to rally a party
behind his administration. That would defeat the whole purpose of
his tenure.

Whether those who had opposed his election would accept his particular view of party history was far from certain. Suspicious by nature, Adams early detected a conspiracy among Jackson, Crawford,
and Calhoun to defeat him.[21] It did not deflect him though from starting immediately on the great work of reconciliation. The first task
was the construction of a cabinet. Adams intended that it should be
a microcosm of the larger unity he had in mind, encompassing all
of the leaders of the major factions in the late election. Clay, of course,
was Secretary of State. Jackson was the president's first choice for
the War Department until his blatant hostility made an offer impossible. Crawford was invited to remain at the Treasury, but declined
"in very friendly terms," as Adams was pleased to note.[22] Calhoun,
as vice-president, could accept no office, but two members of Monroe's
cabinet, Secretary of the Navy Samuel Southard and Postmaster-General John McLean, widely regarded as his supporters, were asked to
stay on. Both men agreed. Another holdover was the attorney general,
William Wirt, considered a political neutral. De Witt Clinton, a Jackson supporter, and possessed of a large following outside his own state
(he had received frequent mention as a presidential candidate prior
to 1824), was offered the top diplomatic assignment to London. Much
to Adams's disappointment, Clinton preferred to remain as governor
of New York.[23]

20. James D. Richardson, *A Compilation of the Messages and Papers of the
Presidents, 1789–1897* (Washington, 1896), II, 295–97.
21. Adams, *Memoirs,* VI (Feb. 8, 11, Mar. 7, 1825), 501, 506–7, 525; Memoranda
of Rufus King, Feb. 12, 1825, King, *Life and Correspondence of Rufus King,*
VI, 592.
22. Adams, *Memoirs,* VI (Feb. 11, 1825), 508.
23. W. Plumer, Jr., to W. Plumer, Sr., Feb. 21, 23, Mar. 2, 1825, Brown,
Missouri Compromises, pp. 143–44.

The declinations forced the president to shift ground somewhat, although his resolve to find a ministry of all the talents was still evident. The Treasury went to Richard Rush. As minister to England, Rush had not become deeply involved in the campaign, but he had been a candidate for elector on the pro-Crawford ticket. For the War Department, Adams found a bona fide Radical, Senator James Barbour of Virginia, a longtime member of his state's ruling Republican clique. In place of Clinton for the Court of St. James, he tapped the most famous living Federalist, Senator Rufus King of New York, thus honoring the pledge he had refused Webster.[24]

It was a well-balanced cabinet from almost every standpoint. Rush (Pennsylvania) and Southard (New Jersey) were from the North. Barbour (Virginia) and Wirt (Virginia and Maryland) were from the South. Clay and McLean (Ohio) spoke for the West. Only the president's own section and the deep South were unrepresented. Ideologically, it was also a mixture. Clay was considered a nationalist, but Barbour and Wirt belonged to the strict constructionist school. Rush advocated moderate protective tariffs, but opposed the national bank. Most of the group had supported candidates other than Adams or Clay in the election. The Jacksonians were conspicuous by their absence, but only because of the violence of their opposition.[25]

Adams's situation was perilous. By his own estimate, two-thirds of the nation had opposed his election.[26] To compensate for this, he desperately needed to build a cadre of loyal supporters throughout the nation. Through the appointive power he possessed the means for doing so. He had ample precedents for using patronage in his behalf. He had already squandered his cabinet appointments on the elusive quest for consensus and his policy toward filling the bulk of offices at his command was no less ineffective. He determined to keep the incumbents in office regardless of whether they supported his administration, dismissing only those found guilty of official misconduct in the performance of their duties. When vacancies occurred they would be filled without reference to earlier loyalties; his opponents would receive equal consideration with his friends.[27] Thurlow Weed, a rising

24. Adams, *Memoirs*, VI (Mar. 5, 1825), 523; Rufus King to Christopher Gore, Mar. 22, 1825, King, *Life and Correspondence of Rufus King*, VI, 600.

25. Adams, *Memoirs*, VI (Mar. 5, 1825), 522.

26. *Ibid.*, VII (Jan. 1, 1826), 98.

27. *Ibid.*, VI (Mar. 5, May 13, 1825), 520–21, 546; *ibid.*, VII (Oct. 28, 1826; May 23, Aug. 5, Oct. 23, Nov. 7, 29, Dec. 28, 1827; May 7, 17, 1828), 163–64, 275, 317, 343, 349, 363, 390, 534, 544; *ibid.*, VIII (June 3, July 7, 1828), 25,

figure in New York politics, made this damning observation after a futile trip to the White House to seek positions for the president's friends: "Mr. Adams, during his administration, failed to cherish, strengthen, or even recognize the party to which he owed his election; nor, as far as I am informed, with the great power which he possessed, did he make a single influential political friend."[28]

Taking their cue from the inaugural address, the friends of the administration encouraged the belief, almost as an official party line, that there were no parties. The memory of parties, one pro-administration orator told his audience was "kept alive partially and unworthily for other purposes."[29] The address adopted by the Adams state convention in Virginia summarized this rhetorical effort to convince the voters that old labels were obsolete:

> In the ancient state of political parties, when federalists and republicans contested for ascendancy, there was something in the great questions of foreign policy, in the leading principles of construction applied to the Constitution, bearing strongly on the essential character of the Government, and worthy of a general struggle between the statesmen. . . . But this stage of things have passed away, and the feelings and doctrines to which it gave rise, though not entirely forgotten, are almost unknown in the party distinctions of the day. Federalist and republican mingle together in the ranks of the Opposition—and together, rally around the standard of the Administration. There will be no great principle of political doctrine to distinguish them. . . .[30]

So far as Adams's supporters were concerned, this historical view of parties was not unalloyed altruism. By deploring the continued use of party names, they hoped to undermine their opposition. If all party

---

51; Worthington C. Ford (ed.), "Letters Between Edward Everett and John McLean, 1828, Relating to the Use of Patronage in Elections," *Proceedings of the Massachusetts Historical Society*, 3rd ser., I (Feb., 1908), 359–93.

28. Harriet A. Weed (ed.), *Autobiography of Thurlow Weed* (Boston, 1883), pp. 178–81; Glyndon G. Van Deusen, *Thurlow Weed: Wizard of the Lobby* (Boston, 1947), p. 34.

29. *Report of the Proceedings of the Town Meeting in the City of Philadelphia. July 7, 1828.* n.p., n.d.

30. *The Virginia Address*, n.p., n.d., p. 7. For similar sentiments, see *Proceedings of a Convention of the People of Maine, Friendly to the Present Administration of the General Government* [Jan. 23, 1828]. n.p., n.d., pp. 55–56; Administration meeting at Charleston, South Carolina, reported in the *Albany Argus*, Aug. 10, 1826; *Address of the State Convention of Delegates from the Several Counties of the State of New-York to the People, on the Subject of the Approaching Presidential Election* (Albany, 1828), pp. 14–15.

distinctions were spurious, what excuse could the Jacksonians have for maintaining an organized resistance? The *National Intelligencer*, a leading defender of the administration, denounced the very idea of a concerted opposition to the president.[31]

Because a very substantial segment of the old Republican party refused to give allegiance to the administration, former Federalists were embraced out of necessity. They were needed in Congress, where they provided able spokesmen such as Webster and John Sergeant of Pennsylvania, and back home, where they might compensate for Republican defections to Jackson. The Federalists demanded, in return, equal treatment with the president's Republican followers. In practice this meant the abandonment by Adams of any claim to the Republican mantle. Too proud to assume the name Republican, the Federalists were too ambitious to suffer the onus of Federalism. This placed Adams in a bind. Although eager to dispel the fog of party conflict, he realized that many Republicans deeply resented any welcoming of Federalists, particularly where appointments were concerned, and he had enough perspicacity to realize that "To this disposition justice must sometimes make resistence and policy must often yield."[32] In the end he managed to make both groups unhappy; he appointed too many Federalists to suit the professional Republican politicians, not enough to soothe the Federalists.[33]

The question was much broader than appointments. It involved the whole political process. In areas where the Federalists survived in appreciable numbers they insisted that the Republicans supporting Adams abandon their exclusiveness, and even their name, in making nominations. If they did not, the Federalists would refuse to enlist for service. The consequences of not appeasing the Federalists became clear in 1827 when the New Hampshire Republican leaders drew up resolutions endorsing the administration in a party caucus, excluding the Federalists, for passage by the state legislature. Joining with the Jacksonians, the Federalists were able to prevent a vote being taken, although a majority of the legislators favored Adams.[34] Earlier, the

31. *Daily National Intelligencer*, Mar. 12, 22, Apr. 17, 19, 25, 1826.
32. Adams, *Memoirs*, VII (Dec. 13, 1826), 207–8.
33. Livermore, *Twilight of Federalism*, pp. 188–89, 199, 205–6, 209–14.
34. *Daily National Intelligencer*, July 4, 1827; Webster to Clay, May 18, June 22, 1827, Henry Clay Papers, 1st ser. (Library of Congress), cited hereafter as Clay MSS; Webster to J. Q. Adams, June 30, 1827, C. H. Van Tyne (ed.), *The Letters of Daniel Webster from Documents Owned Principally by the New Hampshire Historical Society* (New York, 1902), pp. 128–29; Ezekiel Web-

Adams Republicans had refused to vote for Jeremiah Mason, a former Federalist, for United States Senator.[35]

This state of affairs spelled possible disaster for the administration cause in the North. Clay, far more astute than the president where practical politics was concerned, recognized the need for a merger of administration Republicans and Federalists. He wrote Webster: "It appears to me to be important that we should on all occasions, inculcate the incontestable truth that *now* there are but two parties to the Union, the friends and the enemies of the administration, and that all reference to obsolete denominations is for the purpose of fraud and deception. In this way, the efforts in particular places to revive old names may be counteracted."[36] Unless this were done the Jacksonians were bound to carry a number of New England states plus New York, Pennsylvania, Maryland, and Delaware, since they comprised the largest portion of the Republican party.[37]

With varying degrees of unhappiness, the president's Republican followers arranged a series of forced marriages with the Federalists.[38] Massachusetts Federalists seconded the nomination of the Republican gubernatorial candidate, but joint Federalist-Republican tickets were chosen for legislative and other offices. In 1827 the Adams Republicans combined with Federalists in elevating Webster to the U.S. Senate. Somewhat similar arrangements were obtained in Connecticut, Rhode Island, and eventually, New Hampshire.[39] In these four states the union was troubled, but successful, the majority of both old parties sanctioning the alliance. In Maine, where the Jacksonians controlled the Republican organization, and Vermont, where the Federalists were only a negligible factor, no nuptials took place.

Only partial success, and that probably creating more difficulties than

---

ster to D. Webster, Jan. 17, July 20, 1827; D. Webster to Joseph Sprague, June 20, 1827, in Webster, *Private Correspondence*, pp. 415-17, 421-22.

35. Livermore, *Twilight of Federalism*, pp. 192-93.

36. Clay to Webster, Apr. 14, 1827, Daniel Webster Papers (Library of Congress), cited hereafter as Webster MSS.

37. John Sergeant to Clay, Aug. 23, Sept. 13, 18, 1827, Clay MSS; Webster to Ezekiel Webster, Feb. 9, June 13, 22, 1827; Webster to J. Q. Adams, Mar. 27, 1827, Van Tyne, *Letters of Webster*, pp. 121, 123-24, 127.

38. Livermore, *Twilight of Federalism*, pp. 189-93, 223-31.

39. Richard Peters to James Barbour, Sept. 1, 1827, Barbour MSS; Lewis Williams to David Call, Jan. 6, 1828, Clay MSS; Webster to Samuel Bell, Oct. 18, 1827, Webster MSS; Webster to Joseph E. Sprague, Mar. 22, 1828, Van Tyne, *Letters of Webster*, pp. 134-35; Webster to Samuel Bell, Oct. 15, 1827, Webster, *Writings and Speeches*, XVI, 158-59.

were solved, resulted from amalgamation in New York and Pennsylvania. Adams Republicans in neither state were eager to relinquish their positions in the party in favor of an unproven hybrid. Factionalism doomed the efforts in New York.[40] Van Buren, now holding the reigns of the Jackson bandwagon, kept the Adamsites off-balance by a series of artful maneuvers. He could do this because while most of the Clintonians supported Adams, their leader professed the warmest admiration for Jackson. Furthermore, the Federalists were deeply split between those aligned with Clinton and those preferring to go along with the Regency. The upshot was that no real merger occurred. The attempts at consolidation in Pennsylvania were marked by bungling.[41] Adams leaders attached too much importance to reaching an understanding with the Philadelphia Federalists, thus offending Republicans elsewhere in the state. Even the Philadelphia arrangements broke down in 1826 when the Federalists persisted in nominating their own congressional candidate. The next year both groups agreed on the same nominees for Congress and local offices, but this did not prevent many Federalists from supporting Jackson.

The Jacksonians did not remain ignorant of what was happening. "You see on what grounds the opposition places itself," Webster wrote in 1826. "The Leading Jackson Journals make the great charge to be, *a tendency, in Mr. Adams, to stand well with Federalists—*"[42] The alliances with the Federalists presented the Jacksonians with an opportunity to read the Adams Republicans out of the Republican party. That Adams had once been a Federalist, and now favored the use of national power reminiscent of Federalism, made him speciously vulnerable even though the man and his measures were by now legitimately Republican. Yet it was the Jacksonians who succeeded to the Republican name and traditions, largely because the administration voluntarily abandoned what should have been its most prized asset. What did it gain in return for surrendering its Republican lineage? Unchallenged supremacy in half of the New England states was the only tangible result. These would undoubtedly have been for Adams in any event. In the South and West there were not enough Federalists to affect the balance against Adams.

40. Livermore, *Twilight of Federalism*, pp. 232–35.
41. *Ibid.*, pp. 235–38; John Sergeant to Clay, Sept. 18, 26, Oct. 27, 1827, Clay MSS.
42. Webster to William Gaston, May 31, 1826, Van Tyne, *Letters of Webster*, p. 120. Also, Webster to Clay, Nov. 5, 1826, Clay MSS.

In New York, association with the Federalists proved a heavy burden to the Adams Republicans. Symptomatic of their plight was the attitude of New York's Representative Silas Wright, Jr. Like other members of the Regency faction he had preferred Adams to Crawford in 1824, and was not, initially, hostile to the administration. Adams soon made his position untenable. With one exception, he noted, every Adams appointee from New York was either a Clintonian or a Federalist. Nor was that all. The administration spokesman in Congress was that notorious Federalist, Webster. "These are facts against which I know not how to contend," Wright lamented. "All say party is done away, but, come to selections for office, federalists are never forgotten, and we should suppose that in the doing away of party, the old line of democrats was done away by annihilation." Although not convinced that Jackson's "political creed" was better than Adams's, Jackson at least could be expected to appoint "democrats and not the federalists" since he kept better company.[43] The number of Republicans alienated by Adams's "no-party" approach cannot be estimated with any precision, but in New York it was considerable judging from the number of complaints by his own friends.[44]

Nor was it accompanied by a mass transfer throughout the country of Federalists to Adams. A large portion, including many of their most able leaders, found their way to the Jackson camp.[45] In trying to win over the Federalists the Adams strategists "made a bad job of it," in the words of the most authoritative historian of Federalism during its "twilight years." "Adams and his advisors compromised and hesitated, never succeeding in attracting the bulk of the old Federalist party, and often swelling the widely held feeling that somehow they had compromised basic Republican principles by opening doors to the ancient enemy."[46] The dichotomy of high-mindedness and expediency in Adams's policy proved politically ruinous.

Nothing illustrates the anomalous position of the Adamsites better than their lack of a title. Their claim to be "the Republican party" had been surrendered in deference to the president's desire to bury

43. Wright to A. C. Flagg, Dec. 20, 1827, Flagg MSS.

44. Henry Wheaton to J. W. Taylor, Mar. 29, 1826; James Tallmadge to Taylor, Feb. 22, May 13, 1826; Feb. 9, 1827; Jan. 5, 1828, Taylor MSS; W. B. Rochester to Clay, Oct. 9, 1827, Clay MSS; J. L. Mallory to A. C. Flagg, July 19, 1825, Flagg MSS; Francis Baylies to G. C. Verplanck, Nov. 13, 1827, Gulian C. Verplanck Papers (New York Historical Society), cited hereafter as Verplanck MSS.

45. Livermore, *Twilight of Federalism*, pp. 196, 220–22, 238–41.

46. *Ibid.*, pp. 199–200.

party distinctions and the Federalists' sensitivities. In New Hampshire, and elsewhere, the Federalists had refused to participate when caucuses, conventions, or meetings were styled "Republican." A new name might have suited the Federalists, but would have remained incompatible with the president's disdain for parties. "National Republican," which some historians in the interest of tidiness have bestowed on the Adams-Clay coalition, was not used in the campaign of 1828 and properly belongs to the Clay party of 1832. Nomination meetings and rallies had to be called under some appellation, but no single one was ever agreed upon. The three most favored, all inglorious, were "The Friends of the Administration," "The Adams Convention" (or whatever the type of meeting), and "Anti-Jackson."

Adams's sins of omission went beyond the failure to give his supporters a name. He neglected the chance to create the national organization that was even more important to his success. Possession of the White House gave the Adamsites a central authority and an affirmative program that were missing in the motley ranks of the Jacksonians. The president could have easily, for example, summoned a national convention to renominate himself and pick a running mate. This, however, was the very sort of thing he wished to avoid; it was not even considered. So the opportunity, like so many others, passed untaken. The failure of Adams to coordinate, in any way, the activities of his supporters across the nation was his most conspicuous shortcoming, since his office afforded him the means to have done so.

It probably seemed totally unnecessary to nominate the president in a national meeting; everyone assumed he would run again. But it would have been immensely helpful in rousing his dispirited followers and for choosing a running mate. Evidence of public support had to be marshaled by diverse means in the states. Beginning late in 1827 his friends sought to create a climate of approval by formal legislative resolutions (Rhode Island and New Hampshire), caucuses (Maine, Massachusetts, Vermont, and New York), state conventions (New Hampshire, New York, Pennsylvania, New Jersey, Maryland, Virginia, North Carolina, Ohio, Kentucky, Indiana, Missouri, and Louisiana), and public meetings (Mississippi and Alabama).

Reliance on state nominations created a problem of how to designate a vice-presidential candidate. A national convention was one solution, and by this date a fairly obvious one, but for a party which denied it was a party it was, of course, not a possibility. At one point some consideration was given to holding a congressional caucus, but this suggestion was not followed up.[47] State nominations would have to suffice. With great consistency the business was badly handled. Everyone realized that there must be a prior agreement on a single ticket. Clay was frequently mentioned as a possible vice-president, but both he and the president inclined to the view that the change of roles offered no advantages.[48] Only William Henry Harrison actively sought the honor, but then, he sought every honor.[49] A few persons suggested that the opposition be raided by nominating Crawford or "Old Republican" Nathaniel Macon of North Carolina. Adams refused to consider these suggestions.[50] Clay, Southard, former speaker Taylor of New York, and others favored James Pleasants, former governor of Virginia.[51] But it was pointed out that Pennsylvania would strongly object to Pleasants since he had denounced protective tariffs and internal improvements as unconstitutional.[52] The strategy was then reversed and Andrew Shulze, the governor of Pennsylvania, was brought forward only to have him decline.[53]

Adams felt strongly that his teammate should be a southerner, an obvious desire to balance the ticket geographically. His personal choice was James Barbour.[54] The Secretary of War evinced no enthusiasm for this elevation, preferring the ministry in London made vacant on King's resignation. It was then suggested that the Adams convention in Virginia, scheduled to meet early in January, 1828, should choose a favorite son who would be taken up elsewhere.[55] But the meeting

47. Clay to Francis Brooke, Nov. 24, 1827, Colton, *Private Correspondence,* p. 183.

48. Adams, *Memoirs,* VII (Dec. 21, 1826; Feb. 13, Nov. 7, 10, 1827), 216–17, 225, 348, 351; C. Hammond to Clay, Jan. 3, 1827; Joseph Kent to Clay, Jan. 26, 1827; John H. Pleasants to Clay, May 4, 1827; W. B. Rochester to Clay, Oct. 12, Nov. 4, 1827, Clay MSS; Storrs MS, Dec. 14, 1827.

49. Adams, *Memoirs,* VII (May 6, 1828), 530; Storrs MS, Dec. 19, 26, 1827; Freeman Cleaves, *Old Tippecanoe: William Henry Harrison and His Times* (New York, 1939), p. 259.

50. Adams, *Memoirs,* VII (Dec. 7, 24, 28, 1827), 374, 388, 390–91.

51. *Ibid.,* VII (Dec. 8, 11, 16, 1827), 375, 378, 381–82; *Daily National Intelligencer,* Oct. 12, Dec. 10, 13, 14, 1827; *Albany Argus,* Dec. 27, 1827; Storrs MS, Dec. 9, 1827; Caleb Atwater to Jackson, Nov. 30, 1827; Atwater to William B. Lewis, Nov. 30, 1827, Andrew Jackson–William B. Lewis Papers (New York Public Library), cited hereafter as Jackson-Lewis MSS.

52. Adams, *Memoirs,* VII (Dec. 16, 1827), 381–82.

53. *Ibid.,* (Dec. 11, 15, 1827), 378, 380.

54. *Ibid.,* (Nov. 12, 1827; Jan. 9, 1828), 352, 400.

55. Samuel L. Southard to R. B. Taylor, Nov. 9, 1827; Southard to Francis Brooke, Nov. 9, 1827, Samuel L. Southard Papers (Library of Congress), cited hereafter as Southard MSS; Southard to Francis Brooke, Dec. 9, 1827, Clay MSS; Adams, *Memoirs,* VII (Dec. 8, 1827), 375.

at Richmond made no nomination because it would be "tauntingly said the bait was her [Virginia's] seduction—and her pride too great to be satisfied with a bait so small—"[56] With no southerners available it was resolved, once again, to propitiate Pennsylvania. Rush, whose report favoring tariffs had elicited favorable notice from the manufacturing interests, was finally picked.[57] Exactly who made the selection is not clear, but it certainly was not the president.[58] A state convention at Harrisburg nominated him and subsequent Adams meetings in other states seconded the choice.[59] By refusing either to exercise personal leadership or permit a substitute for that leadership, such as a national convention or a congressional caucus, Adams ended up with a running mate who was not the man he wanted and was not even from the part of the country he felt would add the most strength to the ticket. It was a fitting climax to his experiment of pretending that he was not the head of a party.

Short of withdrawing from the forthcoming election, Adams could not, no matter how badly he fumbled, prevent his supporters from trying to reelect him. Some admired his great, if misplaced, abilities. Many favored his stand in favor of tariffs and internal improvements. Sectional prejudice among northerners was a plus factor and not a few believed him preferable to a "Military Chieftain." For whatever reason, once they had given fealty they tried to carry their states for him. Voters needed to be informed and brought to the polls. Candidates supporting him, including those for the Electoral College, had to be nominated. In performing these chores and the hundreds of related ones, what amounted to an Adams party was created in almost every state, if only for a brief period before the election. Just by standing for reelection Adams brought a national party into being.

The election of 1828 was critical in bringing about a two-party system in New England, although the formation was not fully completed by the polling day.[60] In 1824 the heavy support for Adams assured him of the backing of the regular Republican election ma-

56. James Barbour to Francis Brooke and Hugh Mercer, Jan. 2, 1828, Clay MSS.
57. Storrs MS, Dec. 19, 1827.
58. Adams, *Memoirs*, VII (Jan. 3, 9, 1828), 398, 400.
59. *Ibid.*, (Jan. 12, May 1, 1828), 403, 525–26; *Democratic Convention* [Jan. 14, 1828] (Harrisburg, n.d.), p. 17.
60. In this and succeeding paragraphs, I am deeply indebted to Richard P. McCormick for his study of *The Second American Party System*. Since his book exceeded my research in the same area, I have borrowed heavily from it.

chinery. In most of New England this consisted chiefly of a legislative caucus which controlled nominations for state offices, elected the central committee, and appointed the county committees. After 1825 schisms occurred within Republican ranks over the presidential question and what remained of the Federalist party melted into the new alignment. So far as the Adamsites are concerned, these were not years for devising new or better party machinery. Their predominant position, in most instances, enabled them to operate the existing apparatus of the Republican party.

Unity in the president's home state crippled any serious effort by the Jacksonians either to take over the Massachusetts Republican party or build a rival organization. The controlling agency of the party, the legislative caucus and its branches in the counties, was overwhelmingly pro-Adams in sentiment. The main difficulty lay in integrating the Federalists into the existing structure rather than in a splitting-off of pro-Jackson elements within it. By the time the caucus met in June, 1828, to nominate Adams electors and appoint the central and county committees, the amalgamation had been achieved. In the election Adams received five-sixths of the popular vote.[61]

The situation in New Hampshire differed from that in Massachusetts in that the Jacksonians were more numerous and more aggressively led. The Republican state organization, nevertheless, remained intact until 1827, when the immediacy of the presidential election forced the leaders to choose sides. Meanwhile, the Adams Republicans and Federalists had effected a merger. In June, 1827, the president's backers staged a giant public meeting in Concord to set in motion a statewide organizational drive. The next year they followed up with a mixed caucus that nominated a full ticket—governor, presidential electors, and congressmen. Two-party politics was in full swing by the end of Adams's term.[62]

Connecticut had been relatively unaffected by presidential politics since 1816, although a loosely organized Republican caucus made nominations for state offices. The state had voted for Adams in 1824 almost as a matter of course. Not until the eve of the 1828 election did a split occur among the state's Republicans, the larger portion siding with Adams. His electors were nominated by the regular party caucus

61. McCormick, *Second Party System,* pp. 36–43.
62. *Ibid.,* pp. 57–60; *Address of the Great State Convention of Friends of the Administration: Assembled at the Capitol in Concord, June 12, 1828* (Concord, 1828).

meeting in May, 1828. As in most of the New England states, the Jacksonians, left holding the short end of the divided party, were compelled to establish a new organizational framework.[63]

By an even older tradition than its western neighbor, Rhode Island had kept state politics separated from national concerns. Sentiment in 1824 and 1828 was overwhelmingly in favor of Adams. The first sign of a new order took place in January, 1828, when a "convention" of state legislators and other administration supporters nominated a state ticket. Simultaneously, the regular mixed caucus of the Republican party chose an almost identical slate. In the autumn, however, the Adams leaders avoided the usual machinery in selecting presidential electors, nominating them at a special public meeting.[64]

Adams's domination was even more complete in Vermont. Nor was there any difficulty with the Federalists as they had ceased to be a factor well before the election of 1824. Lacking a serious challenge from the Jacksonians, the Adamsites exercised an easy mastery over the regular Republican organization. The party caucus duly nominated electors pledged to the president. State offices were not touched by the presidential question.[65]

The long struggle for statehood had submerged the rivalry between Republicans and Federalists in Maine prior to the election of 1824 even though each group maintained a separate identity. Republican unity for the governorship after 1825 was not upset by national considerations; both administration and Jackson supporters attended the nominating caucus. In choosing candidates for the Electoral College, the state legislature, and Congress, however, they went their separate ways. The Adams leaders rallied their legions at a huge mixed caucus, followed up by district conventions which made the nominations.[66]

The revived party system took hold most quickly in the middle Atlantic states.[67] These states, significantly, were the first to apply fully the convention system to all the major electoral units. This, as well as the historical development of political factions, accounts in some measure for the rapidity with which the middle states produced two well-balanced, highly competitive parties.

In New York, the split between the Bucktails (after 1823 the

63. McCormick, *Second Party System*, pp. 64–67.
64. *Ibid.*, pp. 80–82.
65. *Ibid.*, 71–72; *Albany Argus*, Nov. 21, 1827; July 2, 1828.
66. McCormick, *Second Party System*, pp. 50–52; *Daily National Intelligencer*, Feb. 4, 1828; *Proceedings of a Convention of the People of Maine*.
67. McCormick, *Second Party System*, pp. 103–4, 166–69.

Regency) and the Clintonians laid the basis for a two-party system, but it was not until after Adams's election that this polarity coincided with the division in national politics. The Regency became the Jackson party in New York, the Clintonians supported Adams. There were important exceptions to this bifurcation. Many who followed the Regency in state politics preferred Adams, while Clinton himself supported Jackson. But the death of Clinton early in 1828 greatly simplified the political line-up. The remaining Federalists were divided between the two. And in 1827 a new force, the Antimasons, began a spectacular rise although they were not sufficiently strong in 1828 to rival the older factions. Beginning in 1827 the supporters of the president began organizing the state, taking over, more or less intact, the existing Clinton organization. The following year they used the caucus to endorse the administration, held three state conventions, one of which nominated a state ticket, and staged a series of county and district conventions to select other candidates, including presidential electors.[68]

After the election of 1824, New Jersey Republicans temporarily patched up their differences. But the new order was not to be denied. At the regular state convention in 1826 to nominate congressmen a rupture took place between the Jackson and Adams men and each group put up a separate slate. In 1828 the Adamsites held two state conventions, one to nominate the congressional ticket, the other for electors.[69]

Pennsylvania stands out as an exception to the balanced two-party system in the middle states. Jackson's popularity in 1824 swept aside the factionalism that had rent the Republicans for decades. His supporters retained firm control of the pervasive convention structure of the party after 1825. The friends of Adams made no attempt to counter this sentiment until late in 1827, when a public meeting at York summoned a state convention for Harrisburg to nominate elec-

68. *Albany Argus,* May 29, June 3, 9, 10, 12, 14, Oct. 8, 20, 1828; *Buffalo Emporium and General Advertiser,* May 1, 29, June 19, July 17, Aug. 7, Oct. 2, 1828; *Daily National Intelligencer,* Apr. 30, June 16, July 29, 1828; *Free Press* [Auburn, N.Y.], June 4, July 2, 30, 1828; *Niles' Weekly Register,* XXXV (Nov. 1, 1828), 147; *Address to the Republican Citizens of the State of New York,* (Albany, 1828).

69. McCormick, *Second Party System,* pp. 129–30; *Daily National Intelligencer,* Nov. 15, 1827; Feb. 25, Oct. 21, 1828; *Niles' Weekly Register,* XXXI (Sept. 30, 1826), 67; *Proceedings and Address of the New-Jersey Delegates in Favor of the Present Administration of the General Government, Assembled in Convention at Trenton, February 22, 1828* (Trenton, 1828).

tors. Unable to mount county or district conventions, the Adams party elected delegates to the state convention at open meetings. Nevertheless, 109 of 114 counties were represented at the Harrisburg convention. After agreeing on the electoral ticket, the delegates offered the vice-presidential nomination to Rush. By the election of 1828 the administration leaders had built an extensive, if shallow, organization.[70]

Delaware was "a model" state so far as the party system is concerned. It had quickly developed after 1792 two well-organized, stable, and competitive parties. The Federalists remained a viable, cohesive force up to and beyond the election of 1824. Both Federalists and Republicans used the county and state conventions to make nominations and conduct party business. The shift to the second party system caused only the most temporary dislocation. Following a short-lived confusion in 1827 among the older parties over the nomination of candidates for Delaware's congressional seat, a new alignment took the place of the old. Federalist and Republican backers of Adams eventually agreed on a single candidate, the Jacksonians likewise. The bulk of the Federalists became Adamsites while most Republicans apparently supported Jackson.[17] Both continued to use the convention system.

The new party system did not make much headway in the south Atlantic states before 1828. During the early national period the area had been overwhelmingly Jeffersonian except for Maryland and the Federalist enclaves in Virginia and the Carolinas. This tendency toward a monolithic outlook continued despite the impact of the Adams-Jackson rivalry.[72]

Maryland did possess a strong two-party tradition, the Federalists managing to hold together until about 1821. Both of the older parties had adopted the convention system for making county and district nominations, but the absence of any officials elected at-large had precluded the development of the state nominating convention. As the party contest lost intensity after 1813, the voter's allegiance to the nominees of these conventions diminished, but the practice survived. In 1827 both of the new parties revived the use of the convention in the process of creating new organizations. And both drew heavily

70. McCormick, *Second Party System*, pp. 139–41; *Daily National Intelligencer*, Nov. 16, 21, Dec. 19, 1827; Jan. 7, 9, 1828.
71. *Richmond Enquirer*, Sept. 21, 1827; McCormick, *Second Party System*, p. 147, 151–53.
72. McCormick, *Second Party System*, pp. 177–78.

from the ranks of the old parties. The Jacksonians and Adamsites improved upon the old structure by holding state conventions. The Adams state convention met in Baltimore in July, 1827, attended by delegates chosen at county meetings or conventions.[73] Its purpose was not to nominate candidates, but to inspirit the president's followers and perfect the state and local organizations. Electors pledged to Adams were nominated by district conventions the next year.[74] In Maryland, Adams had the benefit of a far-flung grass roots organization.

Virginia had no surviving Federalist party. A semblance of Republican unity was preserved by the Richmond Junto which dominated the caucus and the county committees. As the Junto decided to support Jackson in 1828, the president's friends faced the formidable task of creating a new organization. They did so by ignoring the caucus in favor of summoning a state convention to nominate an electoral ticket, the first meeting of this type in the state's history.[75]

The Adamsites were also responsible for staging the first state convention in North Carolina. There the situation was even more discouraging than in Virginia, for the older Republican leadership merged after 1825 with the broad popular support that Jackson had shown in 1824. In June, 1827, the *Raleigh Register* suggested a state meeting to organize the administration's backers. A county meeting formalized this into a call for a state convention at Raleigh in December. Other public meetings around the state responded by electing delegates. Only fifty-five delegates, including a number of legislators, attended the Raleigh convention, but these nominated an electoral ticket loyal to the president.[76]

South Carolina and Georgia failed to respond to the new duality of national politics. Opinion in both leaned so heavily toward Jackson

73. *Daily National Intelligencer*, May 19, 24, June 6, 8, 12, 21, 23, 27, July 25, 26, 31, 1827; *Proceedings of the Administration Meeting in Baltimore County, June, 1827* (Baltimore, 1827); *Proceedings of the Maryland Administration Convention Delegated by the People, and Held in Baltimore, on Monday and Tuesday, July 23d and 24th, 1827.* (Baltimore, 1827); Robert H. Goldsborough to Clay, Aug. 9, 1827, Clay MSS.

74. *Daily National Intelligencer*, June 8, 1827; Apr. 3, May 20, June 9, 1828; *Meeting of the Friends of the Administration, in Hartford County, Md.* [Mar. 13, 1828], n.p., n.d.

75. The details of the Virginia Adams convention are given in the Conclusion.

76. *Daily National Intelligencer*, Nov. 24, Dec. 13, 28, 29, 1827; *Albany Argus*, Jan. 3, 1828; William S. Hoffman, *Andrew Jackson and North Carolina Politics* (Chapel Hill, 1958), pp. 17–18.

that it prevented any serious activity on behalf of Adams. South Carolina lacked the constitutional basis for popular parties, and in Georgia both factions of the Republican party were solidly committed to Jackson as the result of the administration's advocacy of Cherokee autonomy.[77]

Political sentiment crystallized unevenly in the old Northwest, the degree determined by the length of time each state had been a member of the Union. Ohio adjusted the most quickly to the new parties, Illinois the slowest, and Indiana occupied a midpoint. These states had entered too late to have developed parties before the Era of Good Feelings. All voters considered themselves Republicans, but there were few continuing organizational structures or stable factions.

Not until 1827 did the politicians of Ohio react in a concrete fashion to the impending fight between Adams and Jackson. Leaders of the Adams cause, perhaps taking their cue from the Jacksonians in 1824, decided to hold a state convention. Delegates representing sixty-three of seventy-three counties assembled on December 28, 1827, at Columbus. Electors were nominated and a state central committee was appointed.[78] "The Adams convention," Richard P. McCormick writes, "might properly be regarded as the first full-fledged state party convention in Ohio, for the meetings that had been held during the 1824 campaign hardly merited that designation."[79] In the campaign the Adamsites mounted a full-scale effort and were able to compete on nearly equal terms with the Jacksonians.

Parties were much slower in forming in Indiana. Factionalism rather than two clearly defined parties continued to be the rule well after the election of 1828, and friends of both Adams and Jackson carried on their organizing activities independently of state politics. The Adams men held a thinly attended state convention at Indianapolis early in 1828 to nominate electors and appoint a central correspondence committee. Counties and townships were urged to elect committees of correspondence and vigilance for the forthcoming campaign.[80] In

---

77. McCormick, *Second Party System*, p. 240.

78. Joshua Phillips to Daniel Webster [Dec. 10, 1827], Van Tyne, *Letters of Webster*, p. 131; *Daily National Intelligencer*, Dec. 14, 1827; Jan. 7, 1828; *Proceedings and Address of the Convention of Delegates, That Met at Columbus, Ohio, Dec. 28, 1827, to Nominate a Ticket of Electors Favorable to the Reelection of John Quincy Adams, President of the United States* (n.p., 1827).

79. McCormick, *Second Party System*, p. 264.

80. *Ibid.*, pp. 273–74; *Daily National Intelligencer*, Dec. 14, 1827; *Proceedings of the Administration Convention Held at Indianapolis, January 12, 1828* (Indianapolis, n.d.).

spite of this the administration forces did not command an effective organization in the Hoosier state.

Illinois still retained all the earmarks of a frontier state in that its politics was conducted without reference to stable groupings. The elections of 1824 and 1828 did not measurably affect this chaotic state of affairs. Adams evidenced support in the northern part of the state, but his friends raised no effective organization in his behalf.[81]

Of the newer slave states only Kentucky produced a two-party system before the election of 1828. Like the states of the Northwest, they had never experienced the first party system; their politics tended toward that loose factionalism characteristic of recently settled areas. Furthermore, it was a region which strongly identified with Jackson. The result of these two factors was a generally weak effort on the part of those favoring Adams.

Kentucky's deviation from the pattern was attributable to Clay. His own popularity and his network of faithful lieutenants created an Adams party of considerable strength. District conventions had been held on rare occasions before 1824, but the first state convention was the work of Clay's supporters who had followed him into the Adams camp. Meeting at Frankfort in December, 1827, the delegates not only nominated electors, but chose candidates for governor and lieutenant governor as well.[82] This last action effectively tied state politics to presidential politics, a unique condition among the western states.

Jackson's home state contrasted sharply with Kentucky. Tennessee politics had long been conducted on an unorganized basis. The candidacy of a favorite son only reinforced this confusion. Adams supporters were in such short supply that they made no effort at all—there simply was no contest.[83]

Politics in Louisiana revolved around an ethnic division, the older French settlers pitted against the American newcomers. But this split did not carry over to national politics, since the Creoles took relatively little interest in presidential elections. Adams's cause was immensely aided by Clay's association with it, as the Kentuckian was popular

81. McCormick, *Second Party System*, pp. 280–81.

82. *Ibid.*, pp. 210, 217–20; Thomas Smith to Henry Clay, Oct. 7, 1827, Clay MSS; *Proceedings of the Administration Convention Held at Frankfort, Kentucky on Monday, December 17, 1827* (n.p., n.d.); Leonard R. Curry, "Election Year—Kentucky, 1828," *Register of the Kentucky Historical Society*, LV (July, 1957), 199–200.

83. McCormick, *Second Party System*, pp. 222–23, 227.

there and had strong personal ties with important leaders. The administration men resorted to a state convention to nominate an electoral ticket. Delegates from half the parishes, chosen at public meetings, assembled at Baton Rouge in November, 1827, to take the necessary steps to see that the voters would have the opportunity of reelecting the president.[84]

Chaos was the main feature of politics in Alabama and Mississippi. Neither Jacksonians nor Adamsites attempted much in the way of organizing the state. In both states Adams's electors were appointed at a public meeting which drew persons from all parts of the state.[85] So great was Jackson's grip on the Southwest, however, that an Adams party did not really exist.

Sentiment in Missouri coalesced around the two United States senators, Thomas Hart Benton, who was for Jackson, and David Barton, who backed Adams. Responding to a call by a public meeting in St. Louis, the friends of the administration nominated electors at a state convention at Jefferson City in March, 1828. Nominations for state and local offices were untouched by this development and the largely undefined factionalism existing before 1828 continued.[86] Jackson's greater popularity and Senator Benton's more effective leadership decisively swept aside the efforts of Adams's admirers.

By November, 1828, the friends of the administration had succeeded in establishing organizations of varying degrees of effectiveness in all but three states (South Carolina, Georgia, and Tennessee). In New England they had been able either to preempt the regular Republican election machinery (Massachusetts, Connecticut, and Vermont) or establish new and comprehensive substitutes. Although less strong in the middle Atlantic states, they had, except in Pennsylvania, built viable organizations based on a coalition of Federalists and Republicans. Their record in the South and West was poor. Only in Ohio, Ken-

84. *Ibid.*, pp. 314–15; *Daily National Intelligencer*, Dec. 13, 1827; *Proceedings of the Delegates of the Friends of the Administration of John Quincy Adams. Assembled in Convention at Baton Rouge* [Nov. 5, 1827] (New Orleans, 1827).

85. McCormick, *Second Party System*, pp. 289–90, 297; *Daily National Intelligencer*, June 14, 1828; *Niles' Weekly Register*, XXIV (Mar. 8, 1828), 25; Miles, *Jacksonian Democracy in Mississippi*, pp. 13–14.

86. Leota Newhard, "The Beginnings of the Whig Party in Missouri, 1824–1840," *Missouri Historical Review*, XXV (Jan., 1931), 254–62; Hattie M. Anderson, "The Jackson Men in Missouri in 1828," *Missouri Historical Review*, XXXIV (Apr., 1940), 315–16; William Russell to J. W. Taylor, Feb. 21, 1828, Taylor MSS.

tucky, and Louisiana did Adams make a creditable showing, and in six states he either had no organized backing (South Carolina, Georgia, and Tennessee) or it was so weak as to give Jackson the election by default (Illinois, Alabama, and Mississippi).

Yet in view of the president's attitude toward the party concept, and his general political ineptness, the achievement of his friends in organizing eighteen of the twenty-four states is not unimpressive. The favorite instrument for uniting the president's friends was the state convention. Four of these conventions were the first statewide meetings of delegates for partisan purposes held in their respective states (Virginia, North Carolina, Kentucky, and Louisiana).[87] These innovations occurred in the regions where Adams was weakest, which suggests that the convention was looked upon as the most attractive and efficient method for creating an organization where none existed. The caucus continued to predominate in New England and both parties employed the convention in the middle states where it had become customary. Had the president taken a greater interest in his reelection, or at least not frustrated those among his followers who had a better grasp of political reality, more uniform and effective state organizations might have been constructed. The creation of a national organization encompassing the states was even possible. But the opportunity was never exploited; it was not compatible with the president's image of himself. Surveying his course from the perspective of defeat, he could say with a clear conscience: "In looking back, I see nothing that I could have avoided, nothing that I ought to repent."[88]

87. This credits the Ohio Jackson convention of 1824 as being the first in the state rather than the Adams convention of 1827.
88. Adams, *Memoirs*, VIII (Dec. 31, 1828), 88.

FOUR

The Jacksonians

The Adams-Clay coalition created a second political party as well as it did a first. A mixture of personal ambition, political opportunism, and genuine disapproval of the new administration fused the "losers" of the election of 1825 into a rival combination under the ostensible leadership of "Old Hickory." The union of Jackson enthusiasts, Crawford Radicals, and Calhoun admirers became, in time, the Democratic party. The forging of this confederacy was a difficult undertaking, far more complex than the joining of Clay with Adams. Four possible presidential candidates, if Clinton is included, were involved instead of two. Jackson and Crawford held each other in contempt. Calhoun and Jackson had always professed great mutual respect, but Calhoun and Crawford were beyond hope of reconciliation. Clinton made it a studied policy to remain aloof from national politics, but he was the head of one New York faction locked in a hoary feud with another whose preceptor was the national manager of the Radicals. Even assuming that these proud and sensitive personalities could somehow forget their hostilities sufficiently to agree on a single candidate for the presidency, there seemed utterly no possibility that they could unite on a vice-presidential candidate.

Circumstance dictated that Jackson should be placed in the forefront of the opponents of the administration. He alone had demonstrated national popularity in 1824. A divided opposition could not prevail against an incumbent president; the only hope lay in consolidating behind the strongest contender. Crawford, old and ill, had returned home to nurse his grievances and ambitions. Both remained immense, but only his grievances needed to be treated seriously. Calhoun, on the other hand, had youth and health as well as ambition. But Jackson's advanced age and debility as well as his promise to serve a single term meant that Calhoun could afford to wait. In any event, Crawford's unwavering antagonism made his candidacy untenable in 1828. Clinton's course defied prediction, but his endorsement of Jackson in 1824 and the lack of solid support in his own state weighed against an independent effort.

As it turned out, Jackson never gave the others a chance. He entered the lists so quickly that he preempted the field. Adams's election instantly made him a candidate again.[1] Jackson's second campaign, however, differed markedly from his first. The change owed less to his new ardor than to fresh managers. Instead of "the grog shop politicians" that flocked to his standard in 1824, his campaign was guided by skilled and seasoned politicians of national stature, men immune to the mindless devotion that inspired the original Jacksonians. The new recruits were interested in power and Jackson was an instrument to gain that end. They set out to surround the hero so that his triumph would seem their doing. Their plan, in essence, was to make Jackson the head of a party not of his own creation, one that existed prior to his candidacy and was not totally dependent on him. That way he would become the captain, yet obligated to conduct himself with a due regard for the safety of the ship and crew. More explicitly, he would be made the standard-bearer of the Republican party.

Many persons were involved in this maneuver, but three were of paramount importance: Van Buren, Calhoun, and Ritchie. Each played a vital part, but Van Buren's role was crucial. As the head of the strongest faction in the largest state, he operated from an impressive political base. New York seemed essential to Jackson's election, and his only chance of carrying it rested with the Regency. Jackson had no great personal following there; in 1824 he had received not one of New York's thirty-six electoral votes. Despite Clinton's endorsement of him, the Clintonians as a group supported Adams. In the campaign of 1824 Van Buren had shrewdly used his position in New York to project himself to the front of national politics. His work in the late election had given him valuable contacts throughout the country,

1. Jackson to W. B. Lewis, Feb. 14, 1825; Edward Satchell to Jackson, Mar. 4, 1825; Isaac Baker to Jackson, Mar. 5, 1825; James Buchanan to Jackson, May 29, 1825; Jackson to Joseph Desha, June 21, 1825, Andrew Jackson Papers, 1st ser. (Library of Congress), cited hereafter as Jackson MSS.

particularly in the South, where he was well regarded.[2] He was also the most conscious of the need to tie Jackson to a party, and he pursued this goal with the greatest diligence. He brought to his task a conviction that the Republican party still lived, a belief that there was an unbroken continuity from Jefferson down to Crawford and now Jackson.[3]

Calhoun and Ritchie were willing accomplices. As vice-president, Calhoun contributed the prestige of his office in addition to his own abilities as a strategist and a group of able followers. Ritchie, spokesman for the powerful Richmond Junto, was the key to winning over the southerners who valued "measures above men" or above party names. Together these three would add New York and the Southeast to Jackson's proven popularity in Pennsylvania and the West.

While Calhoun and Ritchie made little effort to conceal their antagonism toward the administration (although neither publicly declared for Jackson until the proper moment), Van Buren was more cautious.[4] For a year following Adams's election, the New York senator and his allies feigned neutrality. Why did Van Buren tarry so long before getting behind Jackson? Was he waiting to see if Adams might prove sufficiently popular to compel his support? It seems unlikely. In any event, the president already had a strong party in New York, so that Van Buren had no stake in his success, and could not reasonably expect to have much voice in the administration. Adams's offer of London to Clinton did not indicate a friendly disposition. Most of all, support of Adams would destroy his influence outside New York, in Virginia, Georgia, and the other southern states where Adams had only a feeble band of adherents and where the Radicals had been strongest. Van Buren could not deliver the Crawfordites to Adams and his nationalist policies. To have tried would have destroyed his position as a national leader. Crawford could not plausibly run again; backing Clinton was unthinkable and Calhoun's bid in 1824 had fallen flat. Jackson was the only alternative.

Expediency dictated that Van Buren should dissemble for a time.

2. Joseph Hobson Harrison, Jr., "Martin Van Buren and His Southern Supporters," *JSH*, XXLL (Nov., 1956), 438–58.

3. For Van Buren's views on the continuity of parties see his *Inquiry into the Origins and Course of Political Parties in the United States* (New York, 1867). Although written many years after the events described here, the book accurately reflects his opinions during these years.

4. *Richmond Enquirer*, Feb. 12, 15, June 21, Nov. 18, Dec. 8, 1825; Van Buren to Butler, Dec. 25, 1825, Van Buren MSS (LC).

Too early an opposition to the administration would appear to be unseemly factiousness. Months would be required before the tangled relationships between Crawford, Calhoun, Clinton, and Jackson could be smoothed out. Assuming that all agreed to support Jackson, some decision had to be reached on the thorny question of a running mate. Considerations of a more local nature also enforced caution. A number of the Regency's supporters had favored Adams or Clay in 1824 and a premature agitation of the presidential question might cause them to bolt the organization. This would be especially regrettable, as both Van Buren's Senate seat and the governorship were subject to an impending election. The "American Tallyrand's" resources would be severely tested in the next two years.

The road that the "Magnus Apollo" would travel was murky. Although he had rebuffed Adams's olive branch, Clinton did not close the door tightly against a future alliance. It was also conceivable that he might opt to run for president. An even stronger possibility existed that he would offer himself as a suitable vice-president for Jackson. This would jeopardize any understanding between Jackson and Calhoun. Clinton was certainly Van Buren's most delicate problem. To successfully neutralize him required that he abandon his ambitions for both the presidency and vice-presidency. It also required a cessation in the constant warfare between the Regency and the Clintonians in New York. In the end suspicions of Clinton's intentions toward the presidency were not well founded.[5] He could count no state, not even his own, as likely to support him. Yet it was not until November, 1827, that Clinton authorized a public denial of his intention to seek the office, reaffirming at the same time his support of Jackson.[6] For the vice-presidency he was more difficult to shake loose.

Well before his final withdrawal as a presidential candidate, Clinton had been moving toward a truce with Van Buren in New York. Clinton was a candidate for reelection in the fall of 1826, Van Buren in the winter of 1827. The followers of both men were anathema to each other. Furthermore, most of Clinton's party were warm advocates of Adams while a small but significant element attached to the Regency opposed Jackson. An attempt by Van Buren to deliver votes to Clinton for governor or Jackson for president could split his own party. Clinton faced a similar rebellion if he supported Van Buren

5. [Thomas H.] B[enton] to Jackson, Feb. 9, 1827, Jackson MSS. 1st ser.
6. *Daily National Intelligencer*, Nov. 15, 1827, quoting a letter from a close associate of Clinton's as printed in the *New York Evening Post*.

or Jackson.[7] Nevertheless, informal conferences took place between the two factions during 1825–26 to explore their rapport over the presidential question. The result was a limited cooperation between the governor and the Regency legislative majority over patronage.[8] "The coquetry between Van Buren & Clinton," a dismayed Adamsite wrote Clay in the spring of 1826, "begins to assume the appearance of open prostitution."[9] A more correct, and certainly more romantic, allusion to the relationship was given by Jabez Hammond who described Van Buren and Clinton as "a kind of Pyramus & Thisbe kissing, with a wall between."[10]

For the governorship, Van Buren wanted to support Clinton at least to the extent of not making a nomination to oppose him. He was prevented from doing this by the refusal of the Bucktail rank and file to countenance aiding the man they had so spitefully and consistently opposed.[11] To defeat Clinton, however, required a conciliatory attitude toward the Adams administration lest the pro-Adams portion of the Regency be driven to support Clinton for governor.[12] With some difficulty Van Buren found the right candidate to oppose Clinton—a relatively unknown former congressman, William B. Rochester, son of the western New York pioneer. Rochester had two important qualifications: he would not be the strongest candidate and he was an Adams supporter.[13] Rochester's nomination would appease the Regency voters who demanded an opposition to Clinton. Of equal importance, it would divide Adams's supporters by forcing them to choose between Rochester, who favored the president but was sponsored by the party which opposed him, and Clinton, who opposed the president but who was the head of their state party. No matter who won it would be interpreted as a victory for Jackson. Van Buren maintained that Rochester was given "a faithful support" and the closeness of the election would bear him out. Yet he also admitted that "[we]

7. Hammond, *Political Parties in New York*, II, 211–12; Taylor to Charles Miner, Apr. 16, 1827; Taylor to J. C. Wright, Apr. 14, 1827, Taylor MSS.

8. Fitzpatrick, *Autobiography of Van Buren*, pp. 158–59; Peter B. Porter to Clay, Mar. 4, 1826; Jabez D. Hammond to Clay, Mar. 16, 1826; Charles King to Clay, Mar. 20, 1826, Clay MSS.

9. Charles King to Clay, Mar. 21, 1826, Clay MSS.

10. Hammond to Clay, Mar. 16, 1826, *ibid.*

11. Fitzpatrick, *Autobiography of Van Buren*, pp. 156–60.

12. Edwin Croswell to Van Buren, Apr. 3, 1826, Van Buren MSS (LC).

13. Silas Wright to Alva Hunt, Sept. 20, 1844, R. H. Gillet, *The Life and Times of Silas Wright* (Albany, 1874), I, 115.

had not much reason as a party to grieve at the result."[14] Adams, for once, concurred with Van Buren.[15]

In February, 1827, Van Buren received, if any were due, his *quid pro quo* when he was reelected to the Senate without serious opposition from the Clintonians. Some Adams supporters in the Clinton party, with a keen sense of political irony, attempted without success to rally an opposition around Rochester.[16] With their own offices secure, only the vice-presidency kept Van Buren and Clinton from complete harmony.

While Clinton and Van Buren were in the midst of making their peace in New York, the senator was also developing his master plan for the presidential campaign. It was boldly conceived. Jackson, Crawford, and Calhoun would be brought together in a grand alliance that would lay exclusive claim to the Republican party, the Adams-Clay coalition to be branded as Federalist. Central to the scheme was the holding of a national nominating convention. It would simultaneously bind the participants to Jackson, supply physical proof of the party's existence, and commit Jackson to support the convention's sponsors.

During the winter of 1826 Van Buren indicated the direction of his thinking by mildly opposing the administration's internal improvement policies and the Panama Congress.[17] Still, he did not endorse Jackson. At the same time he held cordial conversations with Calhoun at the vice-president's Georgetown home. Van Buren and Calhoun agreed to combine behind Jackson and revive the old Republican coalition of southern planter and northern commoner, the compact to be sealed by a national convention.[18] Together, and with the concurring opinion of Calhoun's spokesman in Pennsylvania, Representative Ingham, they worked out the details in a letter to Ritchie.

Virginia, obviously, would be a highly desirable partner in any effort to resurrect the party of Jefferson. But with the relative decline of the state's power Virginians had become apathetic toward national

14. Fitzpatrick, *Autobiography of Van Buren*, p. 164.

15. Adams, *Memoirs*, VII (Nov. 13, 1826), 177.

16. J. Hoyt to Van Buren, June 11, 1826; William L. Marcy to Van Buren, Dec. 10, 1826, Van Buren MSS (LC).

17. Remini, *Martin Van Buren*, pp. 104–5.

18. Fitzpatrick, *Autobiography of Van Buren*, p. 514; Calhoun to Jackson, June 4, 1826, Jackson MSS, 1st ser.; Wiltse, *John C. Calhoun: Nationalist*, pp. 347–48; Remini, *Martin Van Buren*, pp. 129–30.

politics. The Old Dominion's part in the coming struggle was negative. After Adams's first annual message indicated his strongly nationalist outlook, it was unlikely that Virginia would support him. Yet there was no enthusiasm for Jackson or anyone else. "Virginia," as Webster expressed it, "says little about the men whom she would trust, but opposes those actually in power."[19] Other southern states seemed similarly disposed. Senator Willie P. Mangum of North Carolina, a former Crawford man, did not in January, 1826, regard Jackson's new candidacy as serious.[20] A correspondent of Mangum's thought the South should ignore Adams and Jackson and find a more congenial candidate.[21] And even after it was known that Adams would be opposed by an organized party, the senator was not convinced that Jackson should lead it. In April he wrote his wife that "the Administration are both weak & wicked, I fear,—and the present prospect is that the Members of Congress from south of Washington will unite to put down Adams, & if they can get no better, they will take up Gen. Jackson for that purpose."[22]

Bringing the Radicals into the Jackson fold necessitated personal missionary work by Van Buren, but before undertaking it he launched the first stage of the plan that he and Calhoun had contrived. On January 6, 1827, the *Albany Argus* asked the question that was on no one's lips:

> It is suggested to the consideration of republicans throughout the Union, whether a National Convention, composed of delegates from the several states, may not be the best mode to concentrate the public opinion in the nomination of President and Vice-President of the U.S.? The convention may be held early or late in the ensuing fall, under the recommendation of the republican representatives in congress, at any central place,—at Philadelphia, Baltimore, or elsewhere. The choice of delegates might devolve on the republicans in state or county conventions; or on the members of the respective legislatures. It is also suggested whether the results of such a convention would not prevent a recurrence of the bitter animosities that characterized the previous election; strengthen the republican party; and avoid an ultimate resort to the House of Representatives.

19. Webster to Jeremiah Mason, written sometime during the winter of 1826 and quoted in John Bach McMaster, *Daniel Webster* (New York, 1902), p. 140.
20. Mangum to Bartlett Yancey, Jan. 15, 1826, Shanks, *Papers of Mangum*, I, 232–33.
21. Bartlett Yancey to Mangum, Jan. 25, 1826, *ibid.*, 240–41.
22. Mangum to Charity A. Mangum, Apr. 8, 1826, *ibid.*, 268.

A week later Van Buren wrote a long letter to Ritchie amplifying the suggestion and asking the Virginia editor to further it.[23] The idea of the convention he acknowledged as Calhoun's. He noted that the Clintonian newspapers in New York had already declared against the convention, which he attributed to the governor's presidential aspirations. For his part, Van Buren confessed indifference to whether the nomination was made by a congressional caucus or a national convention, although a convention would perhaps be preferable since it "would remove the embarrassment of those who have or profess to have scruples" about attending a caucus, and it "would be fresher & perhaps more in union with the spirit of the times, especially at the seat of the war Pennsylvania & New York." He then listed the advantages of a national convention:

First, It is the best and probably the only practicable mode of concentrating the entire vote of the opposition & of effecting what is of still greater importance, the substantial reorganization of the Old Republican Party.

2nd Its first result cannot be doubtful. Mr. Adams occupying the seat and being determined not to surrender it except *in extremis* will not submit his pretensions to the convention. [Mordecai M.] Noah's real or affected apprehensions upon that subject are idle. I have long been satisfied that we can only get rid of the present, & restore a better state of things, by combining Genl. Jacksons personal popularity with the portion of old party feeling yet remaining. This sentiment is spreading, and would of itself be sufficient to nominate him at the Convention.

3rd. The call of such a convention, its exclusive Republican character, & the refusal of Mr. Adams and his friends to become parties to it, would draw anew the old Party lines & the subsequent contest would reestablish them. State nominations alone would fall far short of that object.

4th. It would greatly improve the condition of the Republicans of the North and Middle States by substituting *party principles* for *personal preferences* as one of the leading points in the contest. The location of the candidates would in great degree, be merged in its consideration. Instead of the question being between a northern and

23. Van Buren to Ritchie, copy, Jan. 13, 1827, Van Buren MSS (LC). Whether the convention scheme was planned in Washington in the spring of 1826 or in December of the same year, when Van Buren and Calhoun spent the holidays at the home of a mutual friend, is not clear. Van Buren's *Autobiography* (p. 514) suggests the earlier date, but Wiltse (*John C. Calhoun: Nationalist,* pp. 344–48) indicates the latter.

Southern man, it would be whether or not the ties, which have heretofore bound together a great political party should be severed. The differences between the two questions would be found to be immersed in the elective field. Altho' this is a mere party consideration, it is not on that account less likely to be effectual. Considerations of this character not infrequently operate as efficiently as those which bear upon the most important questions of constitutional doctrine. Indeed Genl. Jackson has been so little in public life, that it will be not a little difficult to contrast his opinions on great questions with those of Mr. Adams. His letter to Mr. Monroe [urging the appointment of Federalists] operates agst him in N York by placing him in one respect on the same footing with the present incumbent. Hence the importance, if not, the necessity of collateral matter to secure him a support there.

5thly It would place our Republican friends in New England on new and strong grounds. They would have to decide between indulgence in sectional & personal feelings with an entire separation from their old political friends on the one hand or acquiescence in the fairly expressed will of the party, on the other. . . .

6th Its effects would be highly salutary on your section of the union by the revival of old party distinctions. We must always have party distinctions and the old ones are the best which the nature of the case admits. Political combinations between the inhabitants of the different States are unavoidable & the most natural & beneficial to the country is that between the planters of the South and the plain Republicans of the north. The country has flourished under a party thus constituted & may again. It would take longer than our lives (even if it were practicable) to create new party feelings to keep those masses together. If the old ones are suppressed, Geographical divisions founded on local interests or, what is worse prejudices between the free & slave holding States will inevitably take their place. Party attachment in former times furnished a complete antidote for sectional prejudices by producing counteracting feelings. It was not until that defense had been broken down that the clamour agt Southern Influence and African Slavery could be made effectual in the North. . . . Formerly, attacks upon the Southern Republicans were regarded by those of the north as assaults upon their political brethren & resented accordingly. This all powerful sympathy has been much weakened, if not, destroyed by the amalgamating policy of Mr. Monroe. It can & ought to be restored and the proposed convention would be eminently servicable in effecting that object. . . .

Lastly the effect of such a nomination on Genl. Jackson could not fail to be considerable. His election as the result of his military services without reference to party & so far as he alone is concerned scarcely to principle would be one thing. His election as the result of a combined and concerted effort of a political party, holding in the main, to certain tenets & opposed to certain prevailing principles, might be another & a far different thing.

Van Buren remarked in closing that the main resistance to the convention would come from Jackson's friends, who believed that it would be unnecessary, as no one but Jackson intended to oppose Adams. Van Buren thought this a dangerous error.

Van Buren's letter makes the strategy of the 1828 campaign explicit. Jackson was to be cast as the Republican candidate and Adams as the Federalist in the sure knowledge that a contest fought on those grounds was susceptible to but one outcome. The main objective was to a large extent achieved: the Jacksonians did succeed, not without a little help from their opponents, in capturing the Republican party's name, traditions, and most of its organization. The tactic devised to accomplish this, the national convention, was not used. Contrary to Van Buren's prediction it was not required to insure unity behind the presidential candidate. For the vice-presidency it presented positive dangers.

In the winter of 1826–27 both Clinton and Crawford were still possible threats to Jackson. In Crawford's case it was less a question of his running than of standing aloof out of hatred for Jackson. Bringing him into line and consolidating the Radicals generally behind Jackson clearly fell within Van Buren's province. As soon as the weather turned warm, Van Buren, accompanied by his friend, the New York City congressman Churchill C. Cambreling, began a leisurely trip south of the Potomac. Publicly, the senator was still neutral, but the purpose of the journey could not be disguised.[24] He stopped in Richmond and conferred with Ritchie and other members of the Junto. From there he went to Raleigh where he held confidential talks with Radical leaders. Everywhere he was warmly received. The climax of the tour was a visit with Crawford at his home in Georgia. Exactly what words passed between the senator and the former secretary were kept secret, but Crawford did agree to forget his feud with Jackson and back him in 1828.[25] After that the Radical leaders in Virginia and North Carolina slowly swung over to the general, not because they liked

24. Adams, *Memoirs*, VII (May 12, 1827), 272; *Richmond Constitutional Whig*, May 8, 1827; *United States Telegraph*, May 8, 1827.
25. Crawford to Van Buren, Aug. 15, 1827, Van Buren MSS (LC); Crawford to Alfred Balch, Dec. 14, 1827, printed in the *United States Telegraph*, Dec. 2, 1831.

him, but because, in Mangum's phrase, they could "get no better" candidate to defeat the hated Adams.[26]

Clinton, meanwhile, had been eliminated by the Regency planners as a contender. At least in March, 1827, a Washington correspondent of the *Albany Argus,* possibly Van Buren himself, reported that "but two candidates, *Mr. Adams* and *Gen. Jackson,* are now thought of."[27] Calhoun had retired voluntarily. The concentration of public opinion behind either Adams or Jackson rendered the national convention unnecessary. An alternative plan of launching Jackson as the official Republican candidate in a congressional caucus also came to nothing.[28] The *Albany Argus* defended the proposal, but conceded that (unlike in 1824) a caucus was not required to unify the Republican party.[29] After Crawford's pledge, in fact, the whole idea of a national nomination of any kind seems to have died. Despite the care and thought which preceded the framing of the convention scheme, none of the individuals responsible for it pushed it vigorously. Ritchie virtually ignored it in the *Enquirer* even though he had been captivated by a similar proposal just four years earlier.[30] What killed it was not so much the anti-Adams union behind Jackson as a threatened division over the second place on the ticket. Jackson made a national convention superfluous; Calhoun made it prohibitive.

The South Carolinian did not command the loyalties of all those willing to support Jackson. Throughout the campaign there was constant speculation as to whom the party would choose for vice-president, notwithstanding the fact that Calhoun was the incumbent and had all but declared for Jackson from the moment of Adams's election. Two men, principally, stood in the way of Calhoun's receiving the undivided endorsement of the "new" Republican party—Crawford and Clinton. Crawford's opposition was personal, a continuation of an ancient vendetta, but no less hazardous for that. Although he did

26. Henry R. Simms, *The Rise of the Whigs in Virginia, 1824–1840* (Richmond, 1929), pp. 18–20, 26; Hoffman, *Jackson and North Carolina Politics,* pp. 6–15.
27. *Albany Argus,* Mar. 21, 1827.
28. John Morgan to A. C. Flagg, Dec. 4, 1827, Flagg MSS; *United States Telegraph,* Mar. 15, Ap. 5, 6, 1827; *Richmond Enquirer,* Mar. 20, 1827; *Rochester Telegraph,* July 21, 1827.
29. Apr. 10, 1827; Jan. 5, 1828. In January, 1828, Van Buren wrote "that there is not the least probability of a congressional caucus." Van Buren to B. F. Butler, Jan. 23, 1828, Van Buren MSS (LC).
30. Ritchie tepidly endorsed the national convention, suggesting only that he saw no need for involving congressmen in its calling. But he did not push the idea thereafter. *Richmond Enquirer,* Jan. 23, 1827.

not give public vent to his obvious displeasure over the frequent linking of Jackson and Calhoun, Crawford made certain that Jackson and Van Buren were aware of it, disguising it under dire predictions that the weight of Calhoun's name would sink Jackson.[31] The real danger consisted of the discord which the followers of Crawford and Calhoun might cause in the Jackson ranks. Senator John Branch, a key figure in North Carolina, reported the disruptive effects of the feud there.[32] Even more ominous, the Georgia House of Representatives, in December, 1827, formally nominated Crawford for vice-president.[33] This direct threat to Calhoun amounted to little since no appreciable outpouring of Crawford sentiment followed. Yet Crawford continued his efforts to undermine Calhoun the remainder of the campaign and even beyond the November election.[34]

Another and more disturbing movement developed to run Clinton for vice-president. A Jackson-Clinton ticket would be sectionally balanced, appealing particularly to voters in New England, Ohio, and New York. Informed sources reported that Clinton was receptive to the idea.[35] Rumors of the governor's impending candidacy were assiduously fanned by administration papers which rejoiced at the prospect of a split in the opposition ranks.[36] This gossip unsettled Duff Green, editor of the *United States Telegraph* and the special guardian of Calhoun's interests, who felt compelled to deny time and again that Calhoun would be dropped and Clinton, or anyone else, run in his place.[37] "Mr. Calhoun," the *Telegraph* nervously asserted in June, 1827, "cannot consistently be withdrawn. He will not make a vacancy for any man."[38] The rumors were not stilled by this *ex cathedra* pro-

31. W. H. Crawford to Hugh White, copy, May 27, 1827, Jackson MSS, 1st ser.; Hugh White to Jackson, June 19, 1827, John Spencer Bassett (ed.), *Correspondence of Andrew Jackson* (Washington, 1928), III, 365.

32. John Branch to Andrew Jackson, Dec. 11, 1827, Bassett, *Correspondence of Jackson*, III, 385.

33. *Daily National Intelligencer*, Dec. 31, 1827; Jan. 4, 1828. The Georgia Senate refused to concur.

34. Crawford to Van Buren, Oct. 25, 1828; Van Buren to Crawford, undated draft, Van Buren MSS (LC); Felix Grundy to Jackson, Nov. 20, 1828, Jackson MSS, 1st ser.

35. Cornelius P. Van Ness to Van Buren, Feb. 22, 1827; J. S. Schermerhorn to Van Buren, July 11, 1827, Van Buren MSS (LC); John Sergeant to Clay, Sept. 23, 1827, Clay MSS.

36. *Richmond Constitutional Whig*, May 8, June 8, Sept. 26, 1827; *Richmond Enquirer*, Mar. 20, Apr. 3, 10, 1827.

37. *United States Telegraph*, Jan. 29, 30, Feb. 28, Mar. 20, 23, 29, June 14, Sept. 22, Oct. 4, 11, 13, 22, 27, 1827.

38. *Ibid.*, June 12, 1827.

nouncement. A few months later, Green explained "that although the friends of Mr. Calhoun did not consider the Vice Presidency itself, an object worth contending for," he had been "so assailed" by the partisans of Adams and Clay "as to make it highly improper for the friends of Gen. Jackson, as a party, to take any step which shall have the appearance of abandoning him or bargaining with Governor Clinton."[39]

Transactions in Maryland and New York verified Green's apprehensions. At the Maryland state convention in Baltimore in May, 1827, the committee on resolutions had recommended Calhoun for vice-president. The managers of the convention, however, felt that his inclusion would excite the jealousies of other contenders and his name was expunged before final passage by the delegates, much to the chagrin of the Calhoun supporters.[40] Fear of discord over the vice-presidency contributed to delaying the meeting of a caucus in Albany which had been scheduled to declare formally the Regency's support of Jackson. "Let our party no longer stand like a lewd woman by the way side, solicit[ing] the embraces of this or that presidential candidate," Congressman Michael Hoffman wrote Flagg in disgust from Washington.[41] Yet a Jackson-Calhoun nomination would raise the cry of southern influence and, possibly, force Clinton into an alliance with Adams's New York agent, Peter B. Porter, in the opinion of Congressman Silas Wright, Jr. His advice was to "Save the state, and let the nation save itself."[42] Van Buren concurred with Wright so that the caucus planned for the anniversary of the Battle of New Orleans, January 8, 1828, was not held. The postponement seemed to cast doubt on the Regency's course and under prodding from Washington a caucus was finally convened on January 31.[43] Jackson was nominated, but the vice-presidential situation was too hot to handle. Rather than risk the shaky alliance with Clinton no nomination was made on the plea that the voice of the people had not spoken.[44]

Green did not share this view. On January 17, 1828, he had placed

39. *Ibid.*, Oct. 1, 1827.
40. *Richmond Enquirer*, May 25, 29, June 5, 1827.
41. Hoffmen to Flagg, Jan. 8, 1827, Flagg MSS. Also, Hoffman to Flagg, Dec. 21, 1827, *ibid.*
42. Silas Wright, Jr., to Flagg, Dec. 20, 1827, *ibid.* Also, Charles Butler to Flagg, Dec. 15, 1827, *ibid.*
43. Van Buren to B. F. Butler, Jan. 23, 1828; W. L. Marcy to Van Buren, Jan. 29, 1826, Van Buren MSS (LC); Flagg to Silas Wright, Jan. 10, 22, 31 (two letters), 1828, Flagg MSS.
44. Silas Wright to Flagg, Jan. 16, 1828, Flagg MSS.

Calhoun's name along with Jackson's under the *Telegraph*'s masthead as the "REPUBLICAN TICKET." "It is true," he wrote in justification, that the ticket had "not been nominated by a Congressional caucus" as was traditional. A caucus was neither necessary nor proper since "Public sentiment has already been expressed through the ballot box and the press, in terms so distinct as not to be misunderstood."

Some substance lay behind this assertion, as Calhoun had been nominated by the end of January at a number of important Jackson meetings, including the state conventions of Pennsylvania, Ohio, New Jersey, and Kentucky, and by caucuses in Virginia, North Carolina, and South Carolina.[45] But these nominations could not mask the existence or danger of vice-presidential rivalries. Underneath the superficial harmony among those supporting Jackson there lurked sectional as well as personal discords that might shatter the fragile coalition. Major William B. Lewis, Jackson's friend and confidant, understood this from the beginning. "I hope," he wrote in March of 1827, that "no jealousies, either on the part of Governor Clinton or Mr. Calhoun, would be suffered to exist." Jackson, also aware of the problem, had no personal preference according to Lewis. "This is a delicate subject and ought to be touched with great caution. It is a rock upon which we may split. . . ."[46]

Van Buren, with his usual insight, saw exactly what course must be followed. He expressed himself plainly in a letter to Jackson in the fall of 1827 when speculation about the vice-presidency was raging: "Attempts will doubtless be made," he wrote, "to entangle your friends in the Vice-Presidential & other questions but they will I am persuaded have good sense enough not to meddle in these. I have no other feelings in relation to the Vice Presidency than as it may operate on the main question. Let it be left to the natural course of public sentiment & it will fare best. It is as far as I can see the only point upon which we can have difficulty & the true policy in regard to it for the present, clearly is, to let it alone."[47] Although Van Buren never said so, he undoubtedly realized that a national convention might be fatal. The party he had built was composed of elements magnetized by a negative force—opposition to the administration. Jackson was already before the nation, all the anti-Adams blocs acquiescing in his candidacy. Why jeopardize that unity by exposing differences over

45. *United States Telegraph*, Jan. 17, 30, Feb. 6, 1828.
46. Lewis to Elijah Hayward, Mar. 26, 1827, Jackson-Lewis MSS.
47. Van Buren to Jackson, Sept. 14, 1827, Van Buren MSS (LC).

an office that counted for little? Crawford, Calhoun, and Clinton were unwilling to defer to one another. Though the national convention was designed for the purpose of concentrating support behind a single ticket, it could not manufacture an identity of interest where none existed. A national convention in 1828 would have been united solely by Jackson's name; an attempt to tighten the bond by forcing agreement on a vice-presidential nominee was to court a senseless splintering of the coalition.

Ironically, a national convention could have been safely held by the spring of 1828. Crawford had made little headway either in his efforts to sabotage Calhoun or promote himself. Clinton died early in February, 1828. After Clinton's death Calhoun was the first choice of everyone except a handful of Radicals. Of all the Jackson electors chosen in November, only the nine from Georgia failed to cast their ballots for him. But Van Buren could not have foreseen this in 1827 when the decision to hold a national convention had to be made. He decided at that time to move cautiously and let events define his policy. Absolute consistency as to means never hobbled Van Buren or his organization. In 1824 the Regency had gone down the line (and to defeat) in defense of a national nomination, denouncing local and state nominations for president. Now its interests were not served by that policy and Regency-sponsored public meetings called after the Albany caucus of January endorsed state nominations for president as the proper method.[48]

The essential feature of the campaign master plan concocted with the aid of Calhoun was retained, although the specific means envisioned—the national convention—was not. That feature was, of course, the re-creation of the Republican party. The decision not to hold the convention robbed the design of its most visible symbol, but did not totally destroy it. In its place the Jackson managers substituted rhetoric and a series of ad hoc committees.

The necessary rhetorical materials were close at hand; they only required a little refurbishing to include recent events. A strong historical sense of party had existed among the northern Radicals since 1824, especially among the members of the Regency. "That *political parties are inseparable from free government*," trumpeted the *Albany Argus* in 1825, "is a truth which experience has reduced to absolute demonstration."[49] Undeviating loyalty to those who bore the scars of faithful

48. *Buffalo Republican*, Apr. 9, 1828.
49. *Albany Argus*, Oct. 25, 1825.

service was ever the code of the Regency.[50] The same partisan temper
would now be reapplied to national politics. Two assertions, one positive and one negative, were required. The first called upon the Jacksonians to claim sole title to the Jeffersonian tradition, the second for
the Adams-Clay coalition to be stigmatized as a continuation of the
Federalist party.

The Jacksonians never tired of painting themselves as the only true
Republicans, while picturing Adams and his legions as Federalists.[51]
The "old lines" remained intact, the issue was the same as it had
been in '98—aristocracy against democracy.[52] The very idea that
parties had ever been extinguished was ridiculed as a Federalist (i.e.
administration) subterfuge.[53] To counter the Adams view that parties
no longer existed, Isaac Hill and others produced a rival history:
Monroe's visit to New England in 1817 had been the first act of a
Federalist plot to regain power. On that occasion "the crafty Aristocracy" surrounded the guileless president whom they had so recently
reviled and won his confidence by artful flattery while loyal Republicans were kept at a distance. They "proclaimed an 'era of good feelings' " in order to lay the foundation for "that craven 'amalgamation' "
that has since "in the election of the second Adams, restored to power
the party which fell with the first Adams. . . ."[54] Representative Hoffman of New York was more direct: "The Adams' men have made
a *sad* beginning in our State. Their call of a convention is made by
men of every political gender & neutrality. It can never go for republican—it is assertably *federal* and no pains should be spared to fix the
true brand on the papers."[55] The cry was taken up everywhere: the
administration, its policies, measures, and personnel were Federalist,
pure and undiluted.[56]

50. W. L. Marcy to Flagg, Nov. 26, 1823; Oct. 20, 1825; Charles Butler to
Flagg, Dec. 15, 1827, Flagg MSS; Hammond, *Political Parties in New York*,
II, 234–35.
51. Isaac Hill to Henry Lee, Sept. 10, 1828, Jackson MSS, 1st ser.
52. J. C. Calhoun to Levi Woodbury, Sept. 21, 1826, Woodbury MSS;
James Campbell to G. C. Verplanck, Feb. 20, 1826, Verplanck MSS.
53. *Albany Argus*, May 25, 1827.
54. *Proceedings and Address of the New Hampshire Republican State Convention of Delegates Friendly to the Election of Andrew Jackson to the Next
Presidency of the United States, Assembled at Concord, June 11 and 12, 1828*
(Concord, n.d.), pp. 10–11. Also *United States Telegraph*, Jan. 24, Mar. 22,
1827; June 3, 1828.
55. Michael Hoffman to Henry Ashley, typed copy, Apr. 4, 1828, Flagg MSS.
56. *Richmond Enquirer*, Sept. 12, 29, 1826; *United States Telegraph*, Apr. 10,
29, May 1, 4, 15, 18, 23, Aug. 20, 1826; June 11, Nov. 22, 1827; July 8, 23,
24, 28, Aug. 28, Sept. 2, 11, 1828.

Even as the Jacksonians were successfully labeling their opponents as Federalists, they were winning over a substantial number of Federalists. The critical difference was that while the "Adams Republicans tended to treat the Federalists as a bloc," making politically costly concessions in regard to names and nominations, the Jackson leaders cultivated them as individuals without conceding anything to them as a group.[57] Their attitude was succinctly stated by an upstate New Yorker who reported to Flagg that the Federalists in his county were urging that local meetings be called to nominate Jackson. But, he wrote, "we shall not be hasty in taking their advice—we are not anxious of their company, tho' their assistence may be welcome—"[58] In dealing with the Federalists the Jacksonians played the same as the Adamsites, but avoided the name. They carried off the Republican title in the states where it counted and simultaneously won sufficient Federalist votes to provide an extra margin of victory.

Adams's rejection of parties had effectively stifled the labor of his friends. Did the success of Van Buren and his confederates indicate that their candidate accepted the restoration of the party system? Far less literary than Adams, Jackson committed fewer opinions to paper than his adversary. He was not, moreover, given to the introspective musings capable of producing a diary and hence his opinions cannot be documented with the same degree of thoroughness as those of Adams. Jackson was a man of decided views on most subjects, but his opinion of political parties underwent a marked change between the elections of 1824 and 1828.

Prior to 1825, his attitude toward parties was remarkably similar to Adams's, although for different reasons. Adams recoiled as a young man from the bitterness of party warfare because he felt victimized by it. Jackson's political environment was marked by the absence of meaningful party labels and an emphasis on the merits of the individual. It was in that spirit that he had lectured Monroe in 1816 about the virtue of ignoring parties when he selected a cabinet, specifically pleading for the appointment of a Federalist. That letter accounted for much of the Federalist support Jackson attracted. As late as the spring of 1824 he was willing to subscribe to this earlier position:

> If I am elected to fill the Presidential chair it must be by the people;
> and I will be the President of the nation, and not of a party. I have

57. Livermore, *Twilight of Federalism*, p. 223.
58. John Morgan to Flagg, Dec. 4, 1827, Flagg MSS.

allways been a republican, and acted with them, but the constitution secures to every man equal rights and privileges; and the very moment I proscribe an individual from office, on account of his political opinion; I become a despot, call me by what name you please—because the other has just as good aright to enjoy his opinion as I have. Therefore as Mr. Jefferson said, "we are all Federalists, we are all Republicans". . . ."[59]

These are sentiments worthy of John Quincy Adams. How then did Jackson, a man who prided himself on the firmness of his opinions, succeed as a party leader and Adams fail? The answer lies in the temperament of the two men. Adams was self-righteous to a degree which betrayed an inner doubt, as if he were continual prey to temptations he feared he could not resist. Jackson knew no doubts, never questioned his own motives. After becoming convinced that he, and the people, had been cheated out of the presidency by a wicked bargain, he subordinated whatever misgivings he may have had about his fitness for the office to concentrate on winning it. He forgot old quarrels, embraced erstwhile foes, and carefully measured his public words and acts for their political effect. Most significantly, he was willing to turn over the actual running of the campaign to experts such as Van Buren, many of whom he did know first hand. To vindicate himself, he allowed these men to make him the figurehead of a revived Republican party, the existence of which he had not previously exhibited the slightest concern.[60] Adams destroyed the opportunity to build a party around himself by what he did not do and would not permit others to do for him. Jackson created a party by allowing his friends to do those tasks that he had no deep interest in. His attitude toward parties, unlike that of Adams, was not decisive in shaping his campaign.

Flaying the ghost of Federalism achieved only a portion of the strategy outlined by Van Buren in his letter to Ritchie. It identified the Jacksonians as the Republican party, but no bombast could bring into being the national organizational network which the New Yorker had envisioned. The national convention was intended to give the party a physical existence. For reasons of expediency it could not be held, but the need to coordinate Jackson's campaign remained. Only now the job must be done informally.

59. Jackson to Andrew Jackson Donelson, Apr. 11, 1824, Bassett, *Correspondence of Jackson*, III, 246–47.
60. Jackson to J. C. Calhoun, July 26, 1826, *ibid.*, 307–8.

Two national control centers developed, one in Nashville and the other in Washington.[61] The Tennessee group was officially constituted at a public meeting in March, 1827. A committee presided over by Jackson's crony, John Overton, and including other close associates such as Major Lewis, was elected for the purpose of refuting the many charges leveled at Jackson. It earned for its efforts the nickname "Whitewashing Committee."[62] In practice the Nashville group also functioned as a national correspondence committee, keeping in touch with the central committees in the states, feeding them propaganda and giving advice as to how they should conduct themselves.[63] According to Robert V. Remini, it was the Nashville committee which "helped to unite the state organizations, after they formed, into something resembling a national party."[64]

The Washington overseers were really two groups, but their personnel and activities overlapped. The first was the central committee for the District of Columbia headed by John P. Van Ness and numbering important Jackson leaders outside Congress such as Duff Green. Its main concern was funneling the propaganda generated by the pro-Jackson congressmen into the states for general dissemination. The members worked closely, however, with the second and more important group. This was the Jacksonian high command in Congress. Van Buren was the most influential member but other notables were included: Calhoun, Thomas Hart Benton, John Randolph, and Edward Livingston. They met frequently and casually to plan congressional tactics, raise money to subsidize party newspapers, supervise the formation of state committees, distribute campaign literature, and coordinate the endorsements of Jackson by caucuses and conventions. They combined many of the functions both of the present day legislative caucus and national committee.[65]

Effective as it may have been for the 1828 campaign, the informality of the Jackson command posts betrayed the looseness of the coalition. The national organization was designed for a single battle. Once the

61. The best account of this and other aspects of the campaign is Robert V. Remini's *The Election of Andrew Jackson* (Philadelphia, 1963).

62. *Richmond Enquirer*, Apr. 10, 1827; Oct. 3, 7, 1828; *United States Telegraph*, Sept. 27, 1828; Louis R. Harlow, "Public Career of William Berkeley Lewis," *Tennessee Historical Quarterly*, VII (Mar., 1948), 22–27.

63. Remini, *Election of Andrew Jackson*, pp. 63–68.

64. *Ibid.*, p. 63.

65. *Ibid.*, pp. 68–71; 166–80; *Albany Argus*, Jan. 1, 1827; *Monroe Republican* [Rochester], Jan. 16, 1827; Marquis James, *The Life of Andrew Jackson* (Indianapolis, 1938), p. 455.

election was over there would be no way of perpetuating it. What had been done contrasted favorably with the headless Adams campaign, but it was clear that no organization had been devised capable of giving the national party continuity between elections. In the states the Jacksonians also made, as a rule, a more vigorous effort than their opponents although they used, in most instances, the same methods.

New England was Jackson's weak spot. He had few visible supporters there in 1824 and the addition of the Radicals and Calhounites added relatively few recruits except in New Hampshire and Maine. For the most part the friends of the administration controlled the regular Republican caucuses. Thus the Jacksonians were compelled to resort to other means for nominating their electors and conducting their campaign. The expedient devised in Massachusetts, the enemy's home country, was a meeting of friendly legislators and so-called delegates from Boston and nearby towns which convened in June, 1828, to choose the candidates for the Electoral College and the members of a central committee.[66] Under the guidance of Isaac Hill, the New Hampshire Jacksonians made the greatest progress in the region toward creating a vigorous state party. A state convention (which included a number of legislators) met at Concord and not only appointed a central committee and electoral ticket but also nominated candidates for Congress and state offices.[67] This was the first state convention in the history of New Hampshire. In Connecticut the Jackson men also initiated the first state nominating convention, the move virtually forced on them by Adams's domination of the Republican legislative caucus.[68]

Electors for Jackson in Rhode Island and Vermont were nominated at statewide public meetings, indicative of Jackson's relative lack of strength in those two states.[69] The situation was more promising in Maine, where his supporters were sufficiently well placed and numerous to stage a mixed caucus and district conventions in his behalf.[70]

In the middle Atlantic states Jackson benefited from the support

66. McCormick *Second Party System*, pp. 44–46; *United States Telegraph*, July 17, 1828.

67. McCormick, *Second Party System*, pp. 58–60; *New Hampshire Republican State Convention . . . at Concord, June 11 and 12, 1828; Albany Argus*, May 23, July 2, 1828.

68. McCormick, *Second Party System*, pp. 65–67; *Albany Argus*, July 2, Aug. 13, 1828; *Address to the People of Connecticut Adopted at the State Convention, Held at Middletown, August 7, 1828, with the Proceedings of the Convention* (Hartford, 1828).

69. McCormick, *Second Party System*, pp. 71–72, 82.

70. *Ibid.*, p. 52.

of an appreciable, if not the predominant, part of the Republican party. The regular state convention in Pennsylvania nominated his electoral slate.[71] The Regency in New York nominated him in a legislative caucus and let the district conventions choose his electors.[72] In New Jersey and Delaware the party split in two, but each half continued as before to conduct its business by means of state conventions.[73] The only novelty in the way of organization between 1824 and 1828 in the middle states occurred in New York, and although not directly related to the presidential contest, it sheds some light on the growing practice of holding conventions in preference to caucuses.

The Regency had long used district and county conventions for local offices, yet the nomination of the governor and all other critical decisions remained the prerogative of the caucus. In 1824 the Clintonians had introduced the state convention, but the Regency had clung to the caucus even at the cost of defeat. In 1826 Clinton was renominated by a state convention.[74] This time the Regency decided to imitate its opponents. The change had been contemplated for some time. The new state constitution adopted in 1821 had advanced the date of the gubernatorial election from spring to autumn. Under this arrangement a caucus nomination would have to be made some six months before the election, since the legislature adjourned in the early spring. Samuel A. Talcott, a member of the Regency, had warned Van Buren in 1822 that "there are but few men who can run from spring to fall without getting in some measure out of breath. Besides, so long an interval between the nomination & election would afford too good an opportunity to organize cabals of every description, and God only knows where all the under currents & counter currents would drift us." Talcott proposed to solve this problem by calling a special session of the legislature for August, using as an excuse the need of legislation to implement the new constitution, so that the caucus nominations could be made closer to election day. He opposed holding a convention instead of a caucus because "there are certain folks that understand managing a convention too well."[75] Talcott's ad-

71. *Richmond Enquirer*, Jan. 12, 15, 1828.
72. *Albany Argus*, Aug. 22, 25, 29, Sept. 10, 18, 23, 1823.
73. *Richmond Enquirer*, Sept. 28, 1827, Jan. 29, 1828; *United States Telegraph*, Sept. 27, 1827; June 9, 1828.
74. *Albany Daily Advertiser*, June 9, Aug. 30, Sept. 16, 25, 1826; *Free Press* [Auburn, N.Y.], Oct. 4, 1826; Hammond, *Political Parties in New York*, II 230–31.
75. Talcott to Van Buren, Feb. 7, 1822, Van Buren MSS (LC).

vice to move the date of the caucus went unheeded and the caucuses of 1822 and 1824 made their nominations at the usual time.[76]

Yet when the caucus met in the spring of 1826, instead of nominating candidates it authorized a state convention. Having previously defended the caucus against all detractors, the Regency could not admit the substitution involved the sacrifice of a principle. The announcement of the switch was accompanied by a declaration that the caucus was still preferable to the convention "because the members of the legislature, from their general knowledge of the wants of the state, their particular knowledge of men, their responsible character, and their facilities of forming correct opinions, are decidedly the most judicious source of such nominations."[77] The only reason cited publicly for the change was that given by Talcott in 1822—the shift in the time of the election and the dangers resulting from an early nomination. What was probably the most potent reason was never mentioned—the success of Clinton two years previously against the caucus candidate. The Regency embraced the convention only after getting licked. Thereafter, all parties of any significance in New York nominated their gubernatorial candidate in a state convention.

In the south Atlantic states the regional favoritism that made Adams the overwhelming choice of New England worked heavily against him. The fusion of the Radicals and Calhounites with the original Jackson men presented an impregnable front. Only in Maryland, in many ways more akin politically to its northern than to its southern neighbors, did the administration muster a formidable party. But the Jacksonians were also strong. Their party resulted from the convergence of disparate groups cut loose by the dissolution of the old party lines after 1821. Republican stalwarts such as Samuel Smith joined with old Federalists and younger politicians of no particular allegiance in order to ride the general's popularity into office and power.[78] In the spring of 1827, after careful preparations, the organizing efforts of the Jackson leaders were brought to a head at a state convention, followed by nominating conventions in the counties and districts. The next year another state convention met to galvanize the Jackson forces while electors were chosen in district conventions.

76. Benjamin Knower to Van Buren, Mar. 4, 1822; M. Ulshoeffer to Van Buren, Mar. 11, 19, 1822, *ibid.; Albany Argus,* Apr. 6, 1824.

77. *Albany Argus,* May. 27, 1826. Also Apr. 17, May 1, 5, June 7, 1826, *ibid.*

78. Mark A. Haller, "The Rise of the Jackson Party in Maryland, 1820–1829," *JSH,* XXVIII (Aug. 1962), 307–26; *Richmond Enquirer,* June 12, 1827; *United States Telegraph,* May 30, 1827; May 24, 1828.

Elsewhere in the South the exertions of the Maryland Jacksonians were not matched. They did not need to be. The Richmond Junto altered its usual mode of operations only to the extent of allowing counties represented by state legislators favorable to Adams to elect special delegates to attend its caucus.[79] In North Carolina, where politics was conducted more informally, the Jackson electors were picked by a state central committee elected at a public meeting in Raleigh. Subsequently, district conventions were assembled to go through the motions of nominating them.[80] Since the choice of electors in South Carolina remained the privilege of the legislature, Jackson's nomination by a caucus in 1827 ended the campaign there.[81] In Georgia the only contest in the presidential election lay between two sets of Jackson electors offered by rival Republican factions, and agreed upon, apparently, by the leaders of each group.[82]

The election of 1828 brought no alteration in organizational techniques in the Northwest, but rather intensified those that had become evident four years earlier. After the 1824 election the Jackson organization in Ohio was abandoned until 1826, when the Hamilton County (Cincinnati) central committee reorganized itself and assumed the role of an unofficial state committee. Preceded by county meetings, a state convention met on January 8, 1828, to nominate electors. After it had adjourned, many of the delegates remained in Columbus and, together with members of the legislature and local citizens, put up a slate of state officers.[83] In Indiana the 1824 Jackson organization had also decayed. The new version formed in 1827 was far more thorough than the first edition. At its apex stood the state convention which nominated the electors and appointed a central committee. Local committees were established in almost every county and in many townships.[84]

79. *Richmond Enquirer,* Jan. 17, 1828.
80. Hoffman, *Jackson and North Carolina Politics,* pp. 19–20; *United States Telegraph,* Apr. 2, 10, 22, 1828.
81. *Richmond Enquirer,* Jan. 6, 1827.
82. McCormick, *Second Party System,* p. 240.
83. Francis P. Weisenburger, *Passing of the Frontier, 1825–1850,* vol. III, *The History of the State of Ohio* (Columbus, 1941), pp. 215–28; Webster, *Democratic Party Organization,* pp. 15–25; *The Proceedings and Address of the Ohio Jackson Convention Assembled at Columbus, on the Eighth of January, 1828, to Nominate an Electoral Ticket* (n.p., 1828); *Niles' Weekly Register,* XXXIII (Jan. 26, 1828), 357.
84. Esarey, *Proceedings of the Mississippi Valley Historical Association for the Year 1913–1914,* VII, 235–41; Webster, *Democratic Party Organization,* pp. 25–27; *Niles' Weekly Register,* XXXIII (Feb. 9, 1828), 388; Israel T. Canby to Jackson, May 19, 1828, Andrew Jackson, MSS, 1st ser.

National affairs took longer to affect politics in Illinois mainly because the state was so overwhelmingly for Jackson. Early in 1827 the lower house of the legislature officially nominated him for the presidency, and he was also endorsed by public meetings throughout the state. No state convention was held and the Jackson electors were nominated by self-styled district conventions.[85]

The newer slave states presented an uneven picture. The Adams-Clay organization in Kentucky was equaled by that of the Jacksonians. At first the work had been carried on with some secrecy. The creation of a committee system in Louisville in 1826 was so novel that it was deemed worthy of reporting directly to Jackson in great detail.[86] In 1828, partially as a result of the labors of two former Clay supporters who deserted to Jackson, Amos Kendall and Francis Preston Blair, a state convention, backed up by county committees, was held to nominate candidates for Congress and the Electoral College.[87]

In the other states of the Southwest there were few innovations. Self-nomination remained the rule in Tennessee, the challenge of Adams being too weak to force the politicians of Jackson's home state to change their ways.[88] Alabama, where Jackson also reigned supreme, nominated his electors at a statewide public meeting.[89] Next door in Mississippi public opinion was massively behind Jackson, but his friends broke the frontier tradition of self-nomination by holding a thinly attended state convention to choose his electors.[90] A more vigorous fight occurred in Louisiana, as the Adamsites were not without sources of strength. To counter them, the Jacksonians summoned a state convention to nominate electors; nearly all of the parishes sent delegates.[91] The state convention was also used by the party for electors in Missouri, although it did not betoken any extensive organizing activities in the counties and towns.[92]

85. Pease, *The Frontier State, 1818–1848*, pp. 114–49; *United States Telegraph*, Apr. 11, 1828.

86. A. Campbell to Jackson, Feb. 4, 1828, Jackson MSS, 1st ser.

87. McCormick, *Second Party System*, pp. 216–19; *Niles' Weekly Register*, XXXIII (Jan. 26, 1828), 357.

88. McCormick, *Second Party System*, p. 227.

89. *Ibid.*, pp. 289–90; *Daily National Intelligencer*, June 14, 1828; *United States Telegraph*, June 9, 1828.

90. McCormick, *Second Party System*, p. 297; Miles, *Jacksonian Democracy in Mississippi*, p. 13.

91. *United States Telegraph*, Dec. 31, 1827; Jan. 3, Feb. 13, 1828.

92. McCormick, *Second Party System*, p. 306; *Richmond Enquirer*, Feb. 14, 1828.

In twelve states the principal device used by the Jacksonians to organize their followers was the state convention, and in three of them (New Hampshire, Connecticut, and Mississippi) it was used for the first time. District conventions in four states (Maine, New York, Maryland, and North Carolina) nominated the Jackson electors. Mixed caucuses were used in two (Massachusetts and Virginia), and public meetings served in four states (Rhode Island, Vermont, Illinois, and Alabama). Only three states (South Carolina, Georgia, and Tennessee) failed to develop some central agency for party control. State and local politics were penetrated by the presidential race in over half the states; candidates for Congress, for governor, and for minor offices lined up behind either Jackson or Adams. The two areas where this was least true were New England and the South, regions that were firmly in the grip of one presidential candidate or the other. Lively competition for the presidency was conducive to the growth of formal organizational techniques in the states.

The election of 1828 was not a landslide for Jackson, although he won handily. The popular vote gave Adams approximately 508,000 while Jackson's total stood at somewhat over 647,000.[93] In the Electoral College Adams received 83 votes to Jackson's 178. The president carried all of New England (save one electoral vote from Maine) plus New Jersey and Delaware. Jackson swept the South and West and took all of Pennsylvania. The votes of New York and Maryland were divided between them. No one factor can ever explain the result of any national election and that of 1828 was perhaps more complex than most. Jackson had many assets as a candidate, Adams grave handicaps. Most of Jackson's advantages were "built-in," beyond the reach of professional politicians, the chief one, of course, being his status as a popular hero. But it is worth noting that in the one area most subject to manipulation, the building of an effective organization with national as well as state centers of control, the Jacksonians enjoyed a distinct edge.

93. *Historical Statistics of the United States, Colonial Times to 1957* (Washington, 1960), p. 683.

III

The Antimasons
1829–32

"Now, if it were an agreeable subject, I would describe to you all the hustle, excitement, collision, irritation, ennunciation, suspicion, confusion, obstinacy, foolhardiness, and humor, of a convention of one hundred and thirteen men, from twelve different States, assembled for the purpose of nominating candidates for President and Vice-President of the United States."

William H. Seward, letter of October 2, 1831

FIVE

The Rise of Antimasonry

The two-party system formed around the Adams and Jackson standards was soon threatened by a third party, the Antimasonic. Although the new entrant's membership and area of influence were still too small in 1828 to affect the contest for the presidency, Antimasonry grew rapidly thereafter and by 1832 figured in the calculations of every politician interested in controlling the national government. The Antimasonic party was the country's first third party, and in many ways the strangest. It has a strong claim on the attention of the social, as well as the political, historian.[1] The party's celebrity, however, derives chiefly from the fact that its 1831 convention to designate a presidential candidate was clearly the prototype of all subsequent national nominating conventions.[2]

1. Whitney R. Cross, *The Burned-over District* (Ithaca, 1950), pp. 3–123; Arthur B. Darling, "Jacksonian Democracy in Massachusetts, 1824–1848," *AHR*, XXIX (Oct., 1923), 277–79; David M. Ludlum, *Social Ferment in Vermont, 1791–1850* (New York, 1939), pp. 3–89, 97–113; J. Cutler Andrews, "The Antimasonic Movement in Western Pennsylvania," *Western Pennsylvania Historical Magazine*, XVIII (Dec., 1935), 255–66; John D. Hicks, "The Third Party Tradition in American Politics," *Mississippi Valley Historical Review*, XX (June, 1933), 6–7; Klein, *Pennsylvania Politics, 1817–1832*, pp. 277–79; Frederick Jackson Turner, *The United States, 1830–1850* (New York, 1935), pp. 118–20; Glyndon G. Van Deusen, *The Jacksonian Era, 1828–1848*, New American Nation Series, ed. Henry Steele Commager and Richard B. Morris (New York, 1959), pp. 55–56; Leland Milburn Griffen, "The Antimasonic Persuasion: A Study of Public Address in the American Antimasonic Movement, 1826–1838" (Ph.D. dissertation, Cornell University, 1950).

2. In 1808 and 1812 the top national leaders of the Federalist party met in New York City to discuss whom they would support for president. The claim that these meetings were the first national nominating conventions is, in my opinion, spurious. Neither purported to be a delegated meeting, which is the essence of a convention. Those who attended were not elected or chosen on

Why and how the Antimasons pioneered the device has never been adequately explained even though the history of the party is familiar enough.[3] Historians agree that Antimasonry began with the hue and cry over the kidnapping and presumed murder of William Morgan in 1826 by a group of Masons. But the intimate connection between the criminal act and the calling of the first presidential convention has been overlooked. To understand why the Antimasons were the initiators of this important institution requires a careful scrutiny of the circumstances surrounding Morgan's disappearance and the events which followed it. The early years of the party merit close study for another reason. Because Antimasonry originated in a single historical incident the process of party development, the means by which a small group of men gradually expanded their following and authority, can be traced with unusual precision. The major parties embodied broad movements and amorphous forces, but the Antimasonic party furnishes material for a case study.

Nothing about Morgan's life foreshadowed a martyr's death. His acquaintances in the small, upstate New York village of Batavia knew him as a chronic failure. Yet he was not entirely lacking in enterprise. Through publication of the secrets of the Freemasons, whose brotherhood he had recently joined, Morgan expected to reap a tidy profit.[4] News of his apostasy, unfortunately, provoked Masons living in the region to conspire for the purpose of punishing his planned exposure of the order's mysteries. Whatever the original intention, their retribution bore all the marks of a highly organized and elaborately executed lynching.[5]

---

the basis of any system of geographic or demographic apportionment, and only in the vaguest sense could they be said to represent the rank and file of the party. The meetings were simply informal and secret gatherings of the great men of the party. For a different interpretation, see John S. Murdock, "The First National Nominating Convention," *AHR*, I (July, 1896), 680–83 and Samuel Eliot Morison, "The First National Nominating Convention, 1808," *ibid.*, XVII (July, 1912), 744–63.

3. The standard monograph is Charles McCarthy's *The Antimasonic Party: A Study of Political Antimasonry in the United States, 1827–1840*, vol. I, *Annual Report of the American Historical Association for the Year 1902* (Washington, 1903).

4. William Morgan, *Illustrations of Masonry* (York, Canada, 1827).

5. Antimasonic accounts of the abduction by those contemporary to the event include *A Narrative of the Facts Relating to the Kidnapping and Presumed Murder of William Morgan* (Batavia, N.Y., 1827); "Report on the Abduction and Murder of William Morgan," *The Proceedings of the United States Anti-Masonic Convention. Sept. 11, 1830* (Philadelphia, 1830), pp. 11–18; [John Canfield

Shortly after sunrise on the morning of September 11, 1826, Morgan was arrested by the sheriff on a trumped-up charge of petty larceny and taken to Canandaigua, forty-eight miles east of Batavia. After he had spent the day in the county jail Morgan's fine was paid by some Rochester Masons and he was released, only to be immediately seized on the street and forced into a waiting carriage. A lengthy journey over the circuitous Ridge Road, with numerous stops for food, rest, and a change of horses or vehicles, brought the man-stealers and their victim to old Fort Niagara, which did service as a prison for the hapless author. A few days later, on or about September 19, he was dropped, tied and weighted, into the middle of the Niagara River.

Three aspects of the crime help explain not only why it gave rise to a political party but why the Antimasons proved such careful students of the convention system. One was the large number of persons involved in the kidnapping, either as perpetrators or as witnesses. Several dozen men were privy to the intrigue and many others had unknowingly assisted them by providing food, shelter, or fresh horses. The second factor was the great geographic diffusion of the outrage. The participants lived in a score of towns scattered over seven counties. Wherever the avenging Masons resided, conferred, or paused on their mortal journey they fortuitously planted the seeds of Antimasonry and defined the boundaries of a political movement. And last, all of the guilty were members of an esoteric society sworn by bloody oaths to stand together against outsiders, so that Morgan's death seemed less an isolated act of violence than an extensive and elaborate conspiracy against the rule of law. An entire region had the thrill of participating in an individual tragedy which touched the very foundations of civil society.

On hearing of her husband's arrest, Mrs. Morgan went to Canandaigua to retrieve him. There she learned of the odd circumstances of his liberation and second disappearance. Returning home, she told her story to sympathetic neighbors, one of whom, Timothy Fitch, undertook to gather testimony from those persons known to have had contact with Morgan on that day. The evidence uncovered by Fitch linking Morgan's abduction to Masonry was so sensational that two public

Spencer,] *Report of the Special Counsel on the Subject of the Morgan Abduction. Jan. 27, 1830. Submitted to the N.Y. State Senate by Enos T. Throop, Gov.*, n.d.; Samuel D. Greene, *The Broken Seal; or Personal Reminiscences of the Morgan Abduction and Murder* (Boston, 1870); and Weed, *Autobiography*, pp. 213-25. Robert Daniel Burns, "The Abduction of William Morgan," *Rochester Historical Society, Publication Fund Series* (Rochester, 1927), VI, 219-30, is a more recent version, but differs little from the story told by the Antimasons.

meetings, on September 26 and October 4, were held in Batavia to consider it.[6] A committee appointed at the second meeting dispatched agents to continue the investigation by making inquiries along the road to Fort Niagara, instructing them to take sworn statements from witnesses. Copies of these depositions were sent to Governor Clinton, accompanied by a demand that he give aid in ferreting out the malefactors. The committee members also published an appeal to the public in the Batavia *Republican Advocate* giving the disquieting facts so far as they were known. "All persons who are willing to serve the cause of humanity," it concluded, "are earnestly requested to communicate to one of the committee named below . . . any facts or circumstances which have come to their knowledge, and are calculated to lead to the discovery of his present situation, or the particulars of his fate, if he has been murdered." Other newspapers were urged to reprint this plea.[7]

Here was an invitation to the inhabitants of half a dozen counties to play detective. Soon there were public meetings in other towns connected with the kidnapping, usually resulting in the appointment of additional investigating committees.[8] But despite all the information amassed by these amateur sleuths, law enforcement officers performed their duties with an overly scrupulous regard for the rules of evidence, although grand juries were eventually summoned in five counties. The wheels of justice seemed mysteriously clogged as sheriffs, juries, and judges reacted slowly, while the governor (a Mason) and the legislature were at first indifferent to requests for special assistance in the difficult task of apprehension. When indictments were secured, juries frequently would not convict, and, when convictions were attained, judges handed down sentences so light that they insulted the common conception of justice. Most of the people of western New York, not belonging to the brotherhood and stung by the apparent breakdown of law and order at the command of an insidious empire, anxiously sought to punish the culprits.[9]

6. *A Narrative of the Facts*, 11–14, 35–42; Weed, *Autobiography*, pp. 223–25; Burns, *Rochester Historical Society, Publication Fund Series*, VI, 227.

7. *A Narrative of the Facts*, pp. 42–43; Weed, *Autobiography*, pp. 225–26; Green, *Broken Seal*, pp. 117–19.

8. Henry Brown, *A Narrative of the Anti-Masonick Excitement* (Batavia, N.Y., 1829), pp. 46–47; Hammond, *Political Parties in New York*, II 371.

9. *Anti-Masonic Enquirer*, Apr. 5, 19, 1831; Greene, *Broken Seal*, pp. 237–78; Weed, *Autobiography*, pp. 231–98; *Proceedings of the United States Anti-Masonic Convention. Sept. 11, 1830*, pp. 21–32; *Anti-Masonic Review and Magazine*, I, 71–72.

Failure of a Monroe County grand jury in December, 1826, to bring in an indictment for conspiracy so vexed the citizens of Rochester that a protest meeting was called immediately after the jury's dismissal.[10] On the executive committee elected at the assembly were two frustrated members of the jury, including Thurlow Weed. Although he was only twenty-nine at the time, Weed was an experienced, skillful politician and the able editor of the *Rochester Telegraph*. The intricacies of party organization were well known to the versatile Weed before 1826. He had been among those responsible for the meeting of the first New York state convention in 1824, which had nominated Clinton for governor in opposition to the candidate of the Regency's caucus. He had also helped organize the town meetings and county conventions of the People's party in 1823 and 1824, one of which had nominated him for the New York General Assembly. Weed was obviously well on his way up when he undertook to ride the Antimasonic whirlwind.[11]

Prior to his grand jury duty and his election to Rochester's Morgan committee, Weed's interest in the kidnapping had been limited to standard editorial comments deploring violence. Afterward, he devoted all his energies to the Antimasonic cause, withdrawing from the *Telegraph* in the fall of 1827 to establish the Rochester *Anti-Masonic Enquirer*, the leading organ of the movement until he became editor of the *Albany Evening Journal* in 1830.[12] No other man was to exert so great and continuous an influence on the Antimasonic party. To William H. Seward, himself a convert to Antimasonry, he was "the magician whose wand controls and directs the operations of the Antimasonic party. . . ."[13]

In January, 1827, the investigating committees elected at the town or county meetings, such as the one in Rochester, took the natural step of consulting with each other for the more efficient prosecution of their common goal. For four days members of seven committees met at Lewiston, where Morgan's death reportedly had been arranged

10. *Monroe Republican* [Rochester], Dec. 19, 1826; *Free Press* [Auburn, N.Y.], Dec. 20, 1826; Weed, *Autobiography*, pp. 231-32.

11. Van Deusen, *Thurlow Weed*, pp. 6-37; Charles G. Haines to Thurlow Weed, Aug. 3, 1824, Thurlow Weed Papers (University of Rochester Library), cited hereafter as Weed MSS; Weed, *Autobiography*, pp. 117-20.

12. *Free Press* [Auburn, N.Y.], Oct. 10, 1827; Weed, *Autobiography*, 212-15, 360-63; Van Deusen, *Thurlow Weed*, pp. 6-37, 40-41, 44-45.

13. Letter of Feb. 6, 1831, in William H. and Frederick W. Seward, *Autobiography and Memoir of William H. Seward* (New York, 1877), p. 176.

during a Masonic encampment. Many of the future state and national leaders of the Antimasonic party were there, among them Trumbull Cary, Frederick F. Backus, Frederick Whittlesey, Timothy Fitch, and Samuel Works.[14] Weed did not attend, possibly because of Masonic threats made against him.[15] The conference brought together for the first time the scattered groups concerned about the kidnapping. A central correspondence committee of three persons was chosen, all residents of Rochester, to serve as the coordinating agency for future inquiries. Local committees of correspondence, consisting of one person for each locality, were also appointed.[16] The movement now had a head with supporting committees for a nerve system.

It is significant that this meeting of committees was commonly referred to as "the Lewiston Convention" although it fulfilled none of the usual conditions for political conventions.[17] Its sessions were, apparently, entirely informal and private. There were no officers or agenda. Those present had not been elected to represent their communities, but to prove a felony. They did not act for similar constituencies; some were members of a county committee, others of township or village committees. Nor was there any provision for delegate apportionment. Yet in spite of these deviations from normal convention practices the title contained an element of truth, for having been chosen at primary meetings in their home towns, the participants bore the character of the people's delegates. Antimasonry, at this point, was not a political party, but in pursuing the murderers of Morgan, in giving structure to a continuing *posse comitatus,* these self-appointed deputies borrowed the type of organization they were most familiar with—the one used to nominate and elect candidates to public office.

The belief that Masonic influence underlay official apathy inflamed local opinion and made the case an issue in the elections for town officers in the spring of 1827. One visitor to "the infected district" reported that he "had heard nothing talked of, in the stages and bar-rooms, but Morgan."[18] Resolutions condemning Masonry as an institu-

14. *A Narrative of the Facts,* pp. 80–81; Weed, *Autobiography,* pp. 264–84; Spencer, *Report of the Special Counsel,* pp. 16–18.
15. Letter of Jan. 30, 1827, Brown, *A Narrative,* p. 91.
16. *Rochester Telegraph,* Feb. 6, 1827; *Monroe Republican* [Rochester], Feb. 6, 1827. The members of the central committee were Heman Norton, Frederick Whittlesey, and Josiah Bissell, Jr.
17. Brown, *A Narrative,* pp. 88–89; Hammond, *Political Parties in New York,* II, 376–77; Weed, *Autobiography,* p. 250.
18. *Rochester Telegraph,* Mar. 6, 1827.

tion, and not just its treatment of Morgan, were passed by village meetings as early as November, 1827, but it was the approach of the town elections that accelerated and intensified this aspect of public sentiment.[19] A meeting in Seneca late in January was among the first pledging that those present would "not knowingly, vote for any free mason for any office whatever, in town, county, or state."[20] Similar resolutions were passed in other towns, giving the excitement for the first time a political turn.[21] A characteristic feature of these meetings was the selection of a correspondence committee authorized to contact other local committees and the central committee appointed at Lewiston. The town elections served thereby to extend the Antimasonic organization to communities where it did not previously exist.

Whether this initial foray at the polls was premeditated is disputed. Henry Brown, a Masonic writer and witness to the proceedings, claimed that the meetings, while called "for the ostensible purpose of devising means to detect the guilty, and raising funds to aid and assist the widow and orphans," had been craftily turned into partisan affairs by the Lewiston committees.[22] Henry O'Rielly, a professional rival of Weed, also asserted that he foresaw the formation of a political party in early March.[23] Weed, on the other hand, contended that those town meetings which vowed to support only candidates opposed to Masonry were spontaneous.[24] Not until summer, he claimed, did the leaders undertake to encourage political activity, a decision made after the election of village officers in Rochester. Frederick Backus, treasurer of Rochester since its incorporation and a member of the Rochester Morgan committee and the Lewiston convention, was de-

19. *Monroe Republican* [Rochester], Nov. 21, 1826.
20. *Ibid.*, Feb. 6, 1827.
21. *Ibid.*, Jan. 16, Apr. 10, 1827; *Rochester Telegraph*, Mar. 2, 30, 1827; *Buffalo Emporium and General Advertiser*, Mar. 8, 1827.
22. Brown, *A Narrative*, p. 116.
23. An article clipped from the *Rochester Daily Advertiser* of Mar. 10, 1827, in the Henry O'Rielly Papers (Rochester Public Library), has an undated endorsement by O'Rielly: "Copy of the first article published denunciatory of the then *suspected* schemes for establishing a Political Antimasonic Party on the basis of the Morgan Excitement." The only evidence I found of coordination in these elections was a reprint of a set of resolutions which the *Batavia Republican Advocate* had suggested as models for the town meetings. The last one read: "Resolved, That we will not support for any office of honor, trust or profit, any candidate who shall be at the time of election a member of the fraternity of Free Masons." *Buffalo Emporium and General Advertiser*, Mar. 27, 1827.
24. Weed, *Autobiography*, pp. 242–43, 299–301.

feated for reelection even though he did not have publicly announced opposition. "This *coup d'etat,* so secretly and successfully accomplished, awakened," in Weed's words, "immediate and wild excitement throughout the village,"[25] Thereafter, Weed and his cohorts methodically set about creating a campaign organization. By the fall of 1827 Antimasonry had acquired, in conjunction with the elections for the state legislature, a frankly political complexion. Subtly, concern for the punishment of individuals was displaced by the desire to root out a privileged class.

Before those autumn elections, control over the movement had shifted from the amorphous committees of the Lewiston convention to the Rochester Morgan committee consisting of Weed, Whittlesey, Backus, and Works. In the course of the investigations during the winter and spring the Rochester group had assumed a leading part. The committee was responsible, for instance, for having the Niagara River dragged in quest of Morgan's body, and when a decayed corpse was found floating on Lake Ontario the members certified it as his.[26] The immediate task facing the committee in the autumn of 1827 was to field candidates for the state legislature. Public interest in the cause was feverish and the organizational structure existed in embryo. Coordination was required, however, to draw the scattered elements together so they would form nominating conventions. The job of organizing the Monroe County convention and that of the Eighth Senatorial District (which included all of the counties involved in the abduction) was accomplished by the Rochester committee.[27] With that step a political party was launched, one firmly committed to the convention technique.

The election returns, in Whittlesey's opinion, "astonished all—even the anti-masons themselves—and opened the eyes of politicians to the growing power of this new party."[28] Azariah C. Flagg was informed

25. *Ibid.,* p. 301.

26. "A Supplementary Report of the Committee Appointed to Ascertain the Fate of Capt. Wm. Morgan," reprinted in *Murderous Character of Freemasonry* (Chicago, 1882); Weed, *Autobiography,* pp. 230–316; *Free Press* [Auburn, N.Y.], Oct. 31, 1827. The Rochester committee began to function as an effective team when those among the original twelve man committee unwilling to participate in a crusade against Masonry resigned. Instead of an unwieldy group representing an impartial selection of the town's leaders, the committee was reduced to a compact body of four like-minded men. Weed, *Autobiography,* p. 230.

27. Weed, *Autobiography,* pp. 301–2, 336–38.

28. Hammond, *Political Parties in New York,* II, 282–83. The section of Hammond's *History* devoted to Antimasonry was authored by Whittlesey.

by a distressed Regency correspondent that within the contaminated area "every political question was merged entirely in the more personal antimasonic feeling—and this feeling would have opposed the best and purest man without reference to party. . . ."[29] The *Albany Argus*, the Regency's mouthpiece, credited the Antimasons with the election of fifteen assemblymen. The counties carried by the party were the same five Morgan had touched on his dreary journey from Batavia to Fort Niagara.[30]

The party's leadership swiftly followed up these victories by attempting to move outside the confines of the Eighth District. For this purpose a "general" or state convention to meet at Le Roy on February 27, 1828, was suggested, but as this date proved too early for the "distant counties" to organize and elect delegates a new time, March 6, was set.[31]

The proceedings at Le Roy were ordered according to the established pattern of political conventions, except that no system of apportionment was followed. Delegations from the twelve western counties varied in size from one to fourteen.[32] Some speculated that the convention might nominate a candidate for governor even though the election was eight months away. A more expedient policy prevailed, one designed to strengthen the party before it ran candidates for state offices. The Le Roy delegates resolved that another convention, with the counties having double the number of delegates as they had representatives in the state Assembly, should meet at Utica on August 4.[33] Unwilling that the response to this invitation be left to chance, the towns were requested to elect committees of correspondence and a state

29. Letter from Charles Butler, Dec. 2, 1827, Flagg MSS.

30. Nov. 14, 21, 1827.

31. *Anti-Masonic Enquirer*, Feb. 19, 1828.

32. *Ibid.*, Mar. 11, 1828; *Proceedings of a Convention of Delegates Opposed to Free Masonry which Met at LeRoy, Genesee Co. N.Y. March 6, 1828* (Rochester, 1828). Among the delegates was Millard Fillmore, just then beginning his political career. In the fall of 1828 he was nominated and elected to the General Assembly as an Antimasonic member from East Aurora, Monroe County. *Anti-Masonic Enquirer*, Feb. 26, 1828; Robert J. Rayback, *Millard Fillmore: Biography of a President* (Buffalo, 1959), pp. 23, 34.

33. Bates Cook to Weed, Feb. 28, 1828; Albert H. Tracy to Weed, Feb. 29, 1828, Weed MSS; Weed to Francis Granger, Mar. 14, 1828, in Francis Granger Papers (Library of Congress), cited hereafter as Granger MSS; Gerrit Smith to Charles H. Carroll, Mar. 4, 1828, in Gideon and Francis Granger Papers (Library of Congress), cited hereafter as Gideon and Francis Granger MSS; *Proceedings at LeRoy March 6, 1828*, p. 5.

central committee, composed of the four-member Rochester committee, was appointed to prod the localities into action. The central committee's authority officially covered correspondence and publication; in practice it functioned as a command post and its members personally supervised the formation of local organizations and drafted candidates for public office.[34]

By now large numbers of New Yorkers living outside the Eighth District, stirred by the events of the previous eighteen months, were ready to join the crusade. During the weeks following the Le Roy convention town meetings across the state mustered to elect county convention delegates who, in turn, chose the delegates to Utica.[35] Although the reasons for calling the convention were never openly stated, it was "very generally understood" by those at Le Roy that the Utica meeting would offer a candidate for governor. Yet in June the newly appointed central committee published a statement of convention purposes which deliberately avoided any mention of possible nominations.[36]

The central committee's reluctance to admit that the Utica convention would nominate a gubernatorial candidate was a maneuver aimed at seizing the leadership of the anti-Jackson forces from the supporters of President Adams. The politicians of Antimasonry were not beginners; their experience antedated Morgan's disappearance and they held opinions on public questions other than those relating to Masonry. They were, as their opponents pointed out, "a band of political aspirants, who have long been associated together for mutual aid and self-advancement."[37] The area of the abduction was Erie Canal country, and with a few exceptions they had backed the canal's builder, De Witt Clinton, in his fight against the Albany Regency. Almost to a man they supported the Adams administration while the Regency, under the guidance of Van Buren, threw its weight behind Jackson.[38] This basic orientation was not altered by the Morgan incident, and

34. *Anti-Masonic Enquirer*, Apr. 29, 1829; *Proceedings at LeRoy March 6, 1828*, p. 4; Hammond, *Political Parties in New York*, II, 385–86; Weed, *Autobiography*, pp. 257, 336–44.

35. *Anti-Masonic Enquirer*, May 20, Aug. 5, 1828; *Free Press* [Auburn, N.Y.], June 2, 18, July 4, 1828.

36. Robert H. Backus to Weed, Sept. 10, 1828, Weed MSS; Hammond, *Political Parties in New York*, II, 386; *Anti-Masonic Enquirer*, June 17, 1828.

37. *Buffalo Emporium and General Advertiser*, Nov. 26, 1827.

38. Weed to Webster, Mar. 7, 1828, in Webster MSS; Webster to Ezekiel Webster, Mar. 18, 1828, Van Tyne, *Letters of Webster*, p. 134.

a coalition with the old Clintonian, anti-Jackson party in the contest
for governor was entirely reasonable, especially as the Adams party
possessed attributes which the Antimasons lacked—prominent men and
strength along the Hudson River.[39]

A merger of the Antimasons with the Adams party for the gubernatorial campaign was certainly requisite to victory since the Regency
normally controlled the state. But there were obstacles to its consum-
mation. Antimasonry contained a strongly emotional element, a fervor,
which, in Webster's phrase, "put party calculations at defiance." There
was "something singular in Antimasonry, in its movements and operations—the people at first and for a time seem almost to run crazy
on the subject. . . ."[40] The Antimasonic leaders had to reckon with
this fanatical element among their followers in making covenants with
persons not touched by the "blessed spirit."

The passion of Antimasonry repelled many of the Adams men and
created friction between the two parties. Except for the Antimasons,
wrote former congressman Albert H. Tracy, the Adams partisans
"would not now have a loop to hang a hoop. Yet such is their fatuity
that they are determined to make scavengers of us to clear channels
for their purposes."[41] One Adams supporter thought the Antimasons
"more base and corrupt than the original actors in the Morgan
affair . . . ," and a friend of Weed's complained that the most serious
opposition to Antimasonry in his area came not from the Regency
but from the administration party.[42] Antimasonry, confided a pro-
Adams member of Congress to his journal, "was made up of a party
that resembled nothing more than the wildest fanatics of Scotch
Cameroonians. . . . With them Morganism is complete fanaticism—
bordering almost on insanity."[43]

By not advertising their intention of entering the governor's race,
the Antimasonic leaders hoped to steal a march on the Adams party,
which had not yet called a state convention. They wanted to get
their candidate nominated first so that the Adamsites would be com-

39. Charles Butler to Flagg, Dec. 2, 1827, Flagg MSS; Weed to Webster,
Mar. 7, 1828, Webster MSS; P. L. Tracy to J. W. Taylor, July 10, 1828, Taylor
MSS; Timothy Childs to Weed, Mar. 27, 1828, Weed MSS; Seward, *Autobiography*, pp. 302–3; Hammond, *Political Parties in New York*, II, 283–85, 383–84.
40. Webster to Jeremiah Mason, Mar. 19, 1830, Van Tyne, *Letters of Webster*,
p. 151.
41. Tracy to Weed, June 19, 1828, Weed MSS.
42. W. A. Langworthy to Taylor, July—, 1828, Taylor MSS; Robert H. Backus
to Weed, Sept. 10, 1828, Weed MSS.
43. Storrs MS, Aug. 7, 1828.

pelled to support the Antimasonic standard-bearer or risk almost certain defeat by splitting the anti-Regency ranks. It was necessary, of course, to find a candidate who would be acceptable to both groups. Francis Granger, son of Jefferson's and Madison's postmaster-general, seemed the perfect choice. Elected to the New York Assembly in 1823 as a Clintonian, he became the champion of Antimasonry in the legislature while remaining on intimate terms with the friends of the president. "Try and get a 'Journey' out of the Morgan business," Weed told Granger in the spring of 1827. "Take an opportunity to say some proper things upon the subject; tempered as you well know how to temper them."[44]

Before the Utica convention met the hope of a fusion with the administration party received a fatal setback. The Adams men declined to play second fiddle to the upstarts. Instead of being lulled into inactivity, their party chieftains arranged, on short notice, a state convention which assembled two weeks before the already scheduled Antimasonic convention. The president's friends narrowly rejected Granger in favor of Smith Thompson, a justice of the United States Supreme Court. The strenuous efforts of Weed and others to persuade them that they must nominate Granger as the price of Antimasonic support had failed.[45] They did, however, nominate Granger for lieutenant governor by acclamation.[46]

The Antimasonic delegates gathered in the Baptist Church of Utica on August 4, 1828, faced a dilemma: they could either acquiesce in the choice of Thompson (even though he made no avowal of their peculiar principles), and have a chance of supporting a winner, or they could make a nomination exclusively their own, but one having no chance of success. The delegates decided to make no compromises. They resolved that the destruction of Masonry required them "wholly to disregard the two great political parties that at this time distract this state of the Union, in the choice of candidates for office, and to nominate Anti-Masonic candidates for Governor and Lt. Gover-

44. Weed to Granger, Mar. 29 [1827], Gideon and Francis Granger MSS.

45. Weed, *Autobiography*, pp. 303–4; Seward, *Autobiography*, pp. 71–72; Trumbull Cary to Granger, July 26, 1828, in Trumbull Cary Papers (Buffalo Historical Society), cited hereafter as Cary MSS; B. Skidmore to Weed, Aug. 1, 1828, Weed MSS; P. L. Tracy to Taylor, July 10, 1828, Taylor MSS; Ebenezer Griffin to Flagg, July 20, 1828; Flagg to Silas Wright, Aug. 24, 1828, Flagg MSS.

46. Brown, *A Narrative*, p. 227; Hammond, *Political Parties in New York*, II, 386.

nor."[47] They then nominated Granger for the first office and John Crary, former state senator from Washington County, for the second.

Despite the inability of the two parties to agree on candidates, the Utica convention marked an important advance in the spread of Antimasonry. The number of counties represented was almost double that at the Le Roy convention. Delegations attended from twenty-three counties, almost all from the western part of the state or from counties touching the Erie Canal.[48] The convention reappointed the central committee chosen at Le Roy and invested it with authority to call future state conventions.

The ensuing campaign demonstrated the peril of mixing fanaticism with politics. The embarrassed Granger, nominated by one convention for governor and by another for lieutenant governor, accepted the more promising nomination for the lesser office and declined that of the Antimasons.[49] This created a crisis for the party. Their most popular stalwart not only refused to fight under their banner, but was matched against their own nominee for lieutenant governor. Many of the more ardent Antimasons were unwilling to acquiesce in supporting Thompson; they craved a candidate of their own. Only too willing to fill this void was Solomon Southwick, a leader in the movement to dissolve Masonry from within by convincing the brothers that they should surrender their membership.[50] Southwick was well known in the state, albeit his reputation as an eccentric was unlikely to make the party more respectable.[51]

Before Utica, Southwick had been endorsed for governor by several meetings of seceding Masons.[52] Flagg had been delighted since his

47. *Anti-Masonic Enquirer*, Aug. 12, 1828.

48. *Ibid.*; David Bernard, *Light on Masonry: A Collection of All the Most Important Documents on the Subject of Speculative Free Masonry* (Utica, 1829), pp. 471–81.

49. *Anti-Masonic Enquirer*, Sept. 2, 1828; Granger to Weed, Sept. 28, 1828, Granger MSS.

50. James C. Odiorne (ed.), *Opinion on Speculative Masonry Relative to Its Origin, Nature, and Tendency* (Boston, 1830), pp. 245–69; *Anti-Masonic Review and Monthly Magazine*, I, 259–61; Appendix, *Proceedings at LeRoy March 6, 1828*, pp. 12–23; Bernard, *Light on Masonry* pp. 452–59; Brown, *A Narrative*, pp. 226–28; Weed, *Autobiography*, pp. 256–300; Hammond, *Political Parties in New York*, II, 389–90; *The Buffalo Republican*, Mar. 28, 1829.

51. Edna L. Jacobsen, "Solomon Southwick," *Dictionary of American Biography*, XVII, 413–14; Levi Beardsley, *Reminiscences* (New York, 1852), pp. 174–75; Weed, *Autobiography*, p. 102; Van Deusen, *Thurlow Weed*, pp. 17, 40, 54–55.

52. Bates Cook to Weed, Feb. 28, 1828, Weed MSS; Brown, *A Narrative*, p. 227; Flagg to S. Wright, Mar. 7, 16, 1828, Flagg MSS.

nomination threw "an air of ridicule" over the entire movement.[53] If the Antimasons and Adams supporters had united, Southwick would have dropped from sight. With Granger's declination he was again brought forward as a candidate, first at public meetings and then at the regular Antimasonic county and district conventions.[54] "The people," Whittlesey apologized, "were excited and determined to have a candidate."[55]

Popular approval of Southwick disturbed the party leaders. Some wished to disavow him either by calling another state convention to name a new candidate or by circulating a statement signed by leading Antimasons endorsing Thompson.[56] Neither of these alternatives was taken, even though Weed publicly admitted his disappointment over the inability of the two anti-Jackson parties to agree on nominees. At the same time he indicated his chagrin over Southwick's candidacy and his intention of voting for Thompson. Nevertheless, by October, popular pressure had compelled him to place Southwick's name in the *Enquirer* at the head of the ticket.[57] "The Anti-Masons all go for Crary and *nearly* all for Southwick," Weed explained to Granger. "My refusal to support S[outhwick] came near to jeopardizing the County Ticket."[58] It was a question of obeying in order to command.

In other phases of the election, for presidential electors and local officers, cooperation between the Antimasons and the Adamsites was effected with misgivings on both sides.[59] Antimasonry, however, played only a small role in the presidential campaign. The leadership of the party, long committed to the president, sought to turn the excitement against Jackson by repeatedly calling attention to the fact that he

53. Flagg to S. Wright, Mar. 13, 1828, Flagg MSS.

54. *Anti-Masonic Enquirer*, Sept. 23, 1828; Granger to Weed, Sept. 12, 1828, Weed MSS.

55. Hammond, *Political Parties in New York*, II, 391.

56. Robert H. Backus to Weed, Sept. 10, 1828; P. C. Fuller to Weed, Sept. 18, 1828; N. Sargent to Weed, Oct. 26, 1828, Weed MSS.

57. *Anti-Masonic Enquirer*, Aug. 19, Sept. 9, 23, Oct. 7, 1828.

58. Weed to Granger, Oct. 26 [1828], Gideon and Francis Granger MSS. Southwick's *National Observer* reported that Weed had been censured by a Rochester Antimasonic meeting "'for giving support to the administration in preference to genuine anti-masonry. . . .'" *Anti-Masonic Enquirer*, Nov. 18, 1828.

59. P. L. Tracy to Taylor, July 10, 1828; William Thompson to Taylor, Jan. 9, 1828; W. A. Langworthy to Taylor, July, 1828, Taylor MSS; Trumbull Cary to Timothy Fitch, Mar. 20, July 11, 1828, Cary MSS; Webster to Ezekiel Webster, Nov. 18, 1828, Van Tyne, *Letters of Webster*, p. 134; Robert H. Backus to Weed, Sept. 10, 1828, Weed MSS; Seward, *Autobiography*, pp. 70–73.

held high office in the mystic brotherhood. Adams manipulated the prejudice against Masonry to the extent of condemning the kidnapping and murder of Morgan, but refrained from attacking the fraternity itself.[60] Webster was openly pleased by developments, writing Clay "that the effects of Antimasonry will not be unfavorable to the Administration."[61]

The results of the 1828 election greatly encouraged the Antimasons. Adams carried their home district and they elected four state senators and seventeen assemblymen. Southwick, not the most satisfactory candidate, did creditably though he ran well behind Van Buren and Thompson. His votes, together with Thompson's, exceeded those given to Van Buren, demonstrating that if the two anti-Jackson parties cooperated they could wrest control of the state from the Regency.[62]

But lingering mutual suspicion prevented a quick and harmonious consolidation. "[T]he Adams party interposed indirectly, every obstacle in their power," Weed complained openly after the election, "to thwart and embarrass our cause."[63] The hostility of the Adams leaders in New York probably only fueled the national ambitions of the Antimasons. In any event, the president's defeat, in contrast to their own successes, was the crucial factor in the party's swift rise thereafter. The "Friends of the Administration" were demoralized. Clay, the heir apparent, was not acceptable to the Antimasons because he refused to renounce his Masonic affiliation. And even before the election the movement had begun to spread outside New York. As Seward later summarized the situation, "The discomfited and overthrown [Adams] party practically withdrew from the field in the Northern States, and left its vacant place to be filled by the new, vigorous, and enthusiastic Antimasonic Party."[64]

The role the convention system might play in realizing the Antimasons' soaring ambition had been explored before the election of 1828. As the selector of candidates and as a propaganda forum, the convention had served the young party well. As a tool for amplifying

60. *Richmond Enquirer,* Aug. 22, 1828; Adams, *Memoirs,* VII (Jan. 22, 1828), 410; Samuel Flagg Bemis, *John Quincy Adams and the Union* (New York, 1956), p. 148.
61. Webster to Clay, Nov. 5, 1827, Clay MSS.
62. Weed, *Autobiography,* pp. 307, 309–10; Hammond, *Political Parties in New York,* II, 391.
63. *Anti-Masonic Enquirer,* Nov. 18, 1828.
64. Seward, *Autobiography,* p. 76. Also, Hammond, *Political Parties in New York,* II, 393; Van Deusen, *Thurlow Weed,* pp. 49–50, 54–57.

the party's embryonic organization it had been invaluable. Its preemptive possibilities had been fully investigated if not successfully applied. These usages of the convention were learned by Antimasonic leaders from personal experience. Their priority in applying them to national politics before any other party was not accidental.

After the election Weed and his cohorts saw themselves riding the crest of a tide that would, if properly managed, eventually engulf the nation. They lost no time taking advantage of their momentum. Before the end of the year the New York central committee scheduled a state convention for February 19, 1829, at Albany. The convention was "to deliberate upon and adopt such measures as may be deemed best calculated to vindicate the laws of the land from Masonic violence. . . ."[65] Behind these tired phrases was hidden the most important decision in the history of the party.

Considered only from the standpoint of the growth of the Antimasonic party in New York, the Albany convention was another milestone in the extension of the state organization. To induce the holding of meetings for the appointment of delegates, the central committee had circulars printed and distributed announcing the convention and urging the counties to send representatives. Weed enclosed one in a letter to an acquaintance, adding hopefully that "if you have become satisfied of the power and the stability, as I know you are of the justice of our cause, its friends would be happy to find you moving the matter in Queens County."[66] This encouragement fell on fertile ground, for when the Albany convention opened there were forty-two county delegations as against the twenty-three at Utica.[67] Each of the three state conventions held thus far had virtually doubled the party's previous grass roots organizations since the selection of county delegates was invariably accompanied by the appointment of a county committee responsible for winning over public opinion.

But the Albany convention was not concerned primarily with New York. Two resolutions vital to the future of Antimasonry were passed

65. *Anti-Masonic Enquirer,* Dec. 30, 1828.
66. Weed to John A. King, Jan., 1829, Papers of Thurlow Weed (New York Historical Society), cited hereafter as Weed MSS (NYHS). Similar letters were undoubtedly written to others.
67. *Anti-Masonic Enquirer,* Jan. 20, Feb. 2, 10, 17, 24, Mar. 3, 1829; *Proceedings of a Convention of Delegates from the Different Counties of New York Opposed to Free-Masonry, Held at the Capitol in the City of Albany, on the 19th, 20th and 21st Days of February,* 1829 (Rochester, 1829).

by the delegates. First, they disavowed "all connection between Anti-Masons and any political party which heretofore existed in the United States." Candidates should be run for every office, "whether local or general, . . . formed on the distinct principle of opposition to Masonry," and for this purpose "meetings and conventions should be universally called. . . ." Second, they issued a summons for a national convention. Timothy Fitch, the first collector of evidence against Masonry following Morgan's disappearance, moved the appointment of a committee "to inquire whether it is expedient for this convention to recommend a convention of delegates from the several United States . . . and if so, whether it is expedient for this convention to designate the time and place and also the suitable number of delegates from each State."[68] The motion carried and a committee of five was appointed, Seward among them, with Granger as chairman.

Granger subsequently reported that the committee had examined the question of whether "the lights which have been shed from this State upon other sections" justified holding a national convention. In Vermont, Massachusetts, Connecticut, and Rhode Island the committee found that Antimasonry was sufficiently advanced that statewide organizations had already formed while local activity was under way in five other states and one territory.[69] The committee, therefore, unanimously recommended "to the citizens of these United States, to meet in Convention at the City of Philadelphia, on the 11th day of September, 1830, by delegates from each state, equal in number to their representatives in the Senate and House of Representatives in Congress, and to be elected in such manner as the several states shall deem most desirable." Adoption of the report carried without dissent.

This declaration of independence and the calling of a national convention gave notice of the Antimasons' intention to transform themselves into a national party by building on the ruins of the Adams-Clay coalition. Just as the Utica convention had attempted to preempt state leadership by nominating a governor before their potential allies could field a candidate, the Philadelphia convention was designed to appropriate leadership of the anti-Jackson forces nationally. As no other business of consequence was transacted at Albany, it was clear that the decision was made by the central committee; the delegates' approval was strictly pro forma. It has not been possible to identify

68. *Proceedings of a Convention . . . Albany . . . February, 1829*, p. 14.
69. These were Pennsylvania, Ohio, New Jersey, Alabama, Kentucky, and Michigan. *Ibid.*, pp. 17–19.

the individual responsible for suggesting a national convention. Weed, unquestionably, exercised a decisive influence, but whether or not he was the originator is not recorded. He never claimed the distinction. To Fitch goes the honor of having moved the key question. Through him the national convention can be traced back directly to Morgan. In fact all of the controlling hands at Albany, notably those of the Rochester (now the state central) committee, had been drawn in by the backlash to the abduction.

The New York central committee's choice of a convention for the realization of their national ambitions should not be surprising. It was predetermined by the early history of the party. The series of crimes culminating in Morgan's death provided the geographic matrix for a political organization. From the meeting at Lewiston in January, 1827, the convention technique had been the inevitable means of connecting the scattered investigating and correspondence committees into a single, ever-lengthening chain. The Albany convention was the third state convention held within a year, each successive election of delegates creating new local organizations until the party had extended itself throughout most of New York. After the virus of Antimasonry infected adjoining states what was more natural than to apply the same unifying process to the formation of a national party?

Granger's report and the actions of the convention called attention to the swelling popularity of Antimasonry. The planting and growth of the party in the surrounding states followed a pattern similar to that in New York. By word of mouth and through newspapers, the kidnapping of Morgan and the involvement of Masonry were carried to scores of communities. Public meetings were held, candidates for local offices nominated, and, through the convention system, a state organization created. In this progression toward maturity the New York leaders acted as godfathers.

New York's part in assisting the broadening of Antimasonry's base is most apparent in Vermont. In the fall of 1827, General Martin Flint of Randolph, a well-known and controversial figure, repudiated his Masonic membership. Following his renunciation, Flint journeyed to western New York for consultations with party leaders. On his return he organized a ticket which swept his hometown in the spring elections of 1828. Thus inspired, others carried the movement throughout the state by summoning town meetings. The work of organization was furthered by county conventions of delegates chosen at these public meetings in the towns.[70] By the summer of 1829, Antimasonry had advanced to the point where it was possible to hold a state convention, the first staged by any party in Vermont.[71] Among those admitted to the deliberations at Montpelier was Henry Dana Ward of New York City, editor of the *Anti-Masonic Review and Magazine* and high in the councils of the party. The convention nominated candidates for all state offices and appointed a correspondence committee for the state and for each county. It empowered the central committee to call future state conventions and, if necessary, to appoint delegates to the national convention in Philadelphia.

In the annual state elections of 1829, the Antimasonic candidate for governor (who never acknowledged the nomination) lost to a Clay supporter, but ran well ahead of the Jacksonian. The Antimasons did succeed in electing one congressman.[72] Shortly after the poll the three members of the central committee, all from Randolph and including General Flint, called another state convention for June, 1830. This convention nominated a gubernatorial candidate (who accepted) and chose Vermont's delegation to Philadelphia.[73] Although defeated the second time, the party did eventually gain the governorship (after another state convention) and win a majority in the legislature in 1831, making Vermont the only state ever completely controlled by the Antimasons.[74]

Antimasonry in Massachusetts achieved its first political expression in town meetings during the summer and fall of 1828 and the winter of 1829. Its greatest strength lay in the counties of the Connecticut Valley.[75] Although a self-styled convention in Dedham, composed of

70. Ludlum, *Social Ferment*, pp. 94–101, 114–16; *Anti-Masonic Enquirer*, May 12, June 3, July 15, Nov. 25, 1828; June 9, July 28, Aug. 18, 1829. Thurlow Weed made two trips to Vermont in connection with legal aspects of the Morgan case and it may be assumed that he was available for political consultation. Walter Hill Crockett, *Vermont: The Green Mountain State* (New York, 1921), III, 227.

71. Ludlum, *Social Ferment*, pp. 116–17; *Proceedings of the Anti-Masonick State Convention, Holden at Montpelier, August 5, 6, & 7: With Address to the People, on the Subject of Speculative Freemasonry* (East Randolph, 1829); *Anti-Masonic Review and Magazine*, I, 281–83.

72. Ludlum, *Social Ferment*, pp. 116–18; Crockett, *Vermont*, III, pp. 229–31.

73. *Proceedings of the Anti-Masonic State Convention Holden at Montpelier, June 23, 24, & 25, 1830* (Middlebury, 1830); *Anti-Masonic Enquirer*, July 13, 1830.

74. Ludlum, *Social Ferment*, p. 118; McCarthy, *Antimasonic Party*, pp. 504–13.

75. McCarthy, *Antimasonic Party*, pp. 515–16; Darling, *AHR*, XXIX (Oct., 1923), 277–78; Harold U. Faulkner, "Political History of Massachusetts (1829–1851)," *Commonwealth History of Massachusetts*, ed. Albert Bushnell

"citizens from all parts of this state and some from neighboring states," suggested early in 1829 the convening of a state convention, it was not implemented until the Suffolk county central committee endorsed the idea at a public meeting in Boston in September so that delegates might be sent to the national convention.[76]

The first Massachusetts Antimasonic convention opened in Faneuil Hall on December 30, 1829.[77] Eight counties were represented by 243 delegates. As there were no state offices up for election, the convention's only concern was with internal party organization. Delegates to the national convention in Philadelphia were chosen for the eight counties; others were requested to select their delegates in county conventions. The Suffolk committee was officially designated a state central committee with authority to call future conventions and fill vacancies in the national delegation. Finally, the convention recommended the formation of county, town, and ward committees throughout the state.[78] The state committee did not call another convention until the spring of 1831, this time for the purpose of picking the delegates to the second national convention in Baltimore.[79] Control of the party after the convention apparently swung to the Antimasonic members of the legislature as the next convention, in the fall of 1832, was summoned by a legislative caucus rather than by the central committee. At this convention candidates for governor, lieutenant governor, and presidential electors were nominated.[80]

Hart (New York, 1930), IV, 81–82; *Anti-Masonic Enquirer*, Dec. 30, 1828; Jan. 20, 1829; *Doings of the Plymouth County Anti-Masonic Convention* [Mar. 10, 1829], n.p., n.d.

76. *Anti-Masonic Enquirer*, Jan. 20, 1829, from the *Boston Free Press*.

77. *An Abstract of the Proceedings of the Antimasonic State Convention of Massachusetts, Held in Faneuil Hall, Boston, May 19 & 20, 1831* (Boston, n.d.), pp. 4–6; *Anti-Masonic Intelligencer*, Oct. 20, 1829.

78. *An Abstract of the Proceedings of the Anti-Masonic State Convention of Massachusetts, Held in Faneuil Hall, Boston, Dec. 30 and 31, 1829, and Jan. 1, 1830* (Boston, 1830); *A Brief Report of the Debates in the Anti-Masonic State Convention of the Commonwealth of Massachusetts, Held in Faneuil Hall, Boston, December 30, 31, 1829, and January 1, 1830* (Boston, 1830); *Anti-Masonic Review and Magazine*, II, 27–31.

79. *Proceedings of the Antimasonic State Convention of Massachusetts, May 19 & 20, 1831*.

80. McCarthy, *Antimasonic Party*, pp. 516–18; *Antimasonic Republican Convention of Massachusetts, Held at Worcester. Sept. 5th and 6th, 1832* (Boston, 1832). Antimasons in Massachusetts never seem to have developed a genuine convention system at the local level.

Connecticut Antimasons quickly adopted the convention system. Public meetings had introduced the movement during 1828. One of these, held in Norwich in December, proposed a state convention.[81] Subsequent town meetings elected delegates to appear at Hartford in February, 1829. The business of the convention consisted of appointing county corresponding committees and a state committee, the latter empowered to call future state conventions.[82] After the Connecticut party experienced its first electoral victories, the central committee shared its authority with a legislative caucus. In February, 1830, a second state convention, recommended by the caucus, met in Hartford with 128 towns represented for the purpose of appointing delegates to Philadelphia. It nominated, in addition, candidates to fill state offices.[83] Ward, who made a habit of attending out of state conventions, was there to lend guidance. The county committees were reappointed, a town committee system encouraged, and it was urged that Antimasonic candidates be run for all elective offices.[84] A third state convention met in December, 1830, the delegates again elected by mass meetings.[85]

In the remainder of the New England states Antimasonry never attained significant proportions. Town meetings and county conventions were held in Rhode Island preparatory to a state convention which met in April, 1829, to appoint four delegates to Philadelphia.[86] Rhode Island Antimasons tended to ally with the Jacksonians in state politics rather than with the dominant National Republicans.[87] Neither Maine nor New Hampshire sent delegates to Philadelphia, and in both states there was only local Antimasonic activity before 1831.[88]

---

81. Jarvis Means Morse, *A Neglected Period of Connecticut's History, 1818–1850* (New Haven, 1933), pp. 106–7.

82. *Anti-Masonic Enquirer*, May 20, Dec. 30, 1828; Jan. 6, 1829; *Anti-Masonic Intelligencer*, Feb. 3, 10, 17, 1829.

83. *Anti-Masonic Intelligencer*, June 9, 1829; Jan. 5, 19, Feb. 9, 1830; *Anti-Masonic Enquirer*, Feb. 16, 23, 1830; *Anti-Masonic Review and Magazine*, II 89–91; *Proceedings of the Antimasonic State Convention of Connecticut, Held at Hartford, Feb. 3 and 4, 1830* (Hartford, 1830).

84. *Anti-Masonic Intelligencer*, Oct. 27, 1829; Jan. 19, Mar. 2, 23, 30, 1830.

85. *Ibid.*, Nov. 16, Dec. 7, 21, 1830.

86. *Albany Evening Journal*, Apr. 10, 1830; *Anti-Masonic Enquirer*, Apr. 13, 1830; *Anti-Masonic Intelligencer*, May 26, 1828.

87. McCarthy, *Antimasonic Party*, pp. 551–52; Darling, *AHR*, XXIX (Oct., 1923), 278–79.

88. McCarthy, *Antimasonic Party*, p. 556; *Anti-Masonic Enquirer*, June 8, 1830; June 28, 1831.

The Antimasonic party in New Jersey was small and unimportant except as it affected the balance between Clay and Jackson.[89] But there was sufficient interest in the cause to hold a state convention in August, 1830, to select delegates to Philadelphia. In December another state convention met in New Brunswick to endorse congressional candidates who had been nominated previously by either the Clay or Jackson parties. This convention also recommended a third state convention to meet at Trenton to choose delegates to Baltimore.[90]

From a national standpoint the only crucial state besides New York where Antimasonry entered into the vitals of political life was Pennsylvania. Newspapers had early brought the movement to public attention in the western part of the commonwealth. By the fall of 1827 there were limited political stirrings. The party in Pennsylvania bore strong resemblances to its New York counterpart—it was concentrated in a particular section of the state; it also attempted a take-over of the existing anti-Jackson organization, and it was involved in sectional and economic rivalries having no direct connection with Masonry.[91] Antimasonry in Pennsylvania proved the sturdiest branch of the party, enduring long after its sponsors in other states, including New York, had abandoned it for the Whigs.

In 1828 and 1829, town and county mass meetings were held to denounce Masonry, appoint committees of correspondence, and nominate candidates for the national and state legislatures.[92] Thaddeus Stevens, who found the party's battle against murder and privilege politically convenient and personally satisfying, organized the first Antimasonic meeting in Adams County in the summer of 1829.[93] "The Anti-masons," Congressman James Buchanan could write Judge McLean in the spring of 1829, "are becoming numerous amongst us and acting with energy and concert."[94] Buchanan correctly predicted

89. McCarthy, *Antimasonic Party*, p. 555.

90. *Anti-Masonic Enquirer*, Aug. 24, 1830; *Anti-Masonic Review and Magazine*, II, 224; *Anti-Masonic Intelligencer*, Dec. 21, 1830; *Albany Evening Journal*, Dec. 16, 1830.

91. McCarthy, *Antimasonic Party*, pp. 437-41; Klein, *Pennsylvania Politics, 1817-1832*, pp. 262-82; Andrews, *Western Pennsylvania Historical Magazine*, XVIII (Dec., 1935), 256-58.

92. *Anti-Masonic Enquirer*, Feb. 19, Sept. 2, 30, Dec. 30, 1828; Aug. 25, 1829.

93. Richard Nelson Current, *Old Thad Stevens: A Story of Ambition* (Madison, 1942), pp. 15, 16. Also, Fawn M. Brodie, *Thaddeus Stevens: Scourge of the South* (New York, 1959), pp. 39-47, 57-59; Thomas Frederick Woodley, *Thaddeus Stevens* (Harrisburg, 1934), pp. 30, 35, 49, 52.

94. Buchanan to McLean, June, 1829, in John McLean Papers (Library of Congress), cited hereafter as McLean MSS.

that the Antis would enter into "a thorough union" with the old Adams party. A short time later, on June 25, 1829, the first Antimasonic state convention of Pennsylvania met in the court house at Harrisburg and unanimously nominated Joseph Ritner, a well-known foe of the dominant Jackson faction, for governor. The convention was a modest affair; only eight counties were represented by delegates chosen at meagerly attended county mass meetings. To augment the thirty-five delegates (a large number of whom were from Lancaster County), onlookers were admitted from absent counties.[95] Whittlesey participated in the proceedings, having been appointed by the New York central committee "as a delegate from our body to act with you in your deliberations on the matters of general interest."[96] A state committee was appointed and authorized to call additional conventions. The delegates approved the national meeting in Philadelphia, but were "at a loss, at this early period, to say definitely, which would be the most eligible mode of choosing delegates to represent Pennsylvania. . . ."[97] That decision was left to the central committee.

Although the Antimasons were unorganized in many counties, the party showed amazing strength in the 1829 state elections. Ritner polled over 60,000 votes, only about 16,000 less than his Democratic opponent. He carried seventeen counties, most of them in the southern and western part of the state. The party elected one state senator, fifteen members of the lower house, and a congressman, Harmar Denny, from Pittsburgh.[98] Another convention was immediately convened by the state central committee on February 25, 1830, in order to select delegates to Philadelphia. This time thirty-six counties were represented by eighty-seven delegates. A standing committee of correspondence and vigilance was appointed for each county, and the delegation to Philadelphia was designated as a special committee on arrangements to find quarters for the national meeting.[99] Stevens took an active part in the convention and in so doing moved from local

95. Klein, *Pennsylvania Politics, 1817–1832,* pp. 225, 280–86; *Proceedings of a Convention of Delegates from the Different Counties in the State of Pennsylvania, Opposed to Free-Masonry Held at the Court House in Harrisburg, on the 25th and 26th Days of June, 1826* (Lancaster, 1829).

96. *Anti-Masonic Enquirer,* July 14, 1829.

97. *Ibid.,* July 21, 1829.

98. McCarthy, *Antimasonic Party,* p. 432; Andrews, *Western Pennsylvania Magazine of History,* XVIII (Dec., 1935), 261–62.

99. *Proceedings of the Anti-Masonic State Convention Held at Harrisburg, on the 25th February, 1830.* n.p., n.d.; *Anti-Masonic Enquirer,* Mar. 16, 1830; *Niles' Weekly Register,* XXXVII (Apr. 10, 1830), 124.

to state politics. The fall elections of 1830 saw the Pennsylvania Anti-masons register solid gains. They elected six congressmen, four state senators, and twenty-seven members of the Assembly. This success was not due entirely to the appeal of Antimasonry's peculiar cause; many voters opposed to the national and state administrations, parti-cularly the Clay adherents, united with them for lack of any other alternative to the Jacksonians.[100]

Outside of New England and the middle Atlantic states, Anti-masonry had no great impact. The boasts of the *Anti-Masonic Enquirer* in the spring of 1830 that the cause was "spreading over the entire west," and that the western states were preparing to send delegates to Philadelphia, was a variation of the truth.[101] Only Ohio, where Antimasonic agitation had started in 1828, sent delegates to the eastern meeting. They were appointed at a state convention at Canton in July, 1830.[102] The strength of the party was focused in the north-eastern portion of the state dominated by New England settlers and adjacent to western New York. In areas where they were weak, the Antis cooperated with the National Republicans, although there was constant friction between them.[103] In the state and local elections of 1830 and 1831, the Antimasons showed surprising strength within the Western Reserve. The territory of Michigan possessed a viable but short-lived Antimasonic party. A town meeting in Detroit on New Year's Day, 1829, had resulted in the calling of a territorial convention in February to nominate a congressional delegate who was sub-sequently elected.[104] Indiana Masonry was hit hard because of the hostility generated by the Morgan affair, but there was no sustained activity by the party before 1832.[105]

In the border states Antimasonry never established a solid organi-

100. McCarthy, *Antimasonic Party*, pp. 435–36.

101. *Anti-Masonic Enquirer*, June 8, 1830.

102. *Ibid.*, June 10, 1828; June 8, Aug. 10, 1830; *Anti-Masonic Intelligencer*, Aug. 10, 1830.

103. Elisha Whittlesey to Webster, June 23, 1831, Webster MSS; *Proceed-ings of the United States Anti-Masonic Convention, Sept. 11, 1830*, pp. 71–72; McCarthy, *Antimasonic Party*, pp. 526–30; Weisenburger, *Passing of the Frontier*, pp. 263–66.

104. *Anti-Masonic Enquirer*, Sept. 9, 1828; Jan. 27, August 26, 1829; *Proceed-ings of the United States Anti-Masonic Convention, Sept. 11, 1830*, p. 71; McCarthy, *Antimasonic Party*, p. 556.

105. William E. English, *A History of Early Indianapolis Masonry and of Center Lodge*, vol. III, *Indiana Historical Society Publications* (Indianapolis, 1895), 19–23; Logan Esarey, *A History of Indiana from Its Exploration to 1850* (Indianapolis, 1915), p. 306.

zation or won over an important segment of public opinion. Maryland and Delaware each had a single delegate at the party's second national convention, but they were mere tokens. In Maryland, as in many other states, the Masonic fraternity suffered a marked decline, but it was not accompanied by any significant political manifestations.[106] Preliminary steps were taken in Delaware in the spring of 1831 for holding a state convention to appoint delegates to Philadelphia. Whether it actually met is doubtful.[107] Kentucky witnessed some agitation against Masonry, but it was never translated into political action.[108]

Not one state destined to join the Confederacy sent a delegate to either of the Antimasonic national conventions. In Alabama a number of public meetings were held and committees formed in opposition to the Masons. A state convention was even proposed, but an Antimasonic party never materialized.[109] The rest of Dixie was impervious to Antimasonry despite the efforts of Whittlesey and others to arouse interest in the region.[110]

Where Antimasonry had already received popular support the Philadelphia convention assisted in the perfection of the party's state organizations. The need to elect delegates to the first national meeting was the sole, ostensible reason for calling the first Antimasonic conventions in Massachusetts, Rhode Island, New Jersey, and Ohio. In Vermont and Connecticut this function was coupled with the nomination of candidates for state offices. The Philadelphia convention was the subject of special state conventions in New York and Pennsylvania which simultaneously aided in extending Antimasonry into previously untouched counties.

Implicit in the calling of the Philadelphia convention was the possibility, even the expectation, that it would make a nomination for president. The *Albany Evening Journal* loftily declared its intention

106. McCarthy, *Antimasonic Party*, p. 556; *Proceedings of the United States Anti-Masonic Convention, Sept. 11, 1830,* p. 72; Edward T. Shultz, *History of Freemasonry in Maryland* (Baltimore, 1886), II, 616–17; *ibid.*, III, 19–40.

107. *Anti-Masonic Enquirer,* June 8, 1830.

108. *A Manual of Masonry and Anti-Masonry* (Louisville, 1833); J. Winston Coleman, Jr., *Masonry in the Bluegrass* (Lexington, 1933), p. 116; *Anti-Masonic Intelligencer,* Mar. 9, 1830.

109. *Anti-Masonic Enquirer,* Nov. 11, 1828; Apr. 20, Oct. 26, 1830; *Anti-Masonic Intelligencer,* July 27, 1830; John C. Spencer, letter of July 15, 1830, in *A Collection of Letters on Freemasonry in Chronological Order* (Boston, 1849), p. 3.

110. Whittlesey to Weed, Jan. 27, Mar. 17, 1830, Weed MSS.

of holding "utterly aloof" from speculation on this topic in order to wait for "the people" who would "in good time, find a candidate for that elevated station, who owes no allegiance, but to the laws and constitution of his country."[111] These words were honored only in the breach; the guessing game commenced at once, and attempts were made to encourage particular candidates.[112] The names of important national politicians were mentioned—Clay, McLean, Webster, Calhoun, and Rush—although none of them, as yet, had made an explicit avowal of the distinctive principle of the party or had acted with it.

There is strong evidence that the New York high command had decided by the spring of 1830 that no nominations should be made at Philadelphia. Agents of McLean, whom Jackson had appointed to the Supreme Court, reported that Antimasonic leaders, including Granger, thought a fall nomination for president imprudent.[113] The tip-off as to the eventual course that was to be followed came in an editorial in the *Albany Evening Journal* on June 2, 1830. Commenting on a report that the Philadelphia convention would nominate Rush, the *Journal* asserted that "It is by no means certain that any candidate will be named; or, indeed that anything relating to the presidency further than the calling of a nominating convention will be transacted at the coming September meeting."

Nevertheless, the possibility that a presidential candidate might be named remained and sentiment in favor of one man or another developed. Participants in a public meeting at Pittsburgh urged a nomination because "several of the present prominent candidates" (i.e., Jackson and Clay) were Masons, and instructed their delegates to Philadelphia "to use their exertions" to see that a candidate was chosen.[114] The *Pittsburgh Examiner* touted Webster as the nominee able to provide the party with a rallying point that would "fling back

111. *Albany Evening Journal,* Apr. 12, 1830.
112. P. C. Fuller to Weed, Sept. 8, 1829; O. Bradley to Weed, Jan. 26, 1829; Whittlesey to Weed, Jan. 27, July 6, 1830, Weed MSS; W. W. Irwin to Webster, Aug. 25, 1830, Webster MSS; John C. Spencer to Van Buren, June 22, 1829, Martin Van Buren Papers (New York State Library), cited hereafter as Van Buren MSS (NYSL); Richard Rush to James Barbour, Aug. 7, 1830, Barbour MSS; Henry O'Rielly to Flagg, Nov. 11, 1829, Flagg MSS; M. T. Simpson to McLean, Dec. 28, 1829; June 15, July 13, 1830; B. W. Richards to McLean, Feb. 4, 1830; Elisha Whittlesey to McLean, copy, Aug. 30, 1830, McLean MSS; Adams, *Memoirs,* VIII (Feb. 22, Mar. 28, 1830), 191–92, 210–11; *Albany Evening Journal,* June 1, 2, 1830.
113. M. T. Simpson to McLean, Mar. 4, 1830; B. W. Richards to McLean, May 15, 1830, McLean MSS.
114. *Albany Evening Journal,* June 1, 1830.

the charge of want of talent and worth in their ranks. . . ."[115] The Ohio delegation was understood to favor an immediate nomination of McLean, and the former postmaster-general received assurances of wide support from among all the delegates.[116]

Some even talked of a Clay nomination. This resulted from the proceedings of the New York Antimasonic state convention in August, 1830, which had nominated candidates for governor and lieutenant governor. The Antimasons in New York were now unquestionably the predominant force opposing the Regency. The old Adams party (now committed to Clay), shattered by defeat, made no fresh attempt to block Antimasonry and, in fact, abandoned their own organization.[117] The Antimasons were aware, however, that some tangible gestures of friendliness toward the National Republicans were necessary to secure their active support. The Antimasonic convention responded in two ways. First, it nominated for lieutenant governor Samuel Stevens, a New York City alderman associated with the Clay faction of the Workingmen's party, but not previously identified with Antimasonry. Second, the convention adopted resolutions that for the first time committed the party to a whole range of state and national issues unrelated to the Masonic question. They adopted the National Republican platform, support for protective tariffs and internal improvements, in virtually every detail.[118] This patent bid for fusion with the Clay party produced threats of a bolt by Antimasonic extremists such as Crary and Southwick who charged the party had been sold to the Kentucky statesman.[119] "If we are to go to Clay," wrote a surprised and confused Antimason to Weed after the convention had adjourned, "I beg you for an early glimmer of light. Have the goodness to open a cranny to my dull vision."[120]

Union between the Clay party and the Antimasons was not to be

115. Reprinted in the *Anti-Masonic Enquirer*, Aug. 24, 1830.
116. M. T. Simpson to McLean, July 13, 1830; Elisha Whittlesey to McLean, copy, Aug. 30, 1830, McLean MSS; *Anti-Masonic Enquirer*, Sept. 21, 1830.
117. R. M. Livingston to Taylor, Mar. 5, 1830; W. A. Langworthy to Taylor, Mar. 9, 1830, Taylor MSS.
118. M. Cadwallader to Weed, Dec. 14, 1829; Whittlesey to Weed, Feb. 5, 1830, Weed MSS; James H. Woods to Seward, Apr. 27, 1830, William Henry Seward Papers (University of Rochester Library), cited hereafter as Seward MSS; *Proceedings of the Anti-Masonic Convention for the State of New York: Held at Utica, Aug. 11, 1830* (Utica, 1830), p. 6; Hammond, *Political Parties in New York*, II, 396; Seward, *Autobiography*, p. 78; McCarthy, *Antimasonic Party*, pp. 395-97, 406-8; Van Deusen, *Thurlow Weed*, pp. 56-57.
119. *Albany Evening Journal*, Aug. 21, 1830; John Willard to Flagg, Aug. 18, 1830, Flagg MSS; Granger to Weed, Aug. 23, 1830, Granger MSS.
120. P. C. Fuller to Weed, Aug. 20, 1830, Weed MSS.

achieved so quickly, but it remained a fixed goal of Weed and the other New York leaders who viewed the movement in frankly political terms and not as a moral crusade. The more zealous members were opposed to any dilution of the party's principles that would result from mixing with the unconverted. But for the time being, Weed and those sharing his pragmatic outlook were in control of the New York party. And so great was New York's influence within the embryonic national party that they were able to dominate the proceedings at Philadelphia. Whittlesey was responsible for the convention's organization; Granger was president; Seward was chairman of two committees; Ward of two, and Whittlesey of one. All of the key decisions, particularly the question of whether to make a nomination, were made in accordance with the wishes of New York. This should not imply any dissatisfaction with New York's hegemony. As the men credited with bringing the party into being, as members of the state party that had attracted the most conspicuous men, and as residents of the state on which the hopes for national success depended, the New York delegates were inevitably looked to for guidance.

Before the Philadelphia convention formally opened, two caucuses were held in the city to complete the arrangements. The first gathered on the morning of September 10 to discuss where the convention would meet. Independence Hall, the inevitable first choice, was not available to them, and the owner of a private building had declined to rent it because, it was said, he was a Mason. The city commissioners came to the rescue by offering the use of the District Court Room.[121] A second, and more important, caucus assembled the next morning with most of the delegates in attendance. A committee, headed by Whittlesey, was elected to prepare the convention's organization.[122]

The first session opened officially at noon on the eleventh of September, the fourth anniversary of Morgan's kidnapping. On Whittlesey's motion Joseph Ritner of Pennsylvania was made president pro tempore. A roll call of the delegates by states followed. Ten states

121. *Albany Evening Journal*, Sept. 15, 1830; *Niles' Weekly Register*, XXIX (Sept. 18, 1830), 58.
122. *Proceedings of the United States Anti-Masonic Convention, Sept. 11, 1830*, p. 85. Samuel Rhea Gammon, Jr., *The Presidential Campaign of 1832*, vol. XL, *Johns Hopkins University Studies in Historical and Political Science* (Baltimore, 1922) is especially useful in taking note of the priorities of the Antimasonic and the other national conventions. It also provides narratives of their formal proceedings.

and one territory were represented by ninety-six delegates, but three states—New York, Pennsylvania, and Massachusetts—accounted for 70 percent of the total.[123] Whittlesey then moved the appointment of permanent officers, a president, four vice-presidents, and two secretaries. Granger was unanimously elected president, accepting the honor with a speech "complimentary to the respectability and importance of the convention. . . ."[124] After the election of the other officers a prayer was offered by a clerical delegate from Massachusetts. Whittlesey next moved the appointment of one delegate from each state and territory as a committee "to lay before this Convention the subjects proper for its consideration."[125] This done, the convention adjourned until 4 P.M.

When the convention reassembled the committee on business submitted fourteen resolutions, each providing for the appointment of a committee. This was to be the work of the convention—to break down into small groups to prepare reports which would then be discussed and acted on by the whole body. The procedure occupied six full days. Nine of these committees were concerned with the investigation of various aspects of Masonry and the Morgan abduction; one was to prepare the rules and orders to govern the proceedings, another to recommend the admission of honorary members, and another to prepare an "Address to the People" setting forth the measures necessary to extinguish Masonry. The thirteenth resolution appointed a committee of five (the standard number) to draw up resolutions expressing the sentiments of the convention, and the last committee was charged with devising a system of national correspondence for the diffusion of information on Masonry.[126] After a few modifications, these resolutions were adopted and the committees appointed. Six other committees, including one to raise funds to defray the costs of the convention, were proposed from the floor and approved.

The Court Room proved too small to handle the delegates and spectators. On Monday the convention reconvened in the saloon of the Musical Fund Society Hall, rented at a cost of two hundred dollars.

---

123. Before the end of the convention the names of sixteen late arrivals were added to the list. *Proceedings of the United States Anti-Masonic Convention, Sept. 11, 1830*, pp. 163–64.
    124. *Ibid.*, p. 85.
    125. *Ibid.*, p. 5.
    126. *Ibid.*, p. 6.

The new auditorium was spacious enough to provide room for a large number of visitors. Granger wrote *"ex cathedra"* that there were at least a thousand men in the room, "garnished with half a dozen ladies."[127]

Most of the committee reports were long and perfunctory recitals of the evils of Masonry. The work of the committee on resolutions cannot be considered except in a vague way as the party platform. The eight resolves contained the usual, hackneyed accusations against Masonry.[128] The "Address to the People of the United States" was the document intended to have the greatest propaganda value.[129] It was written by Myron Holley of Canandaigua, who like many other party leaders combined journalism with an active political career. He would subsequently achieve a measure of fame as an abolitionist. Holley made a specialty of writing the addresses of Antimasonic conventions. His "wit," on the authority of an admirer, did "not consist in its brevity."[130] The address was a tedious review of the crimes and dangers of Masonry framed in a declamatory style. It was, in Seward's words, "the measure in which is to excite public attention and to direct public inquiry."[131]

The most important decision of the Philadelphia convention concerned the nomination of a presidential candidate. The delegates were of three minds. Some, particularly the Pennsylvanians, wanted an immediate nomination. A few thought the idea of contesting for the presidency extraneous to the purposes of the party. Others, including the New York leadership, favored a nomination, but at a later date. The subject was unexpectedly introduced on Monday morning, September 13, when an insignificant New York delegate, John L. Curtenuis, proposed a committee to consider "the most expedient time, place and manner, for making nominations of candidates for the offices of President *and* Vice President of the United States." Objections were voiced questioning the motion's expediency and it was quickly

127. *Ibid.*, p. 86; *Anti-Masonic Enquirer*, Sept. 21, 1830; Granger to Weed, Sept. 14, 1830, Francis and Gideon Granger MSS; William H. Maynard to Weed, Sept. 16, 1830, Weed MSS.

128. *Proceedings of the United States Anti-Masonic Convention, Sept. 11, 1830*, p. 84.

129. *Ibid.*, pp. 145–63.

130. [Elizur Wright,] *Myron Holley, and What He Did for Liberty and True Religion* (Boston, 1882), pp. 34, 166–69.

131. *Proceedings of the United States Anti-Masonic Convention, Sept. 11, 1830*, p. 121.

tabled.[132] The next day Curtenuis withdrew his resolution only to have it instantly renewed by Whittlesey on behalf of the committee on business. This precipitated a debate on the merits and timing of a presidential nomination.[133] Most of those who spoke favored deferring nominations until another time. An amendment offered by a Pennsylvania delegate to force an immediate nomination was lost without debate. Delay was advocated on the grounds that "the people had not instructed us, and did not expect us to act on this subject. When the people wanted a nomination, they would elect delegates for this express purpose." Thaddeus Stevens defended the political approach to Antimasonry and thought it desirable to nominate a presidential candidate as the best way to force a national discussion on the issue.[134] Seward's reason for wanting a postponement was cryptic but revealing. "The termination of the state elections," he said, "might alter materially the aspect of affairs."

Important state contests were scheduled during the next months. New York was electing its governor in a few weeks and an Antimasonic victory there would greatly improve the party's national prospects. Moreover, New York Antimasonic leaders did not want their chances spoiled by anything done in Philadelphia. Their expectations were high. The opposition to the Regency was now united behind the Antimasonic state ticket as the National Republicans had acquiesced in the nomination of Granger and Stevens.[135] Whittlesey believed that the whole future of the party, including its chances to win the presidency, depended on the New York race.[136] For this reason Weed was angered to learn that Granger had been chosen president of the convention. Those responsible were "stark mad, or I am an Ass—a four-legged, long eared Ass," he told Granger. "Will," he demanded, "one doubtful man be gained by this step?" Too close an identification with Antimasonry on Granger's part might cost him as many as 3,000 votes.[137] Granger was apologetic for his blunder, but maintained that he was "*forced*" to be president and urged Weed to "keep cool."[138] Even before he received Weed's rebuke though,

132. *Ibid.*, p. 87.
133. *Ibid.*, pp. 6, 94–96.
134. *Ibid.*, p. 95.
135. Seward, *Autobiography*, p. 78; Wright, *Myron Holley*, p. 170; P. C. Fuller to Weed, Aug. 30, 1830, Weed MSS; *Daily National Journal*, Aug. 17, 1830.
136. Whittlesey to Weed, Jan. 29, 1830, Weed MSS.
137. Weed to Granger, Sept. 13, 1830, Weed MSS (NYHS).
138. Granger to Weed, Sept. 14, 1830, Gideon and Francis Granger MSS.

he knew that he had erred, writing Weed as he sat upon the platform that he felt "an undefined and uncomfortable impression" that he should not have been made convention president.[139]

The nomination of a presidential candidate at Philadelphia would alienate those New Yorkers supporting contenders other than the one chosen. It would also divide the Antimasons since there was no consensus among the members on who the nominee should be. The *Albany Argus* went so far as to say that Granger had gone to Philadelphia for the express purpose of preventing, in his own interest, a presidential nomination. If the convention were to nominate Clay, said the *Argus* with more truth than kindness, it would expose the "cant and insincerity" of Antimasonic leaders who had proclaimed their independence of the old parties. The nomination by the Philadelphia convention of a candidate other than Clay would be equally fatal as it "would necessarily connect Mr. Granger with him; and would jeopardise the support of those friends of Mr. Clay, who are not antimasons, but whose aid is now counted for the anti-masonic candidate for governor."[140]

A correspondent of the *Anti-Masonic Enquirer* (perhaps Whittlesey), reporting from Philadelphia on the day the convention opened, had predicted in authoritative tones that no nomination would be made:

> The delegates here are not disposed to sell their votes to any man, in exchange for the reputation of his name, however exalted that name may be. They seemed inclined to lay down in a mild and moderate, yet firm manner, a chart of the principles by which they will be governed—submit it to the people of these United States, leave them to reflect upon it for 12 or 18 months, and inform them that at the end of the period, a convention will be called to nominate a President upon those principles. This will give all fair warning of this purpose, and leave all to make up their minds as to their course of conduct.[141]

These ideas were embodied in the report of the committee on nominations which was submitted to the convention four days later. The report, delivered to the convention by Amos Ellmaker of Pennsylvania, stressed the necessity of capturing the presidency to prevent Masonry from controlling the national government. A nomination would of itself advance their cause as it would "force the investigation of the

139. Granger to Weed, Sept. 17, 1830, *ibid.*
140. *Albany Argus*, Sept. 17, 1830.
141. Sept. 21, 1830.

principles and practices of the institution into every district of the United States. Anti-Masonry will be more widely extended by one presidential election on anti-masonic grounds, than by many years of exertion through state elections only."[142] The committee thought, however, that nominations should not be made at this time. Not all of the states were represented in the convention. As the election was two years away, they should be given a chance to participate in making the nomination. Furthermore, a year's delay "will enable the people throughout the United States to form an opinion, whether those who may be candidates are firm and decided anti-masons." None of the potential contenders for the presidency in 1832 had committed themselves, in other words, to Antimasonry.

There were other imponderables to be considered. Jackson had not yet announced that he would run for a second term. His decision would materially alter the prospects of those with presidential ambitions. Clay's attitude toward the approaching contest was ambiguous. Although the acknowledged head of the opposition, he had not obligated himself to run. Politicians such as McLean and Calhoun who hoped for Jacksonian support recoiled from making an open bid until the president's wishes were known. Those such as Webster and Rush in the anti-Jackson camp could not accept an Antimasonic nomination without risking an affront to Clay and a mortal schism in the National Republican ranks.

A postponement would give the party a chance to grow and enhance the value of its nomination. It would also give aspirants to the nation's highest office a chance to get "right" with Antimasonry. The committee prudently recommended that delegates representing the people of each state, equal in number to the state's electoral votes, meet in convention on September 26, 1831, in Baltimore "with power to make nominations of suitable candidates for the offices of president and vice president, to be suported at the next election; and for the transaction of such other business as the cause of anti-masonry may require."

After approving the Baltimore convention the delegates made one other important decision before disbanding. The chairman of the committee to devise a system of national correspondence read his report advocating the creation of a national committee charged with responsibility for maintaining communications with the state committees.[143]

142. *Proceedings of the United States Anti-Masonic Convention, Sept. 11, 1830,* pp. 12–13, 73–75, 123, 131–33.
143. *Ibid.,* pp. 13, 77–78, 133–34.

The original instructions to the committee had emphasized that the purpose of national correspondence was propaganda, as if to make clear the intention not to create a policy-making body of the type found among the state committees of correspondence. When Whittlesey moved that the national committee be authorized "to open a correspondence with candid members of the fraternity on the subject of secret societies, and to publish their answers with their consent," strong objections were raised. Stevens of Pennsylvania and others saw a joker in the innocuous resolution; it would "give office-seeking masons a chance of thus promoting their selfish views." Did these delegates fear that the national committee, under the authority of Whittlesey's resolution, might promote the candidacy of a particular contender for the presidency and thereby obligate the party in advance of the Baltimore convention? If so, Seward sought to allay their apprehensions by assuring the delegates that Whittlesey could never be "governed by sinister designs." Always eager to avoid divisions, Whittlesey withdrew his amendment.

Ward and two other editors from New York City were then appointed to be the national committee for correspondence. The selection of journalists indicated the limitation imposed on its activities. The national committee was supposed to generate publicity, not make policy. Yet Ward, something of a fanatic, proved capable of making mischief for the party in the future. Members of the state committees of correspondence were granted ex officio membership on the national committee and could, when present, participate fully in its proceedings. The inclusion of state committeemen, even though nominal, presaged the formation of a permanent agency to manage the business of the party between the meetings of its national governing body.

Care was taken to see that the convention's proceedings were published. A special committee was appointed for that purpose, and the committee to raise funds to pay for the cost of the convention was instructed to turn over its surplus to it. The delegates also resolved that the proceedings should be printed in German as well as in English. At Stevens's suggestion, the committee was requested to transmit fifty copies of the proceedings to each delegate for personal distribution.[144]

The very meeting of a convention, apart from its own publications, gave recognition to the party and its program. Newspaper coverage

144. *Ibid.*, pp. 9, 13.

was assured by virtue of its national pretensions. Masonry would be scrutinized by those who had never given it much thought. The entire convention system, in fact, conspired to promote the Antimasonic cause. As the editor of the *Anti-Masonic Enquirer* wrote later, "Experience has abundantly proved that the assembling together of the people by themselves, in their primary meetings, and by their Delegates in County, State, and National Conventions is among the most efficient means to disseminate information of the true character and principles of Free Masonry. . . ."[145]

The real function of the national convention did not reside in its reports or resolutions or the Address to the People, but in the actual and symbolic joining of thousands of persons from different states in a common cause. In this sense the Philadelphia convention was an undoubted success. Late Friday afternoon, September 17, after a vote of thanks to its officers and a prayer, the first Antimasonic national convention adjourned *sine die*.

145. *Anti-Masonic Enquirer*, Dec. 2, 1830.

SIX

The Antimasonic National Nominating Convention

The Philadelphia convention announced the firm intention of the Antimasons to make their party truly national by running a candidate for president. The party's position as it readied its bid for national power was both promising and precarious. It had grown tremendously in a short time; already it possessed formidable organizations in the nation's two largest states, states that might prove decisive in the election. In half a dozen others the movement gave every sign of developing into a sturdy force. The main opposition to Jackson was divided over both issues and leaders. Part of it looked toward Clay and emphasized economic nationalism. Another portion was simply anti-Jackson and ready to take up the man who could put together the broadest coalition against the president. Calhoun and McLean were the names most frequently mentioned in this connection. Antimasonry offered the anti-Jackson politicians of every stripe an issue which transcended their own differences. It could become a receptacle for all those who, for whatever reason, were unhappy with the new administration. That much was promising.

Yet there were serious questions as to the party's stability, not to mention its dubious respectability. Antimasonry generated tremendous enthusiasm, but could the fervor be sustained? Was opposition to a secret society a sufficient base on which to erect a national party? Masonic numbers were shrinking under the attack. What would happen to the party once the Masonic threat lost its plausibility? On the answers to those questions depended the willingness of national politicians to have their names associated with the party.

In the year preceding the Baltimore convention the Antimasonic leaders conducted a survey to decide on a presidential candidate. There was a general desire to nominate the man who would win the greatest number of votes, for only if they made an impressive showing could they realize their national ambitions. Everyone wanted a "name" to head the ticket, and this made it necessary to look outside the party. The only Antimason mentioned as a possible candidate was Granger, but though easily the best-known figure in the party, he was not nationally prominent. Furthermore, Granger expected to run again in 1832 for the New York governorship (he had been defeated in 1830), a far more solid prospect than the presidency.[1] The publicity value of having a famous candidate was appreciated by even the most zealous. "The more influential his name is," wrote Ward, "the farther their [the Antimasons'] aim will be perceived, and the farther that is *perceived,* the more will it be *approved* by the American people."[2]

The extent to which the nominee should pledge himself to the principles of Antimasonry was not agreed upon. To important leaders in New York, including Weed, Seward, Granger, and Whittlesey, the strength of the candidate's convictions was less important than his ability to attract voters, from Jackson if possible, but at the very least from the National Republicans. They were prepared to settle for an innocuous assurance from the potential nominee, given privately before the convention, that he was opposed to Masonry. The more fanatical Antimasons, including much of the leadership outside New York and those like Ward and Holley inside the state, demanded public evidence of a sincere devotion to the cause before the convention met. To these persons, winning the election was less important than preserving the party's integrity. Pennsylvania's Amos Ellmaker believed that "if a man be nominated who is not a firm, open & decided antimason the party will be deserted in disgust by very many in every part of the country who have heretofore been the most zealous and active."[3] The task of the dominant and pragmatic New York "bosses"

1. Amos Ellmaker to Seward, May 5, 18, 1831; William H. Maynard to Seward, May 31, 1831, Seward MSS; *Albany Evening Journal,* Dec. 20, 1830. It was reported to Adams that Granger was weary of Antimasonry and wanted to withdraw from the party. On the advice of Weed and Whittlesey, he did not attend the Baltimore convention, in order to avoid repeating the embarrassment caused by the Philadelphia convention. Adams, *Memoirs,* VIII (Mar. 3, 1831), 333; Granger to Weed, Aug. 1, 1831, Weed MSS.
2. Reprinted from the *New York Whig* in the *Albany Argus,* July 2, 1831.
3. Ellmaker to Seward, May 5, 1831, Seward MSS.

was to find a candidate acceptable to all of the anti-Jackson groups. Too strong an Antimason would repel the National Republicans and other groups opposed to Jackson, but a candidate unwilling to espouse the principles of Antimasonry might engender a revolt among the party's grass roots.

At one time or another six candidates were under consideration for the nomination—Henry Clay, John McLean, Richard Rush, John Quincy Adams, John C. Calhoun, and Daniel Webster. Each faced a dilemma not unlike that of the party, since Antimasonry was an emotional issue calculated to lose some votes whatever position they took in relation to it. Except for Adams, they had no deeply held opinion on the iniquity of Masonry. More important, support from the Antimasons alone was clearly insufficient to win the election. Only in conjunction with other and more substantial backing did the nomination have value, yet failure to receive Antimasonic support would kill the chances of any candidate competing against Jackson. These men wanted to keep the door to an Antimasonic nomination open, but avoid any obligation until they had lined up additional support. Granger's view of McLean as "anxious for our nomination as a mere political launch upon which to cruise around and see what other cargo he can take on board" could be applied to others with equal aptness.[4]

On the other hand it apparently never crossed the minds of the Antimasonic leaders, except when writing for public consumption, that the rank and file of the party or their delegates might actually designate the party's candidate. All of them, including those with the reputation of being fanatics, assumed that the choice would be made long before the Baltimore convention. The editor of the *Anti-Masonic Intelligencer* wrote with unintentional irony: "No man, no Antimason we mean, yet knows who will be the people's delegates to that Convention; and the Antimasons, poor fellows have no REGENCY of their own to tell them what they *must* do."[5] A waggish letter Seward received was more accurate: "I have made *up my* mind upon McLean & McLean it must be. . . . What says the Auburn Regency the Buffalo R. the Roch[ester] R.—The Weed Regency and all their combinations Collaterals and Ramifications. . . ."[6] The Antimasons had many Regencies, but they held conflicting opinions. By convention

4. Granger to Weed, Aug. 1, 1831, Weed MSS.
5. Dec. 7, 1830.
6. Samuel G. Andrews to Seward, undated, Seward MSS.

time they had resolved their differences, only to have their concert shattered by the last minute duplicity of the chosen candidate.

Any effort to defeat Jackson had to reckon first with Clay. His defeat for president in 1824 and that of Adams in 1828 did not lessen the ardor of his many friends for his elevation. Everyone assumed that he would challenge Jackson in 1832. The Antimasons were decidedly anti-Jackson and inclined to the American System. They were strong in the middle Atlantic states that Clay must carry to win. A decision of the Antis not to support him would be ruinous to his prospects. All that the leaders like Weed asked of Clay was a public declaration censuring secret societies, but this he was not ready to give.[7] Flagg had predicted in 1828 that Clay would "find the danger of playing with torches in a powder house" before he finished with Antimasonry.[8]

In view of the consequences that a hostile Antimasonry presented to his candidacy, Clay's handling of the party is difficult to understand. A possible explanation might be found in his personal involvement with Masonry. He had joined the fraternity in Virginia as a young man and after his transfer to Kentucky had participated actively in the Lexington lodge.[9] In Washington he manifested an occasional interest.[10] When the 1832 campaign was under way, Kentucky Masonic officials published depositions implying that Clay was no longer a member in good standing, but Clay never hinted that he questioned the morality of the organization.[11] On the contrary, Clay did not believe the accusations against Masonry and, hence, he had a low opinion of the Antimasonic party. Clay believed that its only object was power, that to obtain it Antimasons were willing to assume any posture, Jackson or anti-Jackson, that expediency dictated.[12] Other than advising

7. Weed, *Autobiography*, pp. 350–54.

8. Flagg to Wright, Mar. 16, 1828, Flagg MSS.

9. Bernard Mayo, *Henry Clay: Spokesman of the New West* (Boston, 1937), pp. 41, 118; Glyndon G. Van Deusen, *The Life of Henry Clay* (Boston, 1937), pp. 32, 70.

10. "Proceedings of a meeting of Masons in the U.S. Senate chamber on Mar. 9, 1822," and John N. Mouldon to Clay, Feb. 11, 1826, Clay MSS.

11. Statement of John Henry, secretary of Lexington Lodge No. 1 and H. J. Bodley, secretary of the Grand Lodge of Kentucky, signed Nov. 26, 1831, Luther Bradish Papers (New York Historical Society), cited hereafter as Bradish MSS; *Niles' Weekly Register*, XLI (Jan. 7, 1832), 346–47.

12. Clay to John Baihache, Nov. 24, 1830, Colton, *Private Correspondence*, p. 289.

his friends to refrain from attacking the party and to cooperate with Antimasons in local elections, he was not prepared to appease the blessed spirit. Masonry he pronounced harmless.[13] "He has no partiality for the order of masonry," Weed was informed by a friend who had conversed with Clay, "yet would not to insure his election to the Presidency publicly denounce it."[14]

Something more positive would be necessary to bring the Antis out for Clay. Relations between the Antimasons and the National Republicans in New York had been strained since 1828. In the fall of 1830 ill feelings were exacerbated by the results of the New York election for governor. Granger lost that contest because, in the opinion of many Antimasons, a large portion of the National Republicans ("Clay masons") preferred their defeat to victory over the Regency. "Their villainous conduct," Weed fumed, "has destroyed Clay. . . . We must now fight on our own hook."[15] Granger was also bitter. He hoped that "these new fangled Nation'l Reps." would run tickets in western New York because "their corporal's guard," when contrasted with Antimasonry, would "look like the *mouse* under the *mammouth* in Peale's museum."[16]

Party newspapers took up the cudgels against Clay, attacking his candidacy as the work of Masons hoping to reelect Jackson by dividing the opposition since they knew the Antimasons would never go for Clay. The *Albany Evening Journal* reprinted anti-Clay editorials from other newspapers calling for the nomination of an open and decided Antimason.[17] County conventions passed resolutions to the same effect.[18] The New York state convention of February, 1831, meeting to appoint delegates to Baltimore, was clearly hostile to Clay. The delegates, in language too strong for Weed's taste, vigorously reaffirmed their intention never to nominate or support a Mason for any state or national office.[19] The Pennsylvania convention which met a few months later passed a similar resolution after barely defeating

13. Van Deusen, *Henry Clay*, pp. 241–42.
14. James Clark to Weed, Jan. 22, 1831, Weed MSS.
15. Weed to Granger, Nov. 11, 1830, Gideon and Francis Granger MSS.
16. Granger to Weed, Dec. 8, 1830, Weed MSS. Also, *Richmond Daily Whig*, Nov. 11, 12, 13, 1830.
17. *Albany Evening Journal*, Dec. 6, 7, 8, 1830; Jan. 10, Feb. 5, 1831; *Anti-Masonic Enquirer*, Nov. 30, 1830; Feb. 1, 8, 1831.
18. *Albany Evening Journal*, Feb. 9, 1831.
19. *Ibid.*, Feb. 18, Mar. 5, Nov. 19, 21, 26, 1831; Whittlesey to Weed, Mar. 15, 1831; George H. Boughton to Weed, Mar. 15, 1831, Weed MSS.

one which specifically instructed its delegates to the national convention not to vote for Clay.[20] Other state conventions were to echo these sentiments before the autumn. In June, 1831, Weed publicly renounced his preference for Clay as incompatible with Antimasonry.[21]

Despite this rebuff attempts were made up to the eve of the national convention to install Clay in the good graces of the party. In May, 1831, at a convention of manufacturers in New York City, Clay supporters tried unsuccessfully to negotiate with the Antimasons.[22] In early September a committee of Indiana Antimasons wrote him with a view to supporting him for the presidential nomination. Still loath to denounce Masonry, but anxious to avoid unnecessary offence, Clay did not answer the inquiry until after the Baltimore convention.[23] Finally, in a desperate maneuver just before the convention opened, Clay's two leading supporters in western New York, Peter B. Porter and William B. Rochester, castigated Masonry in severe language and recommended that it be abandoned. Clay, they said, shared their Antimasonic sentiments, but "the characteristic delicacy of his feelings" forbade him to announce it publicly as it "might be construed into an effort, on his part, to advance his well earned popularity by indirect means."[24]

No doubt Clay's belief that Antimasonry was a delusion outside the realm of politics was sincere, yet one wonders whether he would have remained intractable if he had believed the party barred his way to the White House. But he refused to treat its pretensions as a serious threat to his own. He was not certain that the Antimasons could find a suitable person disposed to accept their nomination and, if they did, the hopelessness of their cause would force them to abandon him before the election, "virtually if not formally." "Upon the whole," he complacently confided to Francis Brooke, "I do not apprehend any serious mischief from it."[25] He was not even convinced that the leaders wanted

20. *Proceedings of the Anti-Masonic State Convention, Held at Harrisburg, on the 25th of May, 1831*, n.p., n.d.; *Niles' Weekly Register*, XL (June 4, 1831), 237.

21. *Albany Evening Journal*, June 4, 1831. Seward came to the same conclusion in March. Letter of Mar. 3, 1831, Seward, *Autobiography*, p. 184.

22. James A. Hamilton, *Reminiscences* (New York, 1869), p. 220.

23. *Niles' Weekly Register*, XL (Dec. 3, 1831), 260; *Albany Argus*, Dec. 6, 1831, from the *Baltimore Republican*.

24. Correspondence between a group of Masons and Rochester, Porter, reprinted in *Daily National Intelligencer*, Oct. 5, 1831, from the *Buffalo Journal*.

25. Clay to Brooke, June 23, 1831, Colton, *Private Correspondence*, p. 304. Also, Clay to Adam Beatty, June 25, 1831; Clay to Brooke, July 18, Oct. 4, 1831, *ibid.*, pp. 305–6, 316.

a nominee; they were only going through the motions in order to satisfy their followers. If they did make a nomination after all, "our friends," he wrote to Senator Josiah S. Johnston of Louisiana, "should not be deterred from raising their own presidential standard." The folly of dividing the opponents of Jackson and the numerical superiority of the National Republicans would result, if the Antimasons were not abused, in a union of the two forces under his banner.[26]

Even assuming Clay could unite the Antimasons and National Republicans, it was unlikely that he would attract Jacksonian support. McLean could. This made him, from the Antimasonic point of view, a more desirable nominee. He had political lines out to a number of groups, in addition to his personal strength in Ohio and the West. He was an admirer and protégé of Calhoun and had served the South Carolinian's interests as postmaster-general under Monroe. Although retained by Adams, he had used his position to aid Jackson in 1828. After the election he found himself in conflict with the president-elect, but Jackson, reluctant to break with him, appointed him to a Supreme Court vacancy.[27] For a man with presidential ambitions, McLean was almost ideally situated with ties to three major political factions and a perch overlooking the battle. His friends began to encourage his aspirations immediately after Jackson's election. "The delicacy of Genl. Jacksons health—the sudden and severe cramp, to which he is subject (in the body)," made it unlikely that he would survive his term, a close associate wrote McLean a few days after the inauguration. The Ohioan, he said, was the obvious choice to succeed the president.[28] McLean did not discourage these suggestions and as the election of 1832 approached he fancied himself the choice of a great nonpartisan coalition for the presidency.[29]

Inevitably, McLean attracted the attention of the Antimasons.[30] The

26. Clay to Johnston, July 23, 1831, Colton, *ibid.*, pp. 206–9.

27. McLean to J. W. Taylor, July 2, 1829, McLean MSS.

28. M. T. Simpson to McLean, Mar. 11, 1829, *ibid*. Also, John Agg to McLean, Dec. 5, 1828; W. L. Prall to McLean, Dec. 28, 1828; McLean to Prall, Dec. 31, 1828; James M. Gazlay to McLean, Feb. 12, 1830; M. Langhorne to McLean, Mar. 21, 1829; Z. M. Reynolds to McLean, Apr. 10, 1829; Chester Bailey to McLean, June 8, 1829, *ibid*.

29. Francis P. Weisenburger, *The Life of John McLean: A Politician on the United States Supreme Court* (Columbus, 1937), pp. 68–74; Ebner Malcolm Carroll, *Origins of the Whig Party* (Durham, 1925), pp. 40–44, 134.

30. M. T. Simpson to McLean, Dec. 28, 1829; B. W. Richards to McLean, Feb. 4, 1830, McLean MSS.

chairman of the Pennsylvania central committee wrote to him in May, 1830, for his opinions on Masonry. McLean replied that he was not a member of the society and being ignorant of Masonic principles could "neither approve nor condemn them."[31] He was fearful this equivocal response might eliminate him from consideration, but his friends assured him that he had taken the wisest course—only a few fanatics in the party wanted to nominate an avowed Antimason; the majority realized that moderation was necessary to win votes outside the fold.[32] McLean continued to straddle the issue, desirous of retaining the Antimasons' good will, but refusing to identify himself with the party. He was "in principle opposed, to all combinations of men, under whatever name or profession who attempt to [con]trol the public will, for the attainment of [self]ish objects," but he was quite as hesitant as Clay to apply this condemnation specifically to Masonry or to proscribe Masons as unfit for public office. The whole question, he maintained, had nothing to do with politics.[33]

When Whittlesey learned that McLean was not a Mason he was delighted, informing Weed that he was "a President ready made to our hands . . . ."[34] But the more single-minded among the faithful were less enthusiastic. After all, McLean's position did not differ materially from that of Clay; only the fact that McLean was not a Mason made him more acceptable. Dissatisfaction with a McLean nomination became formidable when alternatives appeared.

In the spring and summer of 1831 two prominent politicians aligned themselves unequivocally on the Antimasonic side. Each resided in an area of Antimasonic strength outside of New York and each became the favorite of local Antimasons who pressured the New Yorkers to give up McLean for their honest man.

Pennsylvania Antimasons were inevitably appreciative when Richard Rush took up their cause. His record of service to the Republican party and the nation was lengthy and illustrious. He had recently been Secretary of the Treasury under Adams and had run for vice

31. George W. Harris, Francis Wayatt to McLean, May, 1830; McLean to G. W. Harris, draft, May 24, 1830, *ibid.*

32. Elisha Whittlesey to McLean, June 9, 1830; M. T. Simpson to McLean, June 15, 1830; B. W. Richards to McLean, Sept. 20, 1830; Robert Hanna to McLean, Oct. 11, 1830, *ibid.*

33. McLean to Robert Hanna, Nov. 1, 1830; McLean to Cyrennus Gibbs, *et al.,* Oct. 31, 1830, *ibid.*

34. Whittlesey to Weed, July 6, 1830, Weed MSS.

president in 1828. In response to communications from Antimasonic committees he wrote a series of prolix letters during the spring of 1831 scoring Masonry in the harshest terms.[35] These letters were widely circulated and won Rush support not only from Pennsylvania Antimasons, but from the zealous everywhere. Ellmaker, for one, pressed Rush's claims on New York.[36] Pennsylvania, Seward told Weed, would insist on Rush's nomination; there was "a kind of Jacksonianism in Antimasonry which inclines us all to huzza for such a hero. . . ."[37] Holley, and others equally extreme, came out for the Pennsylvanian in opposition to McLean.[38] New England Antis "who seemed resolved, not to give their suffrages to any individual of equivocal or doubtful opinions" inclined to Rush, so Seward was informed.[39]

The opinion that McLean's expressions on Masonry were too weak to warrant nomination became widespread in the light of Rush's letters. Even Weed was swept up in the admiration for Rush's "more than Roman courage and patriotism."[40] He stated categorically that "McLean will not answer. He is anxious to be our candidate, but not on *exclusive* Anti-Masonic grounds. . . . Rush, as things now stand, is our man."[41] Seward agreed that McLean would have to go farther than give a "silent assent" to the nomination, but he questioned Rush's "political responsibility."[42] William H. Maynard, a state senator, and Albert H. Tracy shared his opinion of Rush.[43] They questioned his fitness for the presidency, suggesting that he was more suitable for the vice-presidential nomination. They still preferred McLean in deference to his superior talents and greater popularity.

35. Richard Rush, *Letter on Freemasonry to the Committee of the Citizens of York County, Pennsylvania* (Boston, 1831); *Boston Free Press—Extra*, May 20, 1831; *Letters of Rush, Adams, and Wirt* (Boston, 1831); *Albany Evening Journal*, Aug. 1, 1831.

36. Ellmaker to Seward, May 13, 1831, Seward MSS; Seward to Weed, June 22, 1831, Weed MSS.

37. Seward to Weed, July 19, 1831, Weed MSS.

38. Holley to Seward, June 6, 1831, Seward MSS; M. Cadwallader to Weed, June 21, 1831; P. C. Fuller to Weed, July 25, 1831; George H. Boughton to Weed, July 24, 1831, Weed MSS.

39. Seth Hunt to Seward, July 15, Aug. 6, 1831, Seward MSS.

40. Weed to Seward, June 18, 1831, *ibid.*

41. Weed to Seward, July 24, 1831, *ibid.*

42. Seward to Weed, June 22, 1831, Weed MSS.

43. William H. Maynard to Seward, May 31, 1831; Albert H. Tracy to Seward, June 2, 1831, Seward MSS; Seward to Weed, July 19, Aug. 2, 1831, Weed MSS.

The doubts as to Rush's reliability were, in retrospect, well founded. After dangling himself in front of the candidate-hungry party he withdrew as a candidate for either president or vice-president on the Antimasonic ticket in late July, 1831.[44] A few persons continued to push for his nomination for one or the other office despite his withdrawal, but there was no serious attempt to draft him prior to the convention itself.[45] Furthermore, Rush's vehement espousal of Antimasonry was, initially at least, a pose, part of a plan he concocted to lure Antimasonry into the Clay camp by using himself as stalking horse. He unveiled this scheme in a letter to James Barbour in the summer of 1830: "As soon as I get into Pennsylvania," he wrote, "all my efforts will be directed towards procuring the nomination of Mr. Clay by the Antimasonic convention, that is to meet in Philadelphia in September. I have already in my correspondence with Antimasons, (the confidance of some of whom I believe myself to possess) been recommending the obvious policy of this step under all present circumstances, even though Clay be a mason; and I shall follow up my efforts with all zeal and discretion when I get into the state."[46]

The following spring Rush asked Clay to conciliate the Antimasons because with their aid "we should carry your banner to glorious victory, even if we do not without."[47] The publication of his views on Masonry, he explained to Webster, would advance "the principles and cause of Mr. Clay among the Anti-Masons, by showing that one attached to both as I am, is nevertheless unequivocally in the A.M. faith on its main points."[48] But Rush was not even loyal to Clay. In August, 1831, he declared that the Antimasonic candidate could not be a Mason.[49] Shortly before the election he moved into the Jackson camp (over the Bank issue), using his great influence among Pennsylvania Antimasonry in an effort to prevent a coalition between the Antimasons and the National Republicans.[50]

The refusal of Rush to be considered for the nomination he had given every impression of seeking forced attention on another national

44. Ellmaker to Seward, Aug. 1, 1831, Seward MSS; *Niles' Weekly Register*, XL (Aug. 27, 1831), 453.

45. Myron Holley to Seward, Aug. 9, 1831; William H. Maynard to Seward, Aug. 12, 1831; Ellmaker to Seward, Aug. 5, 1831, Seward MSS.

46. Rush to Barbour, Aug. 7, 1830, Barbour MSS.

47. Rush to Clay, Apr. 14, 1831, Colton, *Private Correspondence*, p. 299.

48. Rush to Webster, May 19, 1831, Webster MSS. He wrote in a similar vein to Adams. See Bemis, *John Quincy Adams and the Union*, pp. 283–84.

49. *The Globe*, Aug. 29, 1831.

50. J. H. Powell, *Richard Rush: Republican Diplomat, 1780–1859* (Philadelphia, 1942), pp. 231–34.

figure who openly championed the Antimasonic side. If Adams's motives were not so devious as those of his former cabinet officer, neither were they completely frank nor disinterested.[51] Adams had maintained cordial relations with the Antimasons ever since the election of 1828; as the time neared for the party to nominate a candidate he increased his personal involvement in the movement. In May, 1831, he attended an Antimasonic state convention in Faneuil Hall.[52] He took a high view of the dangers of secret societies, declaring the issue was more important than whether Clay or Jackson was elected.[53]

Although Adams urged the nomination of Rush following the publication of his letters, he believed that a harmonious decision arrived at before the convention met was the most important consideration. Otherwise, "the fiend of Masonry would creep into the fold," and by taking advantage of party discords prevent a common nomination.[54] Suggestions that he should be that candidate were deflected with expressions of modest indifference.[55] After Rush's desertion, sentiment for Adams's nomination among New England Antimasons increased. In August, 1831, a committee composed of the two leading Antimasons of Massachusetts called on Adams, proffered their support and asked him if he would decline the nomination. Adams replied that he "saw no necessity for declining any nomination which any one might be pleased to make," but he hoped his name would not be pressed if it appeared that someone else would be more likely to unify the party.[56]

The movement for Adams was not kindly received in New York, and Seward was sent northward to sound out the situation.[57] On September 14 he had a three-hour interview with Adams. While Seward was candid with Adams in discussing the prospects of the party, he did not tell him that the main purpose of his journey was to dissuade Adams's supporters from pushing his candidacy.[58] Adams told Seward

51. Bemis, *John Quincy Adams and the Union*, p. 281. Bemis's biography contains an excellent account of Adams's Antimasonic connections. See *ibid.*, pp. 273–98.
52. Adams, *Memoirs*, VIII (May 20, 31, June 2, 6, 1831), 363, 364–65, 366–67.
53. *Ibid.* (June 10, 1831), 368. His relations with his former supporters were far from cordial. He thought Clay should withdraw to make room for a fusion candidate. *Ibid.* (July 28, Aug. 25, 1831), 389, 400–401.
54. *Ibid.* (July 11, 1831), 380.
55. *Ibid.* (July 11, Aug. 6, 1831), 392–93.
56. *Ibid.* (Aug. 31, 1830), 403–4.
57. Seward to ———, Sept. 6, 1831, Seward, *Autobiography*, p. 198.
58. *Ibid.*, pp. 205–7; Adams, *Memoirs*, VIII (Sept. 14, 1831), 412–13; Seward to Weed, Sept. 14, 1831, Weed MSS.

that he blamed Clay for failing to conciliate the Antimasons; he was sorry that Rush had refused the nomination and that he was opposed to McLean. He also repeated his intention not to turn down the Antimasonic nomination. Seward was impressed by Adams's character and intelligence, but repelled by his cold manner: "[A]s I left the house, I thought I could plainly answer how it happened that he, the best President since Washington, entered and left the office with so few devoted personal friends."[59]

According to Samuel Flagg Bemis, Adams's indifference to the nomination was nothing more than his old pride. The former president earnestly wished to be nominated by the Antimasons in the hope that this would cause the National Republicans to abandon Clay and combine to defeat Jackson "under a Man of the Whole Nation. . . . Only he must not lift a finger for the office. He must await a Call."[60] But there would be no Call. New York Antimasons were not eager to nominate a candidate who bore the stigma of political ineptitude and defeat. They were ambitious enough to think that they could win.

Seward reported to Weed that nothing could be done to prevent the Massachusetts and Rhode Island delegations from going to Baltimore committed to Adams. McLean was disliked in New England because of his association with Calhoun. Happily, the delegates would not insist on Adams's nomination once they discovered in Baltimore that New York did not second them. The New Englanders "will yield to discussion with New York to be conducted on our part upon the disastrous operation of Mr. Adams' nomination upon our cause in that state."[61]

Another citizen of Boston received occasional mention as an Antimasonic nominee. Webster's name was suggested as one that would be the most likely to entice Clay supporters into a union of forces as both men were identified with the protective tariff.[62] Webster was interested, but he never received any sustained encouragement from influential party leaders.

There was one other possibility. Calhoun had hoped to succeed Jackson when the president's first term expired, but Jackson's determination to run again, the estrangement between the two men, and the ascendancy of Van Buren within the administration made it most

59. Seward, *Autobiography*, pp. 206–7.
60. Bemis, *John Quincy Adams and the Union*, p. 292.
61. Seward to Weed, Sept. 14, 1831, Weed MSS.
62. Seth Hunt to Seward, Aug. 31, 1831, Seward MSS.

unlikely he would receive the presidential nod. Still, Calhoun could conceivably gain the White House if he could compound Antimasonic support in the North with his southern backing. In 1829 he had reportedly written to one of his lieutenants in western New York, Christopher Van Deventer, condemning Masonry and applauding Antimasonry.[63] Somewhat later, word came back from Antimasonic congressmen in Washington that Calhoun talked like an Antimason.[64] In May, 1831, Calhoun declared in a letter to Van Deventer that Masonry was worse than useless; it was pernicious. At the same time he attempted to discourage the party from supporting McLean.[65] Duff Green, always busy in his master's interest, made an expedition to the North in September to drum up Antimasonic aid for the South Carolinian.[66]

Calhoun was reluctant to make an open declaration of his Antimasonry.[67] But this lack of candor was less of an obstacle to his preferment than the growing acrimony over the tariff. Seward had written in March, 1831, that "the stain of nullification is too black upon his record to justify any belief that he can receive our support."[68] Even so, he had his partisans. Granger believed him the strongest candidate while John C. Spencer of New York preferred him to all others.[69] By Weed's reckoning a Calhoun nomination would carry as many as four southern states for the Antimasonic cause and add strength in New York City as well.[70]

But Calhoun's plausibility as the nominee vanished when the rhetoric sharpened during a flare-up in the tariff controversy late in 1831.

63. Spencer to Van Buren, June 22, 1829, Van Buren MSS (NYSL); Henry O'Rielly to Flagg, Nov. 11, 1829, Flagg MSS.
64. Whittlesey to Weed, Jan. 27, 1830; Timothy Childs to Weed, Jan. 27, 1830, Weed MSS.
65. Calhoun to Van Deventer, May 25, 1831, Jameson, *Correspondence of Calhoun*, p. 293.
66. John L. Adriance to Weed, July 29, 1831; D. Russell to Weed, Sept. 13, 1831, Weed MSS; M. T. Simpson to McLean, July 13, 1831, McLean MSS; Charles M. Wiltse, *John C. Calhoun: Nullifier, 1820–1839* (Indianapolis, 1949), p. 121.
67. Calhoun to Van Deventer, Aug. 5, 1831, Jameson, *Correspondence of Calhoun*, p. 296.
68. Seward to ———, Mar. 5, 1831, Seward, *Autobiography*, p. 184.
69. Granger to Weed, Aug. 1, 1831; Seward to Weed, Aug. 2, 1831; P. C. Fuller to Weed, July 25, 1831, Weed MSS; ——— to S. L. Gouvernor, Apr. 3, 1831, Gouvernor MSS. Spencer, son of Ambrose Spencer, had been won over to Antimasonry while serving as Special Counsel in the Morgan case.
70. Weed to Seward, July 4, 1831, Seward MSS; *Albany Evening Journal*, June 28, 1831.

The Fort Hill Address published in early September made his position in favor of nullification unmistakable.[71] Even without this declaration, it is doubtful that the convention would have dared to nominate so strong an anti-tariff man. Calhoun's nomination would alienate, as Seward pointed out, the very states Antimasonry expected to carry. It was in "the free the cold, clean intelligent North" that Antimasonry must succeed or fail.[72]

In September, as the delegates made their way to Baltimore, McLean and not Calhoun was still the man most frequently mentioned as the likely nominee.[73] Despite his hesitancy to declare himself a candidate or to avow his adherence to the principles of Antimasonry, McLean had been from the start the choice of the New York directors. During the winter and spring of 1831 they gave him a build-up in the party press.[74] Weed momentarily wavered, but Rush's withdrawal again made him the most available candidate. Adams and Calhoun were politically impossible. Yet McLean's irresolution continued to cause his advocates some uneasiness over whether he would accept the nomination.[75]

Guarantees were sought that McLean would not disappoint the convention. As he seemed unwilling to commit himself in writing, Albert Tracy made a special trip to Ohio in order to reach a verbal understanding. Tracy reported on his return near the end of July that he found the judge ardent to be president, but afraid Antimasonry could not elect him. McLean did agree not to decline the nomination or do anything inconsistent with his position as head of the party. His convictions regarding Antimasonry Tracy found at best lukewarm. "Still he talks sensibly and reasonably," Tracy related to Seward, "as an ambitious man having friends on both sides well could do and I have no doubt will answer our purposes exceedingly well." McLean's name on the ticket would help the party in the coming fall elections in New York and Pennsylvania while a Rush nomination would fasten

71. Wiltse, *John C. Calhoun: Nullifier*, pp. 121–22; Arthur Styron, *The Cast Iron Man: John C. Calhoun and American Democracy* (New York, 1935), pp. 162–64.

72. Seward to Weed, Aug. 2, 1831, Weed MSS.

73. Samuel H. Hopkins to Seward, Sept. 9, 1831, Seward MSS; *Albany Evening Journal*, Sept. 22, 24, 29, 1831; *Albany Argus*, Sept. 24, 1831.

74. *Albany Evening Journal*, Jan. 20, Mar. 4, 9, 22, May 12, 1831; *Anti-Masonic Enquirer*, Feb. 1, 1831.

75. Seward to Weed, July 19, 1831, Weed MSS; Warren Jenkins to McLean, July 17, 1831; James Bradford to McLean, Aug., 1831, McLean MSS.

"old Adamsism" on the party and bring sure defeat. Unless the party intended "to abandon policy altogether and go for the naked principle of our *Praise God Barebones* votaries we *must* make McLean our candidate—"[76]

The "votaries" were far from satisfied with the results of Tracy's mission. Ward and his colleagues on the national committee wanted something more and they wanted it in writing. In August they sought out Benjamin W. Richards, a close friend of McLean, in Philadelphia, to impress upon the coy candidate the necessity of appeasing the zealous Antis as a condition of nomination.[77] Ward asked that in the administration of the government and the appointment of men to office McLean, if elected president, would ignore "the narrow prejudices which find talents and worth chiefly in one combination of men . . . ."[78]

All Ward sought was a pledge that McLean would appoint some non-Masons to federal offices. But when Weed and others of his school discovered what Ward had done, they were disturbed lest Ward's clumsy efforts might offend McLean and cause him to withdraw. Weed wrote at once to the putative candidate: "I have just read the correspondence, the character and tone of which, on the part of Mr. Ward and the Committee, is alike painful and mortifying. The Committee, in opening such a correspondence, wholly mistook the nature of their duties and the objects of their appointment. It was an act of superarrogation, and is so regarded by all the gentlemen (messers Maynard, Whittlesey, Seward and Hopkins of our Senate, now sitting as a Court of Errors) to whom it was read." The national committee members, Weed explained, were sincere but inexperienced. "No pledges or publications were desired or thought of." They were quite satisfied with the promise he had given Tracy. The election prospects, he assured McLean, were good—the Antimasons would certainly carry Pennsylvania, New York, and Vermont, and, if Clay withdrew, "as we all think he must," then a great many more.[79]

76. Tracy to Seward, July 25, 1831, Seward MSS.

77. Richards to McLean, Aug. 13, 1831, McLean MSS. Richards was mayor of Philadelphia. McLean's daughter married an Augustus Richards, also of Philadelphia, whom I suspect from the nature of their correspondence was the mayor's son. *United States Telegraph*, Apr. 17, 1829; Oct. 22, 1831.

78. Ward to Richards, copy, Aug. 10, 1831, McLean MSS. This letter was written for transmission to McLean.

79. Weed to McLean, Aug. 23, 1831; B. W. Richards to McLean, Sept. 8, 1831, McLean MSS.

As the Antimasonic party prepared to hold its second national convention, the success it had obtained during its brief existence was a cause for self-congratulation. No surer sign of this could be found than the names of the politicians willing to flirt for its favor. The party was now "courted by men, who, three months ago, regarded us as things of nought," observed one member proudly.[80] The *Albany Evening Journal* noted with obvious satisfaction that not long ago the opposition had maintained that the party would not be able to persuade a single man of eminence to accept their nomination. "But they have since been willing to admit, that Mr. Rush would consent—then Mr. Adams, and then Mr. M'Lane, and by the grumbling in a late Masonic Mirror against Mr. Webster, and his declaration as to Masonry, it is evident they recon [*sic*] him of the same class."[81]

This boasting proved premature. Waiting in Baltimore for the delegates was a letter from McLean declining to be considered for the nomination. His acceptance of the nomination given orally to Tracy in July had been, he wrote, conditional. Now the public interest compelled him to withdraw. Jackson, Clay, and Calhoun were already before the public. The addition of a fourth name would further distract the public mind and render a decision by the people unlikely at a time when the administration of the national government required public confidence. In any event his judicial position disqualified him from entering the contest "unless the use of his name would be likely to tranquilise the public mind, and advance the prosperity of the country."[82] McLean's high-minded refusal to involve the bench in politics was gross hypocrisy. Not only had he cultivated support from every part of the political spectrum, just two years previously he had written an article vigorously upholding the right of judges to run for president as men uniquely qualified for the office.[83]

McLean's fear of distracting the public mind was undoubtedly exceeded by his fear of losing an election. As long as the possibility of merging the nomination of the Antimasons with the support of the

80. Orville L. Holley to John M. Bailey, Aug. 10, 1831, Myron Holley Papers (New York State Library), cited hereafter as Holley MSS.

81. *Albany Evening Journal*, Sept. 21, 1831.

82. *Ibid.*, Sept. 30, 1831, from the *Journal of Commerce; Niles' Weekly Register*, XLI (Dec. 3, 1831), 259-60. McLean apparently wrote similar letters to a number of people. The earliest was dated Sept. 7 and was addressed to Albert H. Tracy, postmarked Nashville.

83. "Sketch in reference to remarks in the Camden Journal—Judge Story—13 Aug. 1829," McLean MSS.

National Republicans remained alive, he made himself available. This was the theme of the letters he received from his agents and his own inquiries.[84] "As a *secondary* support to an individual nominated on political and more elevated principles," Samuel L. Gouvernor wrote McLean, "it's support would indeed be powerful. As presenting a primary & *leading* principle for a nomination, its power is materially lessened—"[85] By the time McLean made his decision not to accept the offer of the Antimasons every sign indicated that he would receive no other. Jackson, Clay, and Calhoun had cut the ground from under him. If future circumstances warranted abandoning the security of the Supreme Court, a nomination by the Antimasons might prove an embarrassment.[86]

The convention was scheduled to open at noon on Monday, September 26. McLean's letter apparently did not reach its destination until the day before. The consternation of the Antimasonic leaders on receiving it can scarcely be imagined.[87] But they were resourceful men. Its contents were not disclosed while they attempted to repair the damage. A messenger was sent to Philadelphia to talk with B. W. Richards to discover what McLean would do if he were nominated despite his withdrawal. Seward wrote Richards imploring him to come to Baltimore to counteract the effect of McLean's letter.[88] In case the nominaton of McLean proved infeasible, a special courier was dispatched to Rush at his home in nearby York, pleading for permission to use his name.[89] And negotiations were opened with prominent men in Baltimore, among them the former attorney general, William Wirt.[90]

84. B. W. Richards to McLean, June 11, 24, July 28, Sept. 8, 1831; M. T. Simpson to McLean, July 1, Aug. 26, 1831, McLean MSS; Adams, *Memoirs*, VIII (Apr. 20, 1830), 358; Weisenberger, *Life of McLean*, pp. 70–76.

85. Gouvernor to McLean, Sept. 9, 1831, McLean MSS.

86. Richards to McLean, Oct. 1, 1831; P. Bradley to McLean, Oct. 6, 1831, *ibid*.

87. Seward, *Autobiography*, p. 89.

88. Richards to McLean, Oct. 1, 1831, McLean MSS.

89. *Daily National Journal*, Sept. 28, 1831; *Albany Evening Journal*, Sept. 30, 1831, from the *Journal of Commerce;* Rush to McLean, Sept. 27, 1831, McLean MSS.

90. Seward later implied that John Marshall, then in the city, and Charles Carroll of Carrollton were considered for the nomination, but this is difficult to credit. Carroll, although celebrated as the last surviving signer of the Declaration of Independence, would not have made at the age of ninety-four a likely candidate. Marshall had just observed his seventy-fourth birthday and was in poor health. Had the Antimasons, in their desperation, been willing to settle for a "name" without any thought of winning the election they could have fallen back on Adams. Seward, *Autobiography*, p. 90.

Meanwhile, the delegates were arriving in town. As reported by a correspondent of the Washington *National Journal*, the scene at this first national nominating convention differed remarkably little from that of later conventions: "Nothing can exceed the bustle and confusion in this city. Stage after stage, and hack after hack, from the Steamboats, driving to Barnum's, and greeted with the shout—'all full'—then posting away to Beltzhover's to receive the same irritating information. . . . and finally, by way of especial favor, permitted to discharge their freight at Lyford's. . . . Anti-Masonry has done something for Baltimore, whatever it might do for the Union."[91]

On Monday morning the convention opened in "the long room" of the Athenaeum. The physical arrangements for the convention had been taken care of by Ward in the summer on behalf of the national committee.[92] Approximately 120 delegates were present. Most of the states represented, and many of the delegates, were the same ones that had been at Philadelphia.[93] Maine, Delaware, and New Hampshire were fresh additions, but the Michigan territory was missing. A delegate accredited from Maryland was actually a spectator representing no one but himself.[94] All of the delegations, except those from Delaware and New Hampshire, had been chosen at state conventions.

The Baltimore convention also bore a strong resemblance in its organization to its predecessor. A committee "to lay before the Convention the subjects proper for its consideration" was appointed which prescribed the entire agenda of the convention. The rules and orders of the Philadelphia convention were adopted. The chief benefit it derived from previous experience was the greater efficiency of the second convention. It was better organized, more tightly run, less subject to delays from the floor, and lasted half as long. The only thing peculiar to the Baltimore proceedings was the nomination of candidates. Here the procedure was consistent with the practices of state and local conventions, but done with a bit more flourish.

The committee on business recommended that six committees be appointed, all similar to those at Philadelphia. In addition it requested the national committee to make a report on the progress of Anti-

91. *Daily National Journal*, Sept. 27, 1831.
92. Ward to Weed, Aug. 8, 1831, Weed MSS (NYHS).
93. *The Proceedings of the Second United States Antimasonic Convention, Held at Baltimore, September 1831* (Boston, 1832); *Niles' Weekly Register*, XLI (Oct. 1, 8, 1831), 83–85, 107–10.
94. *Baltimore Republican*, Sept. 30, 1831; Shultz, *Freemasonry in Maryland*, II, 19.

masonry during the past year. It also recommended that the convention go into a committee of the whole the next day for the nomination of candidates for president and vice-president and "that the votes be taken by ballot, separately for each of these candidates, and that the votes of three-fourths of all the members present, be considered necessary to constitute a choice." Why the committee advocated the adoption of a three-fourths rule is not clear. The requirement of more than a simple majority for nomination had not been the practice in state or local conventions. In a number of state constitutions a two-thirds or three-fourths vote was required to enact certain classes of legislation, but the similarity between these provisions and the nomination of candidates was not great enough to constitute a precedent.

A more reasonable explanation for the adoption of the rule lies in the emphasis which the party leaders placed upon harmony. Possibly, the committee believed that this rule would prevent the convention from breaking in two. Or, it may have been sensitive to the fact that Pennsylvania and New York controlled well over half of the delegates and wished to avoid accusations of dictation by these two giants. Perhaps it was simply to let the nation and the party's rank and file see how united the delegates were. The danger that the rule itself would become a source of division was avoided by arriving at a consensus beforehand.

On Monday evening after the convention adjourned a committee that included Weed, Spencer, and Abner Phelps called on Wirt.[95] Wirt regretted in later months the occasion which brought these men to his home. Although he had a distinguished public career behind him, having served for twelve years as attorney general under Monroe and Adams, he did not find politics congenial. At the bar his reputation was unexcelled. As a man of letters he had been dubbed the "American Goethe," but the resemblance was more physical than literary even though his life of Patrick Henry, *The Letters of a British Spy*, and other essays had been well received.[96] After retiring from the Adams

95. Weed, *Autobiography*, p. 390. Weed lists Albert H. Tracy as a member of the group, but Tracy was not a delegate to the convention and two observers mention the fact that, because of illness, he was not present. (Richards to McLean, Oct. 1, 1831; Warren Jenkins to McLean, April 23, 1832, McLean MSS.) There was a Phineas L. Tracy in the New York delegation, but nothing indicates his inclusion on the committee.

96. Thomas P. Abernathy's article in the *Dictionary of American Biography*, XX, 418–21, is the best brief account of Wirt's life and career. See also John P. Kennedy, *Memoirs of the Life of William Wirt*, 2 vols., 2nd ed. (New

administration he had devoted his talents to the law, yet had not totally divorced himself from politics. He was an ornament of the National Republican party and had been chosen a delegate to its national convention in December. At the time of the Antimasonic convention he was reportedly at work on the Address of the National Republican convention.[97]

Wirt's eminence, his close identification with the Clay partisans, who were said to have him under consideration for vice-president, and, above all, his presence in Baltimore conspired to make him a suitable candidate.[98] Had the convention met in Boston, New York, or anywhere except in Baltimore, Wirt very likely would not have been thought of for the nomination. His name came into consideration only on the receipt of McLean's letter. The committee made an offer that evening to Wirt's astonishment.[99] His acceptance was delayed by his reluctance to act in a manner inconsistent with his obligations to the National Republican party and to Clay.

His youthful connection with Masonry presented no obstacle, the committee members assured him. They skillfully exploited Wirt's conviction that the nation must be saved from Jackson, which could only be done, he was told, through the union of the opposition on a single candidate. It was out of the question for the Antimasons to nominate Clay, but the National Republicans would support the Antimasonic candidate if Wirt consented to their request. Granger, not Clay, would get the nomination if he declined. Only he could concentrate the two parties. Patriotism required him to accept the nomination. As a citizen, he had no right to refuse the call of a half a million countrymen.

To this heady brew the committee added the usual tales of Masonic conspiracy, embellished with a new twist calculated to appeal to Wirt's southern sensibilities. Negro Masonic groups existed in Boston, Baltimore, and Washington. The committee had no doubt there were "simi-

---

York, 1866); Frederick William Thomas, *John Randolph of Roanoke, and Sketches of Character, Including William Wirt* (Philadelphia, 1853), pp. 33–46; Benjamin F. Perry, *Biographical Sketches of Eminent American Statesmen* (Philadelphia, 1887), pp. 526–34; Margaret Bayard Smith, *The First Forty Years of Washington Society*, ed. Gaillard Hunt (New York, 1906), pp. 244, 316–17.

97. Nathan Sargent, *Public Men and Events* (Philadelphia, 1875), I, 187.

98. George H. Boughton to Weed, Jan. 29, 1832, Weed MSS; *Daily National Intelligencer*, Aug. 1, Sept. 8, 1831.

99. Wirt to Dabney Carr, Sept. 30, 1831, William Wirt Papers (Library of Congress), cited hereafter as Wirt MSS.

lar *black lodges* in Richmond, Charleston, & throughout the Southern states—&, if not, that they may be very easily organized, & thus open a channel of intercourse & concerted insurrection & murder throughout the whole country. . . ."[100] The host expressed interest and promised to inform them of his decision the next day.

When the convention convened on Tuesday the lack of a candidate forced a postponement of the nominations until Wednesday.[101] That evening, September 27, an unofficial and informal meeting of the delegates convened to decide what should be done. At this caucus some of the delegates learned for the first time of McLean's refusal. They may also have been told of Rush's fresh rejection of the nomination. Wirt in the meantime had sent permission for his name to be considered.[102] But the delegates had come prepared to nominate McLean while Wirt's Masonic connection was looked upon with disapproval. Many did not want to give up McLean and tried to force his nomination. "[T]here were those who contended, strongly and ingeniously that the letter did not contain a refusal to accept the nomination," a participant in the caucus told McLean, "but a *wish*, that the nomination might not be made, & that notwithstanding that was your *wish*, & desire yet that you would not refuse to yield your wish to the will of the people."[103] So argued Thaddeus Stevens and Harmar Denny of Pennsylvania, claiming "personal knowledge of Judge McLean's private sentiments. . . ."[104] Others "hinted" that McLean wanted to create the impression of having the nomination "*forced*" on him because it would put him in a better position to receive the nomination of the National Republicans.[105]

The disagreement in the caucus was sharp. The McLean faction was vociferously led by Stevens and seconded by other important figures such as Ward. They were backed by most of the Pennsylvania and Ohio delegations and a portion of the New York delegates. Weed's moderates upheld Wirt, although the Rochester editor did not take

100. Wirt to William H. Cabell, copy, Oct. 3, 1831; Wirt to Dabney Carr, copy, Sept. 30, 1831; Wirt to David Briggs, copy, Oct. 2, 1831; Wirt to Thomas Swann, copy, Oct. 3, 1831, Wirt MSS; Wirt to Salmon P. Chase, Nov. 11, 1831, Kennedy, *Memoirs of Wirt*, pp. 311–12.

101. *Proceedings of the Second United States Anti-Masonic Convention, Held at Baltimore, September, 1831*, p. 14.

102. Weed, *Autobiography*, pp. 390–91; Seward, *Autobiography*, p. 90.

103. Warren Jenkins to McLean, Apr. 23, 1832, McLean MSS.

104. *Baltimore Republican*, Oct. 8, 1831.

105. *Ibid.*

a leading part in the debate. Abner Phelps of Boston put the case for the Marylander. The Wirt contingent, composed of the New England bloc and most of the New York delegates, denounced McLean as "a selfish small intriguer. . . ."[106] The Stevens group thought Wirt "too recent a convert" whose nomination would ruin their prospects in the coming elections. This was countered by the assertion that Wirt's nomination would compel the National Republicans to abandon Clay, thus leaving the Antimasons in sole possession of the opposition to Jackson.[107]

Not until 2 A.M. did the caucus resolve the disagreement. To prevent a schism in the convention when balloting for the record the next day, the caucus conducted a poll of the delegates present. It was decided that a three-fourths vote, just as for the regular proceedings, would be required to designate the nominee. Whoever won in the caucus would then be supported by all at the formal session.[108] There were 105 delegates present, but a large number did not vote on every ballot. On the first ballot, Wirt received 38 votes to McLean's 41, with 5 for Granger, 2 for Webster, and 5 ballots scattered or blank. Wirt moved ahead of McLean on the second ballot, 46 votes to 26, but was still far short of the required number. The third ballot saw Wirt gain 4 votes while his chief opponent lost 7. On the next and final ballot he quickly shot over the top with 94 votes.[109]

Despite the fact that he had written not one but several letters declining the nomination, despite the declaration of a close friend who had recently spoken to him that the intention of his letter was to put his name "totally out of the question," McLean had nearly a majority of the delegates behind him at the start of the poll. Only "the trickery of the Yankees" prevented his nomination, Richards told McLean. The New Englanders (who bore no love for the Ohioan) had supported Wirt, he related, in exchange for a promise to appoint Webster Secretary of the Treasury.[110]

Even the vote of the caucus did not quite end the matter. A few

---

106. *Ibid.*
107. *Ibid.*
108. *Daily National Intelligencer,* Oct. 19, 1831, from the *Rhode Island American* (whose editor was a delegate to the convention).
109. McLean had 9 votes, Granger and Rush 1 each on this last ballot.
110. Richards to McLean, Oct. 1, 1831, McLean MSS. Seward had written Richards that he must come to Baltimore in order to counteract the effect of McLean's letter. Richards could not go, although he was anxious for McLean to be nominated, but he did send his son.

diehards, chief among them Thaddeus Stevens, refused to acquiesce in the decision, and there was apprehension "that the convention would explode the next day by a refusal to nominate Mr. Wirt or by a fatal division on that question."[111] To Seward fell the assignment of reconciling the dissidents, and the argument lasted into the early hours of the morning. Stevens, "unreasonable and impracticable," went to bed as adamant as ever in a room shared by the New Yorker. The next morning Seward was surprised to find him "entirely calm and undisturbed," quite willing to permit Wirt's nomination.[112]

On Wednesday the convention officially made its nominations without the benefit of nominating speeches or even an announcement of who the candidates were. The roll was called and each delegate, rising after his name was read, walked to a table in the center of the hall, where he deposited his ballot in a box. At the conclusion of the roll one teller read aloud the contents of each ballot while another kept the tally. Out of 111 cast Wirt received all but 3. Rush had 1 vote and 2 were blank. On Stevens's motion the nomination of Wirt was declared unanimous and three persons were appointed to inform the nominee of their decision and request his acceptance.[113]

The vice-presidential nomination followed the same procedure. Ellmaker received the identical vote as Wirt. Like Wirt, he had not been discussed previous to the convention's opening as a potential candidate. The preconvention discussion of vice-presidential candidates had been based on the assumption that either Rush or McLean would be nominated for the first office in which case New York was marked as the most likely source for the vice-president.[114] Several persons were mentioned. Granger was the favorite of some, but he was not available. Maynard, Tracy, and Whittlesey received consideration as did John C. Spencer. Seward and Tracy were opposed to Spencer on grounds that he was neither a skillful nor reliable politician. Seward preferred his good friend Tracy, but the former congressman declined and Whittlesey was too unknown. As convention time neared, interest focused on Levi Lincoln, the governor of Massachusetts, who occa-

111. Seward, *Autobiography*, p. 90.
112. *Ibid.*, pp. 90–91.
113. *Proceedings of the Second United States Anti-Masonic Convention, Held at Baltimore, September 1831*, p. 59.
114. Seward to Weed, July 19, Aug. 2, 8, Sept. 10, 14, 1831, Weed MSS; Weed to Seward, July 24, 1831; Tracy to Seward, Sept. 19, 1831; Seth Hunt to Seward, Sept. 19, 1831, Seward MSS; *Albany Evening Journal*, Sept. 13, 1831.

sionally made Antimasonic sounds although a member of the National Republican party. Seward had expected while in Boston in September to advance this project as a means of consoling New England Antimasons for New York's disapproval of Adams. But Lincoln left town before Seward arrived and the necessary arrangements could not be made before the convention met.

Just prior to the balloting Spencer was rumored as the likely choice.[115] No reasons were ever assigned for the last minute switch. Ellmaker's nomination had a certain logic behind it. As former attorney general of Pennsylvania, he was the best known and most reputable leader from a swing state.[116] His zeal in the cause complemented Wirt's coolness. Yet the same could have been said of Spencer. It seems certain that the decision was made off the floor before the roll call. Perhaps Seward's distrust of Spencer prevailed. More likely, the nomination of Ellmaker bore some relation to the bitter caucus of the previous evening when a portion of the Pennsylvania delegation had so vehemently opposed Wirt. More than a good night's sleep might account for Stevens's unexpected amiability.

The convention completed its work during the remainder of the day. Copies of the proceedings were directed to be sent to the executive officers of the national and state governments, former presidents, Supreme Court justices, the mayor of Baltimore, the trustees of the Athenaeum, Charles Carroll, and the Marquis de la Fayette. In its opening session the convention had sought to secure maximum coverage of the proceedings by reserving a special section of the hall for newspaper reporters. The committee on resolutions reported its handiwork for adoption, followed by the report of the committee appointed to wait on the presidential nominee.

They returned bearing a letter of acceptance.[117] At least the convention credited it with being an acceptance. Wirt confessed that previous to the convention he had regarded Antimasonry as an agency of "the vindictive purposes of party proscription and persecution. . . ." He was himself a Mason, and, although inactive for more than thirty years, he had never had reason to believe its members

115. Seth Hunt to Seward, Oct. 3, 1831, Seward MSS; *Albany Evening Journal*, Sept. 30, 1831, from the *Journal of Commerce*.

116. Ellmaker earlier in his career had declined a seat on the Pennsylvania Supreme Court and an offer from Monroe to become Secretary of the Navy. *Daily National Intelligencer*, Oct. 7, 1831.

117. *Proceedings of the Second United States Anti-Masonic Convention, Held at Baltimore, September, 1831*, pp. 63–67.

180 Emergence of the Presidential Nominating Convention

vicious. He had always been "more disposed to smile than to frown" on its mummeries, regarding both Masonry and Antimasonry "as a fitter subject for farce than tragedy. . . ." But the convention, he informed the delegates, had revealed to him the dangers of Masonry. The Morgan case proved that the foolish words of the ritual were meant to be taken literally. Still, he could not believe that the many honorable men, including Washington, who had been or were yet members accepted their oaths as superior to their obligations to God and country. He could not, therefore, administer the government, if he were elected, on the assumption that Masons were disqualified from holding office. It would be an unwarranted punishment of innocent men. If they wanted such a pledge as a condition of nomination, he would decline the honor "with far more pleasure" than he would accept it. In closing he refused to admit the Antimasons were a political party since their cardinal tenet, *"the supremacy of the laws,"* was the sacred principle of the whole nation and not of a single group.

Wirt's letter, designed to avoid too close an association with Antimasonry, which might destroy his chances for a subsequent nomination in December, was followed by a short, straightforward acceptance by Ellmaker. The "Address to the People," composed by Holley, was read and accepted. It contained the customary charges against Masonry, tied loosely to the presidential election.[118] After the ratification of the address the delegates passed resolutions calling for another national convention to meet in Washington in December, 1835. It contained no reference to nominations, but the timing of the projected meeting indicated that the party intended to stay in the president-making business. The holding of another national convention was subject to the approval of the national committee (which had been reappointed for four years). With this additional power the committee resembled in its duties, although not in its personnel, the present day national committees. After a flurry of resolutions thanking those responsible for conducting the convention the delegates adjourned.

The nomination of Wirt gave the Antimasonic party a respectable, even a distinguished, name to put at the head of its ticket. Admittedly, the candidate was neither a popular figure nor one previously considered for the presidency. Whether his nomination was sound policy

118. William H. Maynard to Holley, May 19, 1831, O'Rielly MSS; *Proceedings of the Second United States Anti-Masonic Convention, Held at Baltimore, September, 1831*, pp. 68–84.

was subject to a double test. Would his celebrity as a public man atone for his lukewarm embrace of Antimasonry or would the party faithful be disgusted by the nomination's obvious expediency? The more severe trial, however, was whether his nomination would induce the National Republicans to abandon Clay. That, after all, was the only reason, other than his proximity to the convention, he had been chosen. Wirt appreciated this, for it was on this ground that he allowed himself to be persuaded to lend his name to a party for which he felt but little sympathy.

Unfortunately for the man and the party, Wirt soon demonstrated a lack of aptitude for office-seeking. His letters following his nomination were defensive, apologetic in tone. He despaired of the result before the campaign had begun. He needed to convince the National Republicans that unless they nominated him they faced certain defeat. Instead, he was concerned with defending himself against the imputation of duplicity. He wanted everyone to know that he had not betrayed Clay or his party. He shrank from the battle and dreaded attacks on his integrity that had not yet been made.[119]

The Baltimore convention had made the best of a bad situation. The alternatives to Wirt were the nomination of a man likely to turn down the honor or adjournment without a candidate. The National Republican convention in December would determine how well they had done.

119. Wirt to Rush, copy, Oct. 3, 1831; Wirt to Dabney Carr, copy, Oct. 5, 1831; Wirt to Rush, copy, Oct. 6, 1831; Wirt to Carr, copy, Oct. 7, 1831; Wirt to Joseph M. White, Oct. 10, 1831; Wirt to Robert Walsh, Oct. 14, 1831; Wirt to John Meredith, Oct. 19, 1831; Wirt to William H. Cabell, Oct. 28, 1831; Wirt to Abner Phelps, Oct. 28, 1831, Wirt MSS.

IV

The National Republicans
1829–32

"A voice comes from all parts of the Union, fresh from the people, uniform and loud for Henry Clay."

Maysville Eagle, February 22, 1832

SEVEN

The Formation of the
National Republican Party

Less than three months after the Antimasons deserted Baltimore, the delegates to another national convention crowded into the Athenaeum's Long Room. The first meeting bore heavily on the second. In nominating Wirt, a witness to the Antimasonic convention observed, "a dead set is now to be made against the Clay party, and particularly at the next Baltimore convention."[1] Officially, the name of the group sponsoring the convention was the National Republican party, but the writer was correct in identifying it with Henry Clay. The National Republican party and its convention were little more than fronts for the presidential ambitions of the Kentucky statesman. If the Antimasonic convention illustrated the national convention's usefulness as an instrument for gaining a wider recognition, that of the National Republicans exemplified its possibilities as a party rally.

In all essentials the National Republican party was an extension of the defeated administration. The only visible changes were the substitution of a new head and the addition of a title. Clay automatically advanced to first place in the opposition ranks. After the catastrophe of 1828 any desire Adams harbored to continue as leader was unrealistic. The only possible intraparty rival to Clay was Daniel Webster. Elected to the Senate in 1827, Webster had distinguished himself as a defender of Adams in congressional debate and had performed yeoman service in the prosaic work of building the party's organization. But he suffered from the stain of New England Federalism and his identification with national interests was just beginning.

1. *Baltimore Republican*, Oct. 8, 1831.

The laurels won in defense of the Union had not been bestowed in 1829. Because the designation "friends of the Administration" had been rendered obsolete, the Adams-Clay supporters were compelled to take another name. The method of adoption was informal; Clay partisans in the Kentucky spring elections of 1829 branded themselves "National Republicans" to differentiate their Republicanism from the narrow, sectional variety personified by the Jacksonians. The old Adams party elsewhere in the nation quickly embraced it.[2]

The strong continuity between the Adams party of 1828 and the Clay party of 1832 should not disguise the contribution of the National Republicans to the development of the second party system. The bitterness of the 1828 election precluded, of course, the restoration of the Republican party. Adherents of Clay immediately began opposing the Jackson administration with all the means at their command. But the Adams-inspired myth that parties did not exist, or were undesirable if they did, was hastily discarded. Clay frankly accepted the party concept and openly attempted to turn it to his advantage. The election of 1832 was the first since 1816 fought between parties with clearly distinguishable names. The National Republicans also demonstrated, thanks largely to Clay, a far keener appreciation of the importance of thorough organization. The meeting of the national convention in December was the most obvious product, even if unplanned, of that awareness.

As a party leader, Clay had great assets. Adams had summed them up back in 1821 when he noted that "Clay has large and liberal views of public affairs, and that sort of generosity which attaches individuals to his person."[3] His American System had been artfully framed to appeal to large sections of the electorate and it was sufficiently flexible in its application that tariff and internal improvement legislation could be manipulated for maximum political benefit. As a master parliamentarian, Clay was ever ready to compromise if it would result in advantages for himself. His charm made disciples of thousands. The author of his campaign biography exaggerated only a little when he remarked that "Probably he has more personal friends, who, in the fulness of their enthusiastick love, would almost shed their blood for him, than any other man in the United States."[4]

2. *United States Telegraph,* July 13, 1829.
3. Adams, *Memoirs,* V (Mar. 9, 1821), 326.
4. George D. Prentice, *Biography of Henry Clay* (Hartford, 1831), p. 11.

But for all his skill in Congress and the devotion of countless friends, Clay had serious faults as a political strategist. The American System, despite its latitude, had no overriding appeal to a nation of small farmers; his economic nationalism was a generation away from widespread popularity. Indeed, he lacked any real insight into the popular mind. He was, consequently, often a poor judge of what constituted an effective issue, his most notable lapse being the championing of the Bank of the United States in 1832. Instead of reading the minds of the voters, he often relied on his instinct as a gambler. Adams had also perceived that by temperament he was "impetuous and his ambition impatient."[5] Given Jackson's intuitive understanding of what the average citizen wanted from government, these were dangerous qualities.

Clay sensed that his wisest course lay in not launching an immediate drive for the White House. He wrote in November, 1828, to Webster that "Above all I think *we* ought not to prematurely agitate the question of the succession. The agitations of the last six years entitle us to rest. If it is again immediately disturbed let others not us assume the responsibility."[6] This judicious advice was not followed. Clay could not keep his friends from bringing his name forward. And he loved public attention too much to isolate himself at Ashland, craved the presidency too deeply not to improve his prospects at every opportunity, disliked Jackson too intensely to withhold his attack. Just a month after writing Webster, Clay "embarrassed" Edward Everett of Massachusetts by asking whether "he might depend upon the support of the Eastern States at the next Presidential election," adding that he was certain of the West.[7]

Clay's readiness to assume command of the opposition was revealed in every word and action. He told Adams before Jackson had taken office "that he intended to freely express his opinions" on political subjects.[8] He was true to that vow. At a large testimonial dinner given by his Washington admirers before his departure for Kentucky he lashed out at the incoming president as unfit for the office.[9] All along his homeward route his followers feted him at innumerable and noisy receptions and dinners.[10] At Lexington he defended his past

5. Adams, *Memoirs,* V (Mar. 9, 1821), 325.
6. Clay to Webster, Nov. 30, 1828, Webster MSS.
7. Adams, *Memoirs,* VIII (Dec. 27, 1828), 86.
8. *Ibid.,* (Mar. 12, 1829), 110.
9. *Daily National Journal,* Mar. 7, 10, 1829.
10. *Ibid.,* Mar. 18, 21, 24, Apr. 2, 1829; *Kentucky Reporter,* Apr. 1, 8, 15, 22, 1829.

political conduct and assailed Jackson's patronage policies.[11] Cheered by this outpouring, Clay continued his tour during the summer and fall, visiting most of the important towns in the state.[12] Perhaps he wanted reassurance that Kentucky did not repudiate him by voting for Jackson; undoubtedly, fences needed mending after a long absence. The following winter a family reunion in New Orleans furnished his well-wishers new occasions to pay homage.[13] These trips restored his confidence in his popularity.[14]

During the year following his involuntary retirement, while he was collecting applause at personal appearances, Clay was also being lavishly praised in friendly newspapers across the country.[15] "At present," related the *Massachusetts Journal* in September 1829, "we believe that the eyes and minds of the late administration party are turned towards Kentucky; and that Mr. Clay, without being formally nominated, is a candidate for the presidency. . . . We had rather fail with him than succeed with any other gentleman we know."[16] In the ensuing months he gathered in an impressive number of such endorsements.[17] The Jackson papers did not doubt that he was already a candidate. Every speech and visit was attacked as a campaign venture.[18]

Whether he was actually an "avowed candidate," as the Jacksonians charged, was an open question so far as his own supporters were concerned. Some, including the editor of the *Providence Journal*, believed that "Mr. Clay is fairly, by common consent, before the people, as their candidate. He needs no other nomination."[19] But those more

11. *Kentucky Reporter,* June 3, 1829.

12. *Ibid.,* June 17, July 1, 8; Aug. 2, Sept. 2, 30, Oct. 7, 14, 21, 28, Nov. 18, 1829.

13. *Ibid.,* Mar. 3, 31, Apr. 7, 1830; *Daily National Journal,* Feb. 20, 22, Mar. 8, 12, 20, Apr. 3, 1830.

14. Clay to Johnston, Apr. 1, Oct. 5, 1829, Colton, *Private Correspondence,* pp. 226, 244; Clay to Brooke, Sept. 5, 1829, *ibid.,* p. 242; Clay to Webster, Nov. 30, 1828, Webster MSS.

15. *Kentucky Reporter,* July 22, 29, Aug. 5, 12, 26, Sept. 9, 1829; *Daily National Journal,* June 26, July 8, Aug. 3, 10, Sept. 14, 15, 16, 17, 23, 25, Nov. 26, Dec. 2, 1829.

16. Quoted in the *Kentucky Reporter,* Sept. 23, 1829.

17. *Daily National Journal,* Feb. 6, 22, Apr. 6, May 1, 3, 4, 19, 26, 1830.

18. *United States Telegraph,* Jan. 28, Mar. 11, 16, 25, Apr. 24, June 30, Aug. 13, Sept. 1, 18, 26, Oct. 23, Nov. 14, 1829; *Argus of Western America* [Frankfort, Ky.], June 10, Sept. 23, Oct. 14, 21, 1829; *New Hampshire Patriot,* Sept. 6, 1830.

19. Quoted in *Daily National Journal,* June 8, 1830.

privy to his thoughts were careful to deny that either Clay or his friends had "made any decisive movement" in regard to running for president.[20] In September, 1829, Clay once again expressly stated that he did not wish the succession question to be agitated.[21] His hometown organ, the *Kentucky Reporter*, edited by Thomas Smith, the husband of Mrs. Clay's niece, declared that "whatever may be the wishes or views of his numerous friends, there has not been any such formal annunciation of his name as a candidate as to place him in that attitude before the American people."[22] The editor found it necessary to repeat this assertion three weeks later.[23] If Clay were not a candidate it was only because he did not choose to consider himself one. Obviously, he and his advisers did not think the time or manner of these early nominations propitious. Francis Preston Blair's *Argus of Western America* penetrated this disguise and wondered why Clay's friends bothered denying that he had been nominated.[24]

Why indeed? There is the possibility that Clay had not yet made an irrevocable decision to seek the presidency. The evidence is scanty. He wrote Brooke in the spring of 1830 that his "attachment to rural occupation every day acquires more strength, and if it continues to increase another year as it has the last, I shall be fully prepared to renounce forever the strifes of public life."[25] In view of Clay's activities up to that time this could not have been meant seriously. Clay was incapable of renouncing public life. At fifty-three, his powers were undiminished and he could not have realized that his great ambition would go unfulfilled. He had run once in an abnormal, five-cornered free-for-all. The letter which expressed satisfaction with life on the farm also recounted the triumphal visit to New Orleans and reviewed the political outlook for 1832.

A more plausible explanation of Clay's coyness: an admission of candidacy would narrow his room to maneuver. His alleged intention to oppose the president was being tied to events over which he had little control. The Jacksonians made it an issue, for example, in the Kentucky legislative elections in the summer of 1829, claiming that a National Republican victory would mean his formal nomination

20. From the *Boston Courier*, quoted in *Daily National Journal*, June 18, 1829. Also *ibid.*, June 26, Aug. 21, Sept. 29, 1829.
21. Clay to Johnston, Oct. 5, 1829, Colton, *Private Correspondence*, p. 244.
22. Oct. 28, 1829; also, *United States Telegraph*, Nov. 30, 1826.
23. Nov. 18, 1829.
24. Nov. 11, 1829.
25. Clay to Brooke, Apr. 19, 1830, Colton, *Private Correspondence*, p. 261.

by the state legislature.[26] The *Reporter* denied this, but did acknowledge that an attempt had been made to secure the election of persons
friendly to Clay as an "expression of affection and confidence. . . ."[27]
Clay certainly considered an endorsement by the Kentucky legislature
a possibility, although he was willing to settle for a vote of confidence
rather than an explicit nomination.[28] Subsequent National Republican
reverses in Kentucky and other western states made clear the dangers
of bringing Clay forward too early.[29]

When and how he should be nominated were the subjects of a
lively debate among his friends during the winter and spring of 1830.
Even though the editors of a number of National Republican papers
considered him before the people, most ignored the obvious, pretending
that he was not yet a candidate. Of these, a few urged a nomination
by a congressional caucus before the session adjourned in June, 1830.[30]
The Jackson papers were full of dark tales of an impending congressional nomination, delighted at the prospect of another campaign
against King Caucus.[31] The decision was too important, however, to
be left to the newspapers whether friendly or hostile.

Reminiscent of the Jackson campaign of 1828, the National Republicans developed dual control centers. The first was Clay himself; any
plans made in his name could only be implemented with his approval.
The second was a strategy board in Washington composed principally
of congressmen, but including, at least occasionally, other important
personages, such as Joseph Gales, Jr., editor of the *National Intelligencer*, and Peter Force and, later, John Agg, editors of the *National
Journal*. Spokesman for this ad hoc group appears to have been Webster. In any event it was the Massachusetts senator who communicated
their advice to the candidate. The exchange of opinions and the process
of decision-making by its members were achieved informally—they
talked among themselves and then relayed their consensus to
Kentucky.

At no time did the congressional opposition to Jackson seriously
contemplate backing any other candidate. In March, 1830, Webster

26. *Argus of Western America*, July 19, 1829; *New Hampshire Patriot*, Sept.
21, 1829; *United States Telegraph*, May 2, June 18, 1829.
27. Sept. 2, 1829. Also see issue of Sept. 23, 1829.
28. Clay to Johnston, Aug. 26, Oct. 5, Dec. 31, 1829, Colton, *Private Correspondence*, pp. 240, 244, 249; Clay to Brooke, Sept. 5, 1829, *ibid.*, pp. 242–43.
29. *United States Telegraph*, Aug. 21, 22, Nov. 12, Dec. 3, 1829.
30. *Daily National Journal*, May 21, June 4, 1830.
31. *Ibid.*, June 25, 1830.

informed James Pleasants, editor of the leading anti-Jackson paper in Virginia, the *Richmond Whig*, that "the general impression is that Mr. Clay stands first and foremost in the ranks of those who would desire a change. I do not think there is the least abatement of the respect and confidence entertained for him."[32] "You are necessarily at the head of one party," he told Clay, "and Jackson will be, if he is not already, identified with the other."[33]

Sentiment among the pro-Clay members of Congress in January, 1830, leaned toward a caucus nomination during the present session, so John W. Taylor informed Adams on the basis of a letter from Clay. The former president believed that a nomination from Washington "would be fatal to the prospects of Mr. Clay. . . ."[34] Further conferences produced a change. Late in May, Webster wrote Clay that now only a few members desired a caucus nomination before adjournment. Most, said Webster, agreed "that a formal nomination would not be popular enough in its character and origin, to do good." It would be immediately proclaimed "to be the act of your friends acting at your instance."[35] A later nomination emanating from the states would be preferable.

From where should the nomination come, and when? The current session of the Massachusetts legislature was suggested, but Webster thought this was a poor choice; everyone new Massachusetts was safe. Besides, a nomination from that source would "only raise the cry of coalition revived." Maryland would provide "the proper scene;" the state held elections in October and a National Republican victory seemed certain. A nomination by the Maryland legislature in December would be the most advantageous, especially as neither New York nor Pennsylvania were "likely to be so soon ready for it." Finally, Webster counseled Clay to keep in the background for the time being: "The people will bring you out, *nolens volens*. Let them do it. I advise you, as you will be much watched, to stay at home; or , if you wish to travel, visit your old friends in Virginia. We should be glad to see you at the North, but not now. You will hear from the North, every town and village in it, on the 4th of July."

32. Webster to Pleasants, draft, Mar. 6, 1830, Webster, *Correspondence of Webster*, I, 492.
33. Webster to Clay, May 29, 1830, Colton, *Private Correspondence*, p. 276.
34. Adams, *Memoirs*, VIII (Jan. 24, 1830), 180.
35. Webster to Clay, May 29, 1830, Colton, *Private Correspondence*, p. 275; also, Adams, *Memoirs*, VIII (June 19, 22, 1830), 231–32.

Clay approved these plans: "The decision of my friends at Washington to stand still for the present, and to leave the first movement to Maryland, was best under all circumstances." And he also agreed that he should not undertake additional tours.[36] Yet he immediately proceeded to violate his pledge. The failure to heed the advice of his congressional consultants not only upset their campaign strategy, but led unwittingly to the holding of a national convention.

Clay's decision to take the initiative was a response to an unexpected event—Jackson's veto of the bill authorizing the purchase with federal funds of stock in a company engaged in building a turnpike between Maysville and Lexington. The veto message, based on constitutional grounds, cast a dark shadow over all future internal improvements financed by the national government. Combined with southern threats to leave the Union if the tariff were not reduced, threats at that moment gaining in intensity, the Maysville veto shook the foundations of the American System. That System was the edifice on which Clay had based his whole career in national politics; if it toppled he would fall with it. He could not afford to allow Jackson's act to pass unchallenged unless he was willing to bury his ambitions for the White House. But the veto was an opportunity as well as a threat. It was certain to be unpopular not only in the West, especially in Kentucky where its effect would be most immediately felt, but also in those coastal states, such as Maryland, which counted on federal aid in opening commerce with the West.

Responding instantly to the challenge laid down by Jackson, Clay dashed off a letter to one of his Kentucky agents outlining a course of action directly contrary to his agreement with Webster penned only the day before. "We are all shocked and mortified," Clay wrote Adam Beatty, "by the rejection of the Maysville road and other events occurring at the close of the late session." He urged Beatty, perhaps others in Kentucky, to call protest meetings, even listing exactly what resolutions they should pass. In addition to disapproving the veto he recommended that "the nullifying doctrines of the South" be condemned and hinted, none too subtly, that now was the time to present his name for the presidency:

It is thought by my friends that these public meetings will furnish suitable occasions for making a nomination for the next Presidency,

36. Clay to Webster, June 7, 1830, Webster, *Correspondence of Webster,* I, 504.

and recommending to the next Legislature to second and support it. They urge that this will be a popular measure, and not one of caucus agency. That the nomination connects itself naturally with the question of Internal Improvements. That the time has come. That Congress having adjourned, no counteracting measure can be adopted by members of Congress at Washington. That other States look to Kentucky for the first movement. That it will have a good effect on the August elections [for the Kentucky legislature]. That it can do no harm, and may do much good, etc.[37]

On June 21, only thirteen days later, the citizens of Clay's own Fayette County held a public meeting in accordance with his suggestion. The corresponding commitee appointed at the meeting issued an address that stopped just short of a formal nomination "lest it be charged with partiality toward a friend and neighbor. Whether that consideration is or is not applicable to other parts of the State of Kentucky than Mr. Clay's immediate vicinity, they are the most competent judges."[38] Other county meetings called about the same time to protest the veto were not so backward and made the desired nomination.[39]

Everywhere, in fact, the veto touched off demonstrations for Clay. More than any other event it transformed the scattered fragments of the former Adams coalition into the National Republican party. Literally hundreds of newspapers were provoked into an open defense of the American System and support for Clay.[40] Public meetings, local or state conventions in Virginia, New Jersey, Maryland, Connecticut, Tennessee, Maine, and Delaware formally nominated him.[41] Thus fortified, Clay began an extended tour of Ohio in July for the purpose of galvanizing his partisans. At Cincinnati he delivered a full scale defense of the American System designed to set the keynote for the coming campaign.[42] "The voice of the people, like the rushing together of many waters," rhapsodized the *Western Citizen* (Paris, Ky.), "pro-

37. Clay to Beatty, June 8, 1830, Colton, *Private Correspondence*, pp. 276–77.
38. *Kentucky Reporter–Extra*, July 7, 1830.
39. *Maysville Eagle*, July 6, 13, 1830; *Kentucky Reporter*, June 30, July 7, 21, 1830.
40. *Kentucky Reporter*, June 30, July 7, 14, 21, Aug. 4, 11, 1830; *The Commentator* [Frankfort, Ky.], July 6, 27, Aug. 31, 1830; *Daily National Journal*, June 8, 9, 16, 17, 18, 22, 24, 25, July 2, 13, 16, 20, 27, Aug. 3, 1830.
41. *Kentucky Reporter*, Aug. 18, Sept. 1, 22, Oct. 13, 1830; *The Commentator*, Sept. 28, Oct. 19, 1830; *Daily National Intelligencer*, Aug. 6, 11, 19, 21, Oct. 2, 1830; *Niles' Weekly Register*, XXXVIII (Aug. 14, 1830); *Maysville Eagle*, Aug. 24, 1830; P. Sprague to Webster, July 15, 1830, Webster MSS.
42. *Kentucky Reporter*, July 28, Aug. 4, 11, 18, 25, Sept. 1, 8, 1830; *Louisville Public Advertiser*, Aug. 24, 1830.

claim Mr. Clay a candidate for the next Presidency—"[43] From Washington came word that it was "idle to talk of any other candidate."[44]

The meetings occasioned by the veto greatly accelerated local party organization as almost all of them elected correspondence committees, the members of which formed a leadership nucleus in hundreds of communities. The Massachusetts state committee endeavored to pull these scattered groups together in order to create a national network for Clay's benefit.[45] Nothing came of this undertaking, but in a number of states the veto meetings did produce tangible results. A New Jersey public meeting late in July called to nominate Clay also summoned a state convention to prepare for the congressional elections in November.[46] In August, National Republicans in Maryland were inspired to begin a thorough and systemic reorganization of their party.[47] The veto provided, as the critical *United States Telegraph* had predicted, an excuse "for unfurling Mr. Clay's standard."[48] Clay's instinctive realization that it demanded action more immediate and dramatic than what Webster had counseled was sound.

The spontaneous nominations of Clay by the meetings and conventions following in the wake of the Maysville veto intensified the debate over whether he should receive an authoritative nomination that would make him a candidate beyond all question. There were those who believed no further nomination was necessary.[49] Wrote one Louisiana editor: "*He* cannot be more emphatically before the public, than he is *now*, except by his own announcement, and this course we greatly prefer to any that has yet been suggested, of nominating him from a responsible source."[50] But Clay's most fervent partisans wished for something more impressive than these local endorsements. It was "time that his friends should organize and act in concert."[51] "[T]he sooner Henry Clay is nominated," fretted a Rhode Island editor, "the better will it be for him, for the country, and for posterity. How can a

43. Quoted in *The Commentator*, Aug. 3, 1830.
44. Samuel Burch to Taylor, July 31, 1830, Taylor MSS.
45. A. H. Everett, N. Hale, J. B. David to Taylor, copy, July 19, 1830, *ibid.*
46. *Daily National Journal*, Aug. 4, 1830.
47. *Daily National Intelligencer*, Aug. 7, 1830.
48. May 23, 1830.
49. *The Commentator*, Aug. 10, 1830; *Daily National Journal*, July 2, 13, 20, Aug. 3, 1830.
50. From the *Louisiana Argus*, quoted in the *Louisville Public Advertiser*, Aug. 16, 1830.
51. *Daily National Journal*, June 29, 1830.

large and respectable party," he questioned, "be sustained without an acknowledged leader? Are the National Republicans willing to fight in the dark longer? We say again, let us have the nomination of Mr. Clay from some responsible source. The people are ready for this movement, and to delay is extreme folly."[52]

The most desirable location for a "responsible" nomination was the candidate's own state, as it would indicate that he was supported by the people who knew him best. Presidential candidates were as sensitive then as they are today to the necessity of having a secure home base as a prelude to running. Accordingly, the project of the previous summer of having the Kentucky legislature nominate him was revived. No doubt his friends counted on the favorable effects of the Maysville veto on the impending August elections.[53] The returns, however, were a stunning setback. Instead of the majority of twenty (counting both houses) enjoyed by the National Republicans in the previous legislature, they would now be a minority by a small but critical margin.[54] That, of course, ended all hopes of a legislative nomination by Kentucky.[55]

But Clay's friends could not abandon the idea of providing evidence of favorite son support if they wished him to continue in the race. Now they had to find a new instrument. To meet this need a public meeting was convened in the town of Winchester, Clarke County, in the middle of September. By resolution the participants invited "the friends of the Union of the States and the American System" to meet in a state convention on December 9, 1830, in Frankfort "to take into consideration the next Presidential election, and to nominate such person to that office as will secure the triumph of the American System and the Union of the States, against the new and alarming doctrines of dissolution and nullification. . . ."[56]

The *Kentucky Reporter*, a reliable guide to Clay's thinking, found the Winchester summons entirely to its liking. Making a virtue out of a necessity, the *Reporter* claimed that a state convention was superior to a nomination by the legislature: "Issuing directly from the people, it will bear and proclaim their genuine sentiments. Essentially

52. *Ibid.*

53. *Louisville Public Advertiser,* July 24, 1830.

54. *Ibid.*, Aug. 13, Sept. 2, 11, 1830. Estimates of the losses suffered by the Clay party varied, depending on which side was doing the estimating.

55. Adams, *Memoirs,* VIII (Aug. 24, 1830), 236; *Argus of Western America,* Aug. 25, 1830.

56. *Kentucky Reporter,* Sept. 15, 1830; *Louisville Public Advertiser,* Sept. 22, 1830.

popular in its character and composition, it will command respect and secure confidence by its plain straight-forward movement, without intrigue, without any other motive or origin but the spontaneous impulse of the people themselves."[57] As a bonus, the state convention could "devise some means of effective co-operation" that would prevent more than one National Republican candidate from running for the same office in future state elections. The plural candidacies had been largely responsible, the *Reporter* contended, for the recent Jackson gains. Judging from the quickness with which other counties reacted to the Winchester proposal, the state convention must have been approved by the Kentucky party leaders. Duff Green traced the idea back to Clay himself, communicated through his friend, James Clarke, who served as chairman of the Winchester meeting.[58]

However that may be, public meetings in every county of the state chose delegates for Frankfort.[59] Outside the state the scheme was also widely applauded; only a few National Republican papers took exception. Conspicuous among these was the *Cincinnati Gazette*, edited by Charles Hammond, once a strong ally of the Adams administration. In the *Gazette's* opinion "No adventitious aid of a convention" was required to put Clay in nomination. In any event it was too early for any nomination; "public sentiment" needed to develop. The outlook, at this time, was exceedingly poor. When there were "some decisive indications" of a more favorable climate of opinion there would "be time enough for the friends of the American system to name their candidate. . . ." Getting now to the heart of the matter, the *Gazette* went on to say that Clay was not the man to oppose Jackson, as he was more disliked personally than were the measures of the Jackson administration. Van Buren had deliberately concocted the Maysville veto because he knew that it would force Clay to become a candidate. Ohio, the editor predicted, would remain aloof from following the lead which the forthcoming Kentucky convention would attempt to give.[60] These opinions were not common among National

57. *Kentucky Reporter*, Sept. 22, 1830. Also, *Daily National Journal*, Sept. 23, 1830.

58. *United States Telegraph*, Sept. 24, Oct. 14, 1830. Clarke was a friend of Clay and succeeded to his seat in the House of Representatives. No evidence that I was able to find supports the *Telegraph's* (and others') assertion, but it is not unreasonable.

59. *The Commentator*, Oct. 12–Dec. 8, 1830; *Kentucky Reporter*, Sept. 29–Dec. 1, 1830; *Maysville Eagle*, Oct. 12, 26, Nov. 23, Dec. 7, 1830.

60. *Louisville Public Advertiser*, Oct. 4, 1830.

Republicans, but they were evidence that not all of them were ena-
mored of Clay, at least not of his chances of winning.[61]

Out of the meetings to elect delegates to the Frankfort convention
came the first definite proposal to hold a National Republican presidential nominating convention. At the Jefferson County meeting in
Louisville on October 30, 1830, M. R. Wigginton offered a resolution
"That our Delegates [to the state convention] be and are hereby instructed to propose and vote for the appointment of Delegates to a
National Convention friendly to the election of H. Clay, to be holden
in the City of Washington at some suitable period." It carried
unanimously.[62]

The proposal originated, so far as I have been able to discover,
quite independently of Clay or other important directors of the party
in Kentucky or elsewhere. Wigginton was active in National Republican affairs in Kentucky, but there is nothing to link him with those
who made the important decisions within the party.[63] Subsequent developments point strongly to the conclusion that his motion was not
the fruit of consultations among those high in the party councils. Several contemporary sources attributed it to the example of the Anti-
masonic national convention which had been held the previous month
in Philadelphia, but this is speculation.[64] A presidential nomination
by delegates from all the states was a logical extension of a nomination
by a single state, and would supply Clay with a far more imposing
sponsorship. The Antimasonic model may well have furnished the
immediate inspiration to Wigginton, yet it was not vital to his motion.

Other meetings preparatory to the Kentucky state convention did
not endorse the Louisville resolution, but it did catch the attention
of National Republican editors outside the state. And it was the publicity given the national convention by these men that was responsible
for its meeting rather than the sanction of party leaders, who had
not anticipated it. The enthusiasm of the newspapers soon transmitted
itself to the second echelon politicians in the states, some of whom
took immediate steps to implement the election of delegates. So rapidly
did the movement snowball that Clay and his advisors in Washington

61. *Ibid.*, Oct. 5, 9, 1830; *New Hampshire Patriot*, Sept. 13, 1830.
62. *Kentucky Reporter*, Nov. 10, 1830; *Louisville Public Advertiser*, Nov. 5,
1830.
63. *The Focus* [Louisville], Oct. 18, 1831; *The Commentator*, Jan. 3, 1832.
64. *Louisville Public Advertiser*, Nov. 5, 1830.

were compelled, with some reluctance, to bestow a tardy blessing on the enterprise. One editor rates special mention: John Agg of the *Daily National Journal.* Together with the initiators at Winchester, perhaps even more than they, he must be credited with the meeting of the second national convention.

Relatively little is known of Agg. Born in England, he apparently emigrated at a sufficiently mature age to retain the characteristics of his native country. Contemporaries referred to him as English; Duff Green sneeringly called him "the little Englishman from Picadilly."[65] He had lived in Washington for some years before the election of 1832, and is chiefly remembered as the author of light verses about capital society and, more weightedly, two long epic poems frequently attributed to Lord Byron ("two of the more important Byron apocrypha," according to Howard Mumford Jones).[66] His role as editor–party leader was brief. He became editor of the faltering *National Journal* in August, 1830, continuing in that post until the paper's demise in January, 1832. The *National Journal* had been founded during the Adams administration by Peter Force with the intention of making it the semi-official voice of the executive branch. Force disposed of the property in February, 1830, and it had changed owners and editors twice more before Agg assumed working control.[67] Following the *Journal's* collapse, he began editing the proceedings of Congress, but only one volume was ever printed and he disappeared from view thereafter.[68] It is appropriate that the dates of his tenure at the *Journal* bracket, roughly, the initial call of the National Republican convention in October, 1830, and its meeting in December, 1831.

Agg used the *Journal* as the catalyst for the convention idea, pushing it at every opportunity and forcing consideration of it on the party's solons. From the first report of the Louisville meeting Agg recognized the value of holding a national convention: "We trust this proposition will be acted on."[69] A few days later he wrote:

> We have seen no movement on the part of the friends of Mr. Clay, which more entirely meets approbation than the proposition for a

65. Anne Hollingsworth Wharton, *Social Life in the Early Republic* (Philadelphia, 1902), p. 230; *United States Telegraph,* Aug. 18, 1830.

66. Wharton, *Social Life,* p. 213; Howard Mumford Jones, "The Author of Two Byron Apocrypha," *Modern Language Notes,* XLI (Feb., 1926), 129–31; [John Agg,] *The Ocean Harp: A Poem* (Philadelphia, 1819).

67. *Daily National Journal,* Feb. 2, Aug. 16, 1830.

68. [John Agg,] *History of Congress from March 4, 1789 To March 3, 1793* (Philadelphia, 1834).

69. *Daily National Journal,* Nov. 12, 1830.

National Convention to meet at the City of Washington. . . . Of the miraculous results which can be achieved by union, activity and systematic energy, the last four or five years have given striking testimony. . . . The declarations, sentiments and nominations, should be concentrated; and for this purpose we call all the friends of their country to sweep forward and appoint delegates to the National Convention. It is only in such a Convention, appointed by the people themselves for this specific object, and this alone, that the union of feeling which is necessary to the production of energetic action, can be consummated.[70]

Thereafter, Agg began reprinting editorial comments from other papers relating to the convention, the overwhelming majority of them highly favorable.[71] In this manner news of the proposed convention gained wide currency.

As the idea spread it was impelled by its own momentum to realization. The *New York Commercial Advertiser* contributed a specific day, February 22, 1831, Washington's birthday, when it should open.[72] Other papers, such as the *Alexandria Gazette* and the *Kentucky Reporter*, picked this up, many assuming that the date was official when, in fact, the convention had not yet been called.[73] All the Louisville meeting had done was instruct its delegates to the state convention at Frankfort to propose and vote for a national convention. The *National Journal* warned that February 22, though highly appropriate symbolically, was probably too early for the necessary arrangements to be made.[74] The regular New Jersey state convention meeting on November 24 took no chances. It appointed delegates then and there to attend the national convention whenever it might be held.[75]

The *National Journal* noted that objections to the convention had been raised in "two or three quarters."[76] Two reasons were cited for this dissent. The first was that "no convention should be called to sustain any personal interest, but exclusively with reference to the principles to be sustained." This was a veiled but obvious reference to Clay's domination. Second, some believed that no convention was necessary as Clay was "already sufficiently before the people, nominated by acclamation." Agg dismissed the first criticsm by declaring that "The principle will vindicate the man." To the second he admitted

70. *Ibid.,* Nov. 17, 1830.
71. *Ibid.,* Nov. 22, 25, 26, 27, 30, Dec. 1, 7, 29, 1830; Jan. 10, 13, 24, 1831.
72. As reported in *ibid.,* Nov. 26, 1830.
73. *Ibid.,* Dec. 7, 16, 1830; *Kentucky Reporter,* Dec. 8, 1830.
74. *Daily National Journal,* Nov. 22, 1830.
75. *Richmond Enquirer,* Dec. 3, 1830.
76. Dec. 16, 1830.

a specious validity. But, he argued, a national convention would be far more efficient "in concentrating measures to secure his election" than "the people *en masse.*" "[W]hen the Delegates should have matured their measures, and returned to their homes, its ramifications would be spread throughout the Union. A system of correspondence would be adopted, by which the most distant States would be enabled to communicate with each other; and a concert of action would be established, from which great benefits might be expected to flow."

As the time for the Kentucky convention approached, the Washington leaders still had not made up their minds as to what should be done. Gales, an editor of the prestigious *National Intelligencer,* wrote John W. Taylor in New York early in December, inserting some editorials endorsing the national convention. "I enclose you two extracts from papers received today," Gales wrote, "which show the high consequence of early determination upon the subject I spoke to you. Pray communicate them to your friends."[77] Taylor and those he consulted must have approved because important meetings in New York City and Buffalo met shortly afterward and explicitly endorsed the national convention.[78] The Buffalo meeting, presided over by Peter B. Porter, recommended a state convention at Albany in January in order to organize the party and "with a discretionary power" to choose delegates to a national convention. The meeting in New York suggested that the national convention be postponed from February until autumn (1831). Agg, delighted by this impressive reinforcement, declared that "the *timid* friends of the American System and its founder are cheered and inspirited, and some who doubted—yes, doubted—the expediency of a National Convention, begin to see things in a different light. . . ."[79]

Nevertheless, an air of uncertainty still hung over the project when the Kentucky convention opened on December 9. Clay was nominated by acclamation. William P. Thomasson, a delegate from Jefferson County, introduced a resolution proposing a national convention in accordance with the instructions from the meeting which had elected him. Thomasson was an important figure in Kentucky politics and a close friend of Clay, but in this instance he was only carrying out

77. Gales to Taylor, Dec. 6, 1830, Taylor MSS.
78. *Daily National Intelligencer,* Dec. 17, 29, 1830. The Buffalo meeting convened before the Kentucky state convention; the one in New York met a few days after, but not in time to be influenced by it.
79. *Daily National Journal,* Dec. 21, 1830.

the wishes of his constituents.[80] His resolution was referred to the committee on business which reported that it was not expedient to act on it. The delegates "had already made a nomination of President—a citizen of their own State; and it might not therefore," it was explained, "be entirely becoming *in them, to propose* a National Convention for the same object."[81] This was consistent with Fayette County's modesty in not nominating Clay, but hinting that others should do so.

Thomasson did not give up easily. He moved to amend the committee's report by striking the word "not." The convention's leaders were divided, but Thomasson's motion was defeated.[82] In the end, though, the delegates went as far as it was possible to go without actually calling a national convention. They resolved "That in the event that a national convention shall be held in the city of Washington or elsewhere, by the friends to our principles, previous to the next Presidential election, that twelve delegates be, and they are hereby appointed, to meet in said convention, and represent Kentucky therein."[83] They were willing to appoint delegates to a national convention, but not to invite anyone else to attend.

Opposition to the national convention did not disappear entirely after the Kentucky convention.[84] Its sources are difficult to locate. Agg blamed it on *"insincere* friends among us, or if not insincere, friends of such timid characters and fluctuating purposes, that, unless they can be controled and fixed by some great operation of the party, they may prove injurious, rather than beneficial to us and our cause."[85] He did not name them, but cited the writer, "One of Many," whose letter had recently been published in the *National Intelligencer*, the *Journal*'s rival for the honor of being the party's premier national paper. He might have been referring obliquely to the editors of the *Intelligencer* who had never exhibited much warmth for the national convention. With studied coolness Gales's paper noted Kentucky's tepid invitation only by observing that "Convention or no convention, Henry

80. *Louisville Public Advertiser*, July 23, Aug. 19, 1830; *Memorial History of Louisville from Its First Settlement to the Year 1896*, ed. J. Stoddard Johnston (Chicago, 1896), I, 131, 134; *ibid.*, II, 621–23.

81. *The Commentator*, Dec. 14, 1830.

82. *Louisville Public Advertiser*, Dec. 13, 1830.

83. *Proceedings of the National Republican Convention, Held at Frankfort, Kentucky, on Thursday, December 9, 1830.* n.p., n.d., p. 5.

84. *Daily National Journal*, Jan. 10, 1831.

85. *Ibid.*, Jan. 24, 1831.

Clay already stands in full view of the people as the National Republican candidate. . . ."[86] The *United States Gazette* was equally opaque. After stating that "some considerable opposition from quarters where dissonance of opinion was not looked for," it intimated that those resisting the national convention were really enemies of Clay.[87]

The National Republican editors and politicians were exceedingly discreet about airing their differences, if indeed differences existed. Green, not always a reliable source as he had no love for Clay, professed to see an East-West split within National Republican ranks.[88] Kentucky's tentative summons of a national convention *"pledged to nominate Mr. Clay"* showed that Clay distrusted "the attachment of the prominent men of his own party" and sought to use the convention as a means of forcing himself on them. "What claims," asked the *Telegraph*, "can Mr. Clay have upon a party, if he thrusts himself upon it as a candidate, by a movement which ex facie declares, that he is resolved to be a candidate against their will, and adopts his measures more with a view to exclude competition, than to unite the strength of those with whom he professes to act?"[89]

At least partial confirmation of Green's suspicions of a National Republican division was provided by the comments of the *Boston Courier*, an anti-Jackson paper. It was of the opinion that a national convention "might be assembled for a better purpose" than the nomination of Clay, and called upon those opposed to Jackson (Clay, Calhoun, Webster, and Rush) to sacrifice "personal animosities" in order to beat the president.[90] Months later, the *Richmond Constitutional Whig*, another National Republican paper evincing no enthusiasm for Clay, advocated dropping the national convention for a congressional caucus of all anti-Jackson members, including others besides National Republicans, that could unite them behind a single candidate.[91]

But the hour was too late to deflect the course of the party. The *National Intelligencer*, commenting on the *Whig's* opposition, revealed that the convention had been approved by the National Republican members of Congress during the last session (1831). The congressmen had ruled out a caucus "to obviate the objections which very generally

86. *Daily National Intelligencer*, Dec. 28, 1830.
87. Quoted in the *Maysville Eagle*, Mar. 1, 1831.
88. *United States Telegraph*, Nov. 27, 1830.
89. *Ibid.*, Dec. 22, 1830.
90. From the *Richmond Enquirer*, Feb. 12, 1831.
91. June 16, Aug. 29, 1831.

exist, to nomination by legislative caucus, composed of persons who are not generally authorized to represent the People of their respective districts in this particular." The national convention, "though first proposed without concert, was not finally determined upon without great previous deliberation and consultation." Furthermore, the *Intelligencer* went on, a convention would not preclude subsequent action by the members of Congress to solidify the opposition to Jackson. But the editors were certain that the convention would "be found the best agent in producing harmony and cooperation" and that the intervention of a congressional caucus would not be necessary.[92] The *Whig*, along with other dissidents in the party, eventually fell into line and accepted the inevitable nomination of Clay by a national convention.[93]

In the meantime, details of the convention's meeting had been worked out. The February date was discarded as "impracticable" because of winter road conditions.[94] The *National Journal* expected the New York state convention, originally scheduled to meet late in January, to name the time and place.[95] Although the New York convention did not meet until later in the year, a public meeting in New York City on February 9 did specify that the national conclave should convene the first Wednesday in September at Philadelphia.[96] This decision was unsatisfactory to the Washington strategy board. Agg announced "that it is the opinion of our friends" in Washington that a "December date," coinciding with the beginning of the new session, might be more suitable "in order that there may be a facility of intercourse between members of Congress and members of the Convention." Although careful to say that the "character and functions" of each were "essentially distinct, and such as ought not, and will not, interfere with each other," he felt that "there may be much information of value, requisite for the purposes of the Convention, which cannot be so well or so readily obtained from any other source as from the Halls of Congress."[97] The *National Intelligencer*, burying its opposition to the convention after New York had come out for it, concurred

92. *Daily National Intelligencer*, Aug. 23, 1831.
93. *Daily National Journal*, Mar. 29, Sept. 8, 1831; *Richmond Constitutional Whig*, Sept. 8, 1831.
94. *Daily National Journal*, Dec. 17, 28, 1830.
95. *Ibid.*, Jan. 13, 1831.
96. *Ibid.*, Feb. 16, 1831.
97. *Ibid.*, Feb. 18, 1831.

in the choice of dates, but expressed a decided preference for Baltimore over Philadelphia because of its proximity to Washington.[98]

These suggestions from the leading Clay newspapers in the nation were accepted as commands. They represented the final progression of an idea first advanced by a county meeting in Kentucky the previous October for a national convention to meet in Washington sometime before the election. Others, in response, had proposed that it meet in February, 1831, but that date obviously did not allow the states sufficient time to appoint delegates and the New York City meeting had recommended September instead, also substituting Philadelphia for Washington. The *National Journal* and *National Intelligencer*, wanting the convention close enough so that congressmen might attend, yet sufficiently far away to avoid any imputation of congressional dictation, designated Baltimore as the site and moved the time forward to December.[99] All that remained to be done was to find an agency to make the calling of the convention official. The Maryland legislative caucus, which Webster had once marked as the source of Clay's candidacy, was selected. Events had bypassed that scheme even though Maryland had produced the expected Clay victory in its legislative elections.[100] Now the state's function was reduced to playing the host for others.

A caucus of the National Republican members of the Maryland legislature on February 17, 1831, resolved "That it is expedient that a national convention be held, to which the people of all the states shall be invited to send Delegates, in which their will can be authentically ascertained, and that concert of action produced, which is essential to our cause."[101] Arrangements for a state convention to appoint the national convention delegates were made, after which the caucus issued the call: "Resolved, That our brethren of other states . . . be, and they are, hereby invited to meet in general convention, at Baltimore on the second Monday of December next by delegates equal in number to the electors for president to which their states are respectively entitled, in order that after full consultation, the convention may present as candidates for the presidency and vice presidency, statesmen the best established in public confidence, and calculated

98. Quoted in the *Maysville Eagle*, Mar. 1, 1831; *New Hampshire Patriot*, Mar. 7, 1831.

99. Adams, *Memoirs*, VIII (Jan. 24, 1830), 180.

100. *Maysville Eagle*, Oct. 26, 1830 (from the *Maryland Journal*); *Daily National Journal*, Oct. 7, 1830; Haller, *JSH*, XXVIII (Aug., 1962), 324.

101. *Niles' Weekly Register*, XL (Mar. 12, 1831), 28–29.

to promote our common object, the safety and welfare of the country."
Only six days later, so close as to imply coordination, a Connecticut
convention nominated Clay and recommended that a national convention be held at Baltimore in December.[102] The Clay phalanx was beginning to move at last. Agg could not resist giving himself several pats
on the back for having been responsible for the national convention's
acceptance by party leaders.[103]

102. *Ibid.*, XL (Apr. 16, 1831), 127; *Maysville Eagle*, Mar. 22, 1831.
103. *Daily National Journal*, Feb. 18, Apr. 28, 1831.

EIGHT

Clay's Convention

Henry Clay's opinion on the wisdom of the national convention proposal was never recorded. Despite the assumption of his enemies that he must be responsible since he stood to profit from the meeting, there is no proof that he manipulated the necessary strings. So far as the Baltimore convention is concerned, the council in Washington was more important than the individual in Lexington, although it originated with neither. But once the decision was made Clay could not afford to have the project fail. "Whatever doubts might originally have existed about the movement," he wrote Brooke in October, 1831, "it has now proceeded too far to be abandoned." His tone implied reservation on his part so he quickly added: "And it is therefore desirable that there should be a full and respectable assembly."[1]

Clay was writing Brooke to encourage party leaders in Virginia to make certain that the state was well represented at Baltimore. But no one was more concerned about the success of the convention than John Agg, who repeatedly exhorted the faithful to guarantee that "every state of the Union should be heard in the National Convention. . . ."[2] There was a pervasive consciousness among National Republicans that their organization was inferior to that of their opponents. The triumph of Jackson was attributed to the excellence of the Democrat's state and local machinery and the energy it imparted. The national convention provided an unparalled opportunity to redress the balance.[3] It did not pass untaken.

1. Clay to Brooke, Oct. 4, 1831, Colton, *Private Correspondence*, p. 317.
2. *Daily National Journal*, Aug. 9, 1831.
3. *Ibid.*, June 16, Sept. 12, 19, Nov. 25, 1831.

The appointment of delegates to Baltimore proved a most effective spur to the systematic organization of the National Republican party in the states, counties, and towns where it possessed measurable voter support. It could not, however, as the Antimasons had already discovered, generate support in the absence of an already favorably disposed public opinion.

New Jersey had picked its delegation before the half-hearted invitation of the Kentucky convention. Connecticut moved as soon as the Maryland caucus issued the official invitation in February, 1831. During the interval between the calling and the assembling of the Baltimore convention the remaining states chose their delegates, some waiting until the last possible moment. All methods of selection were invoked, the national managers declining to impose any uniformity on the process. The variety of devices furnishes an index to the use of the convention by the National Republican party. State conventions (including those attended by some state legislators) elected the entire delegations from five states: New Jersey, Connecticut, New York, Indiana, and Rhode Island.[4] In Kentucky the Frankfort convention neglected to appoint the two at-large delegates and these vacancies were filled by a public meeting in Louisville.[5] This procedure was reversed in Vermont, where a state convention chose the senatorial delegates while either public meetings or district conventions selected the bulk of the delegation.[6] A similar order prevailed in Maine, but a caucus rather than convention designated the at-large members.[7] Caucuses were used exclusively in New Hampshire and Massachusetts.[8] District conventions and, occasionally, public meetings performed the task in Pennsylvania, Maryland, and Ohio.[9] County public meetings served in Delaware, Virginia, and North Carolina.[10] A single, statewide meeting

4. Connecticut: *Daily National Journal*, Mar. 2, 1831; New York: *Albany Daily Advertiser*, June 2, 3, 4, 6, 1831; Indiana: *Daily National Journal*, Nov. 24, 1831; Leonard, *Indiana Magazine of History*, XIX (June, 1923), 137-38; Rhode Island: *Daily National Journal*, Nov. 12, Dec. 24, 1831.

5. *Kentucky Reporter*, Oct. 26, 1831.

6. *Daily National Journal*, July 14, 1831.

7. *Ibid.*, Mar. 2, Aug. 10, 12, 22, 1831.

8. New Hampshire: *ibid.*, July 18, 1831; Massachusetts: *ibid.*, June 16, Aug. 11, 12, 1831.

9. Pennsylvania: *Kentucky Reporter*, Aug. 10, 19, 27, Sept. 1, 8, 14, Oct. 1, 27, 1831; Maryland: *Daily National Intelligencer*, May 7, 17, 27, July 16, 30, 1831; Ohio: *Daily National Journal*, Nov. 7, Dec. 1, 3, 1831.

10. Delaware: *Daily National Journal*, June 24, 25, 1831; Virginia: *Richmond Constitutional Whig*, Sept. 1, 8, 15, Oct. 6, 10, 13, 27, Nov. 3, 17, 21, Dec. 1, 6, 9, 15, 1831; North Carolina: *Daily National Intelligencer*, July 2, 13, 1831.

sufficed in Tennessee and Louisiana.[11] Delegates from the District of Columbia were named by the central committee of Washington City.[12] Six states (South Carolina, Georgia, Alabama, Mississippi, Illinois, and Missouri) were not represented at Baltimore.

The type of meeting which appointed the delegates also provides a guide to the party's vigor in particular states. State conventions, legislative caucuses, and district conventions were indicative of formidable Clay strength, enough to enable him to compete on nearly equal, and in a few instances superior, terms with Jackson. Indiana, where Jackson won an easy, two-to-one victory in 1832, would be an anomaly in this group. Conversely, the use of public meetings alone evinced weakness, Delaware being an exception to this generalization. Why a strong National Republican state with a long addiction to nominating conventions should have abandoned the practice when it was especially appropriate is not clear. The party was weakest of all, obviously, in the states where no action was taken to send delegates. To hold a caucus required a substantial number of legislators openly identified with the party; state and local conventions had to be backed by a relatively large number of voters who elected the delegates. But even a thinly supported party could muster enough persons to stage a statewide public meeting.

The regional pattern of Clay's strength suggested by the way delegates to the national convention were appointed, and borne out by the election returns, closely resembled Adams's pattern in 1828—potent in New England, less strong but competitive in the middle Atlantic states (especially Maryland and Delaware), weak but still viable in Virginia and North Carolina, and feeble or nonexistent in the deep South and West except for Ohio and Kentucky. In popular votes, Clay ran slightly ahead of Adams, but failed to maintain even the semblance of a party in several states. Yet in spite of the soft spots and gaps, Clay succeeded in building a national party, and he did it without the prestige and patronage which Adams had enjoyed as an incumbent president. In 1832 these weapons were wielded against him by one of the great personalities of American history. Clay owed much of his success to the national convention as it was the necessity of electing delegates that first moved his adherents, in many states, to begin the task of creating an organization in their communities.

11. Tennessee: *Daily National Journal,* Dec. 2, 1831; Louisiana: *Daily National Intelligencer,* Nov. 25, 1831; Jan. 27, 1832.
12. *Daily National Journal,* May 6, 1831.

The Maryland caucus had observed the ideology implicit in the convention technique by pretending that the national convention would be a direct expression of the people's will as reflected by their delegates. In theory no one could know in advance whom the people would honor. Of course, everyone knew that the sole purpose of the convention was to nominate Clay. Its origin had been closely associated with his candidacy and many of the meetings to elect delegates were called under his name. Others were convoked in behalf of "the friends of the American System" which identified them beyond the slightest doubt as Clay vehicles. Still, there was no need to take any chances as the *National Journal* made clear: "We trust that the delegates to this Convention will come fully and emphatically instructed." Unless they were, the editor ominously warned, they would be "exposed to temptation and error which must always exist in bodies of men assembled for purposes which have been indistinctly defined. . . ."[13] John Agg feared "the intrigues of weak or false friends" who might "divert any of its deliberations into any other channel than that which the general sense of the advocates of the American System has marked. . . ." He was concerned, specifically, that the delegates might reject Clay even though public opinion had "been sufficiently explicit" as to whom the convention should nominate. The function of the delegates was to "fix" public sentiment "more intensely and more enthusiastically on that candidate who founded the American System, and has done so much to sustain it."[14] Most of the delegates, Agg happily noted, had been instructed to vote only for Clay.[15] He need not have worried; no other potential candidate within the party received an endorsement from an appointing body.

Clay's domination of the National Republican party placed him in a curious position prior to the convention. He was a candidate, yet he was not a candidate. He had been nominated by every conceivable method before the national convention met, but if it were admitted that he was already before the people then the national convention would be exposed as eyewash. The fact of his candidacy could scarcely be denied. "The nomination of Mr. Clay by the National Republican Convention, as we have before remarked," said the editor of the *Alexandria Gazette*, "will be but an echo of public sentiment declared in more than one hundred assemblies of the people in different parts

13. *Ibid.*, Feb. 23, 1831.
14. *Ibid.*, Apr. 28, 1831.
15. *Ibid.*, Feb. 24, Mar. 2, Apr. 7, May 6, Aug. 16, Sept. 23, 29, 1831.

of the country."[16] Clay made no secret that he was running; at least he used it as the reason for declining to attend a public dinner in his honor in the fall of 1831. Blair's *Globe* declared that this admission turned the Baltimore convention into a farce as the delegates "find themselves anticipated, and their candidate named without the *god-fatherly* aid, which they had been hustling to provide."[17]

The trouble was that Clay would not stay nominated. Jackson papers, or those disliking both Jackson and Clay—the admirers of McLean and Calhoun most notably—kept circulating rumors that Clay would be withdrawn so that the diverse anti-Jackson elements could concentrate their forces. These stories were hotly, and repeatedly, denied by Clay's friends.[18] The logic of such a withdrawal was brought home by the National Republicans' poor showing in the 1831 summer elections in Kentucky.[19] Although they managed to win a narrow majority in the legislature, they were able to take only four out of the state's twelve congressional seats. Coming on top of a series of Jackson victories since 1829, these defeats could not but fail to discourage all but the most devout. William B. Lewis gleefully reported to Van Buren that "The friends of Mr. Clay, in Kentucky, are quite disheartened; and almost ready to surrender him."[20] One discouraged National Republican reported that many persons in Pennsylvania felt that if Mr. Clay could not carry his own state he could certainly never carry the nation. "Have we," he asked, "any alternative?"[21]

The obvious "alternative" was to follow the lead of the Antimasons and back their expected nomination of McLean. Yet Clay's partisans showed no inclination to desert him even after the Kentucky elections.[22] McLean, projected as a candidate ever since 1828, engendered no enthusiasm among the National Republicans, for though he disapproved of the administration's patronage policies, he did not embrace the American System. Webster had declared in 1830 that McLean "must

---

16. Quoted in the *Kentucky Reporter*, Nov. 2, 1831.
17. Nov. 11, 1831.
18. *Daily National Journal*, Mar. 25, Apr. 2, 14, Aug. 20, Sept. 6, 15, 22, 30, Oct. 8, 1831; *Richmond Enquirer*, Aug. 5, 1831; *Baltimore Republican*, Aug. 2, 1831.
19. *New Hampshire Patriot*, Aug. 29, Sept. 5, Oct. 17, 1831.
20. Lewis to Van Buren, Sept. 17, 1831, Van Buren MSS (LC).
21. W. H. Dillingham to Taylor, Sept. 1, 1831, Taylor MSS.
22. *Daily National Intelligencer*, Sept. 17, 24, 1831; *Kentucky Reporter*, Sept. 21, 1831.

not be thought of, for he is not with us."[23] The discussion turned out to be academic because, as Lewis had foreseen, "the Judge is rather timid—he does not like to measure strength with old Hickory."

Then came the bombshell: the Antimasonic selection of a man who had acted with the National Republicans in all things. The effect on the party of Wirt's nomination was like "the swoop of a hawk upon a covey of partridges."[24] Samuel Southard, the former Secretary of the Navy, complained after the Antimasonic convention that "the mist is entirely too thick for Vision—I cannot see beyond the end of my nose."[25] Upon reflection, he decided that Wirt had made a grave miscalculation—not only would the National Republicans reject him, but the Antimasons would not rally behind him either because of his weak confession of their faith. Being a friend of Clay, Southard perhaps could not be expected to make an impartial analysis, but Adams, who had no such bias, was equally negative. Even though he applauded Wirt's nomination, he realized that any hope Clay would withdraw constituted a delusion.[26]

Antimasonic leaders, their future keyed to a joint nomination with the National Republicans, attempted to persuade their potential allies of the desirability of nominating Wirt (in case its expediency escaped their notice). Massachusetts Antimasons importuned Adams to intercede personally with Clay to secure his retirement, but Adams refused.[27] Nor did he think any of Clay's friends would undertake the assignment.[28] The only important National Republican politicians to openly advocate Clay's withdrawal were Ambrose Spencer and Timothy Pickering. If Clay "should be nominated and accept the nomination," Spencer wrote Webster, "our cause is lost, and General Jackson will certainly be re-elected—" But Spencer, chosen to be a delegate to the National Republican convention, accepted the inevitable. Rather

23. Webster to Mr. Pleasants, Mar. 6, 1830, Webster, *Correspondence of Webster*, I, 492.

24. *United States Telegraph*, Oct. 18, 1831.

25. Southard to Gouvernor, Oct. 13, 1831, Gouvernor MSS.

26. Adams, *Memoirs*, VIII (Oct. 27, 1831), 416; Edward and Alexander H. Everett to Clay, Oct. 29, 1832; Henry Dearborn to Clay, Oct. 29, 30, 1832; Abbott Lawrence to Clay, Oct. 30, 1832, Clay MSS.

27. Adams, *Memoirs*, VIII (Oct. 27, 1831), 416.

28. Edward Everett to Francis Granger, Nov. 10, 1831, Gideon and Francis Granger MSS.

than disturb the harmony of the convention, he declined to attend, thereby eliminating a possible source of opposition to Clay at Baltimore.[29] Webster agreed with Spencer about the harmful effect of a division in the anti-Jackson ranks, but foresaw no chance that Clay would not be nominated.[30] Pickering appealed directly to Clay to support Wirt as the only hope of beating Jackson.[31] But neither the old New England Federalist nor Spencer enjoyed wide influence in the party, and Spencer's advice was undoubtedly tainted by his son's high position in the Antimasonic party.

The reaction of the mass of National Republicans to the startling turn of events can best be gauged by the attitudes of the editors of the party's newspapers. There were literally hundreds of these journals, each independently operated, small businesses dependent upon the goodwill of the party's rank and file in order to sustain a precarious existence. A number of them, located in every state where the National Republicans were strong, quickly deserted Clay, advocating either that Wirt be nominated by the December convention or urging (and this amounted to the same thing) that it be postponed, thus leaving Wirt in possession of the field.[32] But out of the total number of papers involved, there were relatively few apostates from the Clay cause, perhaps a dozen. The majority of these were not influential organs. The major exceptions were the *New York American* and the *New York Journal of Commerce*, respected voices in the anti-Jackson camp.[33] National Republicanism in New York, however, had already made compromises with Antimasonry in order to stay alive. Its leaders had been engaged in a desperate, and losing, struggle ever since 1829 to maintain themselves as the second major party in New York. Union with the Antimasons could not fail to appeal to them as it promised the only chance of overcoming the Regency. In no other state was there so powerful an attraction for a merger of the two anti-Jackson parties. The *Richmond Constitutional Whig*, never sold on Clay, also wavered, made eyes at Wirt for a time, but fell back into Clay's

29. Spencer to Webster, Oct. 24, 1831, Van Tyne, *Letters of Webster*, p. 164. Also, see Spencer to James Clarke, Nov. 6, 1831, Clay MSS.

30. Webster to Spencer, Nov. 16, 1831, Van Tyne, *Letters of Webster*, pp. 167–68.

31. Pickering to Clay, Oct. 22, 1831, Colton, *Private Correspondence*, p. 319.

32. *Daily National Journal*, Oct. 29, Nov. 2, 12, 28, 1831; *Baltimore Republican*, Oct. 22, Nov. 5, 8, 9, 10, 11, 14, 1831; *Commercial Chronicle* [Baltimore], Dec. 10, 1831; *Richmond Enquirer*, Oct. 25, Nov. 1, 1831.

33. *Daily National Journal*, Oct. 15, 26, 1831; *Freeman's Banner*, Oct. 29, 1831.

arms before the convention.[34] Significantly, the only paper opposed to the president that persisted in pressing Wirt's nomination on the National Republicans was Green's *Telegraph*.[35] His advice was obviously suspect to the friends of the American System since he spoke for the champion of nullification and had only recently stopped attacking Clay.

Most of the party's newspapers observed, reportedly on Clay's advice, a conciliatory attitude toward the Antimasons and their nominee, yet one which conceded nothing.[36] "If soft phrases, and honied epithets could prevail upon Mr. Wirt's heart," commented a cynical Democratic editor, "he could not resist the gentle wooings of his Washington admirers."[37] National Republicans acknowledged "his splendid talents and unimpeachable character," but were "determined to hold fast to their first love. . . ."[38] The *National Journal* wasted no time after the Antimasonic convention had adjourned in announcing that Clay would "neither be *immediately* nor *unconditionally* withdrawn. . . ."[39]

As the professions of fealty to Clay poured in, arguments in defense of his staying in the race unfolded. It was asserted that Wirt's nomination would help Clay rather than injure him since Wirt would attract more votes from Jackson.[40] Why the Antimasonic nominee would appeal to Democrats was never explained. Clay could not withdraw because "public opinion" had "unequivocally pointed out this man" as the choice of the party; the convention delegates were "obligated to nominate him."[41] Most speciously of all, in view of its short history, the *Journal* invoked party loyalty: "It is asked of us who belong to the National Republican party, to abandon our colors, and to surrender the advanced and powerful position we have gained, for the purpose of permitting a new flag, the colors of which are not yet dry, and the motto on which is not yet determined, to take the place of the

---

34. *Richmond Constitutional Whig*, Oct. 3, 10, 13, Nov. 14, 17, 28, 1831.

35. *United States Telegraph*, Oct. 8, 18, 19, 20, 27, Nov. 5, 9, 17, 19, 23, 1831.

36. *Daily National Intelligencer*, Oct. 5–Nov. 17, 1831; *Kentucky Reporter*, Oct. 12, 19, 26, Nov. 2, 9, 1831; *Freeman's Banner*, Oct. 8, 22, Nov. 29, 1831; *Daily National Journal*, Oct. 12, 18, 21, 22, 24, 28, 31, Nov. 2, 8, 12, 13, 1831; *The Focus*, Nov. 29, 1831.

37. *Baltimore Republican*, Oct. 6, 1831.

38. *Freeman's Banner*, Oct. 15, 1831.

39. *National Journal*, Oct. 18, 1831.

40. *Ibid.; Freeman's Banner*, Nov. 19, 1831.

41. *Daily National Journal*, Oct. 31, 1831.

National Republican standard, whose hues have been kissed by the sun beams of more than a single summer, and whose inscription, 'For Our Country' has received the acclamations of three-fourths of the States of the Union."[42] Agg was on more solid ground when he described Clay as "the centre round which the National Republican party formed itself. . . . How then can he and the party be divorced?"[43] That was the point: to surrender Clay would be to abandon the party itself.

The lack of any ground swell for Wirt was vividly and doubly illustrated in the interval between the Antimasonic and National Republican conventions. At a so-called national convention of the "friends of the tariff" in New York in September, 1831, summoned to counteract the hysterical opposition of the South to protection, there came the news of Wirt's nomination in Baltimore. Virtually all of the delegates in New York were committed to Clay; the tariff convention was little more than an offshoot of the National Republican party. If there had been any desire to dump the Kentuckian it would have surfaced quickly. But while the choice of Wirt "astounded" them, the delegates recovered from their "momentary embarrassment" in short order. All in New York, Clay was assured, believed that the National Republican convention could not alter its predetermined course "without disgrace and infamy"; the party would unquestionably unite behind him despite "the selfish policy" of the Antimasons.[44]

The other incident took place in Baltimore. Wirt, at the time of his presidential nomination, was a duly appointed delegate to the National Republican convention. His resignation necessitated a new ward meeting to select a replacement. Whatever support he possessed within the lines of his former party would have to be demonstrated among his friends and neighbors. Instead, they repudiated him, reaffirming their preference for Clay in clear and ringing language.[45]

Clay certainly showed no inclination to defer to the third party. His opinions on Antimasonry were not flattering. "If the alternative be between Andrew Jackson," he wrote after Wirt's nomination, "and an Anti-Masonic candidate with his exclusive proscriptive principles, I should be embarrassed in the choice. I am not sure that the old

42. *Ibid.*, Nov. 1, 1831.
43. *Ibid.*, Nov. 21, 1831.
44. M. L. Davis to Clay, Nov. 2, 1831, Clay MSS.
45. Wirt to Luke Tierman, copy, undated, Wirt MSS; *Kentucky Reporter*, Nov. 23, 1831; *Niles' Weekly Register*, XLI (Nov. 19, 1831), 221.

tyranny is not better than the new one."[46] It simply was not in Clay
to give up the fight. His intention of remaining in the contest was
unmistakably disclosed later that fall by his election to the United
States Senate where he could direct the crucial struggles scheduled
for the coming session.[47]

Political realists such as Joseph Gales, Jr., understood that Clay's
strength was "not transferable." He also realized that the party's fasci-
nation with the Kentuckian might be as fatal as it was profound,
but along with the rest preferred to die "with the harness on our
backs, having the consolation at least of a noble company of martyrs."[48]
"One of the characteristics of Mr. Clay is the facility with which
he deceives himself and his partisans into a hope of success, against
the opinions of all the world besides," Green sourly agreed.[49] Giving
a higher priority to the nomination than to victory in November was
not an invention of twentieth-century ideologues.

By the end of November, Agg was able to write that "the feverish
impatience which was some time ago manifested for the withdrawal
of Mr. Clay has somewhat abated, and more wholesome symptoms
have succeeded."[50] The panic was over. Once their confidence was
regained, the Clay prints adopted a harder line toward their Anti-
masonic rivals. Wirt was more to be pitied than censured, a dupe
of dishonest men who had falsely told him Clay would withdraw.
The nomination had been the product of a small group of intriguers,
indifferent even to the wishes of their own membership.[51] One paper
professed to see the fine hand of the ubiquitous Van Buren, who somehow (no details were furnished) contrived to rig Wirt's nomination
in order to aid Jackson.[52]

With such optimism as they could muster, the delegates to the National Republican convention descended on Baltimore to do their duty.
The onset of winter had already turned the roads to mud, slowing

46. Clay to Brooke, Oct. 4, 1831, Colton, *Private Correspondence*, p. 316.
47. *Daily National Journal*, Nov. 21, 1831; Webster to Clay, Oct. 5, 1831,
Colton, *Private Correspondence*, pp. 317–19.
48. Gales to Webster, Oct. 19, 1831, George Ticknor Curtis, *Life of Daniel
Webster* (New York, 1870), I, 401–2.
49. *United States Telegraph*, Oct. 19, 1831.
50. *Daily National Journal*, Nov. 26, 1831.
51. *Daily National Intelligencer*, Oct. 28, Nov. 16, 23, 1831; *Daily National
Journal*, Nov. 3, 4, 18, Dec. 9, 1831; *Freeman's Banner*, Nov. 19, 1831.
52. *Daily National Journal*, Oct. 14, 1831.

the arrival of many delegates. Agg regretted that the meeting, contrary to his advice, had been put off so long.[53] There was some discussion of moving the opening session back a few days to allow more time for travel. It was decided to open at the appointed time, but in deference to those who had been delayed no important business was transacted at the first session.

Approximately 130 delegates were gathered at the Athenaeum at noon, Monday, December 12. Peter A. Livingston of New York moved the appointment of Abner Lacock of Pennsylvania as temporary chairman. Lacock, as head of the Senate committee investigating Jackson's Seminole campaign, had won early distinction as an opponent of the impetuous general. On assuming the post, Lacock suggested that each state delegation examine the credentials of its own members and submit a certified list to the convention the following day. It was then moved that editors and reporters "be invited to take seats to be appropriated for their accommodation." Another delegate proposed the substitution of "permitted" for "invited." This elicited a spirited debate which ended with the amendment being withdrawn and the passage of the original motion. That done, the convention adjourned until noon on Tuesday.[54]

The convention thus inauspiciously begun differed little from its predecessor and successor. The general format had been worked out long ago in the states. It did introduce several features that were subsequently to gain prominence, not to say notoriety, in the conduct of national conventions. These were the keynote address, the nominating speech, and the seconding speech. None of them appears to have been part of the planned agenda, but rather all occurred spontaneously, injected by individual delegates acting on a whim of the moment. It would be many years before they acquired the institutional status they later enjoyed and their auditors suffered (until the impact of television). In most respects, however, the National Republican convention was the least exciting or interesting of the first three national conventions. Its major decision was a foregone conclusion and the proceedings produced no surprises or dramatic discords.

The attendance was disappointing. Eventually, 175 delegates from eighteen (of the twenty-four) states and the District of Columbia took their seats.[55] Many of the delegations were far below their as-

53. *Ibid.*, Dec. 12, 1831; *Daily National Intelligencer*, Dec. 10, 1831.
54. *Niles' Weekly Register*, XLI (Dec. 24, 1831), 301.
55. *Ibid.*, (Dec. 17, 1831), 282.

signed strength, while the District of Columbia, with no electoral votes, had 5 delegates. For a major party this was not an impressive response, although a number of prominent party figures attended as delegates— Luther Bradish, Peter Porter, and Henry Wheaton from New York, John Sergeant from Pennsylvania, James Barbour and John Marshall, Jr., from Virginia, Allen Trimble and Jeremiah Morrow from Ohio, and Josiah Johnston from Louisiana.[56] Five of the delegates were incumbent members of Congress, over 20 more were former members. In addition there were four former cabinet officers and four former governors.[57] Webster made the trip from the capital, but came only as a spectator. Many of the most outstanding men of the party, which possessed an abundance of glittering names, were conspicuous by their absence. On Tuesday, after the roll call, a committee on permanent organization was appointed to recommend officers for the convention. Former Secretary of War James Barbour was selected president, and on taking the chair "delivered a brief, but spirited address," the national convention's first keynote speech.[58] Four vice-presidents and two secretaries were also named. Without fanfare, Barbour announced that the moment had come to nominate a presidential candidate. Before commencing with the ballot Barbour reported that he had a few days earlier received a communication from Clay, and as his name had "been repeatedly mentioned as a most fit and proper person to be nominated" Barbour believed it appropriate to read the letter to the delegates.[59] Clay allowed that he was aware that some of the delegates favored his nomination, but he hoped that none would feel bound to vote for him because of a prior commitment. He wanted every delegate to vote only for the man he believed most fit for the presidential office and most likely to defeat Jackson.

Clay's message was a bit of ritualistic modesty designed to create the impression that the delegates were at perfect liberty to vote for Wirt (or anyone else) should they so desire; all pledges were void. If the convention nominated him it would be a free and open decision. This attempt to reverse the universal opinion that the convention was his creature is understandable, but the letter could hardly have been

---

56. *Journal of the National Republican Convention, Which Assembled in the City of Baltimore, Dec. 12, 1831, For the Nominations of Candidates to Fill the Offices of President and Vice President* (Washington, n.d.).

57. *Daily National Journal*, Dec. 21, 1831.

58. *Niles' Weekly Register*, XLI (Dec. 17, 1831), 281.

59. *Journal of the National Republican Convention*, p. 8.

sincere. The character of the meeting was as well known to Clay as to everyone else and nothing less than a flat withdrawal combined with an endorsement of Wirt could have prevented his nomination.

At the letter's conclusion Livingston, "after some pertinent and eloquent remarks, nominated *Henry Clay*, which was received with loud and reiterated plaudits."[60] This was the first nominating speech and the first demonstration (and seems to have been genuinely spontaneous) in the history of national conventions. No further nominations were made. The roll call followed, each delegate rising in his place and naming "the candidate to which he was most favorable." Although Clay was the only candidate before the convention, this presumably did not prevent the delegates from voting for someone else. With one exception all responded with the name of the Kentucky senator. A delegate from North Carolina, according to the official proceedings, was excused from voting because he had not made up his mind. According to other, and more reliable, reports indecisiveness was not what prevented him from casting his ballot. He told the assembly that "I am still, Mr. President, of the same opinion that I expressed last evening. I do not think it *possible* to elect Henry Clay president—and although I entertain as exalted an opinion of him as does the Gentleman from New York [Livingston], I will not, under the circumstances, give him my vote to place him before the people as a candidate. I am opposed to his nomination, and to *deceiving* the people with impressions that we can elect him."[61] With every vote but one Clay was declared the nominee ("repeated cheers") and a committee composed of one delegate from each state was appointed to secure his acceptance. They immediately embarked for Washington.

The near unanimity of the delegates was not accidental. All three conventions were obsessed with presenting an unbroken front to the public. The Antimasons had hammered out their differences at closed caucuses attended by all interested delegates and the National Republicans followed the same procedure. Three caucuses were held. The first, lasting four hours, met Sunday evening before the convention opened, the second on Monday evening, the last on Tuesday evening.[62] None of them were widely reported in the press, as national conventions were not deemed worthy of intensive coverage. Publicity would

60. *Niles' Weekly Register*, XLI (Dec. 24, 1831), 302.
61. *New Hampshire Patriot*, Jan. 2, 1832; *The Globe* [Washington], Dec. 21, 1831.
62. *Richmond Enquirer*, Dec. 17, 1831.

eventually force the delegates' caucus to be abandoned in favor of the boss- and smoke-filled room. The initial caucus on Sunday arranged for the organization of the convention, its agenda and officers. The Monday evening caucus, to which the North Carolina delegate alluded, dealt with the presidential nomination. Like the Antimasons, the National Republicans were determined to reach a consensus on candidates before the official balloting, after which the minority was expected to yield. That way there would be no jarring scenes on the convention floor. Whether the delegates balloted in the caucus, as the Antimasons had done, is not clear. Probably, it was not necessary. The only account I have found reported that some of the delegates wanted to adjourn without making a nomination, "many" advocated nominating Wirt, "and many (a large majority,) [were] for bringing Clay forward."[63] Only the independence of a single delegate spoiled the illusion of total agreement in the formal session the next day. The final caucus on Tuesday evening achieved unity over the vice-presidency after "great difficulty."[64]

On Wednesday the session opened with a prayer. After disposing of some minor procedural matters, the committee to inform Clay of his nomination made its report. Clay accepted the honor in a brief letter, received by the delegates with "immense applause."[65] The next item was the nomination of his running mate. Those most frequently mentioned before the convention met were Wirt, Southard, Ambrose Spencer, Barbour, and Webster.[66] Barbour withdrew his name from consideration. Webster might have been willing to run, but he was from a state and section already solid for Clay. Neither Spencer nor Southard would strengthen the ticket. Wirt would have been ideal, but could not be nominated since he had refused to withdraw for the presidency. The Tuesday caucus, by a process I have been unable to penetrate, ignored all of the early favorites and chose a man "no one thought of as V. President!!!"[67]

63. *Ibid.*
64. *Albany Argus,* Dec. 19, 20, 1831; *Kentucky Reporter,* Jan. 4, 1832.
65. *Niles' Weekly Register,* XLI (Dec. 24, 1831), 304.
66. *Daily National Journal,* Jan. 6, Sept. 7, 1831; *Richmond Constitutional Whig,* Aug. 1, Nov. 10, 1831; *The Focus,* Feb. 3, 1831; *Western Citizen,* Jan. 22, 1831; *Daily National Intelligencer,* Nov. 7, 30, 1831; *Albany Daily Advertiser,* Dec. 17, 1831; *Albany Evening Journal,* Sept. 7, 1831; *Kentucky Reporter,* Aug. 25, Sept. 22, 1830; Jan. 4, 1831; *The Commentator,* Sept. 21, 1831; John L. Lawrence to Clay, Dec. 7, 1831, Clay MSS; S. L. Southard to James Barbour, Dec. 17, 1829, Barbour MSS.
67. Richard M. Johnson to John McLean, Dec. 15, 1831, McLean MSS.

He was John Sergeant of Philadelphia, former Federalist, former congressman (he had been defeated in 1831), former minister to the Panama Congress, and, currently, a mainstay of the National Republican party in Pennsylvania. Sergeant was an enthusiastic supporter of the American System, so his nomination did not signify an effort to balance the ticket ideologically. His nomination was certainly a continuation of the Adams policy (e.g., Rush's selection for vice-president in 1828) of trying to wean the most tariff-minded of states away from its unnatural affection for Jackson. By the usual political reckoning Pennsylvania should have been wild about Harry instead of giving its heart, and twenty-eight electoral votes, to a president who all but ignored the tariff and was preparing to make war on the state's domination of national banking.

On Wednesday Sergeant's name was presented to the convention without benefit of oratory. One enthusiastic delegate from the District of Columbia, however, seconded the nomination "in a speech of considerable length," a pioneer effort that, unfortunately for future generations, was not quashed.[68] His was the only name offered, and on the roll call he received a unanimous vote. That completed the important business of the day.

Little remained to be done, but it took two days to do it. On Thursday the convention urged that central committees of correspondence be appointed in states where none existed. A proposal to hold a National Convention of Young Men in May, 1832, at Washington was approved. Sergeant's letter of acceptance was read. In the afternoon the delegates formed a procession and marched to the home of Charles Carroll of Carrolltown to be introduced to the last living signer of the Declaration of Independence. Friday, December 16, was the last day. The "Address to the People," a scorching attack on Jackson which soft-pedaled the American System, was read and formally adopted. Arrangements were made to have 10,000 copies printed and distributed. After thanking the officers and the "citizens of Baltimore" who paid the convention expenses, the delegates adjourned, most of them going directly to Washington to wait personally on Clay in order to "*give effect* to the proceedings."[69]

Reactions to the convention were predictably partisan. The *Kentucky Reporter* exclaimed that "A more disinterested body of men—a

68. *Journal of the National Republican Convention*, p. 12.
69. *Albany Argus*, Dec. 19, 1831.

band of truer patriots, has not been convened together since the days of the Revolution."[70] *The Globe* resorted to ridicule: "Certainly there was never such a miserable mummery played off before the eyes of an intelligent people, as is presented in the getting up, and going off, of the National Republican Convention. *'Unanimity,'* we are told, prevails, *'touching the nomination of Mr. Clay for the office of President.'* In a convention convoked for this special purpose, and composed of persons, who, we have no doubt were, for the most part, pressed by Mr. Clay himself, to undertake this service, this 'unanimity' is not extraordinary."[71] Jackson was more direct. "The other day," he wrote Van Buren in England, "the convention at Baltimore nominated, as instructed, Mr. Henry Clay. . . ."[72] This was precisely the charge that the Clayites were to make with less truth but more effect against the Democratic convention a few months later.

Clay had few illusions about his prospects. A few days before the convention opened he wrote Brooke that "The impression here is, that the Baltimore Convention will make a nomination of me. I wish I could add that the impression was more favorable than it is of the success of such a nomination." Then, with the characteristic optimism of a true gambler, he added: "Something, however, may turn up (and that must be our encouraging hope) to give a brighter aspect to our affairs."[73]

Adjournment of the National Republican convention did not end the effort to find a common candidate to oppose Jackson. The powerful executive office and the Electoral College, the Founding Fathers' great contributions to the two-party system, were at work. The Antimasons knew they could not elect a president on their own ticket. National Republican leaders wanted to unify the anti-Jackson vote, for unless there were a merger the president's reelection seemed assured.

A union could be achieved in several ways. Obviously, either Clay or Wirt could withdraw in favor of the other. Or both could bow out, throwing their support to a new candidate acceptable to their respective parties. Wirt seemed eager to retire after Clay had been nominated, but refused to do so on his own authority. The Antimasonic nomination had been thrust upon him and only those who had con-

70. Dec. 28, 1831.
71. Dec. 15, 1831.
72. Jackson to Van Buren, Dec. 17, 1831, Van Buren MSS (LC).
73. Clay to Brooke, Dec. 9, 1831, Colton, *Private Correspondence*, p. 321.

ferred the honor could retract it; he was simply a passive spectator. But considerations of his own honor aside, he sincerely hoped a compromise candidate could be found.[74] Clay gave no hint though that he was willing to call it quits. The time for doing that was prior to the National Republican convention. To have deserted his friends after the convention would have left them totally in the lurch and destroyed the main organized force behind the American System.

Who was available as a unity candidate? The Antimasons had no one to offer, otherwise they would never have chosen Wirt. The Nationals had a fuller stable, but no one who showed promise of being able to go the distance. Adams had one foot firmly mired in each party, yet neither wanted him. Rush was unreliable. Webster was the most plausible alternative so far as the Antimasons were concerned. His weakness lay within his own party: Clay so greatly overshadowed him that he had no sizeable following outside New England. Utterly no disposition to drop Clay for Webster, or for anyone else, found support in party newspapers. Outside the two parties, Calhoun and McLean were looking for an excuse to run. Calhoun was pleasing to neither Antimason nor National Republican because his position on the tariff was popular only in the South while they were both oriented toward the North. McLean's friends were certain that he was just the man to fuse the entire anti-Jackson spectrum, and they anticipated that a congressional caucus would eliminate Clay and Wirt by bringing him forward.[75] The Ohioan's artful public silence and the sympathetic hearing he gave to all who complained about the administration caused many of the anti-Jackson elements to believe that he stood with them. Yet none could ever be sufficiently confident of his views to nominate him. As the congressional session drew to a close in the early summer of 1832 McLean was informed that there was no movement to hold a caucus to select a new candidate.[76]

There remained one other possibility. The two parties might effect a devious, but workable, coalition at the state level by nominating

---

74. Wirt to Dabney Carr, Jan. 12, 1832, Kennedy, *Memoirs of Wirt*, pp. 316–20; Wirt to McLean, Apr. 17, 1832, McLean MSS.

75. Morgan Neville to McLean, Nov. 4, 1831; M. T. Simpson to McLean, June 13, 1832; William Russell to McLean, June 14, 1832; Elisha Whittlesey to McLean, June 20, 1832; H. R. W. Hill to McLean, June 27, 1832, McLean MSS. Wirt also thought there might be a congressional caucus to unite the Jackson opposition. Wirt to Dabney Carr, Oct. 7, 1831; Wirt to Rush, Oct. 6, 1831, Wirt MSS.

76. M. T. Simpson to McLean, July 2, 1832, McLean MSS.

the same persons for electors, although continuing to support different presidential candidates. In one respect the strategy was superior to a joint nomination as each party could conduct a separate campaign— the Antimasons could ride their peculiar hobby without fear of offending those National Republicans who were repulsed by it, and the National Republicans could stress the Bank, tariff, and internal improvements while ignoring Masonry. But it also had its drawback—the members of each party had to believe that the electors would vote for their man. The coalition electors would be unpledged, thus exciting mutual suspicion between the two parties. Would they, in the event of election, vote for Clay or Wirt? Furthermore, there were bound to be those in each party, particularly among the Antimasons, who preferred defeat to association with outsiders.

New York and Pennsylvania, the most populous states and the main sources of Antimasonic strength, were the centers of fusionist activity. Antimasons in New York, guided by Weed and other of the less fanatic party leaders, worked out the details of a coalition with National Republicans in the spring of 1832.[77] At their state convention in June the Antimasons nominated Granger for governor, but divided their electoral ticket nominations with the National Republicans.[78] The senatorial electors chosen to head the ticket were Chancellor James Kent, a leading Clay disciple, and John C. Spencer, the best known of the Antimasonic politicians besides Granger. A short time later the National Republican convention made identical nominations.[79] The electors were publicly uncommitted, but the leaders had a private understanding that should the ticket carry they would vote for Clay.[80] The Antimasons, in other words, sacrificed their nebulous national aspirations for a chance to capture the state government. Clay and Wirt both approved their merger even though some of their partisans had serious misgivings.[81]

77. Clay to Weed, Apr. 14, 1832, Thurlow Barnes Weed, *Memoir of Thurlow Weed* (Boston, 1884), p. 42. Hiram Ketchum to Clay, May 12, 1832; P. B. Porter to Clay, May 27, June 6, 1832; Clay MSS; Orville L. Holley to Seward, May 8, 1832; William H. Maynard to Seward, June 8, 1832, Seward MSS.
78. "Anti-Masonic Republican State Convention," *Evening Journal Extra* [Albany, June 21, 1832].
79. *Niles' Weekly Register*, XLII (Aug. 4, 1832), 402.
80. P. B. Porter to Clay, Apr. 22, 1832; Hiram Ketchum to Clay, May 19, 1832, Clay MSS; Granger to E. Sedgwick, Jr., Aug. 31, 1832, Weed MSS.
81. M. L. Davis to Clay, May 30, 1832, Clay MSS; Webster to Abraham Van Vechten, July 2, 1832, Van Tyne, *Letters of Webster*, p. 175; Hiram Ketchum to Clay, June 30, 1832, Clay MSS; R. M. Livingston to J. W. Taylor,

In Pennsylvania the Antimasons were clearly the senior partner. They ignored the National Republicans in nominating Joseph Ritner for governor and an electoral slate pledged to Wirt at a state convention in February, 1832.[82] The National Republicans selected a separate electoral ticket, but did not designate a gubernatorial candidate, in hopes of tempting Governor George Wolf into breaking with Jackson.[83] By summer though the pressure for an alliance had become "irresistable," so Sergeant told Clay, "too powerful to be controlled, if there were a disposition to control it."[84] Shortly thereafter, the National Republican central committee endorsed Ritner.[85] In October the Clay electors were withdrawn.[86] One Antimasonic leader "intimated" that the Antimasonic electors would vote, if victorious, for Wirt and Sergeant.[87]

Both parties nominated separate state and national tickets in Ohio. The National Republican candidate for governor then withdrew in an attempt to force a joint nomination, but his Antimasonic counterpart declined to follow suit. After the state elections in October the Antimasonic central committee urged party members to vote for the National Republican electors.[88] Apparently, there was an understanding that if the Antimasonic electors carried New York, Pennsylvania, and Vermont then the Ohio electors would vote for Wirt; otherwise, they would vote for Clay.[89]

Elsewhere the coalition movement either amounted to little or floundered completely. New England National Republicans were not under the same compulsion to cooperate with the Antimasons as their brothers in New York, Pennsylvania, and Ohio. In three states, Massa-

---

June 27, 1832; Lemuel C. Paine to J. W. Taylor, May 25, 1832; William K. Scott to J. W. Taylor, copy, Aug. 27, 1832, Taylor MSS; J. C. Spencer to Weed, July 13, Sept. 21, 1832, Weed, *Memoir*, pp. 43–44; A. H. Tracy to Seward, May 30, June 12, 1832, Seward MSS; *The Globe*, Aug. 28, 1832.

82. *Proceedings of the Democratic Antimasonic State Convention Held at Harrisburg, February 22, 1832.* n.p., n.d.

83. *Freeman's Banner*, Jan. 21, 1832; *Niles' Weekly Register*, XLII (June 9, 1832), 273–74.

84. Sergeant to Clay, Aug. 3, 1832, Clay MSS.

85. *Daily National Intelligencer*, Sept. 19, 1832.

86. *Ibid.*, Aug. 15, Oct. 19, 1832.

87. *Richmond Enquirer*, Oct. 26, 1832.

88. Weisenburger, *Passing of the Frontier*, pp. 266–70; *Richmond Enquirer*, Oct. 30, 1832.

89. *Niles' Weekly Register*, XLIII (Oct. 20, 27, 1832), 118, 138; *Daily National Intelligencer*, Oct. 25, 1832; *The Globe*, Oct. 27, 1832.

chusetts, Connecticut, and Rhode Island, the National Republicans were the majority party and this forced the Antimasons to league with the Democrats. In Maine and New Hampshire the Antimasons were not strong enough for the Nationals to bother with. The situation was reversed in Vermont where the Antimasons did not need or want help from other parties. So in those six states no coalition took place.[90] The New Jersey Antimasons, though small in numbers, made their own electoral nominations and never surrendered them.[91] In no other states were the Antimasons able to mount the semblance of an independent campaign.

Where it counted the National Republicans and Antimasons were able to come to terms with one another. It may be that the accommodation drained both sets of partisans of some of their zeal, but it seems unlikely that this could have altered the outcome of the election. Clay's poor showing has been attributed to the siphoning off of anti-Jackson votes by the Antimasons.[92] This is conclusively refuted by the coalitions in New York, Pennsylvania, and Ohio. Only in Vermont and New Jersey did the third party conceivably cost Clay electoral votes. Vermont was carried for Wirt with Clay finishing second and Jackson a poor third. Without the Antimasons the National Republicans would undoubtedly have won the state's seven electoral votes. The New Jersey case is more complicated. The Wirt electors received only 485 votes (out of a total of 47,734 cast), but Jackson carried the state by a mere 463 votes so that had Clay received all but 10 of Wirt's votes he would have carried the state. Adding both Vermont and New Jersey's electoral votes to Clay's column, however, would not alter materially the magnitude of Jackson's victory.

To which party, National Republican or Antimasonic, the future belonged was still not clear after the election. It was certain that both could not survive as major parties. The responsible leaders of each had worked out an effective, pragmatic, and temporary liaison in which both parties retained their separate identities. For all practical purposes it turned out that they had been joined forever and would

---

90. *Antimasonic Republican Convention of Massachusetts, Held at Worcester Sept. 5th and 6th, 1832; Albany Evening Journal,* Jan. 26, Feb. 9, 23, 28, July 16, 18, 1832.

91. *Albany Argus,* Sept. 4, 1832.

92. Horace Greeley, *Recollections of a Busy Man* (New York, 1868), p. 108; Thomas Hart Clay, *Henry Clay* (Philadelphia, 1910), pp. 203–4.

soon acknowledge that fact by assuming a common name, the Whig party. Although no one fully realized it, Antimasonry was already a spent force by November, 1832. It proved a bright, brief flame incapable of sustaining itself once the primary inspiration subsided.[93] Except in Pennsylvania, Antimasonic leaders were prepared to abandon the party.[94] Whatever the sins of Masonry, they did not furnish adequate material to build a national political party. One critic of Antimasonry correctly predicted in November "that in a short time, men will look back and wonder, that persons in the exercise of their sober senses, had ever been gulled by it."[95] The Jacksonians, in the meantime, were moving toward a resolution of their own internal conflicts.

93. A. H. Tracy to Seward, Nov. 19, 1831, Seward MSS.
94. ―― to Seward, Apr. 6, 1832, Seward MSS; Adams, *Memoirs,* VIII (Apr. 17, 1833), 543; Weed, *Memoir,* pp. 47–48; Weed, *Autobiography,* pp. 432–35; Seward, *Autobiography,* pp. 101, 147–48; Henry R. Mueller, *The Whig Party in Pennsylvania* (New York, 1922), pp. 13–35.
95. P. N. Nicholas to Flagg, Nov. 14, 1832, Flagg MSS.

V

The Democrats
1829–32

"Rival aspirants for the superiority of position in their own ranks
have always and everywhere been the bane of political organizations, disturbing their peace and impairing their efficiency, and
will continue to be so as long as the nature of man remains what
it is."

Autobiography of Martin Van Buren

NINE

The President's Party

Although last in point of time, and the only one which did not formally nominate a presidential candidate, the Democratic convention of 1832 has been written about far more than its Antimasonic or National Republican forerunners. This results chiefly from the direct involvement in it of two presidents, the incumbent and his immediate successor, and its greater intrinsic drama. The convention was the only one of the three which produced a contest for any office. Then, too, the convention is frequently cited, both in its calling and meeting, as a notorious example of Jackson's power over the Democratic party. By threats, wire-pulling, and a shameless deployment of patronage, we are told, he forced an unpopular nominee for vice-president on the resisting delegates.[1] The tale is clearly adopted, more or less complete, from charges made by hostile contemporaries.[2] While an enemy's account may be a valuable source of information, it cannot be accepted at face value unless it coincides with demonstrable facts. That coincidence, in this instance, is missing. Most of what is known about the Democratic convention of 1832 is wrong. Seen in its true light the convention was the apogee of a slow and painful process by which

---

1. See, for instance, Agar, *The Price of Union*, pp. 246–47; James, *Andrew Jackson*, p. 605; Carl Russell Fish, *The Rise of the Common Man, 1830–1850* (New York, 1927), pp. 45–46; William O. Lynch, *Fifty Years of Party Warfare (1787–1837)* (Indianapolis, 1931), p. 418; M. Ostrogorski, *Democracy and the Organization of Political Parties* (New York, 1902), II, 63–64; McMaster, *A History of the People of the United States*, VI, 141–43; Clay, *Henry Clay*, p. 199; Carl Schurz, *Life of Henry Clay* (Boston, 1887), I, 379; John Spencer Bassett, *Life of Andrew Jackson* (New York, 1931), p. 541.

2. *The Focus*, Dec. 12, 20, 1831; *Richmond Enquirer*, July 22, 1831; *United States Telegraph*, July 12, 19, Aug. 23, 30, Sept. 1, 13, Nov. 7, 17, 1831; Jan. 2, 7, 26, 27, Feb. 2, 16, 25, Mar. 22, 31, May 23, 26, June 6, Sept. 15, 1832.

a temporary and opportunistic alliance was turned into a political party rather than being a charade ordered performed by a dictatorial president.

The Jackson party which triumphed so decisively in 1828 was a variegated collection of hero worshippers, southern disciples of states rights, northern advocates of protection, western farmers, and politicians from everywhere who recognized a winner. Out of necessity, the candidate had straddled the substantive issues. During the campaign he and his supporters shrewdly concealed their disagreements by an endless reference to the "corrupt bargain" which had deprived the general of the presidency in 1825. Coupled with this accusation was a vague, but nonetheless effective, crying out against aristocracy indicative of the common man's increasing political consciousness.

Jackson's platform had been the most basic one possible: Throw the Rascals Out. Once in office he could not escape a confrontation with the leading public questions, but he tried. The first tangible sign of direction did not come until the veto of the Maysville Road bill. It was written in the strict constructionist language dear to southern hearts, yet its application to so insignificant a project cast serious doubt as to whether he intended to prevent enactment of major internal improvements legislation. On the more sensitive tariff issue, the policy of the administration was even more opaque. No compromise seemed possible between advocates of protection and free trade, between the extremes of Pennsylvania and South Carolina, both enthusiastically for Jackson in 1828. The moderate but protectionist act of 1832, although signed by the president, was not his measure. Only South Carolina's growing bitterness over the tariff and its ultimate defiance of the law permitted Jackson to sidestep this explosive topic and replace it with an issue around which he could rally a national consensus—the integrity of the Union. And not until the summer of 1832 did he find the issue, a gift from Clay, that gave his administration its distinctive character—opposition to the rechartering of the second Bank of the United States.

Before the spring of 1832 the very survival of the Jackson party had been threatened by the "great succession question." Following his defeat in 1825, Jackson had advocated amending the Constitution to limit the president to one term. In his annual message in December, 1829, he officially commended this change to the national legislature.[3]

3. *United States Telegraph–Extra,* Dec. 8, 1829.

Given his advanced age (he was sixty-two shortly after the inauguration) and poor health, this stance obliged most politicians to assume
that he would not seek reelection. Intense speculation as to who would
inherit his mantle began early, even before Jackson took office, and
centered almost exclusively on the two men, Calhoun and Van Buren,
whose ability, popularity, and service to the party elevated them over
a host of possible successors.[4]

The South Carolinian had been prominent in national politics for
almost two decades despite his relatively youthful forty-seven years.
His dry run for the presidency in 1824 indicated that he had a national
as well as a local following. Van Buren, although not so widely known
as Calhoun, had earned an enviable reputation in Washington for his
astuteness, and had a long list of influential friends, particularly among
the old Crawford party in the south Atlantic states. Equally important,
he was the acknowledged master (since Clinton's death) of the nation's
most populous state. In the fall elections of 1828 he had been chosen
governor of New York. Recognition of the preeminence of the two
men came when Jackson selected his cabinet. The first place went
to Van Buren who resigned as governor to become Secretary of State.
One of Calhoun's most ardent followers, Representative Ingham, was
given the Treasury. In addition, two other portfolios went to men
considered to be his friends: John Branch of North Carolina was named
to head the Navy Department, and John Berrien of Georgia was made
attorney-general.[5]

"Whenever the Jackson party falls asunder," announced the *National Journal* shortly after the election, "it will be from the cumbrous
character of its materials, and the weakness of the cement which binds
them together."[6] There was more truth here than the Jacksonians
dared admit. The prospect of a single term for the Hero and the
thinness of any ideological agreement opened the way to an early

4. *Daily National Intelligencer*, Dec. 24, 1829; *Kentucky Reporter*, Mar. 4,
1829; Storrs MS, Feb. 9, Dec. 20, 1828; John J. Degraff to Flagg, Dec. 27,
1828; Silas Wright, Jr., to W. L. Marcy, Feb. 1828, Flagg MSS; G. C.
Verplanck to Van Buren, Dec. 6 [1828]; David B. McWilliams to Van Buren,
Nov. 17, 1829; Thomas Cooper to Van Buren, Mar. 24, 1829; W. S. Crawford
to Van Buren, July 11, 1829; William Carroll to Van Buren, Aug. 4, 1829,
Van Buren MSS (LC).

5. Thomas P. Govan, "John Berrien and the Administration of Andrew Jackson," *JSH*, V (Nov., 1939), 451–57, maintains that neither Branch nor Berrien
were Calhoun partisans, but the opinion was common at the time that they
were. See, for example, Louis McLane to Van Buren, Feb. 19, 1829; E. K.
Kane to Van Buren, Feb. 19, 1829, Van Buren MSS (LC).

6. *Daily National Journal*, Jan. 5, 1829.

fight for control of the party. Neither Calhoun nor Van Buren enjoyed the popularity or commanded the same allegiance among party leaders as Jackson. The friends of both devoutly believed their man was entitled to occupy the White House after the president retired. The disciples of each, without the connivance of either one (both were embarrassed by the out of season antics of their followers), sought to steal a march on the other by early nominations of their favorite.[7] Most of these were the work of minor journalists, but in December, 1829, an important Regency paper, the *New York Courier and Enquirer,* edited by James Watson Webb, drew attention to the impending clash by endorsing Van Buren.[8] Because Webb and his partner, Mordecai M. Noah, were generally believed to be spokesmen for the Regency, the *Courier's* nomination was interpreted as "a formal and authorized annunciation" of Van Buren's presidential candidacy.[9] Duff Green reacted violently against Webb's precipitate action, although exonerating Van Buren from any personal responsibility.[10] Other administration papers deplored the open introduction of the rivalry, but the Webb-Green feud over the succession, which continued into 1830, could not be ignored.[11]

The National Republicans, naturally enough, were delighted.[12] "[A]ll that remains," wrote John Agg, "is for both [Calhoun and Van Buren] to delay the open rupture which their selfish passions render inevitable at some time, and to trade a little longer on what remains of the capital of General Jackson's popularity."[13] Democratic editors were mortified that the succession was being publicly fought over, fearing that the Clay partisans would destroy the Democrats by a divide-and-conquer strategy.[14] The split went deep into party ranks. Maryland Congressman Henry Warfield reported to Webster in the spring of 1830 that "The idea of uniting the Jackson party

7. *Ibid.,* Jan. 24, June 25, Sept. 26, 1829; Jan. 4, 1830.
8. *United States Telegraph,* Dec. 22, 1829.
9. *Richmond Enquirer,* Dec. 25, 1829.
10. *United States Telegraph,* Dec. 22, 1829; Mar. 31, 1830.
11. *Richmond Whig,* Nov. 23, 1830; *New Hampshire Patriot,* Apr. 12, 1830; *Richmond Enquirer,* Feb. 11, Mar. 26, 30, June 18, 1830; *United States Telegraph,* Mar. 16, 24, Apr. 30, 1830; *Daily National Journal,* Mar. 31, Apr. 3, 1830.
12. *Daily National Journal,* Dec. 23, 1829; Mar. 23, Apr. 13, May 12, 18, 1830; John S. Barbour to James Barbour, Mar. 1, 1830, Barbour MSS; John Mills to Woodbury, Apr. 12, 1830, Woodbury MSS.
13. *Daily National Journal,* Mar. 25, 1830.
14. *Richmond Enquirer,* Apr. 14, 1829; Feb. 11, 1830; *New Hampshire Patriot,* Jan. 11, Apr. 12, 1830; *United States Telegraph,* Dec. 13, 1829; June 8, 1830.

in this state in support of any individual [for president in 1832] is perfectly preposterous—they are at this moment virtually dissolved—"[15] The administration was faced with internecine warfare before it had fairly begun.

The impending breakup of the party could be forestalled only if Jackson repudiated his one-term pledge. Sentiment in favor of his running again appeared almost immediately after his election, but it was not until the dangers inherent in his not being a candidate had become apparent that real pressure was exerted.[16] Early in 1830 those closest to Jackson mounted the almost inevitable campaign to persuade him to seek reelection. In January, 1830, Francis Preston Blair's *Argus of Western America* (among other vehement Jackson papers), boldly proclaimed not only that the president was receptive to four more years in the White House but that Calhoun and Van Buren also favored a second term.[17] Journals speaking for the Democratic organizations of Virginia and New York added their voices to the growing movement.[18]

More formal pressure was quickly developed. In March, Major William B. Lewis, now living in the White House, suggested to a member of the Pennsylvania legislature that Jackson should be urged to run again and even sent to him a draft of the appeal.[19] A caucus in Harrisburg two weeks later acknowledged that "the unanimity and harmony of the great democratic party of the union will be greatly promoted by again placing the name of Andrew Jackson before the people as a candidate for re-election."[20] Soon afterward, members of the New York congressional delegation wrote Flagg that a legislative caucus should second the sentiments expressed in Pennsylvania.[21] Cambreling cautioned Flagg to frame "the resolutions so as not to require any answer from the General." Evidently, there was some fear that Jackson, if pressed for an immediate decision, might decline to stand. Time was needed to create the atmosphere of public support necessary to

15. Warfield to Webster, Mar. 1, 1830, Webster MSS.

16. *United States Telegraph*, Apr. 11, June 8, Aug. 13, 22, Nov. 23, 1829; *Daily National Journal*, June 18, 19, Nov. 16, 1829; *New Hampshire Patriot*, Dec. 20, 1830.

17. Jan. 30, 1830.

18. *Richmond Enquirer*, Feb. 16, 1830; *United States Telegraph*, Apr. 15, 1830.

19. James Parton, *Life of Andrew Jackson* (Boston, 1888), III, 297–302.

20. *Niles' Weekly Register*, XXXVIII (Apr. 24, 1830), 169.

21. C. C. Cambreling to Flagg, Apr. 5, 1830; C. E. Dudley to Flagg, Apr. 12, 1830, Flagg MSS.

justify his change of mind. The Regency legislative caucus dutifully
implored Jackson to run for the sake of party stability.[22]

During the year and a half following the caucuses in Pennsylvania
and New York, every meeting, caucus, and convention of what was
coming to be termed the Democratic party recommended Jackson
for reelection.[23] In four states the endorsement was made by an official
resolution of at least one house of the legislature.[24] Although everyone
assumed that Jackson would yield to these pleas, not until January,
1831, when *The Globe* announced that he would *"not decline the
summons,"* was there definite assurance he would do so.[25] Jackson
did not break silence on the subject until the next month when he
responded affirmatively to a nomination by an Ohio caucus.[26]

Only one important bloc within the coalition which had supported
Jackson in 1828 failed to join this enthusiastic chorus. Southern opponents of the tariff demanded that measures be given higher priority
than men. The *Charleston Mercury*, voice of the extremists, cautioned
South Carolina and her sister states not to become entangled in the
debate over presidential candidates, but rather to concentrate on the
vindication of sacred rights.[27] Ever since passage of the "Tariff of
Abominations" in 1828 South Carolina had been in the grip of a states'
rights party which loudly asserted the right of a state to judge the
constitutionality of congressional law. Calhoun, swept along by the
tide of opinion, had anonymously authored in 1828 the state legislature's defense of nullification. As South Carolina's opposition to protection hardened, Calhoun's position as a national leader became more
difficult. Already by the early months of 1830 there were rumors
of an imminent break with the administration.

The change in Calhoun's position was reflected in the *United States
Telegraph*, since 1826 the quasi-official mouthpiece of the Jackson

22. *Buffalo Republican*, Apr. 10, 1830.
23. *United States Telegraph*, July 13, 19, 20, 1830; Jan. 19, 20, 27, Feb. 8,
Mar. 2, 10, 1831; *Argus of Western America*, Mar. 31, July 21, Aug. 4, 25,
Nov. 24, Dec. 1, 1830; Feb. 9, 1831; *The Globe*, July 12, 1831; *Niles' Weekly
Register*, XL (Apr. 16, May 7, 1831), 126–27, 173–74; *ibid.*, XXXIX (Feb. 19,
1831), 452; *Daily National Intelligencer*, Dec. 7, 1831.
24. *Maysville Eagle*, Feb. 1, 1831; *Niles' Weekly Register*, XXXIX (Jan. 8,
1831), 341; *Daily National Intelligencer*, Feb. 4, Dec. 7, 1831; *The Globe*, Jan.
17, 1832.
25. *The Globe*, Jan. 22, 1831.
26. *The Commentator*, Mar. 8, 1831.
27. As cited in the *Daily National Journal*, May 7, 1830.

party. Its editor's first loyalty, however, belonged to the vice-president, his mentor and father-in-law. Green had been among the first to propose a second term for Jackson in 1829.[28] Yet in the spring of 1830, when the boom was gaining momentum, the *Telegraph* hung back, pleading that it was too soon to discuss the next election, but carefully avoiding outright opposition.[29] This was in keeping with Calhoun's own coolness to the second term idea, privately expressed.[30] The overwhelming response of all the other Jackson blocs compelled Green in the autumn of 1830 to abandon his fence and unequivocally endorse Jackson for 1832.[31] Failure to support the president would have exposed Calhoun's growing isolation and left the Van Burenites in undisputed possession of the party.

The movement to renominate Jackson headed off for the moment the threatened division of the party, but it did nothing to resolve the basic incongruity of the original coalition except give the president more time to remold it in his own image. The succession problem was only postponed, not solved, and no one could be sure how long the delay might last. On its solution depended the survival of the party.

Looking back at the intense anxiety which the Calhoun–Van Buren rivalry caused the Democrats from 1828 to 1832, it is difficult to understand how contemporary politicians ever doubted the outcome. Van Buren's triumph seems predestined whether viewed from the narrow ground of Jackson's personal relations with both men or the broader context of impersonal economic and political forces. The important fact though is that they did consider the contest doubtful. From that uncertainty sprang the decision to hold a national convention.

Calhoun's estrangement from Jackson, culminating in their dramatic clash over South Carolina's voiding of the tariff law of 1832, is a complicated and separate story. The break is partially explainable as a conflict of two proud and inflexible personalities, a conflict resulting in part from Calhoun's refusal to compel his wife and his friends to accept the wife of Secretary of War John Eaton, Peggy O'Neale (who was believed to have been Eaton's mistress prior to their mar-

28. *United States Telegraph*, Sept. 12, Nov. 18, 1830.
29. *Ibid.*, Mar. 16, 24, Apr. 5, 1830.
30. Calhoun to Christopher Van Deventer, May 12, 1830, Jameson, *Correspondence of Calhoun*, p. 273.
31. *United States Telegraph*, Oct. 16, 1830.

riage), despite the president's partiality for her company, and in part from Jackson's discovery of Calhoun's long duplicity over his opposition to the Seminole expedition. Calhoun's ambition also played a part. He had long been reckoned presidential timber; twice he had deferred to men he considered inferior to himself. Could he afford to be put off again, especially when every sign indicated he would stand worse with the Democratic party in 1836 than in 1832?

Finally, the break can be accounted for by the shifting scales of economic and political power that drove South Carolina to set the Union at defiance. Fixing upon the tariff as the cause of her impoverishment, the state's politicians developed the concept of state sovereignty set forth in the Virginia and Kentucky Resolutions to its logical conclusion. Calhoun had enunciated this doctrine in the *South Carolina Exposition and Protest* in 1828, but South Carolina had not acted then, expecting that Jackson's election would bring relief. Instead, the protectionists continued to hold sway in Congress and the president did not check them. After 1830 it was no longer possible for Calhoun to be both a South Carolina and a national politician—changes within his own state converted him from a nationalist to a nullifier. In the transition Calhoun forfeited whatever chance he had of donning the Jacksonian cloak.

From the start Calhoun's position within the victorious coalition, in spite of his greater fame, was weak when compared to Van Buren's. The New Yorker had guided a large, well-organized group into the Jackson fold. With the support of the Radicals Jackson had carried Virginia, North Carolina, Georgia, and most of New York. He had been the working head in 1828 of the new party.[32] Calhoun had lent his prestige and advice, but little else. His numerous friends, unfortunately, were so scattered that they could not be credited with carrying a single state that Jackson would not have won without them. In attaching himself to Jackson in 1825 Calhoun had acted to save himself since he was by then at odds with every major Republican faction: the Adams-Clay group, the Radicals, the Clintonians, and even many of the original Jacksonians.[33]

Van Buren's political base was far more impressive. New York was the most populous state; it was critical in any presidential election. As a northern state it comported well with Tennessee. Van Buren's

32. Remini, *Martin Van Buren*, p. 162.
33. Wiltse, *Calhoun: Nationalist*, pp. 333–38.

position there was strong; he was the head of a powerful organization, had been reelected to the Senate in 1827 and in 1828 was elected governor. South Carolina was relatively small and its political complexion left no doubt as to which way it would vote in 1828. Nor was Calhoun at that time the dominating figure in its politics. He had not held office at the hands of South Carolina's voters since 1817 and the nationalist views that had projected him to prominence were now exceedingly unpopular. Recognizing this, he had ingratiated himself at home by defending nullification, but this tended to undercut whatever support he had enjoyed in the rest of the country. Calhoun's slide to strict construction left him occupying much the same ground as the southern Radicals with whom he was on poor terms and who already had plenty of leaders.

The subtle and supple Van Buren got along well with Jackson personally, unlike Calhoun, and their rapport extended to the major issues facing the administration. Calhoun, on the other hand, failed to sustain the president in the three most important policy areas. Jackson's first annual message promised a continuation of moderate protection, a position Van Buren favored, but which Calhoun had earlier denounced as "unconstitutional, unequal, and oppressive. . . ."[34] Calhoun had long advocated a vigorous program of internal improvements—it was his principal card in a bid for northern and western support—while Jackson and Van Buren envisioned a far more limited role for the federal government in this field. Finally, Jackson and Van Buren opposed the rechartering of the Bank of the United States; Calhoun never ceased to support it.[35] Soon after Jackson took the presidential oath Calhoun became an anomaly within the administration party.

The particular events preceding the rupture between Jackson and Calhoun merely illustrated preexisting differences. The social warfare which swirled around Peggy O'Neale Eaton, although not a primary cause of the break, contributed to creating an atmosphere of ill will that later ripened into hatred. Of equal importance was Calhoun's growing identification with the nullifiers, an association that received wide advertisement during the Webster-Hayne debates in January, 1830. In April, Jackson and Calhoun faced each other directly over the tariff-nullification question at the Jefferson Day dinner. The next

34. Richard K. Crallé (ed.), *The Works of John C. Calhoun* (New York, 1857), VI, 2.
35. Harrison, *JSH*, XXLL (Nov., 1956), 442–49; Thomas Payne Govan, *Nicholas Biddle* (Chicago, 1959), pp. 113–14, 137.

strain on their relationship occurred late in May with Jackson's veto of the Maysville bill. John Spencer Bassett goes so far as to say that the veto "robbed Calhoun of a popular policy and weakened him so much that his enemies dared to proceed to destroy him. . . ."[36] There is no evidence that Jackson (or Van Buren, who framed the message) aimed the veto at Calhoun, but its effect was to further undermine any constructive role for Calhoun as the maker of policy.

The proverbial final straw was provided shortly thereafter when Calhoun's old enemy, Crawford, furnished conclusive proof that he had advocated, when Secretary of War in 1818, court-martialing Jackson for crossing the Florida boundary in pursuit of the Seminoles.[37] The president demanded an explanation. Calhoun's long and labored answer could not disguise the fact that he had indeed recommended disavowal of Jackson's escapade.[38] Professing himself shocked at Calhoun's deception, Jackson informed his vice-president that "no further communication with you on this subject is necessary."[39] Further communication may not have been necessary, but it persisted nevertheless. Jackson's opinion of Calhoun sank lower and lower until there was no evil he did not attribute to him.[40] For the time being it served the policy of both men not to let the break become public.

Tangible evidence of the president's desire to free himself of Calhoun came with the decision to dump the *Telegraph* in favor of a new administration paper. Green had long been suspect because of his attachment to Calhoun, but it was only after the events of the spring of 1830 that Jackson took the necessary steps. Blair of the Frankfort *Argus* was imported from Kentucky and under his editorship *The Globe* began publication in Washington on December 7, 1830. Still no authorized account of what had taken place between the two men

36. Bassett, *Life of Andrew Jackson*, 496.
37. Jackson to John Coffee, Apr. 10, 1830, Bassett, *Correspondence of Andrew Jackson*, IV, 134; Crawford to John Forsyth, copy, Apr. 30, 1830, Jackson MSS, 2nd ser.
38. Jackson to Calhoun, copy, May 13, 1830, Jackson MSS, 2nd ser.; Calhoun to Jackson, May 13, 1830, *ibid.*, 1st ser.
39. Jackson to Calhoun, May 30, 1830, Bassett, *Correspondence of Andrew Jackson*, IV, 140–41.
40. Jackson to Calhoun, draft, July 19, 1830, Jackson MSS, 2nd ser.; Calhoun to Jackson, May 19, June 1, 22, 1830; Forsyth to Calhoun, May 31, 1830; Calhoun to Forsyth, June 1, 1830; John B. Overton to Jackson, June 6, 1830; Jackson to Forsyth, June 7, 1830; Forsyth to Jackson, June 17, 1830; Crawford to Calhoun, copy, Oct. 2, 1830, *ibid.*, 1st ser.; Jackson to Lewis, Aug. 25, 1830, Bassett, *Correspondence of Andrew Jackson*, IV, 177.

found its way into print. The *Telegraph* retained a portion of the government's printing; *The Globe* carefully avoided giving offense to the vice-president. Green even managed to welcome his rival, saying "it promises to become an efficient co-laborer in the cause of republicanism."[41]

The split became irreversible, however, in February, 1831, when Calhoun published the correspondence relating to Florida. In addition to accusing Jackson of disobeying orders, a charge the president was acutely sensitive to, Calhoun made Jackson the dupe of a sinister plot by Van Buren to ruin Calhoun for his own benefit.[42] The evidence for this accusation was entirely suppositious, although undeniably some of Van Buren's closest associates were implicated. Strangely, Calhoun seems to have suffered from the naive idea that dragging the whole mess into the open would restore him in Jackson's good graces.[43] His misapprehension was complete. Blair called the pamphlet "a firebrand . . . wantonly thrown into the Republican party. . . ."[44] A "thunderstruck" Jackson saw that Calhoun and Green "have cut their own throats and destroyed themselves in a shorter space of time than any two men I ever knew. . . ."[45] He moved quickly to purge the administration of any taint of Calhoun influence. But, as Lewis accurately said, the whole Seminole business was a "pretext," for well before it came to light "the President was, in his heart, totally estranged from Mr. Calhoun. . . ."[46]

What of Van Buren during all of this? He kept busy serving the president. Jackson found him a perfect advisor and companion. Moreover, Van Buren found no difficulty in paying court to Mrs. Eaton, and he shrewdly avoided becoming directly involved in the controversy over the succession. During the imbroglio following Crawford's revelation he protected himself by remaining totally aloof. In pleasing Jackson, the Secretary of State violated no principles, either of personal conduct or on public questions. He was fortunate in that he could serve himself, his state, and his president simultaneously. Calhoun was not so lucky, but this should not make Van Buren seem less honest. Of all the characters in the drama, Jackson included, he

41. *United States Telegraph*, Dec. 11, 1830.
42. Crallé, *Works of Calhoun*, VI, 379–445.
43. Fitzpatrick, *Autobiography of Van Buren*, pp. 378–79.
44. *The Globe*, Feb. 21, 1831.
45. Jackson to Andrew J. Donelson, Mar. 24, 1831; Jackson to Charles J. Love, Mar. 7, 1831, Bassett, *Correspondence of Andrew Jackson*, IV, 245, 253.
46. Parton, *Life of Jackson*, III, 333.

emerges with the cleanest hands. And he had his reward. As early as December, 1829, Jackson had tapped him to be his successor in the White House.[47]

As a capstone to his services, Van Buren resigned from the cabinet in April, 1831, in order to provide an opportunity for Jackson to fire the whole fractious bunch, most of whom he believed were the vice-president's tools.[48] None of the three men fired as Calhoun minions, Ingham, Branch, and Berrien, was willing to go quietly. There ensued a series of personal recriminations, and even an alleged assassination plot (of Ingham by Eaton), before they were packed off.[49] It was a fitting end to a sorry episode, not without a comic opera touch, and great was the embarrassment of the administration before the country. Jackson, reluctant to part with his friend and counselor, appointed Van Buren minister to England, pending the consent of the Senate, as a mark of his continuing esteem.[50] Van Buren left for London as his former State Department subordinate, James A. Hamilton, wrote, "hailed as a most disinterested patriot by his party, . . . removed from the fight for three or four years, with the advantage of having administered the affairs of his department in a successful manner for two years."[51]

Jackson's decision to run again and the elimination of Calhoun as a competitor to Van Buren prevented an immediate and fatal disruption of the coalition. With an extended period of power Jackson, largely as a result of the Bank and nullification controversies, was able to forge a party with sufficient cohesion to outlast his presidential tenure. This durability was not yet apparent in the spring of 1831. Not only the party but the nation seemed in danger of dissolution. Southern ultras, centered in South Carolina, were calculating, in Webster's phrase, the value of the Union. The president and vice-president of the United States were not on speaking terms. The cabinet had been dismissed, churning up innumerable feuds. Both the tariff and Bank questions hung in the balance, keeping the planter, manufacturer, and merchant in a state of anxiety.

47. Jackson to Overton, Dec. 31, 1829, Jackson-Lewis MSS.
48. Jackson to Willie Blount, copy, Aug. 29, 1831; Jackson to R. G. Dunlap, copy, Aug. 29, 1831, Jackson MSS, 1st ser.
49. Bassett, *Life of Jackson*, pp. 523–30.
50. Fitzpatrick, *Autobiography of Van Buren*, pp. 403–5.
51. Hamilton to General Van Sholten, May 28, 1831, Hamilton, *Reminiscences*, p. 222. Also, Hamilton to Van Buren, May 1, 1831, *ibid.*, p. 214.

Jackson's acceptance of a second nomination restored a semblance of party unity, but could not prevent factional and sectional rivalries from sprouting up over the vice-presidency. The nomination for vice-president in 1832 became a matter of unusual concern because the president's health made it uncertain that he would survive another four years and because the choice would indicate which of the diverse elements within the party stood closest to the throne.

The state endorsements of Jackson were accepted as constituting a sufficient nomination. It was the kind of nomination that Clay's managers had originally envisioned until events impelled them to hold a national convention. Had not the question of a running mate loomed so large the Democrats probably would not have held a convention in 1832. Although prepared to accept Jackson's leadership, the Democratic party was much more loosely knit than its rival. Because the Democrats were strong in all sections of the country, regional tensions were more sharply etched than in the National Republican party, which was virtually nonexistent in the deep South and was weak in the upper South and the West. And the more uniform strength of the Jackson party produced a number of conspicuous state leaders whose organizations could fairly claim the vice-presidency as a reward for their contribution to the cause. The fact that the Democrats were in office, and seemed likely to remain there as long as Jackson was at their head, made their vice-presidential nomination worth competing for, especially as it would give its holder an inside track to win party support for the presidency in 1836.

The most outstanding of these state leaders was Van Buren. By every standard, aside from his closeness to the president, he had the most imposing credentials: the offices he had held, his influence in a large and pivotal state, his residence in the North, his past service to the party. Yet every piece of reliable evidence supports the conclusion that he sincerely did not wish to be Jackson's electoral partner and that prior to January, 1832, the leaders of the party did not want him to be. Nothing links the calling of the Democratic national convention with Van Buren except the unsubstantiated charges of his enemies.

The Democratic convention originated in the endless list of names advanced for the vice-presidency and the consequent need to solidify the party behind a single ticket. If this were not done it could throw the vice-presidential election into a hostile Senate and might even jeopardize Jackson's reelection by splitting his vote among rival Democratic electors in the states. By the spring of 1831 a whole host of names had been suggested in addition to Van Buren's—Levi Woodbury of New Hampshire, Mahlon Dickerson of New Jersey, William Smith of South Carolina, Andrew Stevenson and Philip P. Barbour of Virginia, Richard M. Johnson of Kentucky, George M. Dallas, William Wilkins, and James Buchanan of Pennsylvania, and that old favorite, William H. Crawford.[52] Underlying these nominations were sectional as well as state jealousies. Southerners were eager that an anti-tariff man be chosen, Pennsylvania and New England Democrats wanted a protectionist.

But the name that gave the most trouble was that of Calhoun. Quite apart from his difficulties with Jackson and the headstrong policy of his state, Calhoun faced a personal crisis in his career. By 1832 he would have been vice-president for eight years; no other man had served longer in that frustrating position. Although the post was too insignificant to speak of a two-term tradition, the same limitation was as valid for the second office as for the first. Calhoun never indicated that he desired a third term, but what alternatives did he have? Before the separation from Jackson there were rumors that he would run for president with Van Buren as his vice-president, or, in the event Jackson agreed to a second term, would exchange positions with Van Buren.[53] Calhoun's friends were determined that he not be discarded before other opportunities were available. Consequently, in the spring of 1830 Green and others began to hint that he ought to serve again on the Jackson ticket.[54]

After publication of the Seminole correspondence another term for Calhoun was out of the question so far as the Jacksonian inner circle was concerned. The possibility that Calhoun would attempt to retain his office seems remote now, but it was certainly real to those around the president. Amos Kendall, fourth auditor of the Treasury, a member of the Kitchen Cabinet and a powerful voice within the administration, had the dangers of a split over the vice-presidency forcefully brought to mind while visiting his native New Hampshire in the spring of 1831. Duff Green had just made a swing through New England spread-

52. *Richmond Enquirer*, Mar. 26, May 27, 1831; *Daily National Journal*, Mar. 12, 1831; *Richmond Constitutional Whig*, Feb. 18, 1831; *The Globe*, July 27, 1831; *Daily National Intelligencer*, Sept. 14, Nov. 3, 1830; *Kentucky Reporter*, Apr. 6, 1831; J. M. G. Pierce to Levi Woodbury, Apr. 19, 1830, Woodbury MSS.
53. *Daily National Journal*, May 11, Aug. 24, 1830.
54. *Ibid.*, May 7, 22, 1830; *United States Telegraph*, May 20, 1830.

ing the word that Calhoun must run again. Obviously, this would not do. "This subject," a disturbed Kendall wrote Major Lewis, "is one which ought to have our immediate attention."[55] Shortly thereafter, there was an attempt to renominate Calhoun at a public meeting for Jackson in Washington attended by Green. The introduction of the offending resolution was met by "a sudden and violent clamor on the instant—'Lay it on the table,' cried one—'Throw it over the table,' quoth another—'Throw it under the table,' roared a third." The motion was "indefinitely postponed."[56] *The Globe* referred sarcastically to the Calhounites' belief in "their favorite's perpetual claim to the Vice Presidency, with a reversion in the Presidency."[57] Yet it was still possible for pro-Jackson newspapers, and a local meeting in Maryland early in June, to suggest that Calhoun would be an "acceptable" running-mate for Jackson.[58]

This undercurrent of sentiment for Calhoun plus the abundance of potential vice-presidents provided the immediate background for the calling of the Democratic national convention. The question of whom the party should couple with Jackson in 1832 was very much in Kendall's thoughts during his New Hampshire sojourn. Kendall informed Lewis that he and Isaac Hill, Democratic boss of New Hampshire, had discussed the major alternatives to Calhoun. They were agreed that McLean would be the strongest candidate, but the objections to him were "almost, if not quite, insuperable." Senator Dickerson of New Jersey "would do; but the Southern states, I fear, would not be united in his support on account of the tariff." As for Van Buren: "I take it for granted he does not wish to be run for Vice President—I am sure that he ought not to." On balance Hill and Kendall agreed that former congressman Philip P. Barbour of Virginia, currently a federal judge, would be the best choice. Hill was of the opinion that Barbour could secure the North, although there might be some difficulty in Pennsylvania. Kendall believed him "as likely as any other man" to carry the West. And a Barbour candidacy carried an additional advantage in that he would not be a candidate

55. Kendall to Lewis, May 17, 1831, in "Origin of the Democratic National Convention," *American Historical Magazine*, VII (July, 1902), 269.
56. *Daily National Journal*, May 26, 1831.
57. May 28, 1831.
58. *United States Telegraph*, June 4, 1831; *Baltimore Republican*, June 6, 1831.

for president in 1836. Hill and Kendall, eager to effect a union behind Barbour, made plans to have him nominated at the forthcoming session of the New Hampshire legislature.[59]

Lewis, also desirous of heading off a boom to run Calhoun again, consulted "with several of our friends" in Washington. They believed that an immediate nomiation would be premature. Furthermore, they felt that Barbour would be unacceptable to either Pennsylvania or New York; McLean and Dickerson were also objectionable to portions of the party. Van Buren's name was not even discussed. "There will be great difficulty," Lewis wrote, "in selecting an individual who will be satisfactory to the different local interests." He then went on to propose a national convention:

> Surrounded by so many difficulties, as the case is, and taking everything into consideration, many of our friends (and the most judicious of them) think it would be best for the Republican members of the respective Legislatures to propose to the people to elect delegates to a national convention to be holden, for that purpose, at Harrisburg, or some other place, about the middle of next May. That period is preferred to prevent an improper interference by members of Congress who, about that time, will leave this city for their respective homes. If the friends of the administration, when brought together from every part of the Union, in convention, cannot harmonize I know of no other plan by which it can be done. If the Legislature of New Hampshire will propose this, I think it will be followed up by others and have the effect, no doubt, of putting a stop to partial nominations. You had better reflect upon this proposition and, if you think with me, make the suggestion to our friend Hill.[60]

Kendall and Hill found the idea sound. A legislative caucus meeting June 23 and 24, 1831, at the Eagle Coffee House in Concord passed the following resolution:

> That this convention, aware of the salutory effects which may attend the interchange of sentiments of the great republican party throughout the Union—believing that the great interests of the North and the South, the East and the West, can be better conciliated by holding communion with each other, and yielding points of minor local difference, than by a reiteration of epithets, calculated to widen the breach by fanning the flame of local prejudices,—do recommend to their fellow republican brethern in other states, friendly to the re-election of ANDREW JACKSON, to elect delegates equal to the number of electors

59. *American Historical Magazine*, VII (July, 1902), 269–70.
60. Lewis to Kendall, May 25, 1831, *ibid.*, 271.

of President in each state, to attend a general Convention to be holden at Baltimore, in the state of Maryland, on the third Monday of May, 1832; which convention shall have for its object the adoption of such measures as will best promote the re-election of Andrew Jackson, and the nomination of a candidate to be supported as Vice-President at the same election.[61]

There is nothing to connect Van Buren or Jackson with this invitation. Lewis, of course, lived in the White House, but he gave no hint that he was prompted by Jackson. Surely, he would not have hesitated to relay the president's approval had he secured it, especially since the operation was conducted in secrecy. In any event Jackson took little interest in party matters of this sort; I think it likely Lewis never talked over the convention proposal with him. Nor is there evidence that the convention was designed to nominate Van Buren. Kendall and Hill certainly did not favor it. Lewis's failure to mention Van Buren as a possible nominee indicates that he shared their opinion. Blair, another member of Jackson's circle of advisors, and very probably consulted by Lewis, also was opposed to Van Buren's running.[62]

Quite possibly, a national convention would have been called without Lewis's letter. The Antimasons had already staged one national convention and were preparing to hold another while National Republican plans for a similar meeting were well known. A convention's ability to unify a party behind a single candidate was fully appreciated. In fact, before it was definitely known that Jackson would run again, several Democrats had proposed a national convention to nominate a presidential candidate so that the party could be held together.[63] Is it unreasonable to suppose that Lewis, Kendall, Hill, and whoever else was consulted acted out of a desire to maintain a common front against the enemy rather than conspiring, as charged, to find a way of making Van Buren vice-president? Given the diversity of the Democratic party, was there another method, other than the discredited congressional caucus, of preventing the nomination of Democratic electors pledged to different vice-presidential candidates? How else could they prevent Calhoun's renomination by a portion of the party?

The advantages of a national convention were sufficiently obvious to elicit support from most sections of the party. *The Globe* endorsed

61. *New Hampshire Patriot*, July 11, 1831.
62. James Watson Webb to Van Buren, Dec. 21, 1831, Van Buren MSS (LC).
63. *Buffalo Republican*, Mar. 29, 1829; John Mills to Woodbury, Apr. 12, 1830, Woodbury MSS.

it as "probably the best plan which could be adopted to produce entire unanimity in the Republican party, and secure its lasting ascendancy."[64] The *Richmond Enquirer* declared "that if such a course as this were not advisable on other accounts, it would be almost forced upon us, by the conduct of the Opposition.—The friends of Mr. Clay are to have a *Convention* at Baltimore.—They are appointing their Delegates to it—they are rallying all their force and influence around him. . . ."[65] The *Albany Argus* gave the meeting the Regency's blessings, denying at the same time that Van Buren would be a candidate for the nomination.[66] Other Jackson newspapers and party meetings also went on record as favoring the holding of a national convention.[67]

There were few dissonant voices. Green joined the pro-Clay editors in immediately denouncing it as a new installment on an old plot to smuggle Van Buren into the White House by way of the vice-presidency, Jackson to resign after the inauguration.[68] Friends of McLean did not approve because a convention provided little opportunity for independents such as the Supreme Court justice.[69] Most Pennsylvania Democrats were not interested in consulting the rest of the party. Abetted by the Calhoun faction commanded by Ingham, they demanded that Pennsylvania be allowed to name Jackson's running mate both as a reward for devotion to the president and because the state had never been honored by having a son serve as either president or vice-president.[70] The state had a number of possible favorite sons, none with much reputation outside its boundaries. Congressman Buchanan had his backers, but he was a former Federalist and, in addition, was too loyal a Jacksonian to countenance a separatist movement in his behalf.[71] Others preferred one of the state's senators, Dallas or

64. July 6, 1831. Also, issue of July 19, 1831.

65. July 8, 1831.

66. *Albany Argus*, July 23, 1831. Also, issues of July 7, Aug. 12, 1831.

67. *Ibid.*, July 21, 1831; *The Globe*, July 18, Aug. 25, Oct. 27, 1831.

68. *United States Telegraph*, Apr. 22, July 11, 12, 19, Aug. 23, 1831; *Daily National Journal*, Sept. 5, Dec. 24, 1831; *Richmond Constitutional Whig*, Apr. 27, May 20, 1831; *The Focus*, Dec. 20, 1831.

69. Thomas L. Hamen to McLean, Dec. 19, 1831, McLean MSS.

70. *United States Telegraph*, Aug. 6, 1831; *Richmond Enquirer*, June 24, 1831; *The Globe*, June 16, Aug. 25, Oct. 27, 1831; James Buchanan to Jackson, Sept. 10, 1831, in John Bassett Moore (ed.), *The Works of James Buchanan* (Philadelphia, 1908), II, 177–78.

71. George W. Buchanan to James Buchanan, Apr. 29, 1831; James Buchanan to Jackson, Sept. 10, 1831, Moore, *Works of Buchanan*, II, 172, 178; J. M. G. Pierce to Woodbury, Apr. 19, 1831, Woodbury MSS; *Niles' Weekly Register*, XL (Mar. 26, 1831), 61; *The Globe*, Aug. 23, Oct. 5, 1831.

Wilkins.[72] Blair and Ritchie tried to reassure the state that "her voice would have great weight with the proposed convention," but Pennsylvania, in the end, preferred not to take the chance.[73]

The opposition papers, in detecting a plot to make Van Buren president through Jackson's resignation, came closer to the truth than perhaps they realized. In November, 1830, Jackson had indeed proposed such a scheme to Van Buren while the two were taking one of their famous horseback rides. Van Buren had wisely declined that unusual and unworthy offer.[74] Jackson accepted his refusal and although he subsequently renewed the invitation there is no connection between it and the Baltimore meeting. There is abundant evidence, however, that Van Buren did not wish to run for vice-president either before or after the call of the national convention.

The reorganization of the cabinet in April, 1831, gave Van Buren an additional reason not to seek the office. His friend, Dabney Carr of Virginia, stated the case with clarity: "Your enemies, you will have seen, are already anxiously anticipating some false step, which shall lose you the ground they clearly see you have gained by your resignation. They are giving out that it was an arrangement preparatory to your being brought out for the Vice Presidency, and call upon us to show where is the sacrifice in giving up one office to get a higher. Their wish is father to the thought: they would rejoice to see you a candidate for the Vice Presidency; and I, and all your friends here, would regret it."[75] Those whom Van Buren relied upon for advice, the members of the Albany Regency, told him not to try for the vice-presidency.[76] Ritchie, too, was most emphatic after Van Buren's resignation from the cabinet that he should under no circumstances be a candidate.[77] If well-meaning friends persisted in pushing him, he would still not receive Virginia's support. "We certainly shall not," Ritchie declared flatly in an editorial.[78] He spoke

72. *The Globe*, July 14, Aug. 30, 1831; Jan. 25, 1832; *Daily National Intelligencer*, July 14, 1831; B. W. Richards to McLean, Nov. 11, 1831, McLean MSS.

73. *The Globe*, July 19, 1831; *Richmond Enquirer*, Dec. 2, 1831.

74. Fitzpatrick, *Autobiography of Van Buren*, pp. 506-7; J. A. Hamilton to a friend, Nov. 30, 1830, Hamilton, *Reminiscences*, p. 191.

75. Carr to Van Buren, Apr. 30, 1831, Van Buren MSS (LC).

76. The only exception, to my knowledge, was Benjamin F. Butler. Butler to Van Buren, Apr. 22, 1831, Van Buren MSS (LC).

77. *Richmond Enquirer*, Apr. 14, May 13, 17, 31, June 3, 1831.

78. *Ibid.*, May 24, 1831.

as Van Buren's friend and with Van Buren's consent. In the midst of the cabinet crisis Ritchie replied to a letter from Van Buren that he fully shared his opinion that the best policy was to go to England and avoid being "thrust forward as a candidate for the V.P."[79] Lewis, in later years, recalled that Van Buren's personal choice was Senator Dickerson.[80]

Noah and Webb, editors of a Regency paper of questionable character, were the only persons of any note who continuously pushed Van Buren's candidacy. Green delighted in reprinting the *Courier and Enquirer*'s frequent endorsements of Van Buren for vice-president, pretending that they embodied the New Yorker's true wishes (and thus proving his own thesis).[81] He chose to believe that the editors of the *Albany Argus*, *The Globe*, and the *Richmond Enquirer*, all far more in Van Buren's confidence than the shifty Noah or Webb, were engaged in a dishonest game of furthering Van Buren's quest for the nomination by denying that he was a candidate.[82]

Noah and Webb were acting entirely without authority from Van Buren and contrary to his expressed opinion. Webb admitted it explicitly in a letter to Ritchie.[83] In December, 1831, Noah wrote Levi Woodbury, Secretary of the Navy, that "Van Buren had some chance of being President had his friends assented to have pushed him as Vice—but they have neither moral nor personal courage and have positively withdrawn him treating with great rudeness those who would serve him and wished to do so—"[84] Webb was equally disgusted, but he was more hopeful than his colleague: "You may be, and I believe will be rejected by the Senate!" he wrote Van Buren in London. "Nay, I ardently *desire* that such may be the case. Will you not then be elected vice President?"[85] Webb's reference to Van Buren's pending confirmation by the Senate raised one of the two imponderable circumstances affecting the vice-presidential nomination. The other was the attitude of Jackson. In the end both converged to admit but a single conclusion.

The president was a man of strong partialities and he had formed a very high opinion of Van Buren. He was also a man accustomed

79. Ritchie to Van Buren, Apr. 31, 1831, Van Buren MSS (LC).
80. Fitzpatrick, *Autobiography of Van Buren*, p. 285.
81. *United States Telegraph*, Aug. 20, 23, 30, Sept. 13, Dec. 6, 1831.
82. *Ibid.*, July 19, Aug. 20, 31, Sept. 13, Dec. 31, 1831; *Albany Argus*, July 23, Aug. 12, 1831; *The Globe*, Dec. 7, 1831; *Richmond Enquirer*, Dec. 2, 30, 1831.
83. *Richmond Enquirer*, Feb. 14, 1832.
84. Noah to Woodbury, Dec. 21, 1831, Woodbury MSS.
85. Webb to Van Buren, Dec. 21, 1831, Van Buren MSS (LC).

to having his way. All of the fervent denials by Van Buren, Ritchie, or whomever would count for little if Andrew Jackson were determined to have his former Secretary of State for vice-president. And even though he had dropped the subject after Van Buren had refused his offer of November, 1830, he obviously had not forgotten it. Several weeks before the confirmation vote in the Senate, Jackson renewed the proposition to make Van Buren president by abdication.[86] But only two weeks later, he decided not to press Van Buren to accept, writing on December 21, 1831, that he was reconciled to having him remain overseas for two more years, after which he could resume his place as Secretary of State. Yet Jackson realized that the decision might be taken out of their hands: "I would not be surprised, if contrary to your declared wishes, that you should be run for vice-president; as sure as the Senate makes the attempt to reject your nomination. I am told it will be done. This will bring you back in twelve months, if not, then I wish, if reelected, to bring you back as intimated [i.e., as Secretary of State in two years]."[87]

Van Buren was too shrewd not to appreciate the deadly consequences of Jackson's proposition to make him vice-president and then resign. Nothing would more conclusively prove the quip of his enemies that he was the " 'Mistletoe politician, nourished by the sap of the hickory tree.' "[88] Before Van Buren received Jackson's second letter acquiescing in his continued stay abroad Hamilton had written advising him to authorize Marcy to withdraw his name unconditionally from consideration. "If you do not do something of this kind," Hamilton warned, "it will be believed that Noah and Webb are acting with your assent or at least that you are willing to take the chances."[89] Van Buren clearly was disposed to follow Hamilton's admonition, but it would not do to reject Jackson's generous offer out of hand. The old man was sensitive and might misinterpret the reasons why he spurned it. Instead, Van Buren tried to get the president's consent (not realizing he already had it) before he wrote Marcy. "Upon the subject of the Vice Presidency I do not know that I have anything to say different from the views I have before expressed to you," he told Jackson. Then, after relating Hamilton's plan, he added: "There is a good deal of weight in this—think of it if you please and let

86. Jackson to Van Buren, Dec. 6, 1831, *ibid.*
87. Jackson to Van Buren, Dec. 21, 1831, *ibid.*
88. Henry A. Wise, *Seven Decades of the Union* (Philadelphia, 1872), p. 121.
89. Hamilton to Van Buren, Dec. 7, 1831, Van Buren MSS (LC).

me know how it strikes you."[90] Before Jackson had time to respond the Senate rejected Van Buren's nomination as minister to the Court of St. James.

Until the Senate voted it seemed clear beyond all reasonable doubt that Van Buren would not be a candidate for vice-president. His running was opposed by the most influential party leaders in Washington and in the states—Blair, Kendall, Lewis, Hill, and Ritchie. It was opposed by Van Buren's own organization in New York. It was opposed by Van Buren himself. And most decisively, their decision was approved, however reluctantly, by Jackson. A national convention had been called on the assumption that the party must choose between a large number of candidates, none of whom held a clear edge over the others. The prospect of that convention had stimulated their friends to action. Earnest campaigns were well underway by January, 1832, for Woodbury, Dickerson, Stevenson, Johnson, and Barbour.[91] These campaigns, like the convention itself, were all predicated on the belief that Van Buren was not available. So high did he tower over all others within the party that had he been willing to serve as vice-president a national convention to unify the party would have been unnecessary, even without the assistance of the Senate.

90. Van Buren to Jackson, Jan. 13, 1832, *ibid.*
91. *The Globe,* July 27, Dec. 5, 1831; Feb. 3, Apr. 11, 1832; *Kentucky Reporter.* Apr. 6, Dec. 14, 1831; *Richmond Enquirer,* Nov. 11, Dec. 30, 1831.

TEN

Van Buren's Convention

It required almost four years for the alliance of convenience that put Jackson in the White House to become the Democratic party. Calhoun's isolation and the substitution of Van Buren as the heir apparent were vital to the party-building process. The switch betokened Jackson's new mastery over his supporters, public notice that presidential approval was necessary for advancement: autonomous chieftains, as under Monroe and Adams, would no longer be tolerated. The rise of the moderate Van Buren at Calhoun's expense also constituted a shaking off of an extremist element. The South Carolinian's dogmatism, and that of his adherents, would have soon broken the party into pieces had he succeeded to its helm. Getting rid of Calhoun prevented a showdown between the portions of the party representing conflicting regional interests and freed Jackson to concentrate on issues which cut across geographic lines.

The calling of the national convention was a sure sign of the Jacksonians' coming of age as a party. A similar project had been dropped before the 1828 election because it promised division not unity. Another indication of maturity was the adoption of a distinctive title. In the 1828 campaign they made a fetish of being Republicans in deference to their Jeffersonian antecedents. But the Republican name had been adulterated by overuse. After 1815 even the Federalists used it on occasion. When the Clayites affected the style of National Republicans it was totally ruined. Increasingly, the Jacksonians called themselves "Democratic Republicans," a dual form going back to Jefferson's day. In practice the second half was frequently dropped. At a time when popular rule was gaining greater acceptance it was a happy, if casual, selection. The National Republicans conceded that "there seemed to be a magic in the [name] 'Democrat'. . . ."[1]

The risk that the Democratic national convention might divide rather than unify the party was removed by the action of the Senate. A combination of *"Nullifiers"* and *"Consolidators"* conspired to reject Van Buren's appointment to London.[2] All of those voting against confirmation were identified with either Calhoun or Clay. On opposite sides of the fence so far as the powers of the national government were concerned, they had a mutual grudge against Jackson and his protégé. Calhoun and Clay disagreed about the nature of the wound they inflicted, but both foresaw that it would be fatal.

Calhoun believed that the rejection would ruin Van Buren. Thomas Hart Benton overheard him tell a doubting Senator that "'It will kill him, sir, kill him dead. He will never kick sir, never kick'. . . ."[3] When friends of "the Great Rejected" began kicking, Calhoun still could not see how he could survive the blow. "I do not doubt," he told an old ally, "but that the partisans of Mr. V. B. will make the most desperate effort to force him into the V. Presidency, but judging from indications, I am of the impression, that they will fail. I am told by those, who ought to know, that neither Virginia nor Pennsya. will support him, nor consent to send delegates to Baltimore."[4] Green, the inevitable echo, announced that the rejection "can excite no sympathy, and will consign him to lasting retirement."[5]

But Clay realized, if Calhoun did not, that rejection would make Van Buren the candidate of the Baltimore convention. "That is exactly the point to which I wish to see the matter brought," he wrote Brooke. "Do urge our Jackson friends . . . to nominate him. . . ."[6] Aware that his chances of beating Jackson were slim, Clay was on the lookout for ways to damage his opponent. The opportunity to show the nation that the Senate had no confidence in the president while burdening him with an unpopular running mate proved irresistible. It was an election gamble similar to Clay's decision, made soon afterward, to

1. *Daily National Journal*, Sept. 23, 1831.
2. *New Hampshire Patriot*, Feb. 6, 1832.
3. Thomas Hart Benton, *Thirty Years View* (New York, 1854), I, 219.
4. Calhoun to S. L. Gouvernor, Feb. 13, 1832, Jameson, *Correspondence of Calhoun*, p. 310.
5. *United States Telegraph*, Jan. 29, 1832.
6. Clay to Brooke, Feb. 21, 1832, Colton, *Private Correspondence*, pp. 326–27.

inject the rechartering of the Bank into the campaign. Clay wanted the Democrats to feel outraged by the rejection. He counted on it. With Van Buren's nomination for vice-president, said one National Republican paper, "there will be a certain end to the Jackson dynasty. . . ."[7]

Other observers saw the matter in a truer light. Van Buren's confidant, Cambreling, accurately predicted the consequences before the event. "If you," he wrote Van Buren, "could but be rejected—you should return in triumph—we should have . . . the King, Commons, and people against the Lords—you would be identified with the party and without a competitor [for the nomination]—".[8] Thurlow Weed, although hostile to Van Buren, was of the same opinion: "Nothing could be more gratifying to Van Buren," he wrote, "than his rejection by the Senate. It would change the complexion of his prospects from despair to hope. His kennel presses would set up a frightful howl of 'proscription.' He would return home a 'persecuted man[']' —throw himself upon the sympathy of the party—be nominated for Vice President—and huzz'ed into Office on the heels of Gen. Jackson."[9]

Failure of the Senate to confirm opened a new debate among Van Buren's associates as to the course he should follow. Most of those in Washington now believed he should run for vice-president, although there was some difference of opinion over whether or not he should come home immediately. Only a few persons at the capital, most conspicuously Secretary of the Treasury Louis McLane and Senator Samuel Smith, thought he should not become vice-president; they advocated instead a return to the Senate.[10] Major Lewis also favored election to the Senate, but only as a prelude to the vice-presidency.[11] Leaders of the New York congressional bloc opposed an entry into the Senate and advised Van Buren to avoid further controversy by

7. *Freeman's Banner*, Jan. 28, 1832.

8. C. C. Cambreling to Van Buren, Jan. 4, 1832, Van Buren MSS (LC).

9. *Albany Evening Journal*, Dec. 21, 1831. For similar views see McLean to J. W. Taylor, June 5, 1832, Taylor MSS; B. W. Richards to McLean, Jan. 16, 1832, McLean MSS; R. M. Saunders to W. P. Mangum, Jan. 23, 1832, Shanks, *Papers of Mangum*, I, 462.

10. C. C. Cambreling to J. A. Hamilton, Jan. 31, 1832, Hamilton, *Reminiscences*, p. 242; S. Smith to Jackson, Jan. 28, 1832, Jackson MSS, 1st ser.

11. W. B. Lewis to J. A. Hamilton, Jan. 29, 1832, Hamilton, *Reminiscences*, pp. 237–38.

staying abroad until after the convention.[12] On the main question, however, Jackson, the cabinet, the Kitchen Cabinet, and the New York delegation concurred—he ought to run.[13]

From Albany came advice of another sort. Edwin Croswell, editor of the *Albany Argus*, Flagg, and others of the Regency whose primary concern was New York, wanted Van Buren to forego the vice-presidency in favor of the governorship.[14] The state politicians were dubious about the merits of the second office as a stepping stone to the first. They were worried lest Van Buren, by arousing further jealousies within the party and attracting more absue from the opposition, jeopardize his elevation to chief executive in 1836. Moreover, the Regency needed a candidate for governor who could heal the divisions within its own ranks.

The national politicians strenuously objected to this line of reasoning.[15] Lewis told Flagg that Van Buren must run for vice-president if he ever expected to be president: "The wrong has been done to him, the President and the nation, by the *Senate of the U. States,* and it must be redressed by the *people of all the states.* . . . If the party cannot now, under existing circumstances, succeed in electing him Vice President, he can never hope to be president. To run him for any local, or subordinate situation would in my opinion, destroy his prospects for ever. . . . Upon this subject the cabinet is unanimous; and we have the most encouraging accounts from all quarters—not excepting Virginia and Pennsylvania."[16] Others wrote Van Buren directly. "This is your flood tide," Marcy told him, "and if you wish to make your voyage you should not neglected [sic] it. . . . If you do not come forward now upon the great theatre other actors will

---

12. C. C. Cambreling to J. A. Hamilton, Jan. 31, 1832, Hamilton, *Reminiscences,* p. 242; Van Buren to John Van Buren, Feb. 23, 1832, Van Buren MSS (LC); C. C. Cambreling to Van Buren, Jan. 28, 1832, Fitzpatrick, *Autobiography of Van Buren,* p. 503.

13. W. L. Marcy to J. A. Hamilton, Feb. 7, 1832; W. B. Lewis to Hamilton, dated "1832," Hamilton, *Reminiscences,* p. 241, 243; J. A. Hamilton to Van Buren, Feb. 1, 1832; Lewis Cass to Van Buren, Feb. 4, 1832, Van Buren MSS (LC).

14. E. Croswell to J. A. Hamilton, Feb., 1832, Hamilton, *Reminiscences,* p. 242; A. C. Flagg to ——, Feb. 7, 1832, Van Buren MSS (LC).

15. W. B. Lewis to J. A. Hamilton, "1832," Hamilton, *Reminiscences,* p. 243; J. W. Webb to Van Buren, Feb. 5, 1832, Van Buren MSS (LC); J. A. Hamilton to A. C. Flagg, Feb. 17, 1832; Charles Dayan to Flagg, Jan. 29, 1832; Elijah Hayward to Flagg, Feb. 21, 1832, Flagg MSS.

16. W. B. Lewis to A. C. Flagg, ——, 1832, Flagg MSS.

occupy it and soon begin to share in the good wishes of the spectators—the nation."[17]

Van Buren weighed this advice from Marcy and evidently found it sound. He vetoed running for senator or governor and decided to remain in London until June to prevent tales of intrigue from gaining credence.[18] In December, 1831, he had been on the verge of authorizing Marcy to withdraw his name from consideration for vice-president; the Senate had reversed his position. He now wrote that "If the Republicans of the U. States think my elevation to the Vice Presidency the most effectual mode of testifying to the world their sentiment with respect to the act of the President and the vote of the Senate, I can see no justifiable ground for declining their wishes."[19]

The decision must have been an easy one for Van Buren to make. In reality he had no choice. The party demanded that he run. The vote in the Senate touched off demonstrations of support for his nomination all across the country. Newspapers friendly to the administration waxed indignant over the unnatural combination of Clay and Calhoun which had put him down. New York was the center of this movement, but Democrats in other states were not far behind.[20] It would be easy to say that the sentiment was not genuine, that it was the work of Jackson and his far-flung network of agents. Easy to say, but impossible to prove. The outpouring of support for Van Buren was too immediate and too widespread to be the work of puppeteers whose strings were pulled from Washington. This opinion is confirmed by contemporaries: politicians of every persuasion were almost unanimous in their belief that the rejection had strengthened Van Buren politically, virtually assuring him of the vice-presidential nomination.[21]

17. W. L. Marcy to Van Buren, Feb. 12, 1832, Van Buren MSS (LC). Also, see C. C. Cambreling to Van Buren, Feb. 4, 1832, *ibid.*, C. C. Cambreling to Van Buren, Jan. 28, 1832, Fitzpatrick, *Autobiography of Van Buren*, p. 503.

18. Van Buren to Jackson, Feb. 20, Mar. 13, 1832; Van Buren to John Van Buren, Feb. 23, 1832, Van Buren MSS (LC).

19. Van Buren to Marcy, copy, Mar. 14, 1832. Van Buren MSS (LC).

20. *Albany Argus*, Feb. 2–Apr. 19, 1832; *The Globe*, Jan. 28–Apr. 12, 1832; *New Hampshire Patriot*, Feb. 6, 20, 1832; *Freeman's Banner*, Feb. 11, 1832; *Richmond Enquirer*, Jan. 31, Feb. 11, 18, 24, 1832; *Daily Savannah Republican*, Feb. 17, 1832; *Nashville Republican and State Gazette*, Feb. 4, 16, 23, 28, 1832.

21. M. F. Simpson to John McLean, Feb. 2, 1832; J. W. Campbell to McLean, Feb. 11, 1832; George Kesling to McLean, Feb. 18, Mar. 23, 1832, McLean MSS; Thomas Jefferson Sutherland to J. W. Taylor, Feb. 15, 1832; Ebenezer Sage to Taylor, Mar. 5, 1832, Taylor MSS; Daniel Wardwell to A. C. Flagg, Jan. 26, 1832, Flagg MSS; John Coffee to Jackson, Feb. 24, 1832, Jackson

The newspapers and politicians also agreed on the reason: it had made him a martyr for the cause of Jackson. By singling out Van Buren for humiliation the Senate created a special sympathy for him among the party faithful, some of it in places where there was no love for him or a desire to see him vice-president. He became, as Weed predicted, a persecuted man whose enemies had schemed to deny him an office that by all the usual standards he was more than qualified to fill. The real insult, many pointed out, was directed at the man who had chosen him for London. Whatever differences existed among Democrats over the tariff, internal improvements, or the vice-presidency, the rank and file of the party were one in their ardor for Jackson. Clay and Calhoun succeeded in entwining the advancement of Van Buren inextricably with the reelection of Jackson. "The idea of General Jackson 'creeping' or 'crouching' to the British Government, with the people of the U.S. is absolutely ridiculous," an anti-Van Buren Democrat observed.[22] There seemed nothing left to do but vindicate the president's judgment by making Van Buren vice-president: "We shall see," wrote a Virginia editor, "whether the generous and high-minded friends of Jackson who know the able, zealous and efficient support Mr. Van Buren has given to his administration, will stand by with folded arms and permit him to be sacrificed to accomplish the base designs of an unprincipled combination of Southern nullifiers and Hartford Convention federalists. For one we are prepared to 'Hang our banner on the outward walls'—to nail our colors to the mast—and go heart and hand for Martin Van Buren as Vice President."[23]

This vindication would be the more pleasing as it would be a particu-

---

MSS, 1st ser.; C. C. Cambreling to Van Buren, Jan. 27, 1832, Fitzpatrick, *Autobiography of Van Buren*, p. 454; W. L. Marcy to Van Buren, Jan. 26, 1832; Walter Lowrie to Van Buren, Jan. 27, 1832; F. P. Blair to Van Buren, Jan. 28, 1832; John Forsyth to Van Buren, Jan. 28, 1832; Isaac Hill to Van Buren, Jan. 29, Feb. 12, 1832; Elijah Hayward to Van Buren, Jan. 30, 1832; W. A. Duer to Van Buren, Feb. 1, 1832; John M. Niles to Van Buren, Feb. 2, 1832; Richard Parker to John Campbell, Feb. 3, 1832; J. Hoyt to Van Buren, Feb. 7, 1832; J. A. Hamilton to Van Buren, Feb. 12, 1832; N. S. Benton to Flagg, Jan. 31, 1832; Charles Butler to Van Buren, Jan. 31, 1832; Lewis Cass to Van Buren, Feb. 4, 1832, Van Buren MSS (LC). There were a few exceptions to this prevailing opinion: John L. Lawrence to Clay, Jan. 30, 1832; Hiram Ketchum to Clay, Feb. 12, 1832; William H. Underwood to Clay, Feb. 21, 1832; R. W. Stoddard to Clay, Feb. 21, 1832, Clay MSS; Ambrose Spencer to J. W. Taylor, Jan. 31, 1832, Taylor MSS.
    22. George Kesling to McLean, Feb. 18, 1832, McLean MSS.
    23. *Winchester Virginian* as quoted in *The Globe*, Feb. 3, 1832.

larly appropriate act of revenge. Calhoun had cast the deciding vote
against Van Buren. "Upon every view of the subject," editorialized
the *St. Clairsville Gazette* (Ohio), "we do not see any way in which
the Senate can be made to feel the omnipotence of public opinion
so effectually as by placing M. Van Buren in the Chair of the Vice
President."[24] Green was pleased by this reaction to the Senate's refusal
to confirm as it promised to fulfill his long standing prophecy that
the national convention would nominate his favorite whipping boy.[25]

A number of historians have written knowingly of Jackson's use
of patronage to compel the convention to nominate Van Buren.[26] Certainly Jackson made no secret of his disgust with the Senate, but
he rejoiced because he knew that his wish to have Van Buren as
his vice-president would, at last, be gratified.[27] This does not in itself
prove that he personally forced the delegates to accept Van Buren
against their will. He did, it is true, write Governor William Carroll
of Tennessee urging him to see that his home state was represented
at Baltimore.[28] He also asked his old companion-in-arms, General John
Coffee, to promote meetings in Alabama to protest Senator Gabriel
Moore's vote against confirmation.[29] And he made inquiries among
the members of the Tennessee congressional delegation to substantiate
reports that they favored Van Buren.[30] On the basis of these few
and rather tame incidents Jackson is portrayed as cracking the whip
over the heads of his lackeys.

Outside Tennessee or his circle of old friends Jackson did not interfere. No doubt he realized that it would be injudicious and, more
than that, unnecessary for him to meddle with the Baltimore convention. His intervention in Tennessee was less in his capacity as head

24. From *The Globe*, Feb. 24, 1832.
25. *United States Telegraph*, Feb. 4, 1832.
26. At least two historians have attempted to correct this misinterpretation.
Both attribute Van Buren's nomination to the Senate rather than to Jackson. See
Edward M. Shepard, *Martin Van Buren* (Boston, 1899), pp. 230–41; Gammon,
Campaign of 1832, pp. 91–97.
27. Jackson to J. A. Hamilton, Jan. 27, 1832, Hamilton, *Reminiscences*, p.
237; S. R. Hobbie to A. C. Flagg, Jan. 27, 1832; W. L. Marcy to Flagg, Feb.
6 [1832], Flagg MSS; J. A. Hamilton to Van Buren, Feb. 1, 1832, Van Buren
MSS (LC).
28. Carroll to Jackson, Feb. 7, 1832, Jackson MSS, 1st ser.; Carroll to Jackson,
Feb. 20, 1832, Jackson MSS, 2nd ser.
29. Jackson to Coffee, Jan. 27, 1832, Bassett, *Correspondence of Jackson*, IV,
402.
30. Felix Grundy to Jackson, Feb. 4, 1832, Jackson MSS, 1st ser.

of the party than as a colleague of the state's Democratic politicians. No threats were made (or needed to be). The contention that Jackson used his influence, or his control over federal patronage, to shove recalcitrant delegates into line is without proof, unless one accepts the vaporous charges of the anti-Jackson press. Accusing opposition conventions of being "fixed" was an old game and the charge was probably valid enough in many instances. A carefully arranged unanimity was the rule rather than the exception for most conventions of all parties. The remarkable thing about the first Democratic national convention was its openness.

That the Senate rather than Jackson was responsible for Van Buren's nomination becomes clear when the impact of the rejection on the selection of delegates is examined. In almost every state which chose its delegates after the vote in the Senate the appointing body instructed the delegates for Van Buren. Where the delegates had already been selected, public pressure was exerted to compel them to support the former minister.

New York needed no special prodding. Neither did New England, which had no strong native sons to offer. Van Buren was the most acceptable among the prospective nominees, since he was from an adjacent state and was the most outstanding northern man available. The Maine legislative caucus, meeting in February to appoint the Baltimore delegates, declared that Van Buren's "elevation to the *Vice Presidency* would be highly gratifying to the people of this state. . . . "[31] Local conventions in Vermont and New Hampshire also endorsed him (although they did not choose the national delegates).[32] Connecticut's state convention, which commissioned the Baltimore deputation, supported the New Yorker.[33] Members of the Massachusetts caucus, convened to select the two at-large delegates, expressed their confidence in Van Buren and pledged themselves to back whomever the national convention nominated.[34] A New Jersey caucus in March, which authorized public meetings in the counties to select the Baltimore delegates, voiced the will of the state's Democratic party that they should vote first for Dickerson and then for Van Buren.[35] As Dickerson was a forlorn hope this was equivalent to an

31. *Eastern Argus* [Portland, Me.], Mar. 2, 1832.
32. *Albany Argus*, Mar. 14, 1832.
33. *Ibid.*, May 16, 1832.
34. *Ibid.*, Mar. 14, 1832.
35. *The Globe*, Mar. 20, 1832.

endorsement. Public meetings in Maryland, preparatory to choosing delegates, went on record favoring him.[36] Delaware appointed its representatives before the rejection occurred.[37]

Pennsylvania was a problem. Although devoted to Jackson, it was fearful lest the anti-tariff forces within the national party should gain the ascendant. Many of the state's Democrats were also determined that their contribution to the party be recognized by allowing it to pick the vice-president. Before the rejection of Van Buren, when it appeared likely that a Pennsylvanian would be nominated, a state convention had characterized the national convention as "the most effectual, if not the only mode, of coming at a correct knowledge of the wishes of the great Jackson party throughout the Union," and had appointed delegates to it.[38] In March, 1832, a second state convention at Harrisburg reneged on this endorsement. It resolutely declined to send delegates to Baltimore or uphold the nominee of the national convention.[39] Instead, the convention nominated Senator Wilkins for vice-president and invited the rest of the party to follow suit. There was, nevertheless, considerable Van Buren sentiment among the delegates to this convention and among the voters.[40] After the Harrisburg convention adjourned a large number of the die-hard Jacksonians joined in electing national convention delegates at county public meetings.[41] Many of the delegates chosen in this irregular (for Pennsylvania) manner were the same ones who had been appointed to Baltimore by the first state convention.

Most of the western states had designated their national delegates before the Senate's rejection so it is impossible to measure its effect on their choice. In Kentucky a state convention pledged its delegates to Baltimore to vote for Senator Richard M. Johnson, a favorite son.[42] A like body in Missouri also instructed its sole delegate for Johnson.[43] In Ohio (state convention), Indiana (state convention), and Illinois (public meeting) the delegates were not bound for any individual.

36. *Ibid.*, Mar. 9, 20, Apr. 17, 1832; *Albany Argus*, Mar. 17, Apr. 5, 19, 1832.
37. *The Globe*, Oct. 4, 1831.
38. *United States Telegraph*, Jan. 16, 1832.
39. *Ibid.*, Mar. 10, 1832; *Daily National Intelligencer*, Mar. 8, 9, 10, 1832.
40. M. T. Simpson to McLean, Feb. 2, 1832, McLean MSS; *The Globe*, Feb. 29, Mar. 6, 1832; *United States Telegraph*, Mar. 10, 1832. The motion to send delegates to Baltimore was beaten 88 votes to 51.
41. *Albany Argus*, Mar. 13, Apr. 10, 1832.
42. *The Globe*, Jan. 3, 20, 1832.
43. *Ibid.*, Dec. 31, 1831.

Strong sentiment for Van Buren was detected throughout the region even though Johnson was very much in the frontier tradition.[44]

Where the selection of western delegates took place after the rejection its influence was evident. A public meeting in Nashville, including persons from all over the state, chose a huge delegation to the national convention. Other county meetings added to this list, some of them expressing a preference for Van Buren.[45] A caucus which met before the rejection appointed the Alabama delegates and instructed them for Barbour.[46] After the Senate's action public meetings in the counties demanded that Senator Moore's name be stricken from the delegate list because he had voted against Van Buren. Several of them asked their state's representatives to Baltimore to vote for the New Yorker.[47] Public meetings, called on a hit-or-miss basis, picked the national delegates in Mississippi. Many were sympathetic to Van Buren.[48] Louisiana's delegates were chosen at a mixed caucus shortly before the rejection, but subsequently strong Van Buren opinion was manifested at a large public meeting in New Orleans.[49]

The Southeast presented the greatest obstacle to Van Buren's nomination. It was the region most agitated over the continuance of protection and it lacked the intense enthusiasm for Jackson characteristic of the West. County meetings in Georgia requested the state's congressmen to serve as delegates, but gave them no instructions, although there was evidence of popular sympathy for Van Buren.[50] In South Carolina a legislative caucus appointed the delegates prior to the rejection without specifying for whom they were to vote.[51] Delegates from North Carolina were selected at a combination caucus and public meeting in Raleigh and seconded at county meetings throughout the state.[52]

44. George Kesling to McLean, Feb. 18, Mar. 23, 1832, McLean MSS; Elijah Hayward to A. C. Flagg, Feb. 21, 1832, Flagg MSS; Walter Lowrie to Van Buren, Jan. 27, 1832, Van Buren MSS (LC); *The Globe*, May 12, 1832; *Albany Argus*, May 9, 1832; *Richmond Enquirer*, Feb. 14, 1832.

45. *Nashville Republican and State Gazette*, Feb. 16, Apr. 5, 19, 26, May 3, 1832.

46. *Richmond Enquirer*, Feb. 14, 1832.

47. *Ibid.*, Mar. 8, 15, 23, Apr. 17, 1832; *The Globe*, Apr. 6, 17, May 19, 1832.

48. *The Globe*, Apr. 5, 10, 11, 12, 21, May 19, 1832.

49. *Nashville Republican and State Gazette*, Jan. 26, 1832; *Richmond Enquirer*, Mar. 27, 1832; *The Globe*, Jan. 27, Mar. 10, 26, 1832.

50. *Daily Savannah Republican*, Mar. 1, 23, Apr. 23, 1832; *Richmond Enquirer*, Mar. 15, Apr. 17, 1832. Other states distant from Baltimore also appointed their congressmen to be delegates: Missouri, Alabama, Mississippi, and Tennessee.

51. *Daily National Intelligencer*, Jan. 5, 1832.

52. William H. Haywood to W. P. Mangum, Jan. 16, 1832, Shanks, *Papers of Mangum*, I, 444; *The Globe*, Jan. 23, Mar. 2, 12, 26, Apr. 21, 1832.

The Tarheel State's concern with the tariff made it cool toward any northern vice-presidential candidate, but the Senate did its work for Van Buren there as elsewhere.[53]

The ultimate key to the attitude of the south Atlantic states was Virginia, whose size and prestige were still sufficient to give it a preeminent position despite the challenge of South Carolina to its authority. The Old Dominion was opposed to protection and other centralizing legislation, but its leaders were still willing to work within the federal system and through the party system. The Junto caucus met in December, 1831, and declared unanimously for Jackson, but many of its members insisted that the vice-presidential nominee should be steadfastly against the tariff, internal improvements, and the distribution of the Treasury surplus to the states.[54] They required, in other words, that Jackson's running mate be a southerner, preferably Barbour. But moderates led by Ritchie forced an adjournment of the caucus before it could make a nomination.

By the time the caucus met again to nominate electors, the Senate had forced Ritchie to abandon his opposition to Van Buren's candidacy. From that point on he fought to prevent Virginia from taking any steps which might be prejudicial to the unity of the Democratic party.[55] He cautioned his fellow citizens that they must be prepared to support Van Buren "where a much more obnoxious politician is likely to succeed."[56] One letter writer in the *Enquirer* declared that the New Yorker "comes nearer, in his opinions, to the Virginia State Rights doctrines than any other individual likely to be elected."[57]

Even though Ritchie's friends consistently maintained a sizable majority in the new, mixed caucus, they were wise enough not to push the minority to the breaking point. Electors pledged to Jackson were chosen without difficulty. Barbour was endorsed for vice-president, but the electors were not obligated to vote for him unless he seemed likely to be among the two top contenders in the Electoral College. The ticklish problem of whether or not to send delegates to Baltimore,

53. R. M. Saunders to W. P. Mangum, Jan. 23, 1832; James Iredell to Mangum, Feb. 4, 1832; R. J. Yancey to Mangum, Feb. 11, 1832; Spencer O'Brien to Mangum, Feb. 26, 1832, Shanks, *Papers of Mangum*, I, 462, 471-73, 479-80, 494; *Richmond Enquirer*, Mar. 3, 13, 23, Apr. 21, 1832.

54. *Richmond Enquirer*, Dec. 20, 1831; Simms, *Rise of the Whigs*, p. 52.

55. *Richmond Enquirer*, Feb. 4, 24, 28, Mar. 15, Apr. 27, 1832; Andrew Stevenson to Ritchie, Feb. 4, 1832; Van Buren MSS (LC); Harrison, *JSH*, XXII (Nov., 1956), 454-56; Francis Fry Wayland, *Andrew Stevenson, Democrat and Diplomat, 1785-1857* (Philadelphia, 1949), p. 88; Ambler, *Ritchie*, pp. 145-46.

56. *Richmond Enquirer*, Feb. 28, 1832.

57. *Ibid.*, Mar. 8, 1832. Also, see *ibid.*, Mar. 15, Apr. 27, 1832.

bitterly opposed by the extreme anti-tariffites, was swept under the rug by doing nothing.[58] Yet the aims of the Junto were made perfectly clear by its subsequent announcement that "the people" should decide if they wished to be represented at Baltimore.[59] Virginia Democrats responded eagerly to this backhanded invitation, electing delegates several times over the state's quota at county public meetings.[60] Of the 84 delegates who attended the national convention, 45 favored Barbour and 39 Van Buren.[61]

The act of participating in the Baltimore convention, plus the strong grass roots support for Van Buren, helped kill the Barbour movement which threatened to split the Jackson vote not only in Virginia but throughout the South.[62] The decisive event in this sequence was not pressure from Jackson, but the failure of the Senate to confirm Van Buren's appointment. Barbour himself was of this opinion. He had hoped to rally the South and the national party to his own anti-tariff position. After the rejection he saw that this was impossible. "[H]ad it not been for that unwise act," he wrote in the spring, "we should not be placed in our present dilemma."[63]

The Senate helped prevent a possible schism of major proportions in the Democratic party. Until he was rejected Van Buren could not have run without seeming to prove the accusations of his enemies that his resignation from the cabinet was part of a shabby intrigue to become vice-president. But Calhoun and Clay succeeded in doing what Van Buren had not been able to do—fully identifying him in the popular mind with Jackson. Before that, as Walter Lowrie wrote Van Buren, "The Kentucky candidate seemed in a fair way to unite the whole of the West. At the South were Crawford and Smith, and Penna. had two. Many prominent men would hear of no name but yours, and others much more numerous, would not agree that your name be mentioned. The vote of the Senate has brought these two classes together. I have not heard, nor heard of, any opinion but one, and that is, that you are to be the candidate with the Old Chief, and all his friends believe that he and you will be elected. This too is the opinion of many of the friends of Mr. Clay."[64] Now his nomina-

58. *Ibid.*, Mar. 1, 15, 1832.
59. *Ibid.*, Mar. 20, 1832; Ambler, *Ritchie*, p. 147.
60. *Richmond Enquirer*, Mar. 30–June 1, 1832.
61. *Ibid.*; Ambler, *Ritchie*, p. 147.
62. Ambler, *Ritchie*, pp. 147–48; Simms, *Rise of the Whigs*, pp. 52–53.
63. *Richmond Enquirer*, Mar. 23, 1832.
64. Walter Lowrie to Van Buren, Jan. 27, 1832, Van Buren MSS (LC).

tion became a clear-cut test between Jackson and his bitterest foes, and men who would have given their secondary loyalty to Barbour or Johnson or Dickerson now rallied to Van Buren in order to defend their first love.

The Democratic national convention was more fully attended than either of its rivals; 320 delegates were present from every state but Missouri. Massachusetts, Rhode Island, and Connecticut were the only states represented by the same number of delegates as they had electors. Six states had an excess of delegates, Virginia leading with 61 over its quota and New Jersey following with 45. Almost every conceivable method was used to appoint them. State conventions selected all of the delegates in seven states—Delaware, Connecticut, Indiana, Kentucky, New York, Ohio, and Vermont. A state convention chose the senatorial delegates in Massachusetts, but left the choice of district delegates to public meetings. In three states, Maine, New Hampshire, and South Carolina, the legislative caucus prevailed. Louisiana Democrats resorted to a mixed caucus while those in North Carolina and Alabama combined the caucus with public meetings in the counties. Illinois used a single, statewide meeting, but Pennsylvania, Georgia, Mississippi, New Jersey, Tennessee, and Virginia employed multiple county meetings. Maryland used the district convention.

Many prominent characters in the party served as delegates. New York sent a strong group which included Nathaniel Tallmadge, Silas Wright, Jr., Samuel Young, Cambreling, and Flagg. "Whole Hog" Jackson men in Pennsylvania were represented by young Simon Cameron and "Honest George Kremer," whose fearless exposure of the corrupt bargain between Adams and Clay gave him a special place in party affections.[65] From the South came Joel Poinsett of South Carolina, Senator John Forsyth of Georgia, and Senator William King of Alabama. The Tennessee delegation included Overton and Governor Carroll.

Amid "the hurry & hustle" of Baltimore, swollen by an "immense" throng of strangers, the Democratic national convention opened on May 21, 1832, in the Athenaeum. Kremer was the " 'lion' of the Convention," according to one witness. "Men, women, and children—crowds upon crowds—hurried to the convention to see George Kremer," his hair done up in an old-fashioned "cue" that "peculiarly

65. *Albany Argus*, May 25, 1832.

tickled the free hearts of the youth. . . ."[66] To New Hampshire
went the honor of presiding at the first session; Frederick A. Sumner
gaveled the delegates to order and gave the reasons why his state
had called the convention:

> The object . . . was, not to impose on the people, as candidates for
> either of the first two offices . . . any local favorite; but to concentrate
> the opinions of all the states. They [the members of the New Hamp-
> shire caucus] believed that the great body of the people, having but
> one common interest, can and will unite, in the support of important
> principles. . . . They believed that the coming together of representa-
> tives of the people from the extremity of the union, would have
> a tendancy to soothe, if not to unite, the jarring interests, which
> sometimes come in conflict, from the different sections of the country.

Those responsible, he went on to say, had been motivated beyond
the exigencies of the approaching election. "They believed that the
example of this convention would operate favorably in future elections;
that the people would be disposed after seeing the good effects of
this convention in conciliating the different and distant sections of
the country, to continue this mode of nomination."[67]

Sumner proposed that Jackson's close friend, John Overton, be appointed temporary chairman of the convention, but Robert Lucas of
Ohio was substituted when Overton declined, allegedly because of
illness.[68] Lucas assumed his duties after a brief address. Next, two
committees composed of one delegate from each state were appointed,
one to compile a list of the delegates and the other "to prepare the
rules for the government of the convention." An invitation to Charles
Carroll to attend the convention closed the first session.

The following day the delegates reassembled in the larger quarters
of the Universalist Church. The rules committee recommended a slate
of permanent officers and the adoption of two procedural rules destined
to long and mischievous life. First, the committee suggested that two-
thirds of the total number of votes cast be required for the nomination
of a vice-presidential candidate. Second, "That in taking the vote,
the majority of the delegates from each state designate the person
by whom the votes for that state shall be given." Both proposals were
without precedent in state or local conventions.

66. *Richmond Constitutional Whig,* June 1, 1832.
67. *Niles' Weekly Register,* XLII (May 26, 1832), 234.
68. Weisenburger, *Passing of the Frontier,* pp. 259–60.

Senator King, the committee chairman, explained to the delegates that "a nomination made by two-thirds of the whole body . . . would show a more general concurrence of sentiment in favor of a particular individual, would carry with it a greater moral weight, and be more favorably received, than one made by a smaller number. . . ."[69] One delegate opposed the rule as inconsistent with the fundamental concept of democratic government, majority rule, "and because it might possibly be found impracticable to unite the voices of so large a proportion in favor of any one individual. . . ."[70] These sensible objections were overruled by the delegates and the committee's report was adopted.

King's justification of the two-thirds rule was supported by a subsequent address of the Tennessee delegation to its constituents. According to this document, "it was agreed upon in Committee" that "no nomination ought to go forth to the people from this Convention except under circumstances to exclude the idea, that any material differences had found a place amongst us."[71] On its face the rationale seems sufficient: if the candidate were chosen by anything less than a preponderant majority, the nomination would not be considered as binding on the minority as an overwhelming vote, and the whole purpose of the convention might be defeated.

Behind this reasoning, however, was another motive: to meet criticism leveled at the convention prior to its meeting. For months Duff Green had been embroidering the charge that the nominee of the convention would not represent the whole party, since each state was to cast the same number of votes as it had in the Electoral College without reference to its Democratic strength. Some of these states, chiefly the New England ones, had not voted for Jackson in 1828 and were unlikely to do so in 1832. Therefore, in all probability a minority of the national party would force its candidate, Van Buren, who had New York plus New England in his pocket, on the loyal Jackson states.[72] The states responsible for nominating Van Buren would not be found in the Democratic column in November.

Romulus Saunders, a prominent North Carolina delegate, writing

69. *Albany Argus*, May 25, 1832 (from the *Baltimore Republican*).
70. *Ibid.* I found no evidence to support the conclusion of David, Goldman, and Bain that the two-thirds rule "was taken over in modified form and without much thought from the Antimasons. . . ." Paul G. David, Ralph M. Goldman and Richard C. Bain, *The Politics of National Party Conventions* (Washington, 1960), p. 30.
71. *Nashville Republican and State Gazette*, June 4, 1832.
72. *United States Telegraph*, Feb. 2, 25, Mar. 31, Apr. 6, 1832.

after adjournment, admitted that "The question of what States would be allowed to vote, threatened a . . . serious disturbance to the harmony of our proceedings."[73] To have excluded the states where the Democrats were a minority would have been "as unjust as impolitic." It would have destroyed whatever hopes the party had of carrying them in November. Yet it seemed unfair to allow them to name the candidate for vice-president. "To obviate this difficulty, and to guard against the objection of suffering those non-effective States to decide the question, it was resolved that no person should receive the nomination without having in his favor at least two-thirds of the whole electoral vote." In that way the votes of the presumably anti-Jackson New England states could not be decisive. So the two-thirds rule, which was to bedevil the Democratic party for over a century, was spawned, the offspring of a unique situation and in answer to an unfriendly critic. The rule did not, incidentally, prevent the *Telegraph* and other opposition papers from claiming that Van Buren owed his nomination to the states where the Jacksonians were in the minority.[74]

The unit rule, which in some measure counteracted the two-thirds rule, was also adopted.[75] It helped prevent an endless fragmentation of the votes by suppressing the minority members within the delegations. The committee did not give a reason for proposing the rule, but it was obviously connected with the abnormal size of many of the delegations. Some of the states were represented by more delegates than they were entitled to, others by fewer. "It was necessary therefore," Saunders wrote, "to devise some plan which might reflect correctly the relative weight of each State. . . . Hence it was decided that each State without regard to the number of their delegates, should give its electoral vote." The decision to invoke the unit rule was left, however, to each delegation.[76] Four states, Maryland, North Carolina, Illinois, and Alabama, chose to split their votes. "This rule," Saunders commented, "being so manifestly fair and just, one so likely to accommodate the wishes of all, met with no opposition."

Tuesday afternoon, without the benefit of nominations, the delegates

73. *Richmond Enquirer*, July 3, 1832.
74. *United States Telegraph*, May 25, 26, June 5, 1831; *Richmond Enquirer*, July 10, 1832.
75. Carl Becker, "The Unit Rule in National Nominating Conventions," *AHR*, V (Oct. 1899), 64–82.
76. *Richmond Enquirer*, July 3, 1832.

voted for vice-president. In a procedure differing from the Antimasonic and National Republican conventions, states rather than individual delegates were polled. This was the party of states' rights. Provision was made for each delegation to caucus before roll calls and to record its vote on a paper ballot.[77] Only one ballot was required. There were 283 electoral votes represented in the convention; 189 were needed for nomination.[78] Johnson received the undivided vote of Kentucky and Indiana, plus 2 from Illinois for a total of 26. Barbour did better, garnering Virginia's 23 votes, 11 from South Carolina, 6 each from Alabama and North Carolina, and 3 from Maryland for a total of 49. The other 208 went to Van Buren, giving him 19 votes in excess of the required two-thirds.[79] The vote was then made unanimous.

Van Buren's nomination was inevitable. He came to Baltimore with the solid support of New York, most of New England, and strength in all the other sections of the country. Dickerson withdrew from the contest shortly before the convention opened, giving Van Buren New Jersey's eight votes in accordance with the instructions of the legislative caucus.[80] The refusal of Wilkins's friends to attend the convention added the 30 votes of Pennsylvania (cast by the "irregulars") to his column. This was more than enough, but even without the votes of New Jersey and Pennsylvania the decision in all probability would not have been delayed beyond a second ballot. Neither Dickerson nor Wilkins, both protectionists, could have picked up the necessary votes had their names gone before the convention. Levi Woodbury, a suitable compromise candidate, had been knocked out of the race before the convention opened by the hostility of Isaac

77. A report in the *United States Telegraph* (May 24, 1832) indicates that an "informal meeting" of the delegates to vote on the nomination was held before the balloting. I could find no other reference to this meeting.

78. Missouri's 4 electoral votes were not represented and Illinois, although entitled to 5 votes, cast only 4 (the number of delegates present). Other states whose delegations were below their authorized strength cast their full quota Senator Thomas Hart Benton, the sole Missouri delegate, did not attend. I cannot discover why. Perhaps he did not wish to vote for Johnson, as he had been instructed by the Missouri state convention.

79. *Summary of the Proceedings of a Convention of Republican Delegates from the Several States in the Union, for the Purpose of Nominating a Candidate for the Office of Vice-President of the United States; Held at Baltimore, in the State of Maryland, May, 1832* (Albany, 1832), pp. 6–7.

80. Letter of May 20, 1832, in the *Albany Argus*, May 25, 1832; *Richmond Enquirer*, June 12, 1832.

Hill, who controlled the New Hampshire delegation. After the rejection Hill became a strong Van Buren man.[81] The only candidates with an outside chance of displacing Van Buren were Johnson and Barbour. Both had grave liabilities.

Richard M. Johnson was the distinctly western candidate. Like Jackson, he had fought the redskins and the redcoats (he was credited with killing Tecumseh in the Battle of the Thames in 1813). The colorful "Rumsey Dumpsey" also appealed to easterners, but it was in the West that his tangible strength lay.[82] The state conventions of Missouri and Kentucky which appointed delegates to the national meeting had pledged him their support.[83] Johnson's candidacy suffered three handicaps. First, he was not generally considered to possess the requisite ability for so high an office. Second, he came from Kentucky, which meant that a Jackson-Johnson ticket would lack sectional balance. And last, there was the matter of his "domestic arrangements." Johnson lived openly with his mulatto slave, by whom he had two daughters, reared as his own children. Newspapers made snide references to this, which inevitably hurt him, especially in the South.[84] It was for this reason that Johnson was denied the official vice-presidential nomination at the 1836 national convention, although he was subsequently elected by the Senate.

Philip Barbour was the southern candidate. The movement in his behalf was the work of the free-trade wing of the party, which had looked to Calhoun for leadership. Because of Jackson's immense popularity in the South the nullifiers refrained from direct attacks, using Barbour as a stalking horse to force an anti-tariff position on the party.[85] Unfortunately, the Barbour candidacy did not develop until the Senate made Van Buren's nomination at Baltimore a certainty. In any event Barbour's well advertised and adamant stand against pro-

81. *New Hampshire Patriot*, Jan. 30, 1832. Hill had himself experienced the humiliation of a Senate rejection (for second comptroller of the Treasury). He, too, got his revenge. The New Hampshire legislature elected him to the Senate, forcing Woodbury, an old Hill foe, to retire. Jackson subsequently appointed Woodbury to the cabinet. *Ibid.*, Apr. 26, June 14, 1830.

82. *The Globe*, July 27, Aug. 5, 15, Sept. 3, 24, 1831; Jan. 8, Mar. 19, Apr. 19, 1832.

83. *Ibid.*, Dec. 31, 1831; Jan. 20, 1832. A so-called state convention in Illinois also endorsed Johnson, but this body did not represent the regular Democratic organization. *Ibid.*, Apr. 17, 1832.

84. *Maysville Eagle*, Apr. 12, 1831; *The Focus*, July 21, Aug. 19, 1831; *Daily National Journal*, Mar. 29, 1831.

85. Harrison, *JSH*, XXII (Nov., 1956), 454–56.

tection—he had served as president of a national anti-tariff convention in 1831—made his nomination a red flag to large segments of the party.[86]

Johnson was unacceptable to the South and the Northeast; Barbour was unacceptable everywhere outside the South. Both men were regional candidates who enjoyed neither the undivided support of their own sections nor the steady loyalty of their own states. Kentucky was pledged to support whomever the convention nominated. Virginia under the unit rule gave Barbour almost half of his total vote, but the delegation contained strong Van Buren sentiment. Prior to the roll call of the states the caucus of the Virginia delegation decided to support Van Buren as its second choice after giving Barbour "a fair trial of his strength."[87] Had Johnson shown signs of winning, the bulk of Barbour's votes would certainly have shifted to Van Buren, while Johnson's delegates undoubtedly preferred him to the Virginian.[88] Van Buren had the unbeatable advantage of being the first choice of the majority and the second choice of both minority groups. He owed this enviable position to his prominence and skill as a party leader and to his moderation on the most explosive issue which divided the Democratic party, not to threats from Jackson or the Kitchen Cabinet.

In his old age Major Lewis attempted to take a larger share of the credit for Van Buren's nomination than was justly his, and his pretensions have served as the basis for the myth that Jackson and the Kitchen Cabinet bent the delegates to their will.[89] Lewis, never modest in estimating his influence on history, based his claim on two services he supposedly rendered Van Buren.

A few days before the convention opened Lewis maintained that he and Speaker of the House Andrew Stevenson of Virginia had persuaded Johnson to withdraw from the race in order to clear Van Buren's path.[90] Lewis and Stevenson probably attempted to persuade Johnson to withdraw, yet nothing indicates that they succeeded. In an excess of enthusiasm right after the Senate's rejection Johnson did

86. *Richmond Enquirer*, Sept. 30, 1831.
87. *Ibid.*, June 19, 1831.
88. *Ibid.*, July 3, 1832. This was the opinion of Romulus Saunders, a Barbour man, after talking with the western delegates.
89. Fitzpatrick, *Autobiography of Van Buren*, pp. 582–91; Parton, *Life of Jackson*, III, 421.
90. Fitzpatrick, *Autobiography of Van Buren*, pp. 589–90. Wayland (*Andrew Stevenson*, p. 89) accepts this tale at face value.

come out for Van Buren, but he later repented this self-denial and did nothing to discourage delegates from voting for him.[91] His name was before the convention and he received exactly those votes (with the exception of Missouri's four) which were pledged to him. There is no reason to believe that he withdrew prior to the balloting at Lewis's, or anyone else's, request.

The other part of Lewis's boast is more difficult to unravel. It concerns an alleged plot by Overton, William Barry (the postmaster-general), Louis McLane, and Eaton to defeat Van Buren.[92] Shortly before the convention began, Overton (according to Lewis's account) told Lewis that " 'if we should not be able to nominate Mr. Van Buren' " he favored Samuel Smith of Maryland. Lewis saw in this remark the hand of McLane, working through Barry, working through Overton, to remove Van Buren as a rival for the presidency in 1836. McLane's ostensible reason for opposing Van Buren's nomination was that it would jeopardize Jackson's reelection. By a subtle questioning of Barry, Lewis learned that an intrigue was afloat among a group of the western delegates headed by Eaton to block Van Buren. "I well knew," Lewis wrote several years later, "if Mr. Eaton and Judge Overton should be opposed to Mr. Van Buren that he could not get the nomination—They being the personal and confidential friends of General Jackson, would be considered as representing his feelings and wishes in relation to the matter, which would enable them to procure the nomination of almost any person whom they might recommend to the convention."[93] To end this incipient and nebulous revolt, Lewis gave Overton a lecture and wrote Eaton of Jackson's determination to sink with Van Buren rather than go on without him. Lewis reportedly told Eaton not to oppose Van Buren " 'unless he was prepared to quarrel with the General!' "[94] Eaton responded by assuring him in a letter from Baltimore, written the day the convention opened, that Van Buren would be nominated, although he regretted it, believing as he did that Van Buren's interests would be better served if he ran for governor. Lewis did not credit Eaton's reason for his misgivings as sincere.[95]

On the basis of the evidence Lewis presented it is difficult to find

---

91. *United States Telegraph*, Feb. 16, Mar. 3, 1832; *Richmond Enquirer*, Feb. 21, 1832.

92. Fitzpatrick, *Autobiography of Van Buren*, pp. 587–90.

93. *Ibid.*, p. 589.

94. Parton, *Life of Jackson*, III, 421.

95. Fitzpatrick, *Autobiography of Van Buren*, p. 591.

an intrigue to derail Van Buren. McLane's belief that Van Buren's name on the ticket might cost Jackson votes did not necessarily indicate an unfriendly design. Neither did Eaton's opinion that Van Buren would do well to avoid the center of the stage for four years betray a hostile intent. Many of Van Buren's best friends in Albany were of the same mind. In reading Lewis's account of these events one cannot but sense his desire to enlarge his part in the outcome of the convention so as to improve his standing in the eyes of Van Buren and posterity. The fact that both McLane and Eaton were later to become political enemies of Van Buren gives his story a specious plausibility.

Assuming that Lewis did perceive a sinister meaning behind outwardly innocent words, can he be credited with suppressing the plot? Did Eaton and Overton have it within their power to change the minds of the delegates? They were far from being the only persons with a claim on Jackson's confidence. Everyone in Washington, if nowhere else, knew that Jackson wanted Van Buren to be his vice-president. He had expressed his preference in unmistakable language to all who cared to listen. The probability that Overton and Eaton, with winks and nods could have created a contrary opinion and caused Van Buren's delegates to desert him is not high. On its face the plot has little substance and there is no real reason to think that Lewis's intervention was necessary to achieve Van Buren's nomination. Yet this story, told only by Lewis, is the foundation of the prevailing interpretation that Van Buren was nominated only because Jackson forced the convention to do so against its collective will.[96]

Following Van Buren's nomination, the delegates quickly finished their business. Except for the unit and two-thirds rules the convention did not deviate in any significant way from the pattern established by its predecessors. It did not, however, adopt an address to the people as the Antimasons and National Republicans had done, even though a committee was appointed to draw one up. Failing to agree among themselves, the committee members recommended that each delegation prepare a separate address to its constituents.[97] A general central com-

96. Schurz, *Henry Clay*, I, 379; William Graham Sumner, *Andrew Jackson as a Public Man* (Boston, 1900), pp. 317–18; Harlan, *Tennessee Historical Quarterly*, VIII (June, 1948), 132–33; Charles S. Sydnor, *The Development of Southern Sectionalism, 1819–1848* (Baton Rouge, 1948), p. 204; Agar, *Price of Union*, p. 247.

97. *Niles' Weekly Register*, XLII (May 26, 1832), 235; *Daily National Intelligencer*, May 25, 1832 (from the *Baltimore Chronicle*).

mittee (to reside in Washington) was appointed to oversee the campaign. Cameron of Pennsylvania made a motion that a national convention should meet the third Monday in May in Baltimore every four years, but it was withdrawn by its author following a floor discussion.[98] After making arrangements to print the proceedings and a vote of thanks all around, the delegates adjourned to pay their respects to Charles Carroll, their work well finished.

Four years in power left wounds in the Democratic party which the Baltimore convention could not instantly heal. Pennsylvania was piqued by the party's refusal to give her interests and statesmen their due weight. The cotton planters were angrily demanding a reduction of the tariff as the price of party unity. Of these two schisms the southern one was the more dangerous. It ran deeper than Pennsylvania's pathetic effort to gain attention; the weapons it brandished imperiled the nation. And it had a leader of national stature.

During the spring and summer of 1831 there were indications that Calhoun might run for president. Governor John Floyd of Virginia was trying to promote his candidacy while the tireless Green offered his master as the only candidate on whom all the anti-Jackson forces could unite.[99] A meeting in New York City in August actually nominated him.[100] Whatever illusions Calhoun harbored of obtaining his long sought goal in the ensuing election disappeared with the aggravation of the tariff question in 1831 and 1832. He cast his lot irrevocably with the nullifiers by publishing two treatises in the summer of 1831 defending the right of a state to void an act of Congress. By then Calhoun realized that he could not possibly win and considered running only for the purpose of throwing the election into the House of Representatives where his friends might hold the balance of power between Jackson and Clay.[101] By the spring of 1832 he abandoned this scheme and withdrew his name from further consideration.[102]

Even before his final withdrawal, the southern radicals had begun concentrating their energies behind a drive to deprive Van Buren

98. Until 1852 the Democratic convention did meet in Baltimore and, with one exception, on the third Monday in May.

99. Simms, *Rise of the Whigs*, p. 45; Clay to Brooke, Apr. 1, 1832, Colton, *Private Correspondence*, pp. 331–33; Green to S. L. Gouvernor, Apr. 18, 1831, Gouvernor MSS; *United States Telegraph*, Aug. 17, 18, 20, 27, Sept. 1, 6, 1831.

100. *Albany Daily Advertiser*, Aug. 12, 17, 1831.

101. Wiltse, *John C. Calhoun: Nullifier*, p. 121.

102. *Ibid.*, p. 129.

of the vice-presidency by nominating electoral tickets pledged to Jackson and Barbour, notwithstanding the Baltimore convention. They were joined by National Republicans in those states where Clay was weakest, hoping thereby to throw the election for both offices into the Congress.[103]

In Virginia the states' righters held a state convention at Charlottesville in the summer of 1832 to drum up support for Barbour. No electoral ticket was nominated, as it was hoped that the electors nominated by the Junto caucus might pledge themselves to vote for Barbour. Failing to secure such a commitment, the central committee appointed at Charlottesville eventually published its own electoral slate.[104] Other conventions or public meetings during the summer and fall of 1832 nominated Jackson-Barbour electors in North Carolina, Georgia, Mississippi, and Alabama, where they had the covert, and sometimes open, support of the National Republicans.[105] Barbour gave every sign of countenancing this movement, even accepting the nomination of the North Carolina convention in a letter strongly denouncing protection.[106]

In the end the efforts to defeat Van Buren were wrecked on Jackson's popularity and the incompatibility of a marriage between outspoken advocates of tariffs with their bitterest opponents.[107] Van Buren's defeat would be small consolation to the South if it resulted in Clay's election. And although the New Yorker's silence on the tariff was not so pleasing as Barbour's opposition the South had no reason to dislike or fear him. Besides, the southern Democrats, having participated in the national convention, were committed in honor to abide by its decision, even if the result was not entirely to their liking.

103. F. Sydnor to Clay, June 9, 1832, Clay MSS; C. W. Gooch to C. C. Cambreling, Oct. 9, 1832, Van Buren MSS (LC); J. H. Pleasants to James Barbour, Mar. 23, 1832, Barbour MSS; *United States Telegraph*, July 17, Aug. 23, Oct. 15, 19, 1832.

104. *Richmond Enquirer*, May 1, June 8, 19, Sept. 25, Oct. 2, 9, 16, 30, 1832.

105. J. H. Pleasants to James Barbour, Oct. 7, 1832, Barbour MSS; John Randolph to Woodbury, Mar. 26, 1832, Woodbury MSS; *United States Telegraph*, June 6, 8, 13, 20, 25, 1832; *Daily National Intelligencer*, Oct. 13, 1832; Wiltse, *Calhoun; Nationalist*, p. 129; Govan, *JSH*, V (Nov., 1939), 464; Harrison, *JSH*, XXII (Nov., 1956), 454-56; Edwin A. Miles, "Andrew Jackson and Senator George Poindexter," *JSH*, XXIV (Feb., 1958), 57; Hoffman, *Jackson and North Carolina Politics*, pp. 48-55.

106. *United States Telegraph*, July 31, Oct. 9, 1832.

107. Simms, *Rise of the Whigs*, pp. 49-51; Hoffman, *Jackson and North Carolina Politics*, pp. 52-55.

One North Carolina politician wrote Senator Mangum that ". . . it is a question of fair dealing. We sent our Delegates to the Convention—all agreed that Van B is most likely to succeed on the Jackson ticket—and how are *we* to draw back after taking the chance—this [the Barbour movement] seems to me a crooked policy and after full & honest reflexion I will not myself pursue it. . . ."[108] The national convention did double work, keeping the friends of aspiring candidates in the same party in expectation of receiving its nomination and then, because they had participated in it, preventing the losers from going their separate ways after the convention adjourned.

Barbour's inability to make substantial headway against Van Buren was undoubtedly a factor in his decision not to incur the displeasure of Jackson. He effectively killed his own candidacy in late October by publicly urging his friends in Virginia to support the caucus-nominated electors which, although unpledged, were understood to be for Van Buren. At the last possible moment he announced that he could not jeopardize Jackson's reelection.[109] The Barbour letter, which "astounded his friends, and surprised all parties," was regarded by his supporters as "a virtual withdrawal."[110] The Barbour electors who remained in the race did poorly and did not materially affect the vote in a single southern state.[111]

Pennsylvania's rift with the national party was not bridged. Its leaders refused to sanction Wilkins's withdrawal despite a movement within the state to transfer allegiance to Van Buren following the national convention. Rather than risk a split within the state party all Democratic factions in Pennsylvania decided to support the Jackson-Wilkins slate.[112] After the election there was an attempt to recall the state convention so that the victorious electors could vote for Van Buren. It failed, although the state central committee indicated that it would have been willing to make the change had Van Buren's success depended on it.[113]

---

108. W. H. Haywood, Jr., to W. P. Mangum, June 22, 1832, Shanks, *Papers of Mangum*, I, 557.

109. *Richmond Enquirer*, Oct. 30, 1832.

110. *United States Telegraph*, Nov. 6, 13, 1832.

111. *Ibid.*, Nov. 26, 1832; Miles, *Jacksonian Democracy in Mississippi*, pp. 52–53.

112. *The Globe*, Aug. 20, 1832; *Daily National Intelligencer*, June 2, 1832.

113. "Memorandum of the Proceedings of the Democratic Committee of Correspondence at Philadelphia" [Nov. 8, 1832]; "Copy of the Reply of the Central Committee" [Nov. 11, 1832]; and H. Buehler to Van Buren, Nov. 23, 1832, Van Buren MSS (LC); *The Globe*, Dec. 7, 10, 1832.

Pennsylvania's spoil sport attitude made no difference. The November returns were a triumph for Van Buren as well as Jackson. Clay carried only Massachusetts, Rhode Island, Connecticut, Delaware, Kentucky, and a portion of Maryland for 49 electoral votes. Wirt won 7 from Vermont. The South Carolina legislature defiantly threw away its votes, giving them to Floyd for president and Henry Lee of Massachusetts for vice-president. Jackson received 219 electoral votes out of a possible 288.[114] All of the Jackson electors with the exception of the 30 from Pennsylvania also cast their ballots for Van Buren.

By different means the major parties had largely succeeded in consolidating most of the nation's voters in their ranks, the National Republicans through coalition electoral tickets with the Antimasons, the Democrats by adhering to the middle of the road. The November election returns once again described a two-party system except for Vermont. The pressure generated by the desire to win the presidency produced polarity where none could have anticipated in a few months previously. The same pressure had also created an institution that made the job of finding the common denominators necessary to a two-party system much easier for the future.

114. Two of the Maryland electors did not vote.

Conclusion

"However, the people will rule sometime."

V. W. Smith to A. C. Flagg, October 17, 1830.

"You ask about the caucus—yes sir, you are perfectly right—a want of independence—this never enough to be depreciated, prevalent policy, of hunting majorities, is the ruin of the political morals of the Country, and will overwhelm our institutions in the end."

John H. Pleasants to James Barbour, March 23, 1832.

Pervasive as the convention system was in the states and local units of government prior to the election of 1832—pervasiveness that made possible the national convention's unheralded debut—it did not reach into every county or town, or even into all the states. And in a number of states the convention was the rule for one party, but not the other. In some states, district and county conventions were in use, but not the state convention, and vice versa. In others, conventions of any kind were held only sporadically, and in a small number of states they had yet to be introduced.[1]

A full-fledged convention system was firmly established by 1832 in Pennsylvania, New Jersey, Delaware, New York, and Maryland. In New England the convention was widely employed for local nominations, but in Massachusetts, Rhode Island, and New Hampshire it con-

1. I refer the reader, again, to McCormick, *Second Party System*, as well as to earlier chapters of this book.

tinued to share statewide nominations with legislative caucuses for a few more years. Caucuses and ad hoc methods prevailed for a while longer in Virginia and North Carolina despite occasional use of state and local conventions before 1832. Parties in Ohio and Kentucky had largely completed their convention networks; those in Indiana, Illinois, Missouri, Louisiana, Tennessee, Alabama, and Mississippi waited until the late 1830s before doing so. Only the politicians of South Carolina and Georgia had not employed some form of the convention before Jackson's reelection. It required the additional impetus of the presidential contests of 1836 and 1840 to insure the convention's adoption in all parts of the nation.

Credit for the convention system must be widely shared. The initial thrust had come in the middle Atlantic states as a result of Republican efforts against the Federalists. The Jacksonians in 1824 were the first to use the state convention in the Northwest. The Antimasons and the Democrats introduced it into New England in 1828. On the other hand, the Adams and National Republican state conventions of 1828 and 1832 had priority in several southern states. While a number of blank places on a map of convention usage would not be filled in until 1836 or even 1840, the convention method was clearly in the ascendant by 1832.

What accounts for this uneven yet steady growth of the convention apart from factors applicable to all sections—increasing population, lower suffrage requirements, and improved transportation? Why did the middle Atlantic states lead in the application of the convention, followed by New England, while the South and West generally lagged behind? What were the conditions conducive to the rise of the nominating convention? Four were paramount:

(1) *The division of the state into progressively smaller units of government.* Although every state contained counties, the northern states had subdivided them into townships and election districts (or hundreds). Their more numerous towns were also much more likely to be split into wards than those of the South and West. Where the county was the only electoral division, local conventions had no chance to develop since there was no smaller unit from which delegates could be elected. The undifferentiated government of most towns outside the Northeast similarly slowed the adoption of the convention.

(2) *A dense population.* Delegated rather than mass meetings were more essential in populous areas than in thinly inhabited regions, where

all the interested citizens could assemble under one roof or tree. In cities representative party government was necessary to preserve public order. It is not surprising, therefore, to find that conventions were held first in New York, Philadelphia, Baltimore, or Cincinnati before being taken up by the surrounding rural districts or that, in general, the East was ahead of the South and West. In thinly settled counties, characteristic of much of the South and West, the population was simply insufficient to justify delegated meetings. Parties did well to hold primary assemblies.

(3) *A large number of elective offices.* Frequent elections for a myriad of posts forced politicians to create intricate electioneering machinery in order to extend their control over all the spoils. Furthermore, when faced with a long ballot the average voter needed the guidance which convention-backed tickets provided. Obviously, there had to be elective offices for a particular unit of government before a convention could be held to cover it. One reason that the southern states were slow to adopt the state convention was that few of them had popularly chosen governors or other state officials. In such instances state conventions made sense only when presidential electors were chosen on a general ticket.

(4) *A competitive party system.* Rivalry was the greatest single incentive to political organization of all kinds. Party antagonism was sharpest in the middle states, first between Federalists and Republicans, then between Republican factions, and finally between Democrats and National Republicans (or Antimasons). New England, which possessed the other three conditions, tended to be a one-party area. Western voters had an abundance of offices to fill and, eventually, townships, but their allegiance to Jefferson and Jackson retarded the growth of parties. Competition, as a result, was personal and individualistic. The South was almost as backward as the West in developing two strong parties and it was deficient in the other three conditions congenial to the rise of the convention system as well. Only in the middle Atlantic states were all four elements found.

The precise moment when a particular state or community first embraced the convention system was determined by circumstances unique to a time and place—the quality of local leadership, the relative strength of the contending parties and factions, and the attitude of the voters. Yet in spite of the complexities involved in the glacial change from self-announcement, mass meetings, and caucuses to conventions, in spite of the maze of electoral divisions and the welter of competing groups obscuring the transition, it is possible to discern the principal reasons for the convention's triumph. The convention prevailed over other nominating methods because it best satisfied the ideological demands of the Jacksonian era that government should be responsive to the people's direction. It also solved the technical difficulties of conducting politics in a democracy. In the nominating convention, idea and experience harmonized; a popular theory created an institution which passed the pragmatic test imposed by politicians.

The convention's appeal to the democratic instincts of the age is rooted in the historical significance of the word itself. The convention concept derived from the English constitutional struggles of the seventeenth century when two irregularly appointed parliamentary bodies (in 1660 and 1689) settled the government of the kingdom by pretending to express the will of the whole nation. During and immediately after the American Revolution this precedent proved invaluable as both the former colonies and the new nation needed a means compatible with the natural rights philosophy of government for writing and ratifying their constitutions.[2] Implicit in the convention was the idea that its delegates incarnated the sovereignty of the people; its sessions enacted the social compact. Private associations, such as the great religious denominations, whose large and scattered memberships made primary meetings impracticable, also employed the convention after 1776 as the supreme governing body of their organizations. These conventions possessed, on a more modest scale, the same sovereign functions as the state constitutional conventions and their delegates proceeded on the assumption that their authority sprang directly from the rank and file.

Another user of the convention, one particularly active in the age of Jackson, was the pressure group engaged in securing the passage of a favored bill through Congress or a state legislature. Often representing narrow special interests, the lobbyist endeavored through the holding of conventions to give the appearance of speaking for a majority of the voters. The *Richmond Compiler* observed in 1831 that "This seems to be the age of Conventions—not for forming Constitutions, but for shaping the measures of the People."[3] To marshal the support of "the People" for the purpose of impressing legislators, public meet-

2. J. Franklin Jameson, "The Early Political Uses of the Word Convention," *Proceedings of the American Antiquarian Society*, XII (New Ser., 1899), 183–85.
3. Quoted in the *Daily National Intelligencer*, Aug. 6, 1831.

ings appointed delegates to conventions where, obedient to their instructions, they endorsed resolutions requesting their legal representatives to build some internal improvement, raise the tariff (or lower it), encourage observance of the Sabbath, promote temperance, stimulate trade, or revise the militia laws.[4] In 1827, well before the Antimasons held the first national nominating convention, friends of domestic manufactures met in a national convention, and in 1831 both protectionists and free traders convoked similar assemblies.[5] The *Nashville Republican* wondered whether, in view of all these conventions, "The regular constituted government of the country will shortly become a useless affair, and an unnecessary expense and incumbrance."[6] By the time the party warfare was suffiicently developed to warrant its use convention theory and practice were well known and the politicians had an instrument fashioned to their needs.

The convention satisfied the great political touchstone of Jacksonian democracy—popular sovereignty. Every public question was to be decided by the people acting through their representatives; elected officials were considered, even by themselves, mere agents reflecting the voters' desires. A delegate to the Virginia constitutional convention of 1829–30 resigned his post when he could not in good conscience obey the instructions of a public meeting of his constituents.[7] "We disapprove," said an editor on another occasion, "of all delegates and representatives assuming powers not delegated by the people. . . ."[8] Any other course constituted a dangerous tendency toward aristocracy or even monarchy and many legislative careers were ruined by the exercise of independent judgment. The defeat of the western congressmen who voted for Adams in 1825 was an object lesson to those who thought of flouting the orders of the *demos*.

"The cry of aristocracy takes with certain folks," wrote John C. Spencer to Thurlow Weed in 1831, "and there is no way to meet it but to clamor louder than our adversaries. . . ."[9] Few remarks

4. *Daily National Intelligencer*, Nov. 3, 1823; Dec. 21, 1825; Dec. 6, 1826; *Buffalo Republican*, Dec. 17, 1831; *Richmond Enquirer*, July 18, 1828; *Rochester Telegraph*, Jan. 12, Apr. 3, 1827; *Anti-Masonic Enquirer*, Sept. 22, 1829; Jan. 25, 1831.
5. *Daily National Intelligencer*, June 26, 28, 30, July 9, 28, 1827; July 22, Aug. 2, 18, Sept. 10, Oct. 29, 1831.
6. *Nashville Republican and State Gazette*, Nov. 12, 1831.
7. *New Hampshire Patriot*, Nov. 30, 1829.
8. Quoted in the *United States Telegraph*, Apr. 14, 1826.
9. Spencer to Weed, Sept. 21, 1832, Weed, *Memoir*, p. 44.

typify the demands of Jacksonian politics with greater precision, for in their efforts to prove their devotion to democracy politicians were forever clamoring louder than their adversaries. Lip service to the superiority of democratic government was required of all groups competing for power. The convention, composed of delegates directly commissioned by the entire membership to make a nomination for a particular office, certified that the party met this indispensable condition. In a day when polls of steamboat passengers, grand juries, and militia musters were accepted as indices of public opinion the ability to stage conventions was the best available evidence that the party's nominee enjoyed wide approval. The convention was democracy applied to party government.

Homage to popular sovereignty made it necessary to determine the people's choice of candidates, but the consultation did more than implement a theory; it paid off in the mundane task of winning elections. The convention not only united large numbers of voters in support of a candidate but created an organization capable of waging a successful campaign in his behalf. For this reason it had a special appeal to the new breed of managers generated by the rise of national parties in a period of increasing political participation by the masses. These were men vitally interested in ways of holding amorphous groups together within a single organization which they could wield to hoist themselves into power.

To nominate a candidate for Congress in the middle Atlantic states necessitated mass meetings in each township for the election of delegates to a county convention. The delegates from the townships met and appointed delegates to a district convention which nominated the candidate. All of the not inconsiderable number of persons who partook in these meetings and conventions, or who identified themselves with the sponsoring party, were expected to abide by the decision of the majority and support the nominee. The convention's democratic form reduced the chances of intraparty competition for the same office as every geographic and electoral division of government was directly consulted in the choice of nominees. Unless some clear infraction of the democratic process had transpired in the election of delegates there could be little justification (other than thwarted ambition) for a losing aspirant to declare as an independent candidate. "It is the very foundation of the democratic creed," intoned the *New Hampshire Patriot*, "that the minority shall yield to the majority—and consequently when a candidate shall have been fairly designated by a majority of the

Delegates assembled in convention, every republican will cheerfully yield his assent, and come boldly to his support."[10]

Even if the disappointed candidate for the nomination was insensitive to the moral obligation of abiding by the majority's decision, the fact that the convention nominee wore the tag of the "regular" candidate discouraged revolt because the party's label exerted a powerful influence over the voters. An independent candidate favorable to Jackson stood little chance of winning, although he might siphon enough votes from the regular nominee to elect the Adams man. Certainly, the greatest threat to victory at the polls lay in the possibility that the party's vote would be split among several candidates while the opposing forces were solidly behind one man or ticket. In 1830 a Jackson paper in Ohio sounded the alarm that the National Republicans were "encouraging and inducing a multitude of candidates from our ranks to run for various offices . . . in order to cut up our party, and thus by uniting upon some of their own, to break in upon the Jackson Ticket."[11] By providing a device whereby the full weight of the party could be brought to bear in an election, yet one which allowed for a democratic selection and gave scope to individual ambition, the convention helped perpetuate the two-party system.

The convention's efficacy in concentrating the support of a party was not lost on office seekers. One New York politician wrote in 1823: "I am one of six candidates in this District to fill Mr. Rochesters place in Congress, if I succeed in getting the nomination by the District convention (which will shortly take place) I will be elected. . . ."[12] In the West, where the convention developed slowly, the lack of party cohesion was a severe handicap, particularly to the anti-Jackson forces. Henry Clay in 1829 wrote to a congressional candidate in Kentucky that he "should be most happy to learn that any mode had been adopted to concentrate on yourself, or any other friend, the votes of those who concur in their political principles. Can no such mode be fallen upon? Is it not yet practicable to convene persons from all parts of the district?"[13] A Clay newspaper, noting the disastrous results of plural nominations against an undivided enemy, denounced self-nomination as "anti-republican."[14] An easterner in 1832

10. *New Hampshire Patriot*, Jan. 10, 1831. Also, *Eastern Argus*, June 19, 1829.
11. Quoted in the *St. Louis Beacon*, Sept. 30, 1830.
12. George McClure to Clay, July 23, 1823, Clay MSS.
13. Clay to Adam Beatty, July 9, 1829, Colton, *Private Correspondence*, p. 238.
14. *Kentucky Reporter* as quoted in the *Daily National Intelligencer*, Aug. 9, 1830.

asked Clay plaintively if "our Western brethren [could] be sufficiently innoculated with the caucus [i.e., convention] virus to enforce a wholesome political action among them at future elections. In New York the most jarring personal feelings are made to yield to the furtherance of a great publick purpose."[15]

Another advantage enjoyed by the convention nominee over his independent rivals was the campaign organization incidental to the system. Every township meeting, held to elect county convention delegates, appointed a committee of correspondence which, in turn, provided for committees of vigilance for the school districts and polling places. Each county, district, and state convention appointed similar committees. On this network, reaching down to the smallest subdivision of government, rested the burden of winning the battle on election day. Whatever their official duties these committees operated as command posts, coordinating operations against the adversary. They distributed campaign literature, printed ballots, won over the undecided voter, conducted friends to the place of election, and compiled lists of the voters within their jurisdiction, indicating how each would vote, to be forwarded on to the state committee.[16] No maverick could possibly match this organization produced as a by-product of the convention and placed at the disposal of its nominee.

The propaganda value of the convention was immense. Meetings of county and district conventions were reported not only in the local papers but in friendly sheets throughout the state. A state convention for the nomination of governor and lieutenant governor provided copy for several months. The state central committee issued the call to arms, inviting the counties to send delegates to a state convention. Township meetings then chose delegates to county conventions which appointed the delegations to the state convention and, if state senators or congressmen were to be elected, also appointed delegates to a district convention. Each of these meetings adopted without fail resolutions, and sometimes an address, expressing the delegates' opinions on local, state, and national issues, all duly reproduced in the newspapers. Finally, after the preliminary conventions had run their course, the state convention met. The importance of its task made it an object

15. John E. Lawrence to Clay, Aug. 30, 1832, Clay MSS.
16. See, for instance, *Richmond Enquirer*, Oct. 7, 1828; *Albany Argus*, July 12, 1831; New York Central Corresponding Committee to Luther Bradish, Oct. 16, 1828, Bradish MSS; Circular, in the *Proceedings of the Anti-Masonic Republican Convention of the County of Cayuga, Held at Auburn, January 1, 1830* (Auburn, 1830); Broadside, "Proceedings of the National Republican State Convention of Vermont, held July 16, 1832 at Montpelier."

of great interest and opposition newspapers took notice, if only to scorn and ridicule.

Almost without exception the proceedings and the address of the state convention were published as pamphlets for dissemination as campaign literature. Ten thousand was an average issue. In Pennsylvania many copies were printed in German while in Louisiana a large portion was ordered in French. Publication of the proceedings and the address, in addition to their duplication in newspaper columns, put them into the hands of voters who might never attend a partisan rally. Although these closely printed documents would not be considered effective propaganda today, campaign managers in the 1820s eagerly sought them for distribution.[17]

Apart from the benefits of unity, organization, and propaganda the bringing together of like-minded men from scattered communities, many meeting one another for the first time, kindled enthusiasm and fortified party morale. A correspondent of the Rochester *Anti-Masonic Enquirer* exultingly reported his party's state convention: "It is a glorious Convention. Lobbies, galleries, and all, are overflowing. I am proud of Anti-Masonry. What principles beyond all estimation brings honest plain farmers from the extreme bounds of the State, at the dead of winter. The masons and the Regency look pale, at the view, and in the anticipation, with which such a Convention must present to their minds."[18] A discouraged Adams supporter in New York looked forward to the state convention in hopes that "An exhibition such as might and I trust will be made at the convention will create a new feeling among us—and provide the happiest results in the River Counties."[19] In the meetings of delegates, as Alexis de Tocqueville observed in 1831, "men have the opportunity of seeing one another; means of execution are combined; and opinions are maintained with a warmth and energy that written language can never attain."[20] Every convention was a party rally whose enthusiasm was transmitted to the faithful back home.

The convention's advantages become quite real when the meeting of the Adams convention of Virginia in 1828 is examined closely.

17. Isaac Hill to Levi Woodbury, Aug. 4, 1828, Woodbury MSS; R. K. Lansing to Weed, Feb. 27, Mar. 12, 1829, Weed MSS; Elisha Dorr and John Yates to Luther Bradish, July 5, 1831, Bradish MSS.
18. Feb. 22, 1831.
19. A. Bruyn Hasbrouch to J. W. Taylor, Mar. 10, 1828, Taylor MSS.
20. Alexis de Tocqueville, *Democracy in America* (New York, 1959), I, 199.

Called for the purpose of designating presidential electors, the state convention was the first held in Virginia and its influence extended far beyond the Commonwealth's boundaries.

Despite Adams's efforts at reconciling Virginia to his election by appointing its citizens to important positons, a preponderant majority of the old Republican party, under the leadership of the Richmond Junto, showed unmistakable Jackson proclivities. So hopeless did the president's prospects for carrying Virginia appear that for two and a half years following his inauguration his partisans made no serious effort to organize a statewide party in his behalf. Somewhat tardily, in the summer of 1827, important administration leaders attempted to give the president at least a fighting chance to carry the state. The critical feature of their plan was to be a state convention.[21] The proposal was publicly unveiled in James H. Pleasants's *Richmond Whig*, and through its agency popularized among the demoralized friends of the administration who enthusiastically endorsed it as a means of rallying their forces.[22]

Virginians in 1827 bitterly debated the question of revising the state constitution. For years the large western counties had been complaining about the discrimination in favor of the slaveholding eastern counties in the apportionment of legislative seats. A nominating convention would identify the Adams party with the cause of constitutional reform by emphasizing the reliance of the Junto on a legislative caucus to nominate Jackson's electors. Like the legislature, the caucus was controlled by the planter class. A convention would proclaim the democracy of the Adams party while capitalizing on the general unpopularity of caucus nominations, particularly keen in the underrepresented counties.[23] "The plan of a Convention of Anti Jackson delegates at Richmond," wrote an Adams supporter, would be "a strong political weapon, which the opposite party will dread exceedingly. It will give confidence at home and abroad, and neutralize the influence of the small counties in the Legislature."[24] Once the convention was proposed newspapers friendly to Adams began denouncing the caucus as "an absolute despotism," "an unclean thing" and "a self-constituted

21. Hugh Mercer to Henry Clay, Aug. 18, 1827, Clay MSS.
22. *Richmond Constitutional Whig*, Aug. 29, Sept. 1, 15, 19, 1827.
23. Clay to Francis Brooke, Sept. 24, 1827, Colton, *Private Correspondence*, p. 179.
24. Joseph C. Cabell to Francis Brooke, Oct. 8, 1827, Clay MSS. See also George Webb to J. W. Taylor, Nov. 6, 1827, Taylor MSS.

body . . . undertaking to dictate the choice of a President. . . ."[25]
Through a convention the people of Virginia "for the first time" would
be "given an opportunity to form their *own* Ticket, and thus practically to vote for the President of their choice. . . ."[26]

With Clay's blessing a public meeting in September at Fredericks-
burg, presided over by the Secretary of State's good friend, Francis
T. Brooke, officially invited those opposed to Jackson to participate
in a convention at Richmond in early January, 1828. The invitation
stressed the contrast between a convention, emanating from the people,
and the caucus, imposing its will upon the voters.[27] Dozens of counties
subsequently elected delegates at special public meetings. They also
passed resolutions praising the administration, condemning Jackson and
the caucus, and appointed committees of correspondence.[28] For the
first time Adams had a local organization in Virginia, one created
by the necessity of choosing delegates to a state convention "which
like the throbbing of the heart" communicated "its pulsations to the
distant extremities."[29]

Foe as well as friend felt the effects of the scheduled meeting. Congressman William C. Rives tried to minimize its impact by reassuring
a New York colleague, Gulian C. Verplanck, that the Adamsites
"may, no doubt, have a convention, (as indeed what party is so poor
as not have it's convention, in these times), but Virginia will be Virginia no more, if she can ever be propitiated towards Adams & Clay.
Fear not, then, for us."[30] The *Richmond Enquirer,* joined by a chorus
of other Jackson papers, attacked the convention by pointing out the
small percentage of voters who attended the county meetings.[31] Simultaneously, it defended caucus nominations as far more representative
of the people's thinking since the Adams convention acted on dictation
from Washington while the legislators mirrored the opinion of their
constituents.[32]

Nevertheless, it became clear that the Adams maneuver was operat-

25. *Richmond Constitutional Whig,* Sept. 1, Oct. 6, 1827.
26. From the *Virginia Herald* [Lynchburg] as quoted in the *Daily National
Intelligencer,* Sept. 26, 1827.
27. Clay to Brooke, Sept. 24, 1827, Colton, *Private Correspondence,* p. 179;
Richmond Constitutional Whig, Oct. 6, 1827.
28. *Richmond Constitutional Whig,* Oct.–Nov., 1827.
29. *Ibid.,* Sept. 19, 1827.
30. Rives to Verplanck, Oct. 19, 1827, Verplanck MSS.
31. *Richmond Enquirer,* Sept. 25, Oct. 16, 19, 27, 1827; *United States Telegraph,*
Nov. 1, 3, 27, 1827.
32. *Richmond Enquirer,* Sept. 25, Oct. 5, 12, 19, 25, 1827.

ing effectively on the public mind. Several Jacksonian meetings, "aware that strong objections exist on the part of many persons" to caucus nominations, specifically authorized their legislators to nominate electors.[33] One meeting even suggested the caucus be abandoned entirely in deference to popular prejudice.[34] When the caucus met in December it delayed nominating electors so that special delegates could be chosen in those counties whose legislators were not members of the Jackson party. This call for a mixed caucus was the Junto's first cognizance of the inequities of caucus nominations. By allowing the counties represented in the legislature by Adams men to elect delegates, the Jackson managers invested the caucus with the appearance of greater democracy, a reaction to the appeal of the Adams convention. In setting a date for a subsequent meeting, the December caucus nervously avoided convening on the same day as their adversaries "lest it might by possibility be misinterpreted into the slightest alarm about the result of the Adams Convention." Instead, it would meet a week later, on January 14, "so that the antidote should be administered so soon after the poison as possible. . . . By assembling on the 14th, we shall meet at once this Mammouth convention, which is now agglomerating itself and threatening like an Avalanche, to fall upon our heads."[35]

Beginning on January 8, the anti-Jackson delegates met for four days in the state capitol building. The *Enquirer* admitted that the list of delegates "embraced some of the ablest men in Virginia. . . ."[36] An electoral ticket headed by James Madison and James Monroe was nominated which the *Whig* understandably called "the most powerful ever formed by any state of this union."[37] A state central committee was appointed. The convention address received lavish praise and 30,000 copies were ordered printed, each member of a county committee allotted a portion.[38] Other copies of the address were apparently printed outside Virginia and found effective use throughout the

---

33. *Ibid.*, Oct. 30, 1827; also issues in November and December.
34. *Ibid.*, Nov. 23, 1827.
35. *Ibid.*, Dec. 13, 1827.
36. *Ibid.*, Jan. 17, 1828.
37. *Richmond Constitutional Whig*, Jan. 12, 1828. Neither of the former presidents gave prior consent to their nomination and both eventually withdrew their names from the contest.
38. *Richmond Constitutional Whig*, Jan. 16, 23, Feb. 2, 16, Mar. 8, 12, 1828; *Proceedings of the Anti-Jackson Convention; Held at the Capitol, in the City of Richmond: With Their Address to the People of Virginia* (Richmond, 1828).

nation.[39] Congressman Henry Storrs of New York thought the convention had a decidedly good effect on the whole Adams campaign.[40] The Jackson press, including the *Albany Argus,* conspired to ridicule the convention address, but William L. Marcy wrote with some concern to Azariah C. Flagg that Silas Wright's district was flooded with it.[41] From faraway Missouri came news that "the ingenious, and persuasive ability of the address, of the Virginia administration convention, has done some good here."[42]

The fact that Virginia, reputed to be overwhelmingly opposed to the nationalist administration, could muster such a formidable convention heartened the Adams party everywhere. Within Virginia it briefly revived the spirits of the flagging cause. Unquestionably, the convention gave Adams what he previously lacked in the Old Dominion—an organization capable of waging a campaign, one extending into almost every county, but responding to central direction. It also united the party behind a single slate of electors. The convention's effect was hardly less important for members of the Junto since it compelled them to abandon the pure legislative caucus for the mixed variety, and thus move one step closer to the adoption of the convention.

Were conventions more democratic in practice than the caucuses and other nominating methods they replaced? Congressmen and state legislators were elected directly by the people and were answerable to them if their nominations proved unpopular. Furthermore, caucus members were guided in making their nominations by all the devices for measuring public opinion available to convention delegates—letters, newspapers, and public meetings.[43] Conventions could be manipulated no less than caucuses. Legislators were presumed corruptible because they stood to gain patronage and influence if their candidate succeeded. Was this less true of delegates? Most of them, admittedly, could not expect great rewards because they were so numerous, but this did not necessarily prevent them from being bought. Only the price may have been cheaper.

39. *The Virginia Address.* n.p., n.d.
40. Storrs MS, Jan. 12, 1828.
41. *Albany Argus,* Jan. 23, 1828; *United States Telegraph,* Feb. 1, 1828; *Richmond Enquirer,* Jan. 28, Feb. 7, 14, 16, 21, 26, Mar. 7, 16, Apr. 1, 1828; W. L. Marcy to A. C. Flagg, Feb. 18, 1828, Flagg MSS.
42. William Russell to J. W. Taylor, Feb. 21, 1828, Taylor MSS.
43. Charles S. Sydnor, "The One-Party Period of American History," *AHR,* LI (Apr., 1946), 439–51.

An indication of the superficiality of the democracy practiced by most conventions was the disparity between the large number of persons who participated in them and the small coterie who actually selected the nominees. The custom in state and local conventions was to have the candidate recommended to the delegates by a committee on nominations appointed at the convention by its chairman. The committee's report was then approved or rejected by the delegates as a body rather than by balloting individually for one of several contenders. Frequently, the delegates would caucus informally, as at the Antimasonic and National Republican national conventions, and would agree on the candidate beforehand so that the acceptance of the committee's report was only for the record.[44] The large number of delegates made a deliberative assembly virtually impossible; to have pretended otherwise would have invited chaos and encouraged personal and geographic rivalries. Party leaders dreaded an eruption into violence and newspaper accounts of convention proceedings emphasized their "respectable" character. The delegates were only asked to approve a choice made by the inner circle of party leaders.

This power elite, if its members held any official position in the party at all, was embodied in the central corresponding committee. Weed could legitimately claim that "during the five or six years following the organization of a party opposed to Freemasonry, what was known as the Morgan Committee . . . enjoyed its full and uninterrupted confidence. Candidates for all important offices were indicated by our committee, neither of whom would accept office themselves."[45] The process of candidate selection could be, as Weed recalled, disarmingly simple. When the man he had selected as the nominee of an Antimasonic district convention declined the honor, a substitute was required on short notice:

> The difficulty of this task was not diminished by the circumstance that I was compelled to leave Buffalo in the stage at nine o'clock the next morning to attend a senatorial convention in Batavia. Rising at daylight, and on my way to another hotel to find the Chautauqua and Niagara delegates, I encountered Ebenezer F. Norton in the street, and inquired whether he would accept an Anti-Masonic nomination for Congress. His reply was, "I cannot afford to decline any nomination for Congress." . . . I found Colonel Flemming and Mr. Boughton, of Niagara, and Messers. Mixer and Plumb of Chautauqua, and hastily arranged with them the nomination of Mr. Norton. . . ."[46]

44. *Richmond Enquirer*, May 25, 1832.
45. Weed, *Autobiography*, p. 336.
46. *Ibid.*, pp. 338–39.

But the power of decision was not always vested in a committee; anyone possessing the confidence of the party might exercise it. In New York and Virginia, where the Regency and Junto held sway, control was not restricted to the central committee.[47] The Albany Regency took a keen interest in local nominations, its members criss-crossing the state to secure the desired results.[48] Flagg earned the sobriquet of "the Traveling Regency" for his efforts.[49] When the Regency decided to support Jackson for the presidency in 1828 it was able surreptitiously to arrange for the nomination of Jackson men to the legislature, much to the alarm of the Adams men within the Regency-dominated party.[50] But this type of influence was not unique and its presence may be assumed even though the evidence for it seems slight.[51] Elections were too important to leave to chance. "I have neither the time nor inclination at present," wrote a disgusted observer, "to give you a detail of all the paltry intrigues & machinations, which were resorted to, to effect the nomination of some Gentlemen."[52]

The belief that politicians were bent on personal gain at the people's expense persisted throughout the history of the early republic. Whether or not the convention system masked an undemocratic contrivance to carry office-seekers with greater ease to the public trough cannot be answered categorically. Some viewed the convention as a retreat rather than an advance toward greater democracy. A holder of this position unburdened himself to Congressman J. W. Taylor:

> I most heartily congratulate you on your triumph over the caucus [i.e., convention] candidate (Mr. Palmer). Not that I have anything personal against Mr. P. but I think it all important that *this taking out of the hands of the people* the choice of their rulers should have an end. At last fall's election in the State of Ohio several of the Congressional districts had 6 candidates some 5 and some 4, but few

47. Ammon, *Virginia Magazine of History and Biography*, LXI (Oct., 1953), 398–418; Remini, *New York History*, XXXIX (Oct., 1958), 341–55.
48. Silas Wright, Jr., to A. C. Flagg, Aug. 1, 1830; John A. Dix to Flagg, July 21, 1831; J. B. Skinner to Flagg, July 31, 1830, Flagg MSS.
49. Edwin Croswell to A. C. Flagg, June 27, 1830, Flagg MSS.
50. John Sergeant to Clay, Oct. 24, 1827; George McClure to Clay, Oct. 22, 1827; Peter B. Porter to Clay, Oct. 26; Nov. 6, 1827, Clay MSS.
51. Lemuel C. Paine to J. W. Taylor, Oct. 12, 1828, Taylor MSS; Henry Bradley to W. H. Seward, Aug. 11, 1831, Seward MSS; Van Buren to ———, draft, Aug. 31, 1822; Mordecai M. Noah to Van Buren, Dec. 19, 1819, Van Buren MSS (LC); Klein, *Pennsylvania Politics, 1817–1832*, p. 216.
52. James Campbell to G. C. Verplanck, Oct. 18, 1822, Verplanck MSS.

that had only 2. The choices were completely the people's without any forestalling or attempt at it. Many important reforms that we need can never take place until choices of our legislators shall come direct from the people.[53]

Most of the objections to the convention were rooted in the fear that it menaced the sovereignty of the people. The Jacksonian era had immense faith in direct democracy. This was the theme of the complaints against the introduction of the district convention in Virginia during the winter and spring of 1829 when delegates were being elected to the state constitutional convention, one of the rare occasions when the merits of the convention system were the subject of a full public debate. Nominations by conventions, according to resolutions passed at a public meeting in Richmond, "must operate as a restraint upon the free exercise of the elective franchise."[54] "As Virginians, we deplore the introduction of this system in our State—a system, which compels the people, by evil precedent, to vote for the candidate who is nominated over their heads," remonstrated a group of Buckingham county freeholders.[55] Another meeting saw the convention as an immolation of "the freedom of election at the shrine of an ideal phantom." The people "under the delusive semblance of exercising their most estimable right do nothing more than go through the empty and humiliating ceremony of ratifying the decree of the sovereign caucus."[56] The author of "Anti-Caucus" in the *Richmond Enquirer* saw the convention system as "the fruitful parent of intrigue, and which tends inevitably to pass the choice of public men, and the direction of public measures, out of the hands of us, the people, into those of a few crafty managers. . . ."[57] A second writer viewed "the elective franchise, in its virgin purity, the sheetanchor of our liberty, as a right too sacred to be delegated. . . ."[58]

While the opponents of the convention system in Virginia were ringing the changes on the sovereignty of the people, its advocates countered with pragmatic arguments aimed at showing that it made democracy more operative. Delegates to the Northern Neck district convention reminded their critics "that all the influence which our nomination may be supposed to carry along with it flows directly

53. J. Geddes to J. W. Taylor, Feb. 22, 1823, Taylor MSS.
54. *Richmond Enquirer*, Mar. 20, 1829.
55. *Ibid.*, Mar. 24, 1829.
56. *Ibid.*, Mar. 27, 1829.
57. *Ibid.*, Apr. 14, 1829.
58. *Ibid.*, Apr. 28, 1829.

from these assemblages of our fellow-citizens who appointed us. . . . If you do not like them [i.e., the nominees], you are not bound to vote for them." In a district stretching 150 miles and embracing seven counties, "some sort of concert and unity of action" prior to the election was essential if the inhabitants were to be fairly and fully represented. Without concert the largest single county could elect all of the delegates to the constitutional convention.[59] "Harmony" was a favorite word among the defenders of the nominating conventions. Conventions provided the best guarantee that the men elected would represent the majority of the voters. They would, in addition, protect the "uninformed and ignorant" against "designing demagogues" since consultations among several counties, as opposed to self-nomination, would produce tickets composed of the "wisest and most experienced individuals."[60] At issue was the fundamental question of the relative superiority of an unstructured, pure democracy against the winnowing advantages of representative government.

The organization provided by the convention could be, and often was, used for narrow and selfish ends, but the system at least allowed for popular participation in the choice of candidates. The convention was effective only if it reflected public opinion, only if its nominee won elections. If "order & a judicious selection of candidates" were usually achieved by a few professionals, the delegates could, and occasionally did, reject the designated individual.[61] It cannot be assumed that the delegates or the rank and file disagreed with their leaders simply because the vast majority of conventions accepted decisions handed down from above. The price of party victory, desired by leader and led, was discipline. The greatest test for all nominating methods came on election day when the voters registered their approval or disapproval of the candidates preselected for their suffrage. The convention owed its ascendancy to its superior ability to meet the theoretical and practical requirements of democratic politics: candidates nominated by conventions, wrapped in the mantle of popular sovereignty and backed by an organization no independent could equal, were likely to be elected.

The national meetings of 1831–32 offer no answers to the questions about the convention's inherent possibilities, or lack of them, as a

59. *Ibid.*, Apr. 3, 1829.
60. *Ibid.*, Mar. 27, Apr. 3, 7, 17, 21, 28, May 1, 8, 1829.
61. Curry, *Register of the Kentucky Historical Society*, LV (July, 1957), 200; *Niles' Weekly Register*, XXXIII (Jan. 26, 1828), 357.

vehicle for expressing public opinion. With one exception, however, since 1832 the major parties have found the convention the best way of nominating their presidential candidates. In 1836 the Whigs, consisting of the National Republicans augmented by Antimasons and dissident Democrats, professed great scorn for the institution. Part of their disdain was strategic—they decided to defeat Van Buren's presidential bid by nominating a number of regional favorites rather than by agreeing on a single candidate. They had no need, therefore, for a national convention. But they also fell victim to their own propaganda concerning the Democratic convention of 1832. They had stigmatized that convention as a patronage engine to force Van Buren on the party and they foresaw that the Democrats would resort to it again. "Measures should be taken," John W. Taylor told McLean in 1833, "to render such a caucus [convention] odious."[62] Between 1832 and 1836 Whig politicians in every part of the country systematically attempted to discredit the national convention as intrinsically undemocratic.[63]

The national convention has remained odious to many persons ever since. Each quadrennium the air is filled with suggestions for better ways to nominate our presidents. The question now as in the past is whether conventions are "nothing more than a meeting of party bosses hidden behind a noisy political circus, or can they be treated seriously as representative assemblies competent to decide the party's leadership and principles?"[64] It can only be answered that the voters' repeated acceptance of convention-nominated presidents indicates that the system has been capable of choosing men sufficiently reflective of the people's sentiments to satisfy the democratic impulse.

The greatest contribution of the national convention, though, has been in maintaining the two-party system by providing the means through which groups competing for presidential power can find the common denominators necessary to the formation of only two major parties. The Antimasons and Democrats were particularly aware of the national convention as an agency to locate the candidates most likely to appeal to all the elements within an amorphous political bloc.

62. Taylor to McLean, Sept. 19, 1833, Taylor MSS.
63. Charles M. Thompson, "Attitude of the Western Whigs Toward the Convention System," *Proceedings of the Mississippi Valley Historical Association,* V (1911–12), 168–77; Mueller, *Whig Party in Pennsylvania,* pp. 20–21, 29; Miles, *Jacksonian Democracy in Mississippi,* p. 106.
64. David, Goldman, and Bain, *Politics of National Party Conventions,* p. 1.

The Antimasons used the national convention to find a presidential candidate who would compel the National Republicans to unite with them. Their choice of Wirt was sound, but they ran afoul of an irrational element in politics—personal loyalty. The Democrats sought a vice-presidential nominee who could hold the disparate elements of the party together and they found him. "The only hope of the opposition in Va.," Philip N. Nicholas of the Richmond Junto wrote Flagg, "arose from the expectation of a division in our ranks, relative to the Vice Presidency, but after the Baltimore Convention, it soon became apparant, that there would be no essential separation as to this question, among the friends of the administration. . . ."[65] The National Republicans saw no need for common denominators. They were the party of the American System; their candidate was its author. Had the party been more broadly based it would not have nominated Clay in 1832. When the National Republicans joined with the Antimasons and nullifiers the resulting Whig party would discover the advantages of a national convention, as Clay learned to his sorrow in 1839.

The national convention has profoundly shaped the presidency no less than the party structure. In 1824 Webster had predicted that with the passing of the Revolutionary heroes the choice for president would fall "among a greater number, and among those whose merits may not be supposed to be very unequal." The result would be a persistent failure of any candidate to receive an electoral majority with an ultimate resort to the House of Representatives "and the consequence of this will be . . . a diminution of the weight of authority of the Executive Magistrate, and a continued devolution of more of the authority belonging to that department on Congress—" Unless strong parties developed Webster feared "the President's Office may get to be thought too much in the gift of Congress."[66]

The national convention has averted this danger by concentrating the electorate behind two candidates, thus keeping the election from Congress and giving the president a base of support independent of the legislative branch. With the emergence of the national convention the parties completed their reproduction of the federal structure of government. Local and state politicians as well as national leaders were given a direct part in making a president. Local interests and voting

65. P. N. Nicholas to Flagg, Nov. 14, 1832, Flagg MSS.
66. Webster to William Gaston, Sept. 8, 1824, Van Tyne, *Letters of Webster,* p. 108.

blocs underrepresented at Washington received a chance to exert their influence, causing local political factions to polarize around presidential candidates. Rather than being dependent on a few great leaders or the members of Congress for his election, the president is indebted to the great cross section of the nation represented in a body whose delegates have been chosen by a process involving every county of every state. The convention brought president making to the notice, if not within the control, of the common man.

Tocqueville noted during his visit to the United States in 1831 and 1832 that voluntary associations tended to incite people to revolution by their incessant agitations of issues and causes. But he acknowledged, too, that their uninhibited activity provided security from tyranny or the seizure of power by small groups. "In America," he wrote, "there are factions, but no conspiracies."[67] V. O. Key applied the same idea directly to nominating techniques. He called "the development of pacific means, as a substitute for the darker methods of violence and inheritance for determining the succession to positions of power" the greatest achievement of political parties.[68] By this standard the convention system has been vital to democracy in America.

67. Tocqueville, *Democracy in America*, I, 203.
68. Key, *Politics, Parties, and Pressure Groups*, p. 360.

Bibliography

PRIMARY SOURCES

Unpublished Manuscripts

John Bailey Papers. New York Historical Society.
James Barbour Papers. New York Public Library.
Luther Bradish Papers. New York Historical Society.
Trumbull Cary Papers. Buffalo Historical Society.
Henry Clay Papers. Library of Congress.
Azariah C. Flagg Papers. New York Public Library.
Albert Gallatin Papers. New York Historical Society.
Samuel L. Gouvernor Papers. New York Public Library.
Francis Granger Papers. Library of Congress.
Gideon and Francis Granger Papers. Library of Congress.
Myron Holley Papers. New York State Library.
Andrew Jackson Papers. Library of Congress.
Andrew Jackson–William B. Lewis Papers. New York Public Library.
John McLean Papers. Library of Congress.
James Monroe Papers. New York Public Library.
Henry O'Rielly Papers. Rochester Public Library.
Peter A. Porter Papers. Buffalo Historical Society.
Richard Rush Papers. New York Historical Society.
William Henry Seward Papers. University of Rochester Library.
Samuel L. Southard Papers. Library of Congress.
Journal of Henry R. Storrs. Buffalo Historical Society.
John W. Taylor Papers. New York Historical Society.
Martin Van Buren Papers. Library of Congress.
Martin Van Buren Papers. New York State Library.
Gulian C. Verplanck Papers. New York Historical Society.
Daniel Webster Papers. Library of Congress.
Thurlow Weed Papers. New York Historical Society.
Thurlow Weed Papers. The University of Rochester Library.
William Wirt Papers. Library of Congress.
Levi Woodbury Papers. Library of Congress.

Published Correspondence, Works

[Agg, John.] *History of Congress from March 4, 1789, to March 3, 1793.* Philadelphia: Carey, Lea and Blanchard, 1834.

[———.] *The Ocean Harp: A Poem.* Philadelphia: M. Thomas, 1819.

Adams, John Quincy. *Letters and Addresses on Freemasonry.* Dayton: United Brethren Publishing House, 1875.

Baker, George E. (ed.). *The Works of William H. Seward.* 5 vols. Boston: Houghton Mifflin Co., 1887–90.

Bassett, John Spencer (ed.). *Correspondence of Andrew Jackson.* 7 vols. Washington: Carnegie Institution, 1926–35.

Becker, Carl (ed.). "A Letter of James Nicholson, 1803," *American Historical Review,* VIII (Apr., 1903), 511–13.

Brown, Everett Somerville (ed.). *The Missouri Compromises and Presidential Politics, 1820–1825.* St. Louis: Missouri Historical Society, 1926.

"Calendar of the Barbour Papers, 1811–1841," *Bulletin of the New York Public Library,* VI (Jan., 1902), 22–34.

"Calendar of the Jackson-Lewis Letters, 1806–1864," *Bulletin of the New York Public Library,* VI (Sept., 1900), 292–320.

Colton, Calvin (ed.). *The Private Correspondence of Henry Clay.* Cincinnati: H. W. Darby, 1856.

———. *The Works of Henry Clay.* 6 vols. New York: A. S. Barnes and Burr, 1857.

Crallé, Richard K. (ed.). *The Works of John C. Calhoun.* 7 vols. New York: D. Appleton and Co., 1851–79.

De Puy, Henry F. "Some Letters of Andrew Jackson," *Proceedings of the American Antiquarian Society for April, 1921.* Worcester: Published by the Society, 1922.

Ford, Paul Leicester (ed.). *The Works of Thomas Jefferson.* 12 vols. New York: G. P. Putnam's Sons, 1904–1905.

Ford, Worthington C. (ed.). "Letters Between Edward Everett and John McLean, 1828, Relating to the Use of Patronage in Elections," *Proceedings of the Massachusetts Historical Society,* 3rd ser., I (Feb., 1908), 359–93.

Hamilton, J. G. de Roulhac (ed.). *The Papers of Thomas Ruffin.* 2 vols. Raleigh: North Carolina Historical Commission, 1918.

Hamilton, Stanislaus M. (ed.). *The Writings of James Monroe.* 7 vols. New York: G. P. Putnam's Sons, 1898–1903.

Hay, Thomas R. (ed.). "John C. Calhoun and the Presidential Campaign of 1824: Some Unpublished Calhoun Letters," *American Historical Review,* XL (Oct., 1934; Jan., 1935), 82–96, 287–300.

Hopkins, James F. and Hargreaves, Mary W. M. *The Papers of Henry Clay, 1797–1824.* 3 vols. Lexington: University of Kentucky Press, 1959–63.

Hunt, Gaillard (ed.). *The Writings of James Madison.* 9 vols. New York: G. P. Putnam's Sons, 1900–1910.

Jameson, J. Franklin (ed.). *Correspondence of John C. Calhoun.* Vol. II,

Annual Report of the American Historical Association, 1899. Washington: Government Printing Office, 1900.

King, Charles R. *The Life and Correspondence of Rufus King,* 6 vols. New York: G. P. Putnam's Sons, 1894–1900.

"Letters and Papers of Andrew Jackson, Part 2," *Bulletin of the New York Public Library,* VI (June, 1900), 188–98.

"Letters of James Monroe, 1798–1823," *Bulletin of the New York Public Library,* IV (Feb., 1900), 41–61; V (Sept., Nov., 1901), 371–82, 431–33; VI (June, July, 1902), 210–30, 247–57.

McGrane, Reginald C. (ed). *The Correspondence of Nicholas Biddle Dealing with National Affairs, 1807–1844.* Boston: Houghton Mifflin Co., 1919.

McPherson, Elizabeth Gregory (ed.). "Unpublished Letters from North Carolinians to Van Buren," *North Carolina Historical Review,* XV (Jan., 1938), 53–81.

Meriwether, Robert L. and Hemphill, W. Edwin (eds.). *Papers of John C. Calhoun, 1801–1821.* 5 vols. Columbia: University of South Carolina Press, 1959–71.

Moore, John Bassett (ed.). *The Works of James Buchanan.* 12 vols. Philadelphia: J. B. Lippincott Co., 1908–1911.

Newsome, A. R. (ed.). "Correspondence of John C. Calhoun, George McDuffie and Charles Fisher, Relative to the Presidential Campaign of 1824," *North Carolina Historical Review,* VII (Oct., 1930), 477–504.

Phillips, Ulrich B. (ed.). "South Carolina Federalist Correspondence, 1789–1797," *American Historical Review,* XIV (July, 1909), 776–90.

Richardson, James D. (ed.). *A Compilation of the Messages and Papers of the Presidents, 1789–1897.* Washington: Government Printing Office, 1896.

Severance, Frank H. (ed.). *Millard Fillmore Papers.* 2 vols. Buffalo: Buffalo Historical Society, 1907.

Shanks, Henry Thomas (ed.). *The Papers of Willie Person Mangum.* 5 vols. Raleigh: State Department of Archives and History, 1950–56.

Stone, William L. *Letters on Masonry and Anti-Masonry Addressed to the Hon. John Quincy Adams.* New York: O. Halsted, 1832.

Thorpe, Francis N. (ed.). "A Letter of Jefferson on the Political Parties, 1798," *American Historical Review,* II (Apr., 1898), 488–89.

Van Buren, Martin. *Inquiry into the Origins and Course of Political Parties in the United States.* New York: Hurd and Houghton, 1867.

Van Tyne, C. H. (ed.). *The Letters of Daniel Webster from Documents Owned Principally by the New Hampshire Historical Society.* New York: McClure, Phillip and Co., 1902.

Webster, Daniel. *The Writings and Speeches of Daniel Webster.* 18 vols. National edition. Boston: Little, Brown and Co., 1903.

Webster, Fletcher (ed.). *The Private Correspondence of Daniel Webster.* 2 vols. Boston: Little, Brown and Co., 1857.

Autobiographies, Diaries, Memoirs, Reminiscences

Adams, Charles Francis (ed.). *Memoirs of John Quincy Adams, Comprising Portions of His Diary from 1795 to 1848.* 12 vols. Philadelphia: J. B. Lippincott and Co., 1874–77.

Beardsley, Levi. *Reminiscences.* New York: Charles Vinten, 1852.

Benton, Thomas Hart. *Thirty Years View.* 2 vols. New York: D. Appleton and Co., 1854–56.

Binns, John. *Recollections of the Life of John Binns.* Philadelphia: Published by the author, 1854.

Brown, Henry. *A Narrative of the Anti-Masonick Excitement, in the Western Part of the State of New York.* Batavia, N.Y.: Adams and McCleary, 1829.

Butler, William Allen. *A Retrospect of Forty Years, 1825–1865.* Edited by Harriet Allen Butler. New York: Charles Scribner's Sons, 1911.

Carey, Mathew. *The Olive Branch.* Philadelphia: M. Carey and Son, 1818.

Cheetham, James. *The Life of Thomas Paine.* New York: Southwick and Pelsue, 1809.

Dix, Morgan (ed.). *Memoirs of John Adams Dix.* 2 vols. New York: Harper and Brothers, 1883.

Edwards, Ninian W. *History of Illinois, from 1778 to 1833; and Life and Times of Ninian Edwards.* Springfield: Illinois State Journal Co., 1870.

Fitzpatrick, John C. (ed.). *The Autobiography of Martin Van Buren. Annual Report of the American Historical Association for the Year 1918.* Washington: Government Printing Office, 1920.

Greeley, Horace. *Recollections of a Busy Man.* New York: J. B. Ford and Co., 1868.

Greene, Samuel D. *The Broken Seal; Or Personal Reminiscences of the Morgan Abduction and Murder.* Boston: H. H. and T. W. Carter, 1870.

Hamilton, James A. *Reminiscences.* New York: Charles Scribner and Co., 1869.

Hammond, Jabez D. *The History of Political Parties in the State of New York.* 2 vols. Albany: C. Van Benthuysen, 1842.

Kennedy, John P. *Memoirs of the Life of William Wirt.* 2 vols. 2d ed. New York: Hurd and Houghton, 1866.

Morgan, William. *Illustrations of Masonry.* York, Canada: W. L. Mackenzie, 1827.

Sargent, Nathan. *Public Men and Events.* 2 vols. Philadelphia: J. B. Lippincott and Co., 1875.

Seward, William H. and Frederick W. *Autobiography and Memoir of William H. Seward.* New York: D. Appleton and Co., 1877.

Smith, Margaret Bayard. *The First Forty Years of Washington Society.* Edited by Gaillard Hunt. New York: Charles Scribner's Sons, 1906.

Stanton, Henry B. *Random Recollections.* Johnstown, N.Y.: Blunick and Leaning, 1885.

Stickney, William (ed.). *Autobiography by Amos Kendall.* Boston: Lee and Shepard, 1872.

Thomas, Frederick William. *John Randolph of Roanoke, and Sketches of Character, Including William Wirt.* Philadelphia: A. Hart, 1853.

Varle, Charles. *A Complete View of Baltimore.* Baltimore: Samuel Young, 1833.

Weed, Harriet A. (ed.). *Autobiography of Thurlow Weed.* Boston: Houghton Mifflin Co., 1883.

Weed, Thurlow Barnes. *Memoir of Thurlow Weed.* Boston: Houghton Mifflin Co., 1884.

Wise, Henry A. *Seven Decades of the Union.* Philadelphia: J. B. Lippincott and Co., 1872.

[Wright, Elizur.] *Myron Holley, and What He Did for Liberty and True Religion.* Boston: Privately printed, 1882.

Campaign Literature: Convention Proceedings, Addresses, Speeches, Political Pamphlets and Books

An Abstract of the Proceedings of the Anti-Masonic State Convention of Massachusetts, Held in Faneuil Hall, Boston, Dec. 30 and 31, 1829, and Jan, 1, 1830. Boston: John Marsh, 1830.

An Abstract of the Proceedings of the Antimasonic State Convention of Massachusetts, Held in Faneuil Hall, Boston, May 19 & 20, 1831. Boston: Boston Press Office, n.d.

Address and Proceedings of the Ohio State Convention Which Met at Columbus, O. January 9, 1832, To Nominate a Governor and a Ticket for Electors Favorable to the Re-election of Andrew Jackson as President of the United States. Columbus: Sentinel Office, 1832.

Address of the Administration Convention, Held in the Capitol at Raleigh, Dec. 20, 1827. n.p., n.d.

"Address of the Antimasonic Republican Convention, to the People of Massachusetts," [Held September 5–6, 1832, at Worcester.] *Daily Advocate–Extra.* n.d.

Address of the Central Committee. [Appointed by Massachusetts legislative caucus of supporters of Adams and Rush, held June 10, 1828, at Boston.] n.p., n.d.

Address of the Freemasons of Monroe County, to the Public on Returning Their Charters. Rochester: Henry O'Rielly, 1829.

Address of the General Committee of Correspondence to the Democratic Citizens of the State of Pennsylvania on the Subject of the Presidential Election, 1812. Philadelphia: John Binns, n.d.

Address of the Great State Convention of Friends of the Administration, Assembled at the Capitol in Concord, June 12, 1828. Concord: By Order of the Convention, 1828.

Address of the Jackson State Convention to the People of Maryland, on the Late and Approaching Election of President. Baltimore: Jackson Press, 1827.

Address of the Republican Members of the Legislature, Friendly to the Elevation of Henry Clay to the Office of President of the United States. Albany: J. B. Van Steenbergh, 1824.

Address of the Republicans of the City and County of New-York, to Their Republican Fellow-Citizens of the United States. New York: Frank, White, and Co., 1808.

Address of the State Convention of Delegates from the Several Counties of the State of New-York To the People, on the Subject of the Approaching Presidential Election. Albany: Beach, Denio & Richards, 1828.

Address to the People of Connecticut Adopted at the State Convention, Held at Middletown, August 7, 1828 with the Proceedings of the Convention. Hartford: J. Russell, 1828.

Address to the People of Maryland, from Their Delegates in the Late National Republican Convention: Made in Obedience to a Resolution of that Body. Baltimore: Sands and Neilson, 1832.

An Address to the People of Ohio, on the Important Subject of the Next Presidency; by the Committee Appointed for that Purpose at a Convention of Delegates from the Different Sections of the State, Assembled at Columbus, on Wednesday, the 14th Day of July, 1824. Cincinnati: Looker and Reynolds, n.d.

Address. To the People of the State of New York. [By the Antimasonic members of the Legislature, April, 1831.] n.p., n.d.

Address to the Republican Citizens of the State of New York. Albany: Beach, Denio & Richards by Webster and Wood, 1828.

Antimasonic Republican Convention of Massachusetts, Held at Worcester. Sept. 5th & 6th, 1832. Boston: Perkins & Martin, 1832.

"Anti-Masonic Republican State Convention," *Evening Journal Extra.* [Albany, June 21, 1832.]

Bernard, David. *Light on Masonry: A Collection of All the Most Important Documents on the Subject of Speculative Free Masonry.* Utica: William Williams, 1829.

A Brief Report of the Debates in the Anti-Masonic State Convention of the Commonwealth of Massachusetts, Held in Faneuil Hall, Boston, December 30, 31, 1829 and January 1, 1830. Boston: John Marsh, 1830.

A Collection of Letters on Freemasonry in Chronological Order. Boston: T. R. Martin, 1849.

Considerations Against the Appointment of Rufus King to the Senate of the United States; Submitted to the Republican Members of the Legislature of the State of New York by Plain Truth. n.p., n.d.

Crane, Isaac Watts. *Address Delivered Before the Jackson Convention of Delegates, from the Different Townships of the County of Cumberland Association at Bridgeton, July 27, 1824.* Philadelphia: n.p., 1824.

Declaration of the Objects and Measures of the Farmers, Mechanics, and Other Working Men of the City and County of New York; Addressed to the Farmers, Mechanics and Other Workingmen, of the United States. New York: New York Daily Sentinel Office, 1831.

Defense of Truth and Free-Masonry Exposed. Albany: National Observer Office, 1827.

Democratic Convention. [Adams State Convention held January 4, 1828, at Harrisburg.] Harrisburg: Harrisburg Argus Office, n.d.

Doings of the Plymouth County Anti-Masonic Convention. [Mar. 10, 1829.] n.p., n.d.

Essex Jackson Meeting. [Mar. 27, 1828, at Haverhill.] n.p., n.d.

Jones, John R. *An Address Delivered at a Town-Meeting of the Anti-Masonic Citizens of Philadelphia, October 5th, 1830.* Philadelphia: John Clarke, 1830.

Journal of the National Republican Convention, Which Assembled in the City of Baltimore, Dec. 12, 1831, for the Nominations of Candidates to Fill the Offices of President and Vice President. Washington: National Journal Office, n.d.

Journal of the Proceedings of the National Republican Convention, Held at Worcester, October 11, 1832. Boston: Stimpson and Clapp, 1832.

[Lathrop, John H.] *An Address to the People of the United States, on the Subject of the Anti-Masonic Excitement, or New Party.* Albany: J. B. Van Steenbergh, 1830.

Letters of Rush, Adams, and Wirt. Boston: Leonard W. Kimbell and John Marsh, 1831.

Letters on the Richmond Party. By a Virginian. Washington: n.p., 1823.

A Manual of Masonry and Anti-Masonry. Louisville, Ky.: n.p., 1833.

Meeting of the Friends of the Administration, in Hartford County, Md. [March 13, 1828 at Belle Air.] n.p., n.d.

Murderous Character of Freemasonry. Chicago: Ezra A. Cook, 1882.

A Narrative of the Facts Relating to the Kidnapping and Presumed Murder of William Morgan. Batavia, N.Y.: D. C. Miller, 1827.

New-York National Republican State Convention. [June 3, 1831, at Albany.] n.p., n.d.

New-York State Convention. [Adams convention, June 10–11, 1828, at Albany.] n.p., n.d.

Odiorne, James C. (ed.). *Opinion on Speculative Masonry, Relative to Its Origin, Nature, and Tendency.* Boston: Perkins & Marvin, 1830.

Prentice, George D. *Biography of Henry Clay.* Hartford: Samuel Hanmer, Jr., and John Jay Phelps, 1831.

Proceedings and Address of the Convention of Delegates, That Met at Columbus, Ohio, Dec. 28, 1827, to Nominate a Ticket of Electors Favorable to the Reelection of John Quincy Adams President of the United States. P. H. Olmsted, 1827.

Proceedings and Address of the New Hampshire Republican State Convention of Delegates Friendly to the Election of Andrew Jackson to the Next Presidency of the United States, Assembled at Concord, June 11 and 12, 1828. Concord: Patriot Office, n.d.

Proceedings and Address of the New-Jersey Delegates in Favor of the Present Administration of the General Government, Assembled in Convent at Trenton, February 22, 1828. Trenton: William L. Prall, n.d.

Proceedings and Address of the New Jersey State Convention, Assembled at Trenton, on the Eighth Day of January, 1828, which Nominated Andrew Jackson for President, John C. Calhoun for Vice-President of the United States. Trenton: Joseph Justice, 1828.

The Proceedings and Address of the Ohio Jackson Convention, Assembled at Columbus, on the Eighth of January, 1828, to Nominate an Electoral Ticket, Favorable to the Election of Andrew Jackson to the Next Presidency of the United States. David Smith, 1828.

Proceedings—At a Meeting of the Antimasonic Young Men of the City of Schenectady, Held in Said City, on the 21st Day of July, 1831. n.p., n.d.

Proceedings of a Convention of Delegates from the Different Counties of New York, Opposed to Free-Masonry, Held at the Capitol in the City of Albany, on the 19th, 20th and 21st Days of February, 1829. Rochester: Weed and Sprague, 1829.

Proceedings of a Convention of Delegates from the Different Counties in the State of Pennsylvania, Opposed to Free-Masonry Held at the Court House in Harrisburg, on the 25th and 26th Days of June, 1829. Lancaster: Fen & Fenton, 1829.

Proceedings of a Convention of Delegates Opposed to Free Masonry Which Met at LeRoy, Genesee Co. N.Y. March 6, 1828. Rochester: Weed & Heron, 1828.

Proceedings of a Convention of the People of Maine, Friendly to the Present Administration of the General Government. [Jan. 23, 1828, at Portland.] n.p., n.d.

The Proceedings of a Meeting of the Citizens of Albany, Held at the Capitol, on the Evening of the 28th September, 1824. n.p., n.d.

Proceedings of the Administration Convention Held at Frankfort, Kentucky, on Monday, December 17, 1827. n.p., n.d.

Proceedings of the Administration Convention Held at Indianapolis, January 12, 1828. Indianapolis: Indiana Journal Office, n.d.

Proceedings of the Administration Meeting, in Baltimore County, June,— 1827. Baltimore: Baltimore Patriot Office, 1827.

Proceedings of the Anti-Jackson Convention, Held at the Capitol, in the City of Richmond: With Their Address to the People of Virginia. Richmond: Samuel Shepherd & Co., 1828.

Proceedings of the Anti-Masonic Convention for the State of New York: Held at Utica, August 11, 1830. Utica: Wm. Williams, 1830.

Proceedings of the Anti-Masonic Republican Convention of the County of Cayuga, Held at Auburn, January 1, 1830. Auburn: Thomas M. Skinner, 1830.

Proceedings of the Anti-Masonic Republican Convention of the County of Cayuga, Held at Auburn, January 2, 1832, with Their Address to the Freemen of the County. Auburn: T. M. Skinner, 1832.

Proceedings of the Anti-Masonic State Convention, Held at Harrisburg, on the 25th February, 1830. n.p., n.d.

Proceedings of the Anti-Masonic State Convention, Held at Harrisburg, on the 25th of May, 1831. n.p., n.d.

Proceedings of the Antimasonic State Convention of Connecticut, Held at Hartford, Feb. 3, and 4, 1830. Hartford: Packard & Butler, 1830.

Proceedings of the Anti-Masonick State Convention, Holden at Montpelier, August 5, 6, & 7: With Addresses to the People, on the Subject of Speculative Freemasonry. East Randolph, Vt.: Vermont Luminary Office, 1829.

Proceedings of the Anti-Masonic State Convention Holden at Montpelier, June 23, 24, & 25, 1830. Middlebury: O. and J. Miner, 1830.

Proceedings of the Antimasonic State Convention, Holden at Montpelier, June 15 and 16, 1831. Montpelier: Gamaliel Small, 1831.

Proceedings of the Delegates of the Friends of the Administration of

John Quincy Adams, Assembled in Convention at Baton Rouge. [Nov. 5, 1827] New Orleans: Benjamin Levy, 1827.

Proceedings of the Democratic Antimasonic State Convention Held at Harrisburg, February 22, 1832. n.p., n.d.

Proceedings of the Democratic Convention, Held at Harrisburg, Pennsylvania, January 8, 1828. n.p., n.d.

Proceedings of the Democratic Convention Held at Harrisburg, Pennsylvania. March 5, 1832. Harrisburg: Henry Walsh, 1832.

Proceedings of the Democratic Republican State Convention, Holden at Concord, June 20, 1832. Concord: Hill and Barton, 1832.

Proceedings of the Jackson and Barbour Convention of North Carolina. [June 18, 1832, at Raleigh.] n.p., n.d.

Proceedings of the Maryland Administration Convention, Delegated by the People, and Held in Baltimore, on Monday and Tuesday, July 23d. and 24th. 1827. Baltimore: Baltimore Patriot Office, 1827.

Proceedings of the National Republican Convention, Held at Frankfort, Kentucky, on Thursday, December 9, 1830. n.p., n.d.

Proceedings of the National Republican Convention of Pennsylvania Which Assembled at Harrisburg, on the Twenty-ninth Day of May, One Thousand Eight Hundred and Thirty-Two, for the Nomination of an Electoral Ticket. Harrisburg: Intelligencer Office, n.d.

Proceedings of the National Republican Convention of Young Men, Which Assembled in the City of Washington May 7, 1832. Washington: Gales & Seaton, 1832.

"Proceedings of the National Republican State Convention of Vermont, held July 16, 1832 at Montpelier." [Broadside.]

Proceedings of the Rhode-Island Anti-Masonic State Convention. September 14, 1831. Providence: Daily Advertiser Office, 1831.

The Proceedings of the Second United States Anti-Masonic Convention, Held at Baltimore, September 1831. Boston: n.p., 1832.

The Proceedings of the United States Anti-Masonic Convention. Sept. 11, 1830. Philadelphia: I. P. Trimble, 1830.

Public Meeting. [Adams statewide meeting, Dec. 27, 1824, at Trenton.] n.p., n.d.

"Public Meeting of the Friends of Henry Clay," *National Journal–Extra.* [Washington.] July 20, 1831.

Report of the Proceedings of the Town Meeting in the City of Philadelphia. July 7th, 1828. n.p., n.d.

Republican Meeting of the Citizens of Washington City Friendly to the Re-election of Andrew Jackson to the Presidency. [July 24, 1832.] n.p., n.d.

Republican Nomination for Governor and Lt. Governor. With an Address to the Electors of the State of New York. n.p., n.d.

Republican Prox. [Rhode Island Republican state convention in February, 1815.] n.p., n.d.

Rush, Richard. "Letter on Freemasonry," *Boston Free Press—Extra.* May 20, 1831.

————. *Letter on Freemasonry to the Committee of the Citizens of York County, Pennsylvania.* Boston: John Marsh & Co., 1831.

[Spencer, John Canfield.] *Report of the Special Counsel on the Subject of the Abduction of William Morgan. Jan. 27, 1830. Submitted to the N.Y State Senate by Enos T. Throop, Gov.* n.p., n.d.

State Convention. Proceedings and Address of the Republican Young Men of the State of New-York, Assembled at Utica, on the 12th Day of August, 1828. Utica: Northway & Porter, 1828.

Statement of Votes in Congress Given by the Hon. Ebenezer Seaver. Boston: John Eliot, 1812.

Stearns, John G. *An Inquiry into the Nature and Tendency of Speculative Free-Masonry.* Westfield, N.Y.: H. Newcomb, 1828.

Substance of Mr. Storrs' Remarks, at the Meeting of the Friends of the Administration, Held at Whitesboro', July Fourth, 1828, For the Purpose of Nominating an Elector of President, and Vice-President, for the County of Oneida. Utica: Northway & Porter, 1828.

Summary of the Proceedings of a Convention of Republican Delegates from the Several States in the Union, for the Purpose of Nominating a Candidate for the Office of Vice-President of the United States; Held at Baltimore, in the State of Maryland, May, 1832. Albany: Packard and Van Benthuysen, 1832.

A Supplementary Report of the Committee Appointed to Ascertain the Fate of Capt. Wm. Morgan. Rochester: Edward Scranton, 1827.

Thacher, Moses. *An Address Delivered Before the Members of the Anti-Masonic State Convention; Assembled at Augusta, Maine, July 4, 1832.* Hallowell, Me.: Herrick and Farwell, 1832.

Touchstone to the People of the United States, on the Choice of a President. New York: Pelsue & Gould, 1812.

Two Speeches Delivered in the New-York State Convention, September, 1824, with the Proceedings of the Convention. New York: G. F. Hopkins, 1824.

The Virginia Address. [Adams state convention, Jan. 8, 1828, at Richmond.] n.p., n.d.

Virginia Anti-Jackson Convention. Saturday, Dec. 12, 1827. n.p., n.d.

Waldo, Samuel Putnam. *The Tour of James Monroe, President of the United States, Through the Northern and Eastern States, in 1817.* Hartford: Silas Andrews, 1820.

[Ward, Henry Dana.] *Free Masonry.* New York: n.p., 1828.

Ward, Henry Dana. *An Oration, Delivered at Auburn, N.Y. Monday, 5th July, 1830.* Auburn: T. M. Skinner, 1830.

Newspapers and Magazines

Albany Argus
Albany Daily Advertiser
Albany Evening Journal
Anti-Masonic Enquirer [Rochester]
Anti-Masonic Intelligencer [Hartford, Conn.]

Anti-Masonic Review and Magazine [New York, N.Y.]
Argus of Western America [Frankfort, Ky.]
Baltimore Patriot
Baltimore Republican and Commercial Advertiser
Buffalo Emporium and General Advertiser
Buffalo Gazette
Buffalo Republican
The Commentator [Frankfort, Ky.]
Commercial Chronicle [Baltimore, Md.]
Daily Louisville Public Advertiser
Daily National Intelligencer [Washington, D.C.]
Daily National Journal [Washington, D.C.]
Daily Richmond Whig
Daily Savannah Republican
Eastern Argus [Portland, Me.]
The Focus [Louisville, Ky.]
Frankfurt Argus
Freeman's Banner [Baltimore, Md.]
Free Press [Auburn, N.Y.]
Georgia Journal [Milledgeville]
The Globe [Washington, D.C.]
Kentucky Reporter [Lexington]
Maysville Eagle
Monroe Republican [Rochester]
Nashville Republican and State Gazette
National Banner, and Nashville Whig
New Hampshire Patriot and State Gazette [Concord]
Niles' Weekly Register [Baltimore]
Richmond Constitutional Whig
Richmond Enquirer
Rochester Telegraph
St. Louis Beacon
Star, and North Carolina State Gazette [Raleigh]
United States Telegraph [Washington, D.C.]
Western Citizen [Paris, Ky.]

SECONDARY SOURCES

Books

Abernathy, Thomas Perkins. *Formative Period in Alabama, 1815–1828.* Alabama State Department of Archives and History, Historical and Patriotic Series, No. 6. Montgomery: Brown Printing Co., 1922.
———. *From Frontier to Plantation in Tennessee: A Study in Frontier Democracy.* Chapel Hill: University of North Carolina Press, 1932.
Adams, Henry. *John Randolph.* American Statesman Series, edited by John T. Morse. Boston: Houghton Mifflin Co., 1883.

————. *The Life of Albert Gallatin.* Philadelphia: J. B. Lippincott & Co., 1879.

Agar, Herbert. *The Price of Union.* Boston: Houghton Mifflin Co., 1950.

Ambler, Charles Henry. *Thomas Ritchie: A Study in Virginia Politics.* Richmond: Bell Book & Stationery Co., 1913.

Ammon, Harry. *James Monroe: The Quest for National Identity.* New York: McGraw-Hill, 1971.

Anderson, Dice Robbins. *William Branch Giles.* Menasha, Wis.: George Banta Publishing Co., 1914.

Baker, Elizabeth Teaster. *Henry Wheaton, 1785–1848.* Philadelphia: University of Pennsylvania Press, 1937.

Bassett, John Spencer. *The Federalist System, 1789–1801.* Vol. XI, The American Nation: A History, edited by A. B. Hart. New York: Harper and Bros., 1906.

————. *The Life of Andrew Jackson.* New York: Macmillan Co., 1931.

Beard, Charles A. *The American Party Battle.* New York: Macmillan Co., 1928.

————. *Economic Origins of Jeffersonian Democracy.* New York: Macmillan Co., 1927.

Beard, Charles A. and Mary R. *The Rise of American Civilization.* New York: Macmillan Co., 1933.

Bemis, Samuel Flagg. *John Quincy Adams and the Union.* New York: Alfred A. Knopf, 1956.

Binkley, Wilfred E. *American Political Parties.* 2d ed., rev. New York: Alfred A. Knopf, 1947.

Bobbé, Dorothie. *De Witt Clinton.* New York: Minton, Balch & Co., 1933.

Borden, Morton. *Parties and Politics in the Early Republic, 1789–1815.* New York: Thomas Y. Crowell Co., 1967.

Bowers, Claude G. *Jefferson and Hamilton.* Boston: Houghton Mifflin Co., 1925.

————. *Jefferson in Power.* Boston: Houghton Mifflin Co., 1936.

————. *The Party Battles of the Jackson Period.* Boston: Houghton Mifflin Co., 1922.

Brant, Irving. *James Madison: Commander in Chief, 1812–1836.* Indianapolis: Bobbs-Merrill Co., 1961.

————. *James Madison: Father of the Constitution, 1787–1800.* Indianapolis: Bobbs-Merrill Co., 1950.

————. *James Madison: Secretary of State, 1800–1809.* Indianapolis: Bobbs-Merrill Co., 1953.

————. *James Madison: The President, 1809–1812.* Indianapolis: Bobbs-Merrill Co., 1956.

Brodie, Fawn W. *Thaddeus Stevens, Scourge of the South.* New York: W. W. Norton & Co., 1959.

Brown, Stuart Gerry. *The First Republicans.* Syracuse: Syracuse University Press, 1954.

Bryan, George J. *Life of George P. Barker.* Buffalo: Oliver G. Steele, 1849.

Buley, Roscoe Carlyle. *The Old Northwest: Pioneer Period, 1815–1840*. 2 vols. Bloomington: Indiana University Press, 1955.

Carroll, Eber Malcom. *Origins of the Whig Party*. Durham: Duke University Press, 1925.

Celebration of the One Hundred Twenty-fifth Anniversary of the Massachusetts Lodge. Boston: By the Lodge, 1896.

Chambers, William Nisbet. *Political Parties in a New Nation: The American Experience*. New York: Oxford University Press, 1963.

Channing, Edward. *A History of the United States*. 6 vols. New York: Macmillan Co., 1905–25.

Charles, Joseph. *The Origins of the American Party System*. Williamsburg: Institute of Early American History and Culture, 1956.

Clay, Thomas Hart. *Henry Clay*. Completed by Ellis Paxson Oberholtzer. American Crisis Biographies, edited by E. P. Oberholtzer. Philadelphia: George W. Jacobs and Co., 1910.

Cleaves, Freeman. *Old Tippecanoe: William Henry Harrison and His Times*. New York: Charles Scribner's Sons, 1939.

Coit, Margaret L. *John C. Calhoun*. Boston: Houghton Mifflin Co., 1950.

Cole, Arthur Charles. *The Whig Party in the South*. Washington: American Historical Association, 1913.

Coleman, J. Winston, Jr. *Masonry in the Bluegrass*. Lexington: Transylvania Press, 1933.

Cresson, William P. *James Monroe*. Chapel Hill: University of North Carolina Press, 1946.

Crockett, Walter Hill. *Vermont: The Green Mountain State*. 4 vols. New York: Century History Co., 1921.

Cross, Whitney R. *The Burned-over District*. Ithaca: Cornell University Press, 1950.

Cunningham, Noble E., Jr. *The Jeffersonian Republicans: The Formation of Party Organization, 1789–1801*. Chapel Hill: University of North Carolina Press, 1957.

———. *The Jeffersonian Republicans in Power: Party Operations, 1801–1809*. Chapel Hill: University of North Carolina Press, 1963.

Current, Richard Nelson. *Old Thad Stevens, A Story of Ambition*. Madison: University of Wisconsin Press, 1942.

Curtis, George Ticknor. *Life of Daniel Webster*. 2 vols. New York: D. Appleton & Co., 1870.

Dallinger, Frederick W. *Nominations for Elective Office in the United States*. New York: Longmans, Green & Co., 1897.

Dangerfield, George. *The Era of Good Feelings*. New York: Harcourt, Brace and Co., 1952.

David, Paul T.; Goldman, Ralph M.; and Bain, Richard C. *The Politics of National Party Conventions*. Washington, D.C.: Brookings Institution, 1960.

Eaton, Clement. *Henry Clay and the Art of American Politics*. Library of American Biography, edited by Oscar Handlin. Boston: Little, Brown and Co., 1957.

Esary, Logan. *A History of Indiana from Its Exploration to 1850.* Indianapolis: W. K. Stewart Co., 1915.

English, William E. *A History of Early Indianapolis Masonry and of Center Lodge.* Vol. III, Indiana Historical Society Publications. Indianapolis: Bowen-Merrill Co., 1895.

Fee, Walter R. *The Transition from Aristocracy to Democracy in New Jersey, 1789–1829.* Somerville, N.J.: Somerset Press, 1933.

Ferguson, Russell J. *Early Western Pennsylvania Politics.* Pittsburgh: University of Pittsburgh Press, 1938.

Fischer, David Hackett. *The Revolution of American Conservatism: The Federalist Party in the Era of Jeffersonian Democracy.* New York: Harper and Row, 1965.

Fish, Carl Russell. *The Rise of the Common Man, 1830–1850.* Vol. VI, A History of American Life, edited by A. M. Schlesinger and D. R. Fox. New York: Macmillan Co., 1927.

Ford, Henry Jones. *Representative Government.* American Political Science Series, edited by Edward S. Corwin. New York: Henry Holt and Co., 1924.

———. *The Rise and Growth of American Politics.* New York: Macmillan Co., 1900.

———. *Washington and His Colleagues.* Chronicles of America Series. New Haven: Yale University Press, 1921.

Fox, Dixon Ryan. *The Decline of Aristocracy in the Politics of New York.* New York: Longmans, Green & Co., 1919.

Gammon, Samuel Rhea, Jr. *The Presidential Campaign of 1832.* Vol. XL, Johns Hopkins University Studies in Historical and Political Science. Baltimore: Johns Hopkins University Press, 1922.

Garraty, John Arthur. *Silas Wright.* New York: Columbia University Press, 1949.

Gillet, R. H. *The Life and Times of Silas Wright.* 2 vols. Albany: Argus Co., 1874.

Gilman, Daniel C. *James Monroe.* American Statesman Series, edited by John T. Morse. Boston: Houghton Mifflin Co., 1896.

Gilpatrick, Delbert Harold. *Jeffersonian Democracy in North Carolina, 1789–1816.* New York: Columbia University, 1931.

Goldberg, Isaac. *Major Noah: American-Jewish Pioneer.* New York: Alfred A. Knopf, 1937.

Goodman, Paul. *The Democratic-Republicans of Massachusetts: Politics in a Young Republic.* Cambridge: Harvard University Press, 1964.

Govan, Thomas Payne. *Nicholas Biddle: Nationalist and Public Banker, 1786–1844.* Chicago: University of Chicago Press, 1959.

Higginbotham, Sanford W. *The Keystone in the Democratic Arch: Pennsylvania Politics, 1800–1816.* Harrisburg: Pennsylvania Historical and Museum Commission, 1952.

Historical Statistics of the United States, Colonial Times to 1957. Washington: Bureau of the Census, 1960.

Hoffmann, William S. *Andrew Jackson and North Carolina Politics.* Vol.

40, The James Sprunt Studies in History and Political Science. Chapel Hill: University of North Carolina Press, 1958.

Hofstadter, Richard. *The Idea of a Party System: The Rise of Legitimate Opposition in the United States, 1780–1840.* Berkeley: University of California Press, 1969.

James, Marquis. *The Life of Andrew Jackson.* Indianapolis: Bobbs-Merrill Company, 1938.

Jensen, Merrill. *The Articles of Confederation.* Madison: University of Wisconsin Press, 1948.

———. *The New Nation: A History of the United States During the Confederation, 1781–1789.* New York: Alfred A. Knopf, 1950.

Johnston, J. Stoddard. *Memorial History of Louisville from Its First Settlement to the Year 1896.* 2 vols. Chicago: American Biographical Publishing Co., 1896.

July, Robert W. *The Essential New Yorker: Gulian Verplanck.* Durham: Duke University Press, 1951.

Kass, Alvin. *Politics in New York State, 1800–1830.* Syracuse: Syracuse University Press, 1965.

Kehl, James A. *Ill Feeling in the Era of Good Feelings: Western Pennsylvania Political Battles, 1815–1825.* Pittsburgh: University of Pittsburgh Press, 1956.

Key, Vladimer Orlando. *Politics, Parties, and Pressure Groups.* New York: Thomas Y. Crowell, 1958.

Klein, Philip Shriver. *Pennsylvania Politics, 1817–1832.* Philadelphia: Historical Society of Pennsylvania, 1940.

Korngold, Ralph. *Thaddeus Stevens, A Being Darkly Wise and Rudely Great.* New York: Harcourt, Brace and Co., 1955.

Kurtz, Stephen G. *The Presidency of John Adams: The Collapse of Federalism, 1795–1800.* Philadelphia: University of Pennsylvania Press, 1957.

Leiserson, Avery. *Parties and Politics: An Institutional and Behavioral Approach.* New York: Alfred A. Knopf, 1958.

Livermore, Shaw, Jr. *The Twilight of Federalism: The Disintegration of the Federalist Party, 1815–1830.* Princeton: Princeton University Press, 1962.

Ludlum, David M. *Social Ferment in Vermont, 1791–1850.* New York: Columbia University Press, 1939.

Luetscher, George D. *Early Political Machinery in the United States.* Philadelphia: Privately printed, 1903.

Lynch, William O. *Fifty Years of Party Warfare (1787–1837).* Indianapolis: Bobbs-Merrill Co., 1931.

McCarthy, Charles. *The Antimasonic Party: A Study of Political Antimasonry in the United States, 1827–1840.* Vol. I, Annual Report of the American Historical Association for the Year 1902. Washington: Government Printing Office, 1903.

McCormick, Richard P. *The Second American Party System: Party Formation in the Jacksonian Era.* Chapel Hill: University of North Carolina Press, 1966.

McDonald, Forrest. *We the People: The Economic Origins of the Constitution.* Chicago: University of Chicago Press, 1958.

McDonald, Neil A. *The Study of Political Parties.* Short Studies in Political Science. Garden City, N.Y.: Random House, 1955.

McMaster, John Bach. *Daniel Webster.* New York: Century Co., 1902.

————. *A History of the People of the United States, from the Revolution to the Civil War.* 8 vols. New York: D. Appleton and Co., 1885–1913.

Main, Jackson Turner. *The Antifederalists: Critics of the Constitution, 1781–1788.* Chapel Hill: University of North Carolina Press, 1961.

Malone, Dumas. *Jefferson and His Time.* 4 vols. Boston: Little, Brown and Co., 1948–70.

Mayo, Bernard. *Henry Clay: Spokesman of the New West.* Boston: Houghton Mifflin Co., 1937.

Meyer, Ernst Christopher. *Nominating Systems: Direct Primaries Versus Conventions in the United States.* Madison: Privately printed, 1902.

Miles, Edwin Arthur. *Jacksonian Democracy in Mississippi.* Vol. XLII, James Sprunt Studies in History and Political Science. Chapel Hill: University of North Carolina Press, 1960.

Miller, Alphonse B. *Thaddeus Stevens.* New York: Harper and Brothers, 1939.

Moore, Glover. *The Missouri Controversy, 1819–1821.* Lexington: University of Kentucky Press, 1953.

Morison, Samuel Eliot. *The Life and Letters of Harrison Gray Otis.* 2 vols. Boston: Houghton Mifflin Co., 1913.

Morse, Anson Ely. *The Federalist Party in Massachusetts to the Year 1800.* Princeton: The University Library, 1909.

Morse, Jarvis Means. *A Neglected Period of Connecticut's History, 1818–1850.* New Haven: Yale University Press, 1933.

Mueller, Henry R. *The Whig Party in Pennsylvania.* Vol. CI, Studies in History, Economics and Public Law, edited by the Faculty of Political Science of Columbia University. New York: Columbia University, 1922.

Munroe, John A. *Federalist Delaware, 1775–1815.* New Brunswick: Rutgers University Press, 1954.

Murray, Paul. *The Whig Party in Georgia, 1825–1853.* Vol. XXIX, James Sprunt Studies in History and Political Science. Chapel Hill: University of North Carolina Press, 1948.

Nevins, Allan. *The American States During and After the Revolution, 1775–1789.* New York: Macmillan Co., 1924.

Nichols, Roy F. *The Invention of the American Political Parties.* New York: Macmillan Co., 1967.

Ostrogorski, M. *Democracy and the Organization of Political Parties.* 2 vols. New York: Macmillan Co., 1902.

Parton, James. *Life of Andrew Jackson.* 3 vols. Boston: Houghton Mifflin Co., 1887–88.

Pease, Theodore Calvin. *The Frontier State, 1818–1848.* Vol. II, The Centennial History of Illinois, edited by Clarence M. Alvord. Springfield: Illinois Centennial Commission, 1918.

Perry, Benjamin F. *Biographical Sketches of Eminent American Statesmen.* Philadelphia: Ferree Press, 1887.

Phillips, Ulrich Bonnell. *Georgia and States Rights.* Vol. II, *Annual Report of the American Historical Association for the Year 1901.* Washington: Government Printing Office, 1902.

Powell, J. H. *Richard Rush: Republican Diplomat, 1780–1859.* Philadelphia: University of Pennsylvania Press, 1942.

Prince, Carl E. *New Jersey's Jeffersonian Republicans: The Genesis of an Early Party Machine.* Chapel Hill: University of North Carolina Press, 1967.

Rayback, Robert J. *Millard Fillmore, Biography of a President.* Buffalo: Henry Stewart, for the Buffalo Historical Society, 1959.

Remini, Robert V. *The Election of Andrew Jackson.* Philadelphia: J. B. Lippincott, 1963.

———. *Martin Van Buren and the Making of the Democratic Party.* New York: Columbia University Press, 1959.

Robinson, Edgar E. *The Evolution of American Political Parties.* New York: Harcourt, Brace and Co., 1924.

Robinson, William A. *Jeffersonian Democracy in New England.* New Haven: Yale University Press, 1916.

Roseboom, Eugene H. *A History of Presidential Elections.* New York: Macmillan Co., 1964.

Roseboom, Eugene H., and Weisenburger, Francis P. *A History of Ohio.* Columbus: Ohio State Archaeological and Historical Society, 1953.

Scharf, J. Thomas. *The Chronicles of Baltimore.* Baltimore: Turnbull Brothers, 1874.

Schattschneider, E. E. *Party Government.* New York; Rinehart and Co., 1942.

Schlesinger, Arthur M., Jr. *The Age of Jackson.* Boston: Little, Brown and Co., 1945.

Schlesinger, Arthur M., Jr.; Israel, Fred L.; and Hansen, William P. (eds.). *History of American Presidential Elections, 1789–1968.* 4 vols. New York: Chelsea House, 1971.

Schurz, Carl. *Life of Henry Clay.* 2 vols. American Statesmen Series, edited by John T. Morse, Jr. Boston: Houghton Mifflin Co., 1887.

Shepard, Edward M. *Martin Van Buren.* American Statesmen Series, edited by John T. Morse, Jr. Boston: Houghton Mifflin Co., 1899.

Shipp, J. E. D. *Giant Days or the Life and Times of William H. Crawford.* Americus, Ga.: Southern Printers, 1909.

Shultz, Edward T. *History of Freemasonry in Maryland.* 4 vols. Baltimore: J. H. Mediary and Co., 1884–88.

Simms, Henry H. *The Rise of the Whigs in Virginia, 1824–1840.* Richmond: William Byrd Press, 1929.

Smith, William Ernest. *The Francis Preston Blair Family in Politics.* 2 vols. New York: Macmillan Co., 1933.

Spaulding, E. Wilder. *His Excellency George Clinton: Critic of the Constitution.* New York: Macmillan Co., 1938.

———. *New York in the Critical Period, 1783–1789*. New York: Columbia University Press, 1932.

Spencer, Ivor Debenham. *The Victor and the Spoils: A Life of William L. Marcy*. Providence: Brown University Press, 1959.

Stanwood, Edward. *A History of Presidential Elections*. 3rd ed., rev. Cambridge: Riverside Press, 1888.

Stevens, Harry R. *The Early Jackson Party in Ohio*. Durham: Duke University Press, 1957.

Styron, Arthur. *The Cast-Iron Man: John C. Calhoun and American Democracy*. New York: Longmans, Green and Co., 1935.

———. *The Last of the Cocked Hats: James Monroe and the Virginia Dynasty*. Norman: University of Oklahoma Press, 1945.

Sumner, William Graham. *Andrew Jackson as a Public Man*. American Statesman Series, edited by John T. Morse, Jr. Boston: Houghton Mifflin Co., 1900.

Sydnor, Charles S. *The Development of Southern Sectionalism, 1819–1848*. Vol. V, A History of the South, edited by Wendell Holmes and E. Merton Coulter. Baton Rouge: Louisiana State University Press, 1948.

Thompson, Charles Manfred. *The Illinois Whigs Before 1846*. Champaign: University of Illinois Press, 1931.

Tinkcom, Harry Marlin. *The Republicans and Federalists in Pennsylvania, 1790–1801*. Harrisburg: Pennsylvania Historical and Museum Commission, 1950.

Tocqueville, Alexis de. *Democracy in America*. 2 vols. New York: Vintage Books, 1959.

Turner, Frederick Jackson. *Rise of the New West, 1819–1829*. Vol. XVIII, The American Nation: A History, edited by A. B. Hart. New York: Harper and Bros., 1906.

———. *The United States, 1830–1850*. New York: Henry Holt and Co., 1935.

Utter, William T. *The Frontier State, 1803–1825*. Vol. II, *The History of the State of Ohio*. Columbus. Ohio State Archaeological and Historical Society, 1942.

Van Deusen, Glyndon G. *The Life of Henry Clay*. Boston: Little, Brown and Co., 1937.

———. *The Jacksonian Era, 1828–1848*. New American Nation Series, edited by Henry Steele Commager and Richard B. Morris. New York: Harper and Bros., 1959.

———. *Thurlow Weed: Wizard of the Lobby*, Boston: Little, Brown and Co., 1947.

Wagstaff, Henry M. *States' Rights and Political Parties in North Carolina, 1776–1861*. Baltimore: Johns Hopkins University Press, 1906.

Walters, Raymond, Jr. *Albert Gallatin: Jeffersonian Financier and Diplomat*. New York: Macmillan Co., 1957.

———. *Alexander James Dallas: Lawyer–Politician–Financier, 1759–1817*. Philadelphia: University of Pennsylvania Press, 1947.

Wayland, Francis Fry. *Andrew Stevenson, Democrat and Diplomat, 1785–1857*. Philadelphia: University of Pennsylvania Press, 1949.

Webster, Homer J. *History of the Democratic Party Organization in the Northwest.* Columbus, Ohio: F. J. Heer Printing Co., 1915.

Weisenburger, Francis P. *The Life of John McLean, A Politician on the United States Supreme Court.* Columbus: Ohio State University Press, 1937.

——. *The Passing of the Frontier, 1825–1850.* Vol. III, *The History of the State of Ohio,* edited by Carl Wittke. Columbus: Ohio State Archaeological Society, 1941.

Weston, Florence. *The Presidential Election of 1828.* Washington: Catholic University Press, 1938.

Wharton, Anne Hollingsworth. *Social Life in the Early Republic.* Philadelphia: J. B. Lippincott Co., 1902.

Wiltse, Charles M. *John C. Calhoun: Nationalist, 1789–1828.* Indianapolis: Bobbs-Merrill Co., 1944.

——. *John C. Calhoun: Nullifier, 1829–1839.* Indianapolis: Bobbs-Merrill Co., 1949.

Wolfe, John Harold. *Jeffersonian Democracy in South Carolina.* Vol. XXIV, James Sprunt Studies in History and Political Science. Chapel Hill: University of North Carolina Press, 1940.

Woodley, Thomas Frederick. *Thaddeus Stevens.* Harrisburg: Telegraph Press, 1934.

Young, Alfred E. *The Democratic Republicans of New York: The Origins, 1763–1797.* Chapel Hill: University of North Carolina Press, 1967.

Articles

Abernathy, Thomas P. "Andrew Jackson and the Rise of Southwestern Democracy," *American Historical Review,* XXXIII (Oct., 1927), 64–77.

——. "The Origin of the Whig Party in Tennessee," *Mississippi Valley Historical Review,* XII (Mar., 1926), 504–22.

Ammon, Harry, "The Formation of the Republican Party in Virginia, 1789–1796," *Journal of Southern History,* XIX (Aug., 1953), 283–310.

——. "James Monroe and the Election of 1808 in Virginia," *William and Mary Quarterly,* XX (Jan., 1963), 33–56.

——. "The Richmond Junto, 1800–1824," *Virginia Magazine of History and Biography,* LXI (Oct., 1953), 395–418.

Anderson, Hattie M. "The Jackson Men in Missouri in 1828," *Missouri Historical Review,* XXXIV (Apr., 1940), 301–34.

Andrews, J. Cutler. "The Antimasonic Movement in Western Pennsylvania," *Western Pennsylvania Historical Magazine,* XVIII (Dec., 1935), 255–66.

Andrews, Neil, Jr. "The Development of the Nominating Convention in Rhode Island," *Publications of the Rhode Island Historical Society,* I (New ser., 1893), 258–69.

Becker, Carl. "Nominations in Colonial New York," *American Historical Review,* VI (Jan., 1901), 260–75.

——. "The Nominating and Election of Delegates from New York to the First Continental Congress, 1774," *Political Science Quarterly,* XVIII (Mar., 1903), 17–46.

————. "The Unit Rule in National Nominating Conventions," *American Historical Review*, V (Oct., 1899), 64–82.

Brown, Everett S. "The Presidential Election of 1824–1825," *Political Science Quarterly*, XL (Sept., 1925), 385–403.

Burns, Robert Daniel. "The Abduction of William Morgan," *Rochester Historical Society, Publication Fund Series*, VI (1927), 219–30.

Carroll, Eber M. "Politics During the Administration of John Quincy Adams," *South Atlantic Quarterly*, XXIII (Apr., 1924), 141–54.

Channing, Edward, "Washington and Parties, 1789–1797," *Proceedings of the Massachusetts Historical Society*, XLVIII (Oct., 1913/June, 1914), 35–44.

Clifton, Frances. "John Overton as Jackson's Friend," *Tennessee Historical Quarterly*, XI (Mar., 1952), 23–40.

Collins, Loyd. "Anti-Masonic Movement in Early Missouri," *Missouri Historical Review*, XXXIX (Oct., 1944), 45–52.

Cunningham, Noble E., Jr. "John Beckley: An Early American Party Manager," *William and Mary Quarterly*, XIII (Jan., 1956), 40–52.

Curry, Leonard P. "Election Year—Kentucky, 1828," *Register of the Kentucky Historical Society*, LV (July, 1957), 196–212.

Darling, Arthur B. "Jacksonian Democracy in Massachusetts, 1824–1848," *American Historical Review*, XXIX (Oct., 1923), 271–87.

Dennis, Alfred Pearce. "The Anomaly of Our National Convention," *Political Science Quarterly*, XX (June, 1905), 185–202.

Ericksson, Erik McKinley. "Official Newspaper Organs and Jackson's Re-election, 1832," *Tennessee Historical Magazine*, IX (Apr., 1925), 37–58.

————. "Official Newspaper Organs and the Campaign of 1828," *Tennessee Historical Magazine*, VIII (Jan., 1925), 231–47.

Esarey, Logan. "The Organization of the Jacksonian Party in Indiana," *Proceedings of the Mississippi Valley Historical Association for the Year 1913–1914*, VII, 220–43.

————. "Pioneer Politics in Indiana," *Indiana Magazine of History*, XIII (June, 1917), 99–128.

Faulkner, Harold U. "Political History of Massachusetts (1829–1831)," Vol. IV, *Commonwealth History of Massachusetts*, edited by A. B. Hart (New York: State History Co., 1930), pp. 74–100.

Govan, Thomas P. "John M. Berrien and the Administration of Andrew Jackson," *Journal of Southern History*, VI (Nov., 1939), 447–67.

Green, Fletcher M. "Duff Green, Militant Journalist of the Old School," *American Historical Review*, LII (Jan., 1947), 244–64.

Hailperin, Herman. "Pro-Jackson Sentiment in Pennsylvania, 1820–1828," *Pennsylvania Magazine of History and Biography*, L (No. 3, 1926), 193–240.

Haller, Mark H. "The Rise of the Jackson Party in Maryland, 1820–29," *Journal of Southern History*, XXVIII (Aug., 1962), 307–26.

Hamilton, Milton W. "Anti-Masonic Newspapers, 1826–1834," *Papers of the Bibliographic Society of America*, XXXII (1938), 71–97.

Harlan, Louis R. "Public Career of William Berkeley Lewis," *Tennessee Historical Quarterly*, VII (Mar., June, 1948), 3–37, 118–151.

Harrison, Joseph Hobson, Jr. "Martin Van Buren and His Southern Supporters," *Journal of Southern History*, XXLL (Nov., 1956), 438–58.

Hay, Thomas Robson. "John C. Calhoun and the Presidential Campaign of 1824," *North Carolina Historical Review*, XII (Jan., 1935), 20–44.

Hicks, John D. "The Third Party Tradition in American Politics," *Mississippi Valley Historical Review*, XX (June, 1933), 3–28.

Hockett, Homer, C. "The Influence of the West on the Rise and Fall of Political Parties," *Mississippi Valley Historical Review*, IV (Mar., 1918), 459–69.

———. "Western Influence on Political Parties to 1825," *Ohio State University Bulletin*, XXII (Aug., 1917).

Jameson, J. Franklin. "The Early Political Uses of the Word Convention," *Proceedings of the American Antiquarian Society*, XII (New ser., 1899), 183–96.

Jones, Howard Mumford, "The Author of Two Byron Apocrypha," *Modern Language Notes*, XLI (Feb., 1926), 129–31.

Kelsay, Isabel Thompson, "The Presidential Campaign of 1828," *East Tennessee Historical Society's Publications*, V (Jan., 1933), 69–80.

Klein, Philip S. "The Era of Good Feelings in Pennsylvania," *Pennsylvania History*, XXV (Oct., 1938), 410–17.

Leonard, Adam A. "Personal Politics in Indiana, 1816 to 1840," *Indiana Magazine of History*, XIX (Mar., June, Sept., 1923), 1–56, 132–68, 241–81.

Libby, Orin G. "A Sketch of the Early Political Parties in the United States," *Quarterly Journal of the University of North Dakota*, II (Apr., 1912), 205–42.

———. "Political Factions in Washington's Administration," *Quarterly Journal of the University of North Dakota*, III (July, 1913), 293–318.

Lowe, Gabriel L., Jr. "John H. Eaton, Jackson's Campaign Manager," *Tennessee Historical Quarterly*, XI (June, 1952), 99–147.

McCormick, Richard P. "New Perspectives on Jacksonian Politics," *American Historical Review*, LXV (Jan., 1960), 288–301.

———. "Suffrage and Party Alignments: A Study in Voter Behavior," *Mississippi Valley Historical Review*, XLVI (Dec., 1959), 397–410.

Meigs, William M. "Pennsylvania Politics Early in This Century," *Pennsylvania Magazine of History and Biography*, XVII (No. 4, 1893), 462–90.

Miles, Edwin A. "Andrew Jackson and Senator George Poindexter," *Journal of Southern History*, XXIV (Feb., 1958), 51–66.

———. "Franklin E. Plummer: Piney Woods Spokesman of the Jackson Era," *Journal of Mississippi History*, XIV (Jan., 1952), 1–34.

Miller, William. "First Fruits of Republican Organization: Political Aspects of the Congressional Election of 1794," *Pennsylvania Magazine of History and Biography*, LXIII (Apr., 1939), 118–43.

Morison, Samuel Eliot. "The First National Nominating Convention, 1808," *American Historical Review*, XVII (July, 1912), 744–63.

Morse, Anson D. "Causes and Consequences of the Party Revolution of 1800," *Annual Report of the American Historical Association for the Year 1894* (Washington: Government Printing Office, 1895), pp. 531–39.

Murdock, John S. "The First National Nominating Convention," *American Historical Review*, I (July, 1896), 680–83.

Murray, Paul. "Party Organization in Georgia Politics, 1825–1853," *Georgia Historical Quarterly*, XXXIX (Dec., 1945), 195–210.

Newhard, Leota. "The Beginnings of the Whig Party in Missouri, 1824–1840," *Missouri Historical Review*, XXV (Jan., 1931), 254–80.

"Origin of the Democratic National Convention," *American Historical Magazine*, VII (July, 1902), 267–73.

Ostrogorski, M. "The Rise and Fall of the Nominating Caucus, Legislative and Congressional," *American Historical Review*, V (Jan., 1900), 253–83.

Paullin, Charles Oscar. "The First Elections Under the Constitution," *Iowa Journal of History and Politics*, II (Jan., 1904), 3–33.

Phillips, Ulrich B., "The South Carolina Federalists," *American Historical Review*, XIV (Apr., July, 1909), 529–43, 731–43.

Rammelkamp, C. H. "The Campaign of 1824 in New York," *Annual Report of the American Historical Association for the Year 1904* (Washington: Government Printing Office, 1905), pp. 175–201.

Remini, Robert V. "The Albany Regency," *New York History*, XXXIX (Oct., 1958), 341–55.

Robinson, Edgar E. "The Place of Party in the Political History of the United States," *Annual Reports of the American Historical Association for the Years 1927 and 1928* (Washington: Government Printing Office, 1929), pp. 200–205.

Ryan, Mary P. "Party Formation in the United States Congress, 1789 to 1796: A Quantitative Analysis," *William and Mary Quarterly*, XXVIII (Oct., 1971), 523–42.

Sellers, Charles Grier, Jr. "Jackson Men with Feet of Clay," *American Historical Review*, LXII (Apr., 1957), 537–51.

Smith, Culver H. "Propaganda Technique in the Jackson Campaign of 1828," *East Tennessee Historical Society's Publications*, VI (1934), 44–66.

Smith, William E. "Pen-Executive of Andrew Jackson," *Mississippi Valley Historical Review*, XVII (Mar., 1931), 543–56.

Sydnor, Charles S. "The One-Party Period of American History," *American Historical Review*, LI (Apr., 1946), 439–51.

Thompson, Charles Manfred. "Attitude of the Western Whigs Toward the Convention System," *Proceedings of the Mississippi Valley Historical Association*, V (1911–12), 167–89.

———. "Elections and Election Machinery in Illinois, 1818–1848," *Journal of Illinois State Historical Society*, VII (Jan., 1915), 379–88.

Van Deusen, Glyndon G. "Thurlow Weed: A Character Study," *American Historical Review*, XLIX (Apr., 1944), 427–40.

Wagstaff, Henry McGilbert. "Federalism in North Carolina," *James Sprunt Historical Publications*, IX (No. 2). Chapel Hill: University of North Carolina Press, 1910, 2–44.

Wallace, Michael. "Changing Concepts of Party in the United States: New York, 1815–1828," *American Historical Review*, LXXIV (Dec., 1968), 453–91.

Walters, Raymond, Jr. "The Origin of the Jeffersonian Party in Pennsylvania," *Pennsylvania Magazine of History and Biography*, LXVI (Oct., 1942), 442–58.

Walton, Joseph S. "Nominating Conventions in Pennsylvania," *American Historical Review*, II (Jan., 1897), 262–78.

Weisenburger, Francis P. "Caleb Atwater: Pioneer Politician and Historian," *Ohio Historical Quarterly*, LXVII (Jan., 1959), 18–37.

Wilkenson, Norman B. "Thaddeus Stevens: A Case of Libel," *Pennsylvania History*, XVIII (Oct., 1951), 317–25.

Williams, Frederick D. "The Congressional Career of J. F. H. Claiborne," *Journal of Mississippi History*, XVII (Jan., 1955), 24–42.

Unpublished Materials

Becker, Carl. "The National Nominating Convention." Bachelor of Letters thesis, Civic History Course, University of Wisconsin, 1896.

Griffin, Leland Milburn. "The Antimasonic Persuasion: A Study of Public Address in the American Antimasonic Movement, 1826–1838." Ph.D. dissertation, Cornell University, 1950.

Miller, Frank Hayden. "The Nominating System in Pennsylvania." Master's thesis, University of Wisconsin, 1894.

Peoples, Robert M. "A New Look at the Jackson-Calhoun Break." Honors paper, University of Texas, 1966.

Index

Adams, Henry, quoted, 5
Adams, John, 4, 9, 10, 12, 109
Adams, John Quincy: in election of 1824, 42, 50–51, 56, 58–60, 65–66; elected president (1825), 70; in election of 1828, 70–104, 109–11, 116–18; Virginia Adams convention (1828), 89, 284–88; connection with Antimasons, 130–32, 134–35, 147, 158, 166–67, 169, 171, 211; mentioned, xvi, 67, 121, 174, 185–87, 191, 193, 198, 208, 236, 251, 277, 280, 282
Agg, John: editor of *National Journal*, 190; background of, 198; promotes National Republican national convention (1831), 198–201, 203, 205, 206, 209; mentioned, 214, 215, 232
Alabama: early political organization in, 39, 117, 118; in election of 1824, 51, 66; in election of 1828, 82, 92–93; Antimasonry in, 145; in National Republican national convention (1831), 208; in Democratic national convention (1832), 257, 260, 263, 266–67; in election of 1832, 273; mentioned, 277
Albany Argus: proposes national convention in 1827, 100; mentioned, xiii, 45, 104, 108, 129, 152, 248, 254, 288
Albany Evening Journal, 125, 145–46, 160, 171
Albany, N.Y.: Antimasonic state convention calls national convention (1830), 136–38

Albany Regency: in election of 1824, 50, 53–54; adoption of state convention, 63–64, 114–15; in election of 1828, 80, 87, 95, 97–98, 104, 106, 108–109; relations with Antimasonry, 125, 129, 130, 135, 147, 160, 212; in election of 1832, 234; on Van Buren's vice-presidential candidacy (1832), 246, 247, 254; mentioned, 158, 232, 284, 290
Alien and Sedition Acts, 12
American Revolution, 279
American System. *See* Clay, Henry
Antifederalists, 7–8
Anti-Masonic Enquirer [Rochester, N.Y.], 125, 134, 144, 152, 155, 284
Antimasonic party: holds first national nominating convention (1831), ix, xiii, 3, 140, 153, 156–81, 185, 289, 294; in election of 1828, 87, 134–35; origins of, 121–36 *passim*; Philadelphia convention (1830), 137–55 *passim*, 156, 197; fusion with National Republicans (1832), 221–26 *passim*; in election of 1832, 275, 277, 278, 280, 284; mentioned, 69, 245, 271, 289, 293
Anti-Masonic Review and Magazine, 139
Argus of Western America [Frankfort, Ky.], 189, 233, 238
Athenaeum (Baltimore): site of national conventions (1831–32), xiii, 173, 179, 185, 216, 263

321